ORGANIZATION DEVELOPMENT

Behavioral Science Interventions for Organization Improvement

Fourth Edition

WENDELL L. FRENCH
University of Washington

CECIL H. BELL, Jr.
University of Washington

 PRENTICE-HALL INTERNATIONAL, INC.

Editorial/production supervision: Robert C. Walters
Manufacturing buyer: Ed O'Dougherty

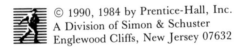
Printed in the United States of America

10   9   8   7   6   5   4   3   2   1

ISBN 0-13-641739-6

Prentice-Hall of Australia Pty. Limited, *Sydney*
Prentice-Hall Canada Inc., *Toronto*
Prentice-Hall Hispanoamericana, S.A., *Mexico*
Prentice-Hall of India, Private Limited, *New Delhi*
Prentice-Hall of Japan, Inc., *Tokyo*
Prentice-Hall of Southeast Asia Pte. Ltd., *Singapore*
Editora Prentice-Hall do Brasil, Ltda, *Rio de Janeiro*
Prentice-Hall Inc., *Englewood Cliffs, New Jersey*

To

MARJORIE

and

DIANNE

CONTENTS

PART III
SOME KEY CONSIDERATIONS AND ISSUES

PREFACE

"This book is about an exciting and profound idea and about the growing body of knowledge related to that idea. The idea is this: it is possible for the people within an organization collaboratively to manage the culture of that organization in such a way that the goals and purposes of the organization are attained at the same time that human values of individuals within the organization are furthered.

"The key to the subject to which this book is addressed, organization development, is contained in the phrase collaborative management of the organization's culture. To *collaborate* is to labor together, as the derivation of the word suggests. To *manage* is to direct and control; to be in command of. *Organization culture* is the prevailing background fabric of prescriptions and proscriptions for behavior, the systems of beliefs and values, and the technology and task of the organization together with the accepted approaches to these. An organization's culture serves powerfully as a determinant of behavior. If the culture supports behaviors appropriate for organization goal attainment, the result will probably be an effective organization; if the culture supports behaviors obviating goal attainment, the result will probably be an ineffective organization.

"In addition, the organization's culture may operate to enhance human values or may operate to thwart them. By human values we mean those goals and strivings of individuals that relate to what they want from the organization and from their participation as organization members. Some human values that seem to be important today are the following: the opportunity to make a meaningful contribution to the organization; the opportunity to have satisfying interpersonal relationships; the opportunity to accept responsibility; the opportunities for recognition and advancement; the opportunities to stretch oneself and to grow."

Thus we began the Prefaces to the first, second, and third editions of *Organization Development* published in 1973, 1978, and 1984. We still believe that organization development represents a viable and robust strategy for improving organization effectiveness and enhancing the quality of work life for organization members. We still believe that a concise exposition of the theory and practice of organization development can be of use to managers, students, boards of directors, and OD practitioners. OD, with its focus on developing total organizations, still represents a significant social invention for the practice of management.

In this spirit we have revised, updated, and expanded the earlier editions of the book. The field of organization development has changed dramatically over two decades: it has grown in popularity and usage; it has expanded into new arenas; it has received additional research attention; and there is now a greater, more reasoned, awareness of its capabilities and limitations. The last decade, in particular, has seen a burgeoning of interest in all aspects of OD—theory, practice, and research. As a result there are compelling reasons for managers and academicians to be knowledgeable about this strategy for intervening in organizations. And there are similar reasons for us to update this book so that readers, new and old, can have a ready reference for understanding organization development—what OD is, what is going on in the field, what the state of the art is, and what the future of OD might be.

This is a book about *organization development,* the applied behavioral science discipline that seeks to improve organizations through planned, systematic, long-range efforts focused on the organization's culture and its human and social processes. The means of OD are are behavioral science and structural interventions into the ongoing organization. The goals of OD are to make the organization more effective, more viable, and better able to achieve both the goals of the organization as an entity and the goals of the individuals within the organization. The world is becoming increasingly complex and interdependent, with the consequence that organization managers and members need all the help they can get to keep work organizations productive as well as hospitable for human beings. Organization development is not a panacea for all the problems of organizations, but it is one strategy for intelligently facing the requirements of a changing world.

We again acknowledge our debt to the work and to the writings of the pioneer practitioner-scholars about whom we write in Chapter 3, "A History of Organization Development." Through correspondence and/or interviews, several of these leading figures provided us with invaluable information and helped us unravel the threads of the early history of OD. In particular, in this regard, we would like to express our deep gratitude to Chris Argyris, Richard Beckhard, Kenneth Benne, Robert Blake, Rensis Likert, Ronald Lippitt, Jane Mouton, Herbert Shepard, and Robert Tannenbaum. We are also indebted to those managers in the client systems and to the internal and external consultants with whom we have worked for helping provide the milieu for much of our learning.

Wendell French
Cecil Bell

1

SOME ILLUSTRATIONS OF ORGANIZATION DEVELOPMENT EFFORTS

This is a book about organization development—a planned, systematic process in which applied behavioral science principles and practices are introduced into an ongoing organization toward the goals of effecting organization improvement, greater organizational competence, and greater organizational effectiveness. The focus is on organizations and their improvement or, to put it another way, on *total system change*. The orientation is on action—achieving desired results as a consequence of planned activities. The setting is real organizations in the real world.

In this book we tell the broad story of organization development (OD); we examine the nature, history, assumptions, strategies and models, intervention activities, and ramifications of organization development. To begin, let us look at some examples of what might happen in an organization as a reseult of instituting OD efforts. Although the settings of the following illustrations are in a variety of types of business and industrial firms, in a public school, a university, and in an American Indian tribe, the settings and organizations could be any of a wide range of organizations. Professional associations, labor unions, volunteer organizations, industrial plants, governmental units, service organizations, small and multinational corporations, colleges and universities, churches, defense units, research and development laboratories—all these offer appropriate settings for organization development programs. The key is that where there are people in organizations who seek to improve those organizations, there is the opportunity for an OD effort.

The reader will note that not everything went perfectly well in all of these OD efforts. For example, in the second illustration, the department head failed to obtain funding—temporarily, at least—for continuing the process into a second year.

1

ILLUSTRATION 1: PROBLEMS IN A BUSINESS FIRM

Problems of lack of cooperation between subunits, increasing complaints from customers, sagging morale, and rapidly increasing costs induced the president of a medium-sized company to confer with an OD consultant about ways to improve the situation. The two talked at length, and it became apparent to the consultant that the executive, while having some apprehensions, was generally agreeable to the desirability of examining the dynamics of the situation, including decision-making processes and his own leadership behavior. He and the consultant agreed that certain organization development efforts might be worthwhile. It was decided that a three-day workshop away from the usual routine, with the executive and his entire work team, might be an appropriate way in which to start.

The president then sounded out several of his subordinates about the possibility of the workshop, and reactions ranged from enthusiasm to some uneasiness. It was agreed to have the consultant meet with the executive and all his immediate subordinates to explain the typical format of such a meeting and to discuss the probable content of such a workshop. At the end of this meeting, the group decided to give it a try.

A few days before the off-site session, the consultant spent an hour interviewing each member of the team. In essence he asked them, "What things are going well?" and "What things are getting in the way of this group and this organization being as successful as you would like it to be?" The purpose of these interviews was to obtain the data around which the design of the workshop was to be built.

At the beginning of the workshop, the consultant first reported back to the group the general themes in the interviews, which he had grouped under these problem headings: "The Boss," "Meetings," "Administrative Services," "Customer Relations," "Relations Between Departments," and "Long-Range Goals." The group then ranked these problem themes in terms of importance and immediacy and chose the problem areas to be worked on. With the consultant acting more as a coach than as a moderator, the group then examined the underlying dynamics of each problem area and examined optional solutions to problems. In addition to making suggestions for breaking into subgroups to tackle certain agenda items, and in addition to providing several 10-minute lectures on such topics as decision making and team effectiveness, the consultant, upon request, intervened from time to time to comment on the way in which the group was working together and to help make explicit the norms under which the group seemed to be operating.

During the three days, time was provided for such recreation activities as jogging, basketball, swimming, and billiards. On two of the three days, the group worked until 6:00 or 6:30 P.M. and then adjourned the sessions for the day to provide for a relaxed dinner and socializing. By and large, the three days, although involving intense work, were fun for the participants. Some misunderstandings and tensions were worked through in the group setting; others were worked out informally during breaks from the work agenda. It seemed to the consultant that there was a sense of enhanced camaraderie and team spirit.

The last morning was spent developing "next action steps" relative to a dozen or so items discussed under the headings listed earlier. One of the decisions was to spend half a day with the consultant three months in the future for the purpose of reviewing progress toward problem solutions.

During a subsequent meeting between the company president and the consultant, the executive reported that the morale of the group was up substantially and customer complaints and costs were beginning to go down but that "we still have a long way to go, including making our staff meetings more effective." The two then agreed to have the consultant sit in on two or three staff meetings prior to the three-month review session.

The three-month review session with the consultant revealed that significant progress had been made on some action steps but that improvement seemed to be bogged down, particularly in areas requiring delegation of certain functions by the president to his key subordinates. This matter was extensively worked on by the group, and the president began to see where and how he could "loosen the reins," thus freeing himself for more long-range planning and for more contacts with key customers.

During the following years, the top-management team institutionalized an annual three-day "problem-solving workshop" involving the consultant. In addition, all the top managers utilized the consultant's services in conducting comparable workshops with their own subordinates. Over this period, the consultant and the personnel director, whose hiring had been a direct outgrowth of one of the sessions, began to work as a consulting team to the organization, with the personnel director gradually assuming more and more of the role of a "change agent." In addition to having planning and control responsibilities in the areas of employment and compensation and in other traditional personnel functions, the new personnel director also coordinated a management development program designed to supplement the company's problem-solving workshops. For example, managers were supported in their requests to attend specialized seminars in such areas as budgeting and finance, group dynamics, and long-range planning. The personnel director thus assumed an expanded role in which he served as an internal OD consultant to the operating divisions, as a linking pin with the external (original) consultant, and as a coordinator of the traditional personnel functions.

ILLUSTRATION 2: TEAM BUILDING IN A UNIVERSITY

Susan Jones, head of the sociology department in a modestly-sized private university, was very concerned. Among members of her department, morale, cooperation and mutual support, and creativity in course design and research were not as high as they should be. These matters also seemed to be affecting relationships with both undergraduate and graduate students. There was not a particular sense of crisis—just an overall tone of malaise.

Through reading and other sources, Susan had some sense of what "team building" might be like. Her hunch was that a team-building process might be productive. She sounded out several professors on an individual basis and, finding these colleagues had similar perceptions of the department, brought up the matter for discussion in a department meeting. Here she received strong support to schedule what she called a "department retreat" and to engage a consultant to help facilitate the workshop.

Prying money loose from the provost's office for consultant fees and workshop expenses was not easy. Susan finally got a green light when she suggested that the university view the retreat as an experiment, with the general results—no information about individuals—reported to the provost.

A qualified consultant/facilitator was selected through recommendations of various professionals and managers. It was agreed that the consultant would spend a day and a half interviewing members of the department, half a day planning the retreat, and two days at the workshop.

The facilitator interviewed each of the 11 department members plus Susan, with the promise that the interviews would be kept anonymous but that themes would be reported out to the group. There were just a few basic questions, although the facilitator frequently asked supplemental questions. The basic questions were:

1. What would this department be like if it were highly successful in its various missions?
2. What things are going well now? What are the strengths?
3. What things are impeding or blocking your being as successful as you want?

The facilitator then extracted the themes from the interviews, and using flip-chart displays, grouped the themes under the three major questions. The facilitator also developed some group or subgroup assignments relative to each of the problem themes; thus, the problems identified in the interviews served to create the agenda for the workshop.

The retreat was held several miles away from campus in an old mansion that had been converted into a retreat center. Lunch and dinner were served both days, but department members returned to their homes at night. The living room served as a general session room, where department members and the facilitator were seated in a large circle in comfortable overstuffed chairs. Other rooms were used from time to time when the facilitator assigned tasks to groups of three or four faculty members. Soft drinks, fresh fruit, coffee, and tea were available during the sessions.

After Susan had welcomed the group and expressed her hopes for the retreat, the facilitator reported out the themes from the interviews. There were six major themes pertaining to strengths, and eight pertaining to problem areas. The interviews had indicated considerable agreement about what people wanted the department to be like, but it was also clear that more work needed to be done on that topic.

One of the strongest deficiencies that had been revealed by the interviews was that people felt somewhat isolated and very unappreciated within the department. Further, they had reported that minor irritations were not being dealt with—for example, irritations toward two or three members who were chronically late to meetings, and so forth—and that these irritations were accumulating and getting in the way of communications. There did not appear to be any serious, long-term conflicts within the department, however. Other themes included a fairly widely-shared perception that the department was not paying enough attention to developing relationships with student organizations and that the curriculum was not allowing faculty members to teach in some leading-edge areas.

One of the first assignments given to the group by the facilitator was as follows:

"First. Jot down some appreciations you have for each member of the group, and later we'll have you read these aloud. Second. There is a lot of good will in this department but, as we've said, there are some minor irritations that are interfering with communications. So, jot down one or two minor irritations or concerns you have about each person— something that the person is doing or not doing that is affecting you. But you be the judge of what concerns you raise—will it be helpful to the relationship? to the department? Can the person do anything about it? Is it a matter just between two people, and would it be better to talk privately with the person?"

The facilitator then gave some examples of constructive feedback and reminded people not to do any labeling or name-calling. The group then carried out this exercise over a period of three hours. One of the outcomes was that several people made agreements to modify behaviors. For example, Susan found out that she would sometimes leaf through her appointment book while talking with faculty members, which they interpreted as signaling impatience or boredom, neither of which Susan intended. Susan agreed to try to stop this, and good-naturedly urged people to remind her when she lapsed into her old habits. The appreciations part of the exercise seemed to give everyone, including Susan, a tremendous lift.

With the exception of the appreciations and concerns exercise, marking pens and flip-chart paper were used to report out all subgroup and individual deliberations during the retreat. Among the approximately eight assignments were the following (each assignment led to discussion followed by tentative action planning):

(1:00 to 2:30 P.M. the first day.) Step 1. "Take a piece of note paper. Draw circles representing the department's various constituencies or stakeholders. Be sure to label them. Vary the size of the circles to indicate which ones you believe are the most important. Then give each circle a letter grade—A, B, C and so on—depending on how you think the department is doing in dealing with that particular constituency." Step 2. "Meet with two other colleagues and consolidate your diagrams, trying to reach agreement. Then report out results to the total group, using flip-chart paper. If you find you do not agree, report out the nature of the disagreement."

(10:30 A.M. until noon, the second morning.) "Spend a half-hour jotting down what you believe the ideal sociology curriculum should look like five years from now. Use course titles mostly, but give a little explanation where needed. Then put your list on flip-chart paper. You may team up with others or go it alone. Then walk around the room and see what others have done...This is obviously very preliminary..."

The last two hours on the second day were spent reaching consensus on next action steps. One action step decided upon was to hold a one-day follow-up session in six months, again using the facilitator. Susan concluded that she could squeeze the funds out of the department budget.

A few weeks after the first two-day retreat, Susan wrote to the provost reporting the faculty's overwhelming enthusiasm for the retreat, and that a number of significant plans were being implemented to enhance cooperation and to improve teaching and the curriculum. The report also recommended that other faculty groups experiment with a similar process. The provost seemed interested in and pleased with the results, but made no commitments about extending the process.

Susan included follow-up items on the agenda of each regular monthly department meeting. The six-month session with the facilitator was held, and there was general consensus that progress had been good in some areas but slow in others. It was clear that people were feeling much better about the department and their relationships, and several said so. Additional action plans were made, including plans for another two-day retreat during the coming academic year.

During the ensuing months, the provost left to take the presidency of another university. At the beginning of the next academic year, Susan wrote a memo to the new provost requesting funds for another retreat. The new provost replied that the fund for "visiting speakers" was depleted and her request was denied. It was clear that the new provost did not understand—or did not appreciate—the process the department had embarked upon, and Susan knew she was confronted with a major challenge.

ILLUSTRATION 3: AN OD PROGRAM TO IMPROVE MINE SAFETY

The U.S. Bureau of Mines gave a contract for a demonstration project to "determine if organization development techniques can have a significant, positive effect on reducing injuries in metal-nonmetal mining." A two-and-one-half-year OD program in a mining company was initiated, conducted, completed, and evaluated. Results showed almost a 50 percent decrease in lost-time injuries at the "experimental" mine and a 20 percent increase in lost-time injuries at a "control" mine.

Organization development techniques had not previously addressed accident prevention. This program indicates that OD can improve mine safety; it suggests that OD is a *generic problem-solving process* applicable to a variety of specific organizational problems.

The principal OD technique used was team building—problem-solving meetings involving a facilitator at all levels of the organization from the president and those reporting to him to the first-line supervisors (called shift bosses) and their crews. Every team examined safety issues as well as issues of effectiveness and efficiency, the more traditional focus of OD interventions.

Actions taken to solve safety problems differed at every level. For example, the president and his top executives declared that mine safety was a high-priority item that would be monitored, evaluated, and rewarded. The OD consultant developed new performance appraisal forms to reflect that emphasis. The vice president of operations and his staff, which included mine managers and the director of safety, introduced structural changes in the safety function by rearranging the reporting relationship of the mine safety specialists and upgrading the authority of their roles. The mine manager of the experimental mine and his top-management team set safety goals, analyzed safety problems, initiated safety policies and procedures, and established new safety incentive programs. The mine manager and his operations team, which included shift bosses and all production managers, developed ways in which to improve mine conditions, enforce safety policies, and analyze causes of injuries and accidents. The shift bosses and crews identified hazardous conditions and work practices and developed plans for immediate corrective action.

The logic behind the program was to involve everyone in systematic problem solving and action taking on a single, critical problem. Accidents occur "where the pick hits the rock." Therefore, the hourly employees had to be involved in problem identification and solution finding. The first-line supervisors play a key role in encouraging safe work practices and maintaining safe working conditions, so they had to be involved with both their crews and their higher management. The mine management had to establish an overall climate where safety was a primary goal, where safe practices were required by everyone, and where organizational resources were expended to correct unsafe conditions. This team had to develop and execute an overall game plan. And the vice president of operations and president of the company had to provide overall direction, emphasis, and a commitment to safety. Although the final payoff was to come primarily from the hourly crews, the program started at the top of the organization to ensure that the total system was pointed in the direction of making mine safety a fact of life at the company.

The power of the OD program to achieve a substantial reduction in lost-time injuries suggests that OD techniques really are generic problem-solving techniques. Mine safety is a complex, relatively intractable problem. But OD procedures were acceptable to the company employees, and OD techniques were effective in improving a long-standing, vitally important problem. Similar, but less dramatic, gains were made in the course of the program in productivity, cost control, absenteeism, and quality of production.

ILLUSTRATION 4: START-UP OF A NEW JUNIOR HIGH SCHOOL

A school district in a suburb outside a middle-sized city had just finished building its third junior high school. The new principal was a young man, well known and liked in the district. He and two vice principals selected the faculty (about 30 persons) and the adjunct staff—librarian, cooks, and custodians. With approval from the school district, the principal contacted a consultant who had been recommended to him and discussed the feasibility of a one-week human relations laboratory for the new school faculty and staff. The consultant and the principal then met and negotiated the general framework of the workshop.

It was apparent to the consultant that this situation represented a typical "start-up" situation in which relative strangers were being called upon to form themselves into an interdependent team to accomplish some organizational mission. Typical issues in this kind of situation are the following: getting acquainted, learning about each other's expressive and communicative styles, clarifying roles, achieving identification with and acceptance of organization goals, determining how each member's activities fit into and contribute to organizational goals, and exploring the nature of the demands of the interdependencies of the organization members.

The week's activities were designed to address these issues. Starting with some get-acquainted activities, the group then turned its attention to exploring the nature of interpersonal communications, improving interpersonal communications skills, and exploring issues of trust, openness, and concern for each other. Next, attention was given to determining what kind of organization the members wanted to build together, what kind of climate they wanted to have, and how they could build themselves into an effective team. The thrust of this latter set of activities related to the school's organization structure and processes, to an understanding of organization dynamics and behavior, and then to building collaboratively the organization structure and processes that the members thought would both allow them to achieve organizational goals and allow them to enhance their individual goals. This included looking at the kind of leadership style and behavior they wanted from the principal and the two assistant principals, and it also included an expression of the desires and expectations of the administrators. Considerable attention was given to what Schein calls the "psychological contract"—the set of expectations that organization members have toward the organization and its hierarchical representatives regarding influence and control and the set of expectations that the organization has toward the members regarding performance and commitment.[1] The group also examined how its members wanted to solve problems and make decisions as a team as they resolved problems common to their task accomplishment. A particularly important theme during the week was how the group was going to make decisions as a group. At the end of what seemed to be a successful week, they indicated that they had grown much closer together, that they valued the individual differences and contributions of the various members, and that they knew how to attack and solve the upcoming task problems of the new year. In addition, they had developed skills enabling them to look at their own processes (the way they got things done). So two major themes identified the week's activities: (1) developing better interpersonal relations and interpersonal skills and (2) building the skills necessary to achieve and maintain an effective organization.

After the week was over, the consultant suggested to the principal that the members of the school staff continue to work at their own organization development through periodically looking at how well they were achieving the goals and procedures that they had established and through taking "refresher" courses in these matters. To this end, three in-service training days (days in which the teachers furthered their professional development) were given over to refresher courses in which the total school staff as a "family group" looked inward at itself and its processes.

The following summer a second one-week laboratory was held with the same participants and the same consultant. There were several focuses. First, the group examined its successes and failures of the past school year in an attempt to learn how to improve its functioning. Second, the group devoted attention to developing the knowledge and skills necessary to generate its own valid data about the organization— its climate, culture, organization dynamics and processes—to manage these better. Again, during the second summer workshop, group members worked on problems relevant to their real-world work problems; again the entire staff and faculty were in attendance; again they worked on interpersonal relations, as these were instrumental in building the organization that they wanted. The second summer was spent almost entirely on understanding organization dynamics and on ways of generating and utilizing valid information about the organization climate and culture. In-service training days following the second summer were again given over to the organization development activities.

Reactions to the program were favorable. Participants subsequently reported that they worked together well and that they enjoyed the climate of the school. They are currently convinced that they are doing a high-quality job of teaching and educating. They call the summer workshops "hard work, but worth it," and they trace organization procedures to the learnings of the workshops. The school is viewed in the district as a model school and a desirable place to which to be transferred. The school has experienced low turnover of staff and faculty.

ILLUSTRATION 5: DEPARTURE FROM TRADITION IN A DIVISION OF A LARGE CORPORATION

Stemming initially from the enthusiasm of the labor relations director and a member of the board, some efforts had been made by a few key executives of a large multidivision company to apply emerging behavioral science ideas to the solution of problems being faced by the corporation. In one division, the top manager and his staff experimented, successfully they felt, with team-building sessions augmented by workshops on leadership style and decision making. In the team-building sessions, intact work groups looked at their tasks and at their ways of working and clarified roles and responsibilities necessary for better task accomplishment. The sessions typically revolved around finding answers to the question, "How can we build ourselves into a more effective team?" The process was then continued at successively lower levels in the organization. In a second division, a major "job enrichment" program was being undertaken that had the immediate consequence of forcing a searching look at the prevailing leadership styles, the structure of the division, and the goals and roles of individuals within the division.

In another division, the top-management team became interested in the use of attitude surveys and requested the help of a consultant through corporate headquarters. The consultant urged that there be extensive participation in the design of an attitude questionnaire, that the data be reported back to all who would participate, and that workshop settings be used. The workshop feature, in particular, was a departure from what the managers thought was traditional business practice, and there was some resistance to the idea because of fears of criticism. This was partially alleviated by a suggestion by the consultant to report the data in such a way as to minimize embarrassment to individual managers, and the management group agreed to go ahead with the questionnaire-plus-workshop approach.

The questionnaire included several items in the following categories: "Organizational Climate," "Pay and Benefits," "Relations with Other Units," "Communications," "Supervisor/Employee Relations," "My Job," and "Opportunities for Personal Growth and Advancement." Subsequently, responses to all items were tabulated for the total division as well as unit by unit. The division summary was reported to all units, but each specific unit tabulation was reported only to the unit involved to avoid misleading and perhaps destructive comparisons.

A team of consultants then worked with all the managers in the organization to design workshops for each unit. During these workshops the data were discussed as well as the probable forces giving rise to the various responses. Emphasis was on "How satisfied are we with the questionnaire responses?" and "What do we wish to improve?" rather than on any external criteria of performance. Action planning, which frequently included recommendations to higher management, was emphasized during the last part of each workshop.

While the workshops had their tense moments and were sometimes heavy going, reactions were generally quite positive. Typically, the manager, the consultants, and the participants agreed afterward that the meetings had been highly successful, that the process should continue throughout the division, and that the questionnaire and the workshops should be repeated in a year or two.

ILLUSTRATION 6: ORGANIZATIONAL IMPROVEMENT IN AN INDIAN TRIBE

A request to a graduate school of business from the tribal council and the executive director of an American Indian tribe for a management development workshop resulted in a counterproposal by a professor who had been approached for his reactions. The professor, who was also an organization development consultant, suggested, with the concurrence and support of a colleague, that the two faculty members visit the reservation, interview the key people in the tribal organization, and develop a workshop around the problems being experienced by the organization. This particular tribal organization was charged with responsibilities for the management of the natural resources of the reservation, for maintenance and development of utilities and services, for welfare and health, for law and order, for economic development, for management of tribal enterprises, and for preservation of the best of the tribal culture. The tribal organization was the governing body of the tribal members.

With the support of the chairman of the five-person tribal council, the council, and the executive director, it was agreed that a group of approximately 20 key people would be invited to the workshop as proposed by the consultants. These people included the total council, the executive director, his key subordinates, the staff of the Community Action Program, the Bureau of Indian Affairs resident forester, and an educator in charge of vocational education in the high school located on the reservation. All these people were interviewed by the consultants and were asked, in effect, What things are going right? and What things in the organization are getting in the way of accomplishing objectives? These two consultants extracted the central positive and negative themes from the interview data. These themes became the basic issues or problems around which the workshop was designed.

The first workshop, spanning an entire week, was held on the university campus and had two basic components that were intermixed throughout the week: (1) a continuation of the use of the *action research model* and (2) a lecture-exercise component. The action research model provided the basic flow of the workshop strategy as follows: data gathering (the preworkshop interviews plus additional data gathering during the workshop), data feedback, ranking of the problems, work on the problems, and action planning to solve the problems. This working of the problems that had been identified by the group served as the backdrop for the week's activities.

Several different types of interventions were initiated by the consultants during the problem-working phases of the workshop. Early in the workshop they presented the *force-field analysis* technique to the participants, who were then asked to use the diagnostic tool in analyzing several of the issues the group had identified as high-priority items. At another point, a modified *role analysis* technique was used relative to the roles of council members and executive director. With the council listening, the other participants discussed the following topic printed on a large sheet of newsprint: "If the council members were operating in an optimally effective and efficient way, what would they be doing?" Responses about which there seemed to be substantial consensus were made visible on large sheets taped on the wall. Council members then were encouraged to respond, and subsequent discussion resulted in some modifications on the sheets. The exercise was then repeated for the executive director's role. With the executive director listening, the rest of the group discussed the question: "If the executive director were operating in an optimally effective and efficient way, what would he be doing?" One of the outcomes of this exercise was a gradual, but significant, shift in delegation of day-to-day operating decisions from the council to the executive director and staff.

The workshop also included several short lectures on a number of relevant topics including leadership, group process, decision making, problem diagnosis, and communications. This component also included some instrumented exercises that permitted participants to compare different decision-making models and to evaluate their usefulness.

The humor of the members of the group appeared frequently and prompted a good deal of laughter. For example, in the review of the roles of the council members and the executive director, it was observed by one of the tribal elders that "We have too many chiefs and not enough Indians." Their humor relative to themselves and to each other usually carried messages of affection and inclusion, including messages of inclusion to the few non-Native American employees on the staff. Ethnic divisions seemed not to be important issues; but problems of role clarification, delegation, and planning were the issues of highest concern.

By the end of the workshop, the participants had worked through a dozen or so important problems or issues and had agreed on next action steps, that is, "who was going to do what when." Results of a questionnaire administered on the last day of the workshop indicated overwhelming enthusiasm for the process and what had been accomplished. The consultants also perceived what they thought was a substantially higher level of openness, trust, and support among the participants at the end of the workshop compared with what was evident during the early part of the workshop.

One of the action steps that was agreed upon was a two-day follow-up visit to the reservation by the consultants to occur in five or six months. During ensuing weeks it became apparent that a follow-up visit sooner than that would be beneficial. The implementation of some action plans had bogged down, although important progress had been made on a number of others.

During the first follow-up visit, the consultants interviewed a cross section of the workshop participants to assess the degree of progress, met with the council to assist in a further review of council activities, and assisted in correcting a misunderstanding as to who was to be on one of the task forces created at the workshop. During the second follow-up visit the time of the consultants was primarily devoted to meetings with the executive director and the council members, although some discussions with key supervisors also occurred.

Subsequently, the council and the executive director requested a second workshop, with the suggestion that this workshop be shorter and that more time be devoted to follow-up on the reservation. The workshop was held at a resort; it started on a Tuesday evening and ended Friday afternoon.

Although the same basic pattern was followed for the second workshop, including preworkshop interviews, less time was spent on lectures and instrumented exercises, and almost all the time was spent on substantive issues. Since tensions between two subunits of the organization and the need for clarification of responsibilities appeared to be the most pressing issues, a significant amount of time was spent on these matters. The first problem was addressed through a three-way intergroup exercise in which each of the major groups—the council, the tribal staff, and the Community Action Program staff—developed the following lists about the other two groups and shared them in a general session:

What we like about what the _____ group is doing.

What concerns us about the _____ group.

What we predict the _____ group will say about us.

During the sharing of the lists, discussion was limited to explanation and questions requesting clarification. This phase was followed by subgroup discussion and, finally, by total group discussion and action planning.

The problem of clarification of responsibilities was addressed by asking each participant to follow a suggested outline in writing his or her own job description, to make the descriptions visible on large newsprint, and to discuss the job descriptions with his or her particular work team, including the supervisor. Revised job descriptions were then posted in the general conference room for perusal and informal discussion during breaks in the sessions.

At the end of the workshop, the consultants, the council chairman, and the executive director agreed on the approximate date of two follow-up sessions at the tribal reservation and agreed to keep in touch by telephone.

ILLUSTRATION 7: A NEW PLANT MANAGER

Several years ago a new plant manager arrived at a continuous process facility (a plant where there is a continuous shaping of raw materials into finished products, as, for example, in a steel-making plant or an oil refinery). He surveyed the scene and found the following characteristics: the plant had over 2,000 employees, there were several layers of managers arranged in functional departments (production, maintenance, technical research, purchasing and stores, engineering, etc.); the plant performed fairly well in terms of productivity and profitability. The new manager's predecessor had been an energetic and autocratic man who had made all the operational and administrative decisions at the plant. The rest of the upper and middle management were called "superintendents"—they superintended their bailiwicks, supplied information to the plant manager, and received orders from the manager about what should be done in their departments and divisions, as the plant was run on a day-to-day basis.

The new manager had a different managerial philosophy and a different leadership style: he believed in delegating as much responsibility to his subordinates as possible; he believed in allowing wide participation in the important decisions affecting the works and the work force; he believed that better information and decisions would come from involved, committed "managers"; he wanted to develop subordinates so that they would move to higher positions of responsibility; and, as he told the managers at one of his first meetings with them, he wanted them to "share in the work and share in the fun." The new manager knew that he needed to build strong individual managers, an effective "management team," and that he needed to change the managerial culture and climate in the plant. He knew that this change in the way things were done would require new skills and a new management climate in the plant. And that would require training; the habits of 10 years could not be changed just by his issuing an order. He called in several consultants, told them his desires, and solicited their aid.

As things evolved, there turned out to be six goals of the change project: (1) to increase the abilities and skills of the individual managers; (2) to build an effective top management team; (3) to build stronger division and department teams; (4) to improve the relations between work groups, such as between production and maintenance, and thus reduce the level of energy spent in competition; (5) to change the managerial culture from one in which one person made all the decisions to one in which all managers made or participated in decisions that affected them; and (6) to improve the long-range planning and decision-making abilities of managers at all levels. These change goals and the ideas of the new plant manager were public knowledge, just as was the information about the consultants and the OD program. Team-building meetings were held with the top management group and the new plant manager. Similar meetings were held with the department managers and their supervisory subordinates. And finally, meetings were held with representatives from several "interface" groups—two or more independent groups with overlapping responsibilities or work flow duties. Also attending these meetings were the external consultants and several internal organization members who were being groomed as internal "change agents." The typical role of the consultants was to assist the groups to identify, work through, and learn from their problems.

This OD program was in operation for four years. During the first year the intervention strategy called mainly for family groups—intact working groups consisting of a superior and key subordinates. These groups met to explore their culture and their methods of problem solving related to their assigned tasks within the organization. It was an important feature of the OD strategy that the first family group meeting involved the plant manager and his key subordinates, the plant division managers. Following this successful venture, the division managers met with their subordinates in team-building sessions in an effort to improve division functioning. Significant issues surfaced during these meetings related to leadership styles, team processes and dynamics, and new ways of solving specific operational problems.

The second year's activities continued the team-building sessions and introduced a new dimension: interface meetings with groups that had problems working together. The fact that the groups had previously been successful in working on their own problems in family groups and analyzing their own dynamics seemed to facilitate the progress of the interface sessions. Greater understanding of the complexities of interdependence and the problems inherent in effective coordination of effort led to rapid and accurate diagnosis of the intergroup problems in most cases. Also during this year, OD task forces were formed to investigate various facets of effectively managing the plant. These task forces were typically temporary problem-solving teams with specific charges, but the charges had far-reaching implications for the plant. For example, task forces have tackled industrial safety problems, labor and union relations issues, and external interface problems with the local community and region. An especially important task force outcome was the development of a new philosophy about career planning and also new career development planning and implementation procedures. These procedures provide better ways for utilizing and developing the manpower talent in the organization and also ensure the development of more managerial talent.

During the third year, the top management team, including the plant manager, turned their attention to developing better long-range strategic planning models. They also instituted some management development programs for the purpose of upgrading the managerial skills of the middle-level supervisors. Some intergroup sessions continued to be utilized when conditions appeared to warrant them. Occasional family group sessions were primarily devoted to problem solving and long-range strategic planning activities.

In the fourth year, the OD activities were moved to the shop floor. One of the consultants became a familiar and friendly face to the hourly employees in several critical areas of the plant. He observed the work and work flow and interacted with the employees to elicit their opinions about how to do the job better and how they felt about the work, the supervision, and the company. The consultant initiated meetings between supervisors and hourly employees in which they systematically evaluated various ideas that had been suggested for improving the work flow and working conditions. The consultant also acted as an "idea conduit" for suggestions that the hourly employees wanted transmitted to higher levels of management.

At the conclusion of the fourth year, the plant manager and the consultants decided to terminate the OD program. It was agreed that the goals of the program had been met. It was noted that many of the "OD activities"—problem-solving task forces, intergroup sessions, strategic planning—were now an integral part of the plant's culture and organizational processes.

ILLUSTRATION 8: PRODUCTIVITY IMPROVEMENTS THROUGH GROUP PROBLEM SOLVING

Production increased from about 825 logs per shift to about 1,500 logs per shift across the "quad saw" at a sawmill in the course of six months. This occurred after a series of one-hour weekly meetings lasting four months between an OD consultant and the crew. The new production level was maintained and even increased after the meetings were discontinued.

What caused the 80 percent increase in productivity?

The background to this story begins with a three-year organization development program conducted by two behavioral scientists at a large wood products company. The program consisted of a variety of activities—first-line supervisor training, survey feedback, team building with various salaried work teams, and numerous other problem-specific interventions. One consultant worked with half of the 2,000-person organization; the other consultant worked with the other half. Some consulting activities, such as supervisor training, cut across the entire organization.

The consultant conducting team-building meetings with sawmill superintendents and their salaried staff members was asked by the superintendent of a large sawmill to help solve production problems with the "quad saw," one of two production lines in the mill. A quad saw is a machine in which four saws cutting simultaneously process small logs into finished-dimension lumber. The quad saw had been installed several years earlier, and the engineers had projected 1,150 logs per shift as the expected production rate. But production had peaked at 800 to 825 logs per shift, and attempts to increase that rate had been unsuccessful. Team problem solving had worked well with the superintendent and his management team; he wanted it applied to the crew on the quad saw. A series of group problem-solving meetings was chosen as the vehicle for understanding and correcting the situation.

The first step was for the consultant to become known to the mill employees and to become familiar with the mill operations, processes, and flows. A total of about 15 persons working at 10 different machine stations comprised the "quad saw system." The entire mill had about 35 employees, all under the direction of a production supervisor. The mill operated two shifts, a day shift and a swing shift.

The next step was to hold a series of weekly problem-solving meetings devoted to understanding and solving whatever problems were getting in the way of production. The meetings were attended by the quad saw crew, their supervisor, the master mechanic servicing that production line, the mechanic's supervisor, and the consultant. The meetings were held immediately after work in the sawmill conference room; they lasted about one hour; hourly employees were paid overtime for attending. The mill superintendent launched the first meeting by saying that he wanted 1,150 logs across the quad saw and was getting only 825. He further stated that he wanted the crew to figure out how to accomplish that goal. He said he would support them in their efforts to improve production. He introduced the consultant as a person who would "help them" as they worked on the problem. Then he answered a few questions and left.

The first meeting was wild and tumultuous: long-standing complaints were aired; dissatisfactions and frustrations were voiced; a general pessimism that nothing could *or would* be done was in evidence. The consultant insisted that they were the people with the knowledge and ability to improve the situation and assured them that the superintendent was sincere in asking for their help. The consultant laid out two broad questions to guide the discussions: How can we do the job better? and How can we make this a better place to work?

At later meetings, the process was more systematic. Every machine station was analyzed in detail by the operators to discover barriers and impediments to production. Every step in the operations flow was examined and studied. At this stage the predominant theme was that mechanical problems were the major source of difficulty. A long list of mechanical and maintenance "wants" was generated. The list was overwhelming for the two maintenance supervisors, so each operator was asked for his three highest-priority items. With the more manageable list, the maintenance people went to work with enthusiasm. Interaction and problem solving between maintenance and operators increased. The weekly meetings were used to report progress and check for effectiveness of repairs, adjustments, and modifications. The equipment began to run significantly better.

Next the group turned to an analysis of "human factors" such as communication, coordination, operator technique, operator training needs, and the like. Again numerous specific problems were raised and systematically addressed, and corrective actions were planned and implemented. Several persons, including the production supervisor, had to modify their behavior for overall system improvements to occur.

As changes were implemented, production began to go up, slowly at first, then more rapidly and dramatically. The superintendent's target of 1,150 was achieved and surpassed about three months after the meetings were begun. But the maintenance people kept improving the equipment, the operators kept improving their flows and technique, and the supervisor kept improving communication and coordination. Production increased to 1,550 logs and then leveled off at a steady, stable 1,500 logs per shift.

The crew members were pleased and proud of their accomplishments. The consultant became even more firmly convinced of the power of group problem solving. The superintendent was amazed at the results.

SUMMARY

These examples are not cited as perfect or ideal organizational interventions but only as fairly typical illustrations of what happens in organization development efforts, particularly in their earlier phases. Although these programs vary in their comprehensiveness, all the illustrations have the following common features: (1) the "client" is a total system or major subunit of a total system, (2) the interventions are primarily directed toward problems and issues identified by the client group, (3) the interventions are directed toward problem solving and improved functioning for the client system, and (4) the interventions are based on behavioral science theory and technology.

In later chapters we will look more closely at many of the techniques, at the underlying theory and assumptions of OD, and at some of the pitfalls and challenges in attempting to improve organizations through behavioral science methods.

NOTE

1. Edgar H. Schein, *Organizational Psychology,* 3rd ed. (Englewood Cliffs, N.J.: Prentice-Hall, 1980), pp. 22–24.

2

A DEFINITION
OF ORGANIZATION
DEVELOPMENT

Although a literal interpretation of the term *organization development* could refer to a wide range of strategies for organization improvement, the phrase has come to take on some fairly specific meanings in the behavioral science literature and in practice. We say "fairly specific" because the boundaries are not entirely clear, perceptions of different authors and practitioners vary somewhat, and the field is evolving.

In the behavioral science, and perhaps ideal, sense of the term, *organization development is a top-management-supported, long-range effort to improve an organization's problem-solving and renewal processes, particularly through a more effective and collaborative diagnosis and management of organization culture—with special emphasis on formal work team, temporary team, and inter-group culture—with the assistance of a consultant-facilitator and the use of the theory and technology of applied behavioral science, including action research.*

By *top-management-supported* we mean general direction and support from the chief executive and members of the top-management group as well as their active involvement. For reasons that will become clear, effective OD requires much more than tacit approval from the power structure.

By *problem-solving processes* we mean the way in which an organization goes about diagnosing and making decisions about the opportunities and challenges of its environment. For example, does it see its environment, and thus its mission, in terms of 10 years ago, or is it continuously redefining its purposes and its methods in terms of the present and the future? Does the organization solve problems in such a way that it taps the creativity and commitment of a select few, or does it tap deeply into the resources, vitality, and common purposes of all organizational members?

The notion of improving problem-solving processes is interrelated with the matter of improving organizational "renewal processes," which is perhaps a broader concept. Lippitt combines these ideas in his definition of *organization renewal,* which he sees as

> the process of initiating, creating, and confronting needed changes so as to make it possible for organizations to become or to remain viable, to adapt to new conditions, to solve problems, to learn from experiences.[1]

Argyris stresses organizational renewal and revitalizing in his description of organization development:

> At the heart of organizational development is the concern for the vitalizing, energizing, actualizing, activating, and renewing of organizations through technical and human resources.[2]

Waterman observes leading companies, writes about revitalization, and distinguishes between renewal and change per se:

> Renewal, after all, is about builders. Many people can introduce change for change's sake and call it renewal. That is illusory. A builder, on the other hand, leads an organization toward renewal that outlives the presence of any single individual and revitalizes even as it changes.[3]

Similarly, Gardner, in writing about organizational *self-renewal,* refers to the avoidance of organizational decay and senility; the regaining of vitality, creativity, and innovation; the furtherance of flexibility and adaptability; the establishment of conditions that encourage individual motivation, development, and fulfillment; and "the process of bringing results of change into line with purposes."[4] Thus, along with ideas about improved problem-solving and renewal processes are the important notions of purpose and direction—all of which are central to organization development activities.

By the term *culture* in our definition we mean prevailing patterns of values, attitudes, beliefs, assumptions,[5] expectations, activities, interactions, norms, and sentiments (including feelings)[6] and as embodied in artifacts.[7] By including artifacts we include technology in our definition.

Our use of the term *culture* includes the notion of the "informal system," which we will be describing in the next chapter as including feelings, informal actions and interactions, group norms, and values.[8] In some ways, the informal system is the hidden or suppressed domain of organizational life—the covert part of the "organizational iceberg," as shown in Figure 2-1.[9] Traditionally, this hidden domain either is not examined at all or is only partially examined. Organization development efforts focus on both the formal and the informal system, but once the OD program is legitimated through the formal system, the initial intervention strategy is usually through the informal system in the sense that perceptions, attitudes, and feelings are usually the first data to be confronted.

By *collaborative diagnosis and management* of the culture, we mean a shared kind of examination and management of organization culture—not a hierarchically imposed

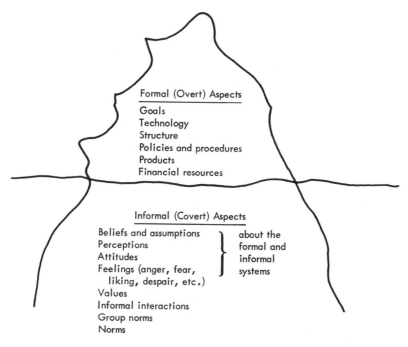

Figure 2-1   Organizational Iceberg

kind. Who does what to whom is an important issue in organization development, and we want to stress that management of group culture must be "owned" as much by the subordinates as it is by the formal leader.

Implicit in the notion of diagnosing organization culture is the assumption that aspects of that culture, while perhaps having some short-term functionality in meeting member or group needs, can be highly dysfunctional in terms of the long-range goals of the organization and its members. A fascinating illustration from the Solomon Islands is provided by the chief executive officer of TRW Inc.:

> On an abandoned military airstrip, islanders wearing tattered GI uniforms marched in formation in front of the control tower. In the tower, a man wearing earphones carved of wood spoke into a wooden microphone and made marks on a clipboard. Other islanders squatted patiently, searching the skies, watching and waiting for a silver airship to arrive in answer to the magic they were making and disgorge its rich cargo. . . .
>
> The cargo cultists saw that our GIs were able to call down bounties from the sky apparently without doing any real work, merely by talking into little boxes, signaling with flags, marching in formations, or even sitting at tables with vases of flowers and sipping ceremonial libations from tall glasses. Lacking any understanding. . .the cultists. . . tried to achieve the same results by imitation.
>
> When their efforts failed to produce the desired results, they often became increasingly fanatical and dogmatic. They would kill off their livestock, consume their food stores and seed corn, destroy their tools, refuse to work, break taboos. Eventually—with luck, before starvation set in—the cult would disintegrate in disillusion, and the local society would begin to repair itself.
>
> I am often struck by the similarities between our behavior and that of these primitives of the South Sea Islands.[10]

While this is an illustration from primitive groups on small islands, the point extends to organizations. Dysfunctional aspects of organization culture, while usually not so starkly visible, are very common phenomena. Organization development is a process of people managing the culture of an organization rather than being managed by that culture.

Our definition recognizes that the key unit in organization development activities is the ongoing *work team,* including both superior and subordinates. (Although we are using the words *team* and *group* more or less synonymously, we will use the former with considerable frequency because of its connotation of interdependency.) As we will elaborate upon in later chapters, this focus on teams in contrast to individuals is different from more conventional ways of improving organizations. To give only one example, in most management development activities the focus is on the individual manager or supervisor—not on his or her work group. Traditionally, the manager has participated in the learning experience in isolation from the dynamics of the work situation. In this case, as Bolman says, the learner is an individual, while in OD *"the learner is a system."*[11]

Although we are emphasizing a focus on relatively permanent work groups to differentiate OD from traditional management development, in comprehensive OD programs extensive attention is also paid to temporary work teams, such as task forces (often called "cross-functional teams" when different specialities or departments are represented), and to intergroup relations, as well as to total system implications. These matters will also be dealt with in subsequent chapters.

The notion of the use of a *consultant-facilitator* (sometimes called a *change agent* or *catalyst*) as one of the distinguishing characteristics of OD has a purpose in our definition. We are somewhat pessimistic about the optimal effectiveness of OD efforts that are do-it-yourself programs. As will be discussed later, in the early phases, at least, the services of a facilitator who is not a part of the prevailing organization culture are essential. This does not mean that the external person cannot be a member of the organization; rather, it means that he or she at least be external to the particular subsystem that is initiating an OD effort.

Part of an effective OD effort is a growing awareness of the significance of the consultant-facilitator role and a growing capability of many organizational members in serving in that role, whether on an ad hoc or a more formalized basis. In an effective OD effort, a significant number of organizational members will increase their consultation skills and utilize these skills in various ways such as helping to run more effective meetings or providing counsel to peers. Some organizational members may be trained to be full- or part-time facilitators. So we need to think of the facilitator *role* in organizations as well as of facilitator *persons*. We believe this role to be extremely important.

And finally, the basic intervention model that runs through most organization development efforts is *action research*. The action research model underlies all the illustrations of organization development described in the first chapter. Basically, the action research model as applied in OD consists of (1) a preliminary diagnosis, (2) data gathering from the client group, (3) data feedback to the client group, (4) data exploration by the client group, (5) action planning by the client group, and (6) action by members of the client group. This model will be discussed in detail in Chapter 8. Parenthetically, because of the extensive applicability of this model to organization development, another definition of organization development could be *organization improvement through participant action research.*

The characteristics of organization development just enumerated, depart substantially from the features of traditional change programs, which Bennis categorizes as follows: "(1) exposition and propagation, (2) elite corps, (3) psychoanalytic insight, (4) staff, (5) scholarly consultations, and (6) circulation of ideas to the elite."[12] Bennis states that *exposition and propagation* are "possibly the most popular" and cites as illustrations the impact of the ideas of philosophers and scientists. The *elite corps* method is basically the infusion of scientists into key power and decision-making posts in organizations. *Psychoanalytic insight* as a change method is similar to the elite corps method but refers to effective change occurring through the medium of executives who have high self-insight and considerable "psychiatric wisdom" relative to subordinates. The *staff* strategy refers to the employment in organizations of social scientists who analyze situations and make policy recommendations. *Scholarly consultations* is a method of change involving "exploratory inquiry, scholarly understanding, scholarly confrontation, discovery of solutions, and, finally, scientific advice to the client." The sixth method described by Bennis is *circulation of ideas to the elite.* One of the illustrations given is the Council of Correspondence, a chain letter that linked rebel leaders in the American Revolution.[13] (See also Chapter 7 for a discussion of Benne and Chin's typology of empirical-rational, normative-reeducative, and power-coercive change strategies.)

Organization development efforts depart substantially from these methods of organizational change as described by Bennis. Of particular relevance are the two organizational consultation methods, "staff" and "scholarly consultations." In both strategies an inside or an external expert studies a situation and makes recommendations; this is the traditional way of consulting. Organization development efforts are different. The OD consultant does *not* make recommendations in the traditional sense; his or her end product is not a written report to top management, concluding with recommendations for the solutions of substantive problems. The client organization, however, is assisted in the way it goes about solving problems. For example, the consultant could be called upon to comment on the way in which a group is working together and might make a number of observations about patterns of interaction, what issues appeared to be avoided, how the agenda appeared to be set, and so forth. Or the consultant could structure situations so as to highlight phenomena, such as in an interpersonal conflict situations where the OD consultant might request two team members to role play each other and each other's point of view. Basically, in most OD interventions the client group is assisted in generating valid data and learning from them.

We see seven characteristics that differentiate organization development interventions from more traditional interventions:

1. An emphasis on the work team and other team configurations as the key units for addressing issues and learning more effective modes of organizational behavior
2. An emphasis, although not exclusively so, on group, intergroup, and organizational processes in contrast to substantive content
3. The use of the action research model
4. An emphasis on the collaborative management of work-team culture, including temporary teams

5. An emphasis on the management of the culture of the total system, including intergroup culture

6. Attention to the management of system ramifications

7. A view of the change effort as an ongoing process in the context of a constantly changing environment.

Another characteristic, a primary emphasis on human and social relationships, does not necessarily differentiate OD from several other change efforts, but it is, nevertheless, an important feature.

If these features characterize organization development (OD), how does OD differ from programs called by such terms as Quality of Work Life (QWL), Organizational Effectiveness (OE), Employee Involvement (EI), and the like? Our answer is that any given change program might have features identical to those listed above and therefore could be called OD, it might be vastly different, or it might have a number of characteristics in common with the above list. Terminology is less important than the activities that are occurring within a particular change effort. By whatever name, we believe that the features listed above comprise an important, comprehensive way of going about organizational improvement that merits being understood, studied, and improved. (We will discuss such programs as QWL, Quality Circles, Management by Objectives, etc. in Chapter 14 to examine some of their characteristics vis-a-vis OD. Organizational Transformation will be discussed in Chapter 21.)

The seven features previously listed will be elaborated upon in the chapters that follow. As we will see in the next chapter, these characteristics have identifiable origins in the recent past and have emerged largely from the behavioral sciences.

NOTES

1. Gordon L. Lippitt, *Organizational Renewal: A Holistic Approach to Organization Development,* 2nd ed. (Englewood Cliffs, N.J.: Prentice-Hall, 1982), p. xiv.

2. Chris Argyris, *Management and Organizational Development: The Path from XA to YB* (New York: McGraw-Hill, 1971), p. ix.

3. Robert H. Waterman, Jr., *The Renewal Factor: How the Best Companies Get and Keep the Competitive Edge* (New York: Bantam Books, 1987), p. 22.

4. John W. Gardner, *Self-Renewal: The Individual and the Innovative Society* (New York: Harper & Row, Harper Colophon Books, 1965). pp. 1–7.

5. Schein defines culture largely in terms of "a pattern of basic assumptions." See Edgar H. Schein, *Organizational Culture and Leadership* (San Francisco: Jossey-Bass Publishers, 1985), p. 9. See also Terrence E. Deal and Allen A. Kennedy, *Corporate Cultures* (Reading, Mass.: Addison-Wesley Publishing Company, 1982).

6. Whyte and Hamilton see sentiments as referring to "the mental and emotional reactions we have to people and physical objects" and as having three elements: "(1) An idea about something or somebody . . . , (2) emotional content or affect, (3) a tendency to recur upon presentation of the same symbols that have been associated with it in the past." See Willian Foote Whyte and Edith Lentz Hamilton, *Action Research for Management* (Homewood, Ill.: Richard D. Irwin, 1965), p. 184.

7. Kroeber and Kluckhohn cite 164 definitions of culture; our definition is congruent with their synthesis: "*Culture consists of patterns, explicit and implicit, of and for behavior acquired and transmitted by symbols, constituting the distinctive achievement of human groups, including their embodiments in artifacts;*

the essential core of culture consists of traditional (i.e., historically derived and selected) ideas and especially their attached values; culture systems may, on the one hand, be considered as products of action, on the other as conditioning elements of further action" [author's emphasis]. See A. L. Kroeber and Clyde Kluckhohn, *Culture: A Critical Review of Concepts and Definitions* (New York: Vintage Books, 1952), pp. 291, 357. See also Ralph H. Kilmann, Mary J. Saxton, Roy Serpa, and Associates, *Gaining Control of the Corporate Culture* (San Francisco: Jossey-Bass Publishers, 1985), p. ix.

8. Our use of the word *culture* includes Argyris's notion of the *living system:* "the way people actually behave, the way they actually think and feel, the way they actually deal with each other. It includes both the formal and informal activities." Chris Argyris, "Some Causes of Organizational Ineffectiveness Within the Department of State," *Occasional Papers,* No. 2 (U.S. Department of State, Center for International Systems Research, 1967), p. 2.

9. This illustration is adapted from an address by Stanley N. Herman, TRW Systems Group, at an organization development conference sponsored jointly by the Industrial Relations Management Association of British Columbia and the NTL Institute for Applied Behavioral Science, Vancouver, B.C., Canada, 1970.

10. Ruben F. Mettler, "The Cargo Cult Mentality in America," *Business Week,* September 22, 1980, p. 22.

11. Lee Bolman, "What Is Organization Development?" in Ernest J. Pavlock, ed., *Organization Development: Managing Transitions* (Washington, D.C.: American Society for Training and Development, 1982), p. 25 [authors' emphasis].

12. Warren G. Bennis, "A New Role for the Behavioral Sciences: Effecting Organizational Change," *Administrative Science Quarterly,* 8 (September 1963), p. 130.

13. Ibid., pp. 130–134.

3

A HISTORY
OF ORGANIZATION
DEVELOPMENT

The history of organization development is rich with the contributions of behavioral scientists and practitioners, many of whom are well known, and the contributions of many people in client organizations. Even if we were aware of all the significant contributors, which we are not, we could not do justice to the richness of this history in a short essay. Therefore, all we can do is write about what we believe to be the central thrusts of that history based on our research to date and hope that the many people who are not mentioned will not be offended by our incompleteness.

Systematic organization development activities have a recent history and, to use the analogy of a mangrove tree, have at least three important trunk stems. One trunk stem of OD consists of innovations in the application of laboratory training insights to complex organizations. A second major stem is survey research and feedback methodology. Both stems are intertwined with a third stem, the emergence of action research. Paralleling these stems, and to some extent linked, was the emergence of the Tavistock sociotechnical and socioclinical approaches. The key actors focused upon in this account interacted with each other and were influenced by experiences and concepts from many fields, as we will see.

THE LABORATORY TRAINING STEM

The T-Group

One stem of OD, laboratory training, essentially unstructured small-group situations in which participants learn from their own interactions and the evolving dynamics of the group, began to develop in about 1946 from various experiments in the use of discussion groups to achieve changes in behavior in back-home situations. In particular, an Inter-Group Relations workshop held at the State Teachers College in New Britain, Connecticut, in the summer of 1946 was important in the emergence of laboratory training. This workshop was sponsored by the Connecticut Interracial Commission and the Research Center for Group Dynamics, then at MIT.

The Research Center for Group Dynamics (RCGD) had been founded in 1945 under the direction of Kurt Lewin, a prolific theorist, researcher, and practitioner in interpersonal, group, intergroup, and community relationships.[1] Lewin had been recruited to MIT largely through the efforts of Douglas McGregor of the Sloan School of Management who had convinced MIT President Carl Compton of the wisdom of establishing a center for group dynamics. Lewin's original staff included Marian Radke, Leon Festinger, Ronald Lippitt, and Dorwin Cartwright.[2] Lewin's field theory and his conceptualizing about group dynamics, change processes, and action research were of profound influence on the people who were associated with the various stems of OD.

What was later to be called the "T-group" began to emerge through a series of events at the New Britain workshop of 1946. The staff consisted of Kurt Lewin, Kenneth Benne, Leland Bradford, and Ronald Lippitt. The latter three, along with other responsibilities, served as leaders of "learning groups." Each group, in addition to group members and a leader, had an observer who made notes about interactions among members. At the end of each day, the observers met with the staff and reported what they had seen. At the second or third evening session, three women members of the workshop asked if they could sit in on the reporting session, and were encouraged to do so. One woman disagreed with the observer as to the meaning of her behavior during the day's sessions, and a lively discussion ensued. The three women then asked to return to the next reporting session, and, because of the liveliness and the richness of the discussions, Lewin and the staff enthusiastically agreed. By the next evening, about half of the 50–60 members of the workshop were attending the feedback session. These sessions soon became the most significant learning experiences of the conference.[3]

From this experience emerged the National Training Laboratory in Group Development, which was organized by Benne, Bradford, and Lippitt (Lewin died in early 1947) and which held a three-week session during the summer of 1947 at the Gould Academy in Bethel, Maine. Participants met with a trainer and an observer in Basic Skill Training Groups (later called T-groups) for a major part of each day. The 1947 laboratory was sponsored by the Research Center for Group Dynamics (MIT), the National Education Association (NEA), Teachers College of Columbia University, University of California at Los Angeles (UCLA), Springfield College, and Cornell University. The work of that summer was to evolve into the National Training Laboratory, later called NTL Institute for Applied Behavioral Science, and into contemporary T-group training. Out of the Bethel experiences and NTL grew a significant number of laboratory training centers sponsored by universities. One of the first was the Western Training Laboratory, headed by Paul Sheats and sponsored by UCLA. The Western Training Laboratory offered its first program in 1952.

In addition to Lewin and his work, influences on Bradford, Lippitt, and Benne relative to the invention of the T-group and the subsequent emergence of OD included extensive experience with role playing and Moreno's psychodrama.[4] Further, Bradford and Benne had been influenced by John Dewey's philosophy of education, including concepts about learning and change and about the transactional nature of humans and their environment.[5] Benne, in collaboration with R. Bruce Raup and others, had built on Dewey's philosophy and focused on the processes by which policy agreements are reached between people who differ.[6] In addition, Benne had been infuenced by the works of Mary Follett, an early management theorist, including her ideas about integrative solutions to problems in organizations.[7]

As a footnote to the emergence of the T-group, the widespread use of flip-chart paper as a convenient way to record, retrieve, and display data in OD activities and in training sessions was invented by Ronald Lippitt and Lee Bradford during the 1946 New Britain sessions. As Lippitt reports,

> The blackboards were very inadequate, and we needed to preserve a lot of the material we produced. So I went down to the local newspaper and got a donation of the end of press runs. The paper was still on the rollers. We had a "cutting bee" of Lee, Ken, myself and several others to roll the sheets out and cut them into standard sizes that we could put up in quantity with masking tape on the blackboards and walls of the classrooms. We took the practice back to MIT and I had the shop make some boards with clamps across the top. We hung them in our offices and the seminar room, and Lee did the same thing at the NEA in Washington. . . . The next summer at Bethel we had a large supply of cut newsprint and used some of the boards on easels, as well as using the walls.[8]

Bradford also reports that he and Ronald Lippitt used "strips of butcher paper " in their early work with organizations.[9]

In a sense, the invention of the T-group grew out of an awareness, that had been growing for a decade or more, of the importance of helping groups and group leaders focus on group and leadership *processes.* This growing awareness was particularly evident in adult education and group therapy.[10]

Over the next decade, as trainers began to work with social systems of more permanency and complexity than T-groups, they began to experience considerable frustration in the transfer of laboratory behavioral skills and insights of individuals into the solution of problems in organizations. Personal skills learned in the "stranger" T-groups setting were very difficult to transfer to complex organizations. However, the training of "teams" from the same organization had emerged early at Bethel and undoubtedly was a link to the total organizational focus of Douglas McGregor, Herbert Shepard, and Robert Blake, and subsequently the focus of Richard Beckhard, Chris Argyris, Jack Gibb, Warren Bennis, and others.[11] All had been T-group trainers in NTL programs.

Robert Tannenbaum

Within our present awareness, some of the earliest sessions of what would now be called "team building" were conducted by Robert Tannenbaum in 1952 and 1953 at the U.S. Naval Ordnance Test Station at China Lake, California.[12] According to Tannenbaum, the term "vertically structured groups" was used, with groups dealing with "personal topics (such as departmental sociometrics, interpersonal relationships, communication, and self-analysis), and with organizational topics (such as deadlines, duties and responsibilities, policies and procedures, and—quite extensively—with interorganizational-group relations).''[13] These sessions, which stimulated a 1954 *Personnel* article by Tannenbaum, Kallejian, and Weschler, were conducted ''with all managers of a given organizational unit present.''[14] The more personally oriented dynamics of such sessions were described in a 1955 *Harvard Business Review* article by the same authors.[15]

Tannenbaum, along with Art Shedlin, also was the leader of what appears to be the first nondegree training program in OD, the Learning Community in Organizational Development at UCLA. This annual program was first offered as a full-time, 10-week, residential program, January–March 1967.[16]

Tannenbaum, who held a Ph.D. in Industrial Relations from the School of Business at the University of Chicago, had early been influenced by such authors as Mary Parker Follett in management theory, V. V. Anderson's *Psychiatry in Industry,* Roethlisberger and Dickson's *Management and the Worker,* and Burleigh Gardner's *Human Relations in Industry.* He was on the planning committee for the Western Training Laboratory (WTL) and a staff member for the first session (1952). During that first session he co-trained with a psychiatric social worker who had attended a Bethel program, and in subsequent sessions, in his words, ''co-trained with a psychiatrist, an educator, a clinical psychologist...and I learned much from them.''[17]

Chris Argyris

Chris Argyris, then a faculty member at Yale University, in 1957, was one of the first to conduct team building sessions with a CEO and the top executive team. Two of Argyris' early clients were IBM and Exxon. His early research and interventions with a top executive group are reported in his 1962 book *Interpersonal Competence and Organizational Effectiveness.*[18]

In 1950, Argyris, while working on a Ph.D. at Cornell University, had visited Bethel as a member of NTL's research staff in order to study T-groups. In his words, ''I became fascinated with what I saw, and wanted to become a trainer. Several years later...I was invited to become a staff member...''[19]

Argyris was later to make extensive contributions to theory and research on laboratory training, OD, and organizational learning. One of his several books on OD, *Intervention Theory and Method,*[20] stands as a classic in the field.

According to Argyris, three people had the greatest impact on his early career:

> Number one was Kurt Lewin[21]...I was at Clark, finishing my undergraduate degree. I would go over (to MIT) and sit in on his seminars[22]...But his writings...had the greatest impact.[23] Next came Roger Barker, and his studies on psychological ecology and behavioral settings. I worked with Roger for several years. His greatest impact was not only on helping me to understand how to study behavioral settings more rigorously, but his whole approach to knowledge, which was to explore, to enquire, and to experiment. Finally, there was Bill White at Cornell University, with whom I received my Ph.D. (in organizational behavior). Bill was not only a very thoughtful and encouraging advisor, but he was very smart and learned about field work. He had a sensitivity for what it meant to be an ethnographer that helped me to learn a lot about what to do in the field.[24]

Argyris interacted with many of the early leaders in the T-group and OD fields. For example, in referring to Douglas McGregor, he states, ''I had many wonderful discussions with him in the advanced president's programs at Bethel and in Florida." In referring to Bradford, with whom he worked numerous times from 1950 on, he states that "he was, without any doubt, the person who helped make NTL come alive."[25]

Douglas McGregor

Douglas McGregor, as a professor-consultant, working with Union Carbide, beginning about 1957, was also one of the first behavioral scientists to begin to solve the transfer problem and to talk systematically about and to help implement the application of T-group skills to complex organizations.[26] John Paul Jones, who had come up through industrial relations at Union Carbide, in collaboration with McGregor and with the support of a corporate executive vice president and director, Birny Mason, Jr. (later president of the corporation), established a small internal consulting group that in large part used behavioral science knowledge in assisting line managers and their subordinates to learn how to be more effective in groups. McGregor's ideas were a dominant force in this consulting group; other behavioral scientists who had had an influence on Jones's thinking were Rensis Likert and Mason Haire. Jones's organization was later called an "organization development group."[27]

Among the many influences on Douglas McGregor, of course, was Kurt Lewin, a colleague at MIT whom McGregor had help recruit. It is also clear that he was influenced by Leland Bradford, Edwin Boring, Irving Knickerbocker, Jay Forrester, and Gordon Allport.[28] McGregor also must have been influenced by Carl Rogers, the leading theorist and practitioner in client-centered therapy, because McGregor assigned Rogers' writings to his classes at MIT.[29] McGregor's classic work, *The Human Side of Enterprise,* which has had such an impact on managers since its publication in 1960, cites an extensive list of psychologists, sociologists, and management theorists, including Peter Drucker.[30] (See the discussion of Richard Beckhard, which refers to the influence of McGregor's consulting work at General Mills on *The Human Side of Enterprise.*)

Herbert Shepard

During the same year, 1957, Herbert Shepard, through introductions by Douglas McGregor, joined the employee relations department of Esso Standard Oil (now Exxon) as a research associate. Shepard was to have a major impact on the emergence of OD. While we will focus mainly on Shepard's work at Esso, it should also be noted that Shepard was later involved in community development activities and, in 1960, at the Case Institute of Technology, founded the first doctoral program devoted to training OD specialists.

Before joining Esso, Shepard had completed his doctorate at MIT and had stayed for a time as a faculty member in the Industrial Relations Section. Among influences on Shepard were Roethlisberger and Dickson's *Management and the Worker* (1939) and a biography of Clarence Hicks. (As a consultant to Standard Oil, Hicks had helped to develop participative approaches to personnel management and labor relations.) Shepard was also influenced by Farrell Toombs, who had been a counselor at the Hawthorne plant and had trained under Carl Rogers. In addition, Shepard had been heavily influenced by the writings of Kurt Lewin. NTL influence was also an important part of Shepard's background; he attended an NTL lab in 1950 and subsequently was a staff member in many of its programs.[31]

In 1958 and 1959 Shepard launched three experiments in organization development at major Esso refineries: Bayonne, New Jersey; Baton Rouge, Louisiana; and Bayway, Texas. At Bayonne an interview survey and diagnosis were made and discussed with top management, followed by a series of three-day laboratories for all members of management.[32] Paul Buchanan, who had worked earlier at the Naval Ordnance Test Station and more recently had been using a somewhat similar approach in Republic Aviation, collaborated with Shepard at Bayonne and subsequently joined the Esso staff.

Blake and Shepard

At Baton Rouge, Robert Blake joined Shepard, and the two initiated a series of two-week laboratories attended by all members of ''middle'' management. At first, an effort was made to combine the case method with the laboratory method, but the designs soon emphasized T-groups, organizational exercises, and lectures. One innovation in this training program was an emphasis on intergroup as well as interpersonal relations. Although working on interpersonal problems affecting work performance was clearly an organizational effort, between-group problem solving had even greater organization development implications in that a broader and more complex segment of the organization was involved.

At Baton Rouge, efforts to involve top management failed, and as a result follow-up resources for implementing organization development were not made available. By the time the Bayway program started, two fundamental OD lessons had been learned: the requirement for active involvement in and leadership of the program by top management and the need for on-the-job application.

At Bayway, there were two significant innovations. First, Shepard, Blake, and Murray Horwitz utilized the instrumented laboratory, which Blake and Jane Mouton had been developing in social psychology classes at the University of Texas and which they later developed into the Managerial Grid approach to organization development.[33] (An essential dimension of the instrumented lab is the use of feedback based on scales and measurements of group and individual behavior during sessions.)[34] Second, at Bayway more resources were devoted to team development, consultation, intergroup conflict resolution, and so forth than were devoted to laboratory training of ''cousins,'' that is, organization members from different departments. As Robert Blake stated, ''It was learning to *reject* T-group stranger-type labs that permitted OD to come into focus,'' and it was intergroup projects, in particular, that ''triggered real OD.''[35]

Robert Blake

As in the case of Shepard and others, influences on Robert Blake up to that point were important in the emergence of OD. While at Berea College majoring in psychology and philosophy (later an M.A., University of Virginia, and a Ph.D., University of Texas), Blake had been strongly influenced by the works of Korzybski and the general semanticists and found that ''seeing discrete things as representative of a continuous series was much more stimulating and rewarding than just seeing two things as 'opposites.'" This thinking contributed in later years to Blake's conceptualization of the Managerial Grid with Jane Mouton and to their intergroup research on win-lose dynamics. This intergroup research and the subsequent design of their intergroup conflict management workshops were also heavily influenced by Muzafer Sherif's fundamental research on intergroup dynamics.[36] Jane Mouton's influence on Blake's thinking and on the development of the Grid stemmed partly, in her words, "from my undergraduate work (at Texas) in pure mathematics and physics which emphasized the significance of measurement, experimental design, and a scientific approach to phenomena."[37] (Mouton later attained an M.A. from the University of Virginia and a Ph.D. from the University of Texas.)

During World War II, Blake served in the Psychological Research Unit of the Army Air Force where he interacted with a large number of behavioral scientists, including sociologists. This contributed to his interest in "looking at the system rather the individuals within the system on an isolated one-by-one basis."[38] (This is probably one of many links between systems concepts or systems theory and OD.)

Another major infuence on Blake had been the work of John Bowlby, a medical member of the Tavistock Clinic in London, who was working in family group therapy. Blake, after completing his Ph.D. work in clinical psychology, went to England for 16 months in 1948 and 1949 to study, observe, and do research at Tavistock. As Blake states it,

> Bowlby had the clear notion that treating mental illness of a individual out of context was an...ineffective way of aiding a person....As a result, John was unprepared to see patients, particularly children, in isolation from their family settings. He would see the intact family: mother, father, siblings....I am sure you can see from what I have said that if you substitute the word organization for family and substitute the concept of development for therapy, the natural next step in my mind was organization development.[39]

Among others at Tavistock who influenced Blake were Wilfred Bion, Henry Ezriel, Eric Trist, and Elliott Jaques.

After returning from Tavistock and taking an appointment at Harvard, Blake joined the staff for the summer NTL programs at Bethel. His first assignment was co-responsibility for a T-group with John R. P. French. Blake was a member of the Bethel staff from 1951 to 1957 and continued after that with NTL labs for managers at Harriman House, Harriman, New York. Among other influences on Blake were Jacob Moreno's action orientation to training through the use of psychodrama and sociodrama and E. C. Tolman's notions of purposive behavior in humans.[40]

Richard Beckhard

Richard Beckhard, another major figure in the emergence and extension of the OD field, came from a career in the theater. In his words,

> I came out of a whole different world—the theatre—and went to NTL in 1950 as a result of some discussions with Lee Bradford and Ron Lippitt. At that time they were interested

in improving the effectiveness of the communications in large meetings and I became involved as head of the general sessions program. But I also got hooked on the whole movement. I made a career change and set up the meetings organization, "Conference Counselors." My first major contact was the staging of the 1950 White House conference on children and youth. . . . I was brought in to stage the large general sessions with six thousand people. . . . I had been doing a lot of large convention participative discussion type things and had written on the subject. . . . At the same time I joined the NTL summer staff. . . . My mentors in the field were Lee Bradford, in the early days, and Ron Lippitt and later, Ren Likert, and very particularly, Doug McGregor, who became both mentor, friend, father figure. . . and in the later years, brother. Doug had left MIT and was at Antioch as president. . . . Doug and I began appearing on similar programs. One day coming back on the train from Cincinnati to Boston, Doug asked if I was interested in joining MIT. . . .

In the period 1958–63, I had worked with him (McGregor) on two or three projects. He brought me to Union Carbide, where I replaced him in working with John Paul Jones, and later, George Murray and the group. We (also) worked together at. . . Pennsylvania Bell and. . . at General Mills.[41]

Beckhard worked with McGregor at General Mills in 1959 or 1960, where McGregor was working with Dewey Balsch, vice president of personnel and industrial relations, in an attempt to facilitate "a total organizational culture change program which today might be called quality of work life or OD." Beckhard goes on to say, "The issues that were being worked were relationships between workers and supervision; roles of supervision and management at various levels; participative management for real. . . . This experience was one of the influences on Doug's original paper, 'The Human Side of Enterprise'. . . and from which the book emerged a year or so later."[42]

Beckhard developed one of the first major nondegree training programs in OD, NTL's Program for Specialists in Organizational Training and Development (PSOTD). The first session was an intensive four-week session held in the summer of 1967 at Bethel, Maine, the same year as UCLA launched its Learning Community in OD. Core staff members the first year in the NTL program were Beckhard as dean, Warner Burke, and Fritz Steele. Additional resource persons the first year were Herbert Shepard, Sheldon Davis, and Chris Argyris. In addition, along with McGregor, Rensis Likert, Chris Argyris, Robert Blake, Lee Bradford, and Jack Gibb, Beckhard was a founder of NTL's Management Work Conferences that are essentially laboratory training experiences for middle managers. As an extension of this program, Beckhard was also active in the development and conducting of NTL's senior executive conferences and presidents' labs.[43]

The Term "Organization Development"

It is not entirely clear who coined the term *organization development,* but it is likely that the term emerged more or less simultaneously in two or three places through the conceptualization of Robert Blake, Herbert Shepard, Jane Mouton, Douglas McGregor, and Richard Beckhard.[44] The phrase *development group* had earlier been used by Blake and Mouton in connection with human relations training at the University of Texas and appeared in their 1956 document that was distributed for use in the Baton Rouge experiment.[45] (The same phrase appeared in a Mouton and Blake article first published in the journal *Group Psychotherapy* in 1957.)[46] The Baton Rouge T-groups run by Shepard and Blake were called *development groups*,[47] and this program of T-groups was called "organization development" to distinguish it from the complementary management development programs already underway.[48]

Referring to his consulting with McGregor at General Mills, Beckhard gives this account of the term emerging there:

> At that time we wanted to put a label on the program at General Mills....We clearly didn't want to call it management development because it was total organization-wide, nor was it human relations training although there was a component of that in it. We didn't want to call it organization improvement because that's a static term, so we labelled the program "Organization Development," meaning system-wide change effort.[49]

Thus, the term emerged as a way of distinguishing a different mode of working with organizations and as a way of highlighting its developmental, systemwide, dynamic thrust.

The Role of Personnel and Industrial Relations Executives

It is of considerable significance that the emergence of organization development efforts in three of the first corporations to be extensively involved, Union Carbide, Esso, and General Mills, included personnel and industrial relations people seeing themselves in new roles. At Union Carbide, John Paul Jones, in industrial relations, now saw himself in the role of a behavioral science consultant to other managers.[50] At Esso, the headquarters human relations research division began to view itself as an internal consulting group offering services to field managers rather than as a research group developing reports for top management.[51] At General Mills, the vice president of personnel and industrial relations, Dewey Balsch, saw his role as including leadership in conceptualizing and coordinating changes in the culture of the total organization.[52] Thus, in the history of OD we see both external consultants and internal staff departments departing from their traditional roles and collaborating in a new approach to organization improvement.

THE SURVEY RESEARCH AND FEEDBACK STEM

Survey research and feedback,[53] a specialized form of action research (see Chapter 8), constitutes the second major stem in the history of organization development. The history of this stem, in particular, revolves around the techniques and approach developed by staff members at the Survey Research Center of the University of Michigan over a period of years.

Rensis Likert

The SRC was founded in 1946 after Rensis Likert, director of the Division of Program Surveys of the Federal Bureau of Agricultural Economics, and other key members of the division, moved to Michigan. Likert held a Ph.D. in psychology from Columbia, and his dissertation, *A Technique for the Measurement of Attitudes,* was the classic study in which the widely used five-point "Likert scale" was developed. After a period of university teaching, Likert had been employed by the Life Insurance Agency Management Association where he conducted research on leadership, motivation, morale, and productivity. He had then moved to the U.S. Department of Agriculture, where his Division of Program Surveys furthered a more scientific approach to survey rsearch in its work with various federal departments, including the Office of War Information.[54] After helping to develop and direct the Survey Research Center, following World War II, in 1948 Likert then became the director of a new Institute for Social Research, which included both the SRC and the Research Center for Group Dynamics, the latter moving to Michigan from MIT after Lewin's death.

Floyd Mann, Rensis Likert, and Others

Part of the emergence of survey research and feedback was based on the refinements made by SRC staff members in survey methodology. Another part was the evolution of the feedback methodology. As related by Rensis Likert,

> In 1947, I was able to interest the Detroit Edison Company in a company-wide study of employee perceptions, behavior, reactions and attitudes which was conducted in 1948. Floyd Mann, who had joined the SRC staff in 1947, was the study director on the project. I provided general direction. Three persons from D.E.: Blair Swartz, Sylvanus Leahy and Robert Schwab with Mann and me worked on the problem of how the company could best use the data from the survey to bring improvement in management and performance. This led to the development and use of the survey-feedback method. Floyd particularly played a key role in this development. He found that when the survey data were reported to a manager (or supervisor) and he or she failed to discuss the results with subordinates and failed to plan with them what the manager and others should do to bring improvement, little change occurred. On the other hand, when the manager discussed the results with subordinates and planned with them what to do to bring improvement, substantial favorable changes occurred.[55]

Another aspect of the Detroit Edison study was the process of feeding back data from an attitude survey to the participating departments in what Mann calls an "interlocking chain of conferences."[56] Additional insights are provided by Baumgartel, who participated in the project and who drew the following conclusions from the Detroit Edison study:

> The results of this experimental study lend support to the idea that an intensive, group discussion procedure for utilizing the results of an employee questionnaire survey can be an effective tool for introducing positive change in a business organization. It may be that the effectiveness of this method, in comparison to traditional training courses, is that it deals with the system of human relationships as a whole (superior and subordinate can change together) and it deals with each manager, supervisor, and employee in the context of his own job, his own problems, and his own work relationships.[57]

Links between the Laboratory Training Stem and the Survey Feedback Stem

Links between people who were later to be key figures in the laboratory training stem of OD and people who were to be key figures in the survey feedback stem occurred as early as 1940 and continued over the years. These links were undoubtedly of significance in the evolution of both stems. Of particular interest are the links between Likert and Lewin and between Likert and key figures in the laboratory training stem of OD. As Likert states it, "I met Lewin at the APA annual meeting at State College, Pa., I believe in 1940. When he came to Washington during the War, I saw him several times and got to know him and his family quite well."[58] In 1944 Likert arranged a dinner at which Douglas McGregor and Kurt Lewin explored the feasibility of a group dynamics center at MIT.[59]

Likert further refers to McGregor: "I met McGregor during the war and came to know him very well after Lewin had set up the RCGD at MIT. After the War, Doug became very interested in the research on leadership and organizations that we were doing in the Institute for Social Research. He visited us frequently and I saw him often at Antioch and at MIT after he returned." Likert goes on to refer to the first NTL lab for managers that was held at Arden House in 1956: "Douglas McGregor and I helped Lee Bradford launch it. . . . Staff members in the 1956 lab were: Beckhard, Benne, Bradford, Gordon Lippit, Malott, Shepard and I. Argyris, Blake and McGregor joined the staff for the 1957 Arden House lab."[60]

Argyris refers to Likert:

> Rensis Likert was also a leader in the field when I was a graduate student, and I had the highest respect for him and his commitment to trying to connect theory with practice. Indeed, I've always been a bit sad to see how many of his colleagues, who saw themselves as more researchers, at times would downplay Rensis' commitment to practice. They saw him as being too. . .committed to the world of practice. I never felt that. I felt that it was the combination of practice and theory that made him an important member of our community. I would put Lewin first on that dimension, and Ren Likert and Doug McGregor next, each in his own way making important contributions.[61]

Links between group dynamics and survey feedback people were extensive, of course, after the RCGD moved to Michigan with the encouragement of Rensis Likert and members of the SRC. Among the top people in the RCGD who moved to Michigan were Leon Festinger, Dorwin Cartwright, Ronald Lippitt, and John R. P. French, Jr. Cartwright, who was selected by the group to be the director of the RCGD, was particularly knowledgeable about survey research, since he had been on the staff of the Division of Program Surveys with Rensis Likert and others during World War II.[62]

THE ACTION RESEARCH STEM

In Chapter 2 we briefly described action research as a collaborative, client-consultant inquiry consisting of preliminary diagnosis, data gathering from the client group, data feedback to the client group, data exploration and action planning by the client group, and action. As we will describe in Chapter 8, there are at least four versions of action research, one of which, participant action research, is used with the most frequency in OD. The laboratory training stem in the history of OD has a heavy component of action research; the survey feedback stem is the history of a specialized form of action research; and Tavistock projects have had a strong action research thrust, as we will discuss shortly.

Because we will treat the history of action research in some detail in Chapter 8, we will mention only a few aspects here. For example, William F. Whyte and Edith L. Hamilton were using action research in their work with Chicago's Tremont Hotel in 1945 and 1946; John Collier, commissioner of Indian Affairs, was describing action research in a publication in 1945; Kurt Lewin and his students conducted numerous action research projects in the mid-1940s and early 1950s. The work of these and other scholars and practitioners in the invention and utilization of action research was basic in the evolution of OD.

SOCIOTECHNICAL AND SOCIOCLINICAL PARALLELS

Somewhat parallel to the work of the RCGD, the SRC, and NTL was the work of the Tavistock Clinic in England. The clinic had been founded in 1920 as an outpatient facility to provide psychotherapy based on psychoanalytic theory and insights from the treatment of battle neurosis in World War I. A group focus emerged early in the work of Tavistock in the context of family therapy in which the child and the parent received treatment simultaneously.[63] The action research mode also emerged at Tavistock in attempts to give practical help to families, organizations, and communities.

W. R. Bion, John Rickman, and Others

The staff of the Tavistock Clinic was extensively influenced by such innovations as World War II applications of social psychology to psychiatry, the work of W. R. Bion and John Rickman and others in group therapy, Lewin's notions about the "social field" in which a problem was occurring, and Lewin's theory and experience with action research. Bion, Rickman, and others had been involved with the six-week "Northfield Experiment" at a military hospital near Birmingham during World War II. In this experiment each soldier was required to join a group that both performed some task such as handicraft or map reading and discussed feelings, interpersonal relations, and administrative and managerial problems as well. Insights from this experiment were to carry over into Bion's theory of group behavior.[64]

Eric Trist

It is of significance that Tavistock's sociotechnical approach to restructuring work grew out of Eric Trist's visit to a coal mine and his insights as to the relevance of Lewin's work on group dynamics and Bion's work on leaderless groups to mining problems.[65] Trist was also influenced by the systems concepts of Von Bertalanffy and Andras Angyal.[66] Trist's subsequent experiments in work redesign and the use of semiautonomous work teams in coal mining were the forerunners of other work redesign experiments in various industries in Europe, India, and the United States. Thus, there is a clear historical link between the group dynamics field and sociotechnical approaches to assisting organizations.

Tavistock–U.S. Links

Tavistock leaders, including Trist and Bion, had frequent contact with Kurt Lewin, Rensis Likert, Chris Argyris, and others in the United States. One product of this collaboration was the decision to publish *Human Relations* as a joint publication between Tavistock and MIT's Research Center for Group Dynamics.[67] Some Americans prominent in the emergence and evolution of the OD field, for example, Robert Blake, as we noted earlier, and Warren Bennis,[68] studied at Tavistock. Chris Argyris held several seminars with Tavistock leaders in 1954.[69]

Although the sociotechnical approach focused on the nonexecutive ranks of organizations and was therefore not a complete systemwide approach, many aspects were congruent with OD as we have characterized it in Chapter 2. The focus on teams and the use of action research and participation were certainly consistent with contemporary OD approaches. (As we will discuss in Chapter 14, some contemporary quality of work life, [QWL] programs are an amalgamation of OD, sociotechnical, and other approaches. Further, some OD efforts have been criticized as not involving rank-and-file employees; sociotechnical approaches are additions to the repertoire of improvement strategies that clearly focus on this level.)

EXTENT OF APPLICATION

Applications emerging from one or more of the stems just described are evident in the organization development efforts now occurring in many countries, including England, Japan, Norway, Canada, Sweden, Finland, Australia, New Zealand, the Philippines, Venezuela, and Holland, as well as in the United States. Among the large number of organizations in America that have embarked on organization development efforts are Union Carbide and Exxon (the first two companies), Connecticut General Insurance Company, Hewlett-Packard, Tektronix, Graphic Controls, Equitable Life Assurance Company, Digital Equipment Corporation, Procter & Gamble, Microelectronics and Computer Technology Corporation (MCC), Mountain Bell Telephone, Searle Laboratories, General Motors, Bankers Trust, Ford Motor Company, Heinz Foods, IBM, Polaroid, Sun Oil, and TRW Inc.

Applications vary, with the total organization involved in many instances, but with only some divisions or plants in others. Further, some efforts have moved ahead rapidly, only to flounder at a later time. In many situations, OD approaches have become an ongoing way of managing with little program visibility and under different terminology. Thus, it is difficult to report with any precision the extent of application. However, one study of a random sample of *Fortune* 500 companies, yielding 71 respondents, found 46 percent (33) of the responding firms to be using organization development techniques.[70]

Applications at TRW Space & Defense Sector (formerly TRW Defense and Systems Group), a large research and development organization in the aerospace field, commenced in the early 1960s, have been as extensive and innovative as those found anywhere in the world, and are of major significance in the emergence and history of OD. (TRW Space & Defense Sector is divided into four groups: Electronic Systems Group,

Defense Systems Group, Space & Technology Group, and Operations & Support Group.) Among the key figures in the emergence of the OD effort at the early TRW Systems were Jim Dunlap, director of industrial relations; Shel Davis, who was later promoted to that position; Ruben Mettler, president; and Herb Shepard. T-group labs conducted by internal trainers, NTL, and UCLA staff members were also important in providing impetus to the effort in its early phases. Efforts at TRW Systems and in the total organiza- tion, TRW, have included team building, intergroup team building, interface laboratories between departments and between company and customers, laboratory training, career assessment workshops, and organization redesign and structuring for improved produc- tivity and quality of working life.[71]

As an indication of how durable organization development has been and how extensively OD is built into the ongoing management processes at TRW, in 1987, *approx- imately 25 years after OD started at TRW,* some 200 offsite OD meetings were held by teams of the four groups of TRW Space & Defense Sector. These meetings included team building, intergroup team building, organization planning, employee sensing, and other OD interventions. According to Sam Shirley, Director of Human Relations, Electronic Systems Group,

> The entire responsibility for designing these meetings is centered in the line Human Rela- tions staffs at both division and group level. . . Our Human Relations professionals are continually called upon to provide a wide variety of internal consulting to their "client system". . . We are continuing to train our internal Human Relations staff in organiza- tion dynamics and consulting skills.[72]

It should be noted that the divisional Human Relations managers are personnel/human resources managers along with being internal OD consultants.[73]

Business and industrial organizations are by no means the only kinds of institu- tions involved. There are applications, for example, in public school systems; colleges; medical schools; social welfare agencies; police departments; professional associations; governmental units at the local, county, state, and national levels; various health care delivery systems; churches; American Indian tribes; and the U.S. military.

OD activities in the U.S. military have waxed and waned, partly depending upon top command interest and support. Reduced support for the program in the Army appears to be partly due to lack of systematic measurement of the results. At one time, the Army ran an Organizational Effectiveness Center and School at Fort Ord, California and graduated some 1,702 officers as internal consultants. The Center started in 1975 with a complement of 19 officers, six enlisted personnel, and 21 civilians; 10 years later the complement had been reduced to three officers and one civilian who were reassigned to the Soldier Support Center to teach basic human resource skills.[74] The Navy, on the other hand, conducted a year-long study of all aspects of its OE program and concluded that the program had "definite value but would be best utilized with a major change in its structure."[75]

Some "community development" strategies have a number of elements in common with organization development, such as the use of action research, the use of a change agent, and an emphasis on facilitating decision-making and problem-solving processes.[76] Undoubtedly, some of the commonality stems from OD practitioners working in the community development field. For example, in 1961 Herbert Shepard conducted community development laboratories at China Lake, California, sponsored by the Naval Ordnance Test Station. These one-week labs involved military persons and civilians and people of all ages and socioeconomic levels. Outcomes included the resolution of some community and intercommunity issues.[77]

In addition to emphasizing the diversity of types of systems using OD consultants, we want to emphasize that intraorganization development efforts have not focused on just top-management teams, although the importance of top-management involvement will be discussed in later chapters. The wide range of occupational roles that have been involved in OD is almost limitless and has included production workers,[78] managers, soldiers, military officers, miners, scientists and engineers, ministers, psychologists, geologists, lawyers, accountants, nurses, physicians, teachers, computer specialists, foresters, technicians, secretaries, clerical employees, board members, and flight crews.

Symptomatic of the widespread application of organization development concepts is the emergence and growth of the OD Network, which began in 1964 and in early 1988 had a membership of about 1,700. Most members either have major roles in the OD efforts of organization or are scholar-practitioners in the OD field. While most OD Network members reside in the U.S., the 1988–89 roster listed 135 international members, the majority from Canada. Nineteen countries were represented in addition to the U.S.

The OD Network began with discussions at the Case Institute of Technology between Herbert Shepard, Sheldon Davis of TRW Systems, and Floyd Mann of the University of Michigan,[79] and through the initiative of Leland Bradford and Jerry Harvey of NTL and a number of industrial people who had attended labs at Bethel. Among the industrial founders of the organization, originally called the Industrial Trainers Network, were Sheldon Davis of TRW Systems, George Murray of Union Carbide, John Vail of Dow Chemical, and Carl Albers of the Hotel Corporation of America. Other early members were from Procter & Gamble, Weyerhaeuser, Bankers Trust, West Virginia Pulp and Paper Company, the U.S. State Department, the U.S. National Security Agency, Pillsbury, Eli Lilly, Polaroid, Esso, Parker Pen, American Airlines, Goodrich-Gulf Chemicals, RCA, Sandia, National Association of Manufacturers, General Foods, Armour & Company, Heublein, and Dupont. Jerry Harvey was the first secretary/coordinator of the emerging organization, and Warner Burke assumed that role in 1967 shortly after joining NTL on a full-time basis. There were fewer than 50 members at that time; when Warner Burke stepped aside as executive director in 1975, there were approximately 1,400 members.[80] That same year the OD Network became independent of NTL.

An OD Division of the American Society for Training and Development was established in 1968 and had more than 4,000 members by the summer of 1981. It is also significant that the Academy of Management, whose members are mostly professors in management and related areas, established a Division of Organization Development within its structure in 1971, and this unit had approximately 1,100 members in late 1987. The Society of Industrial–Organizational Psychology of the American Psychological Association has held workshops on organization development at the annual APA conventions; several annual conventions going back at least to 1965 have included papers or symposia on organization development or related topics.[81] In 1974 the *Annual Review of Psychology* for the first time devoted a chapter entirely to a review of research on organization development.[82] Chapters on OD have appeared at other times, for example, 1977,[83] 1982, and 1987.[84] The 1982 chapter was written by authors from the Netherlands and France, indicative of OD's international applications.[85]

The first doctoral program devoted to training OD specialists was founded by Herbert Shepard in 1960 at the Case Institute of Technology. Originally called The Organizational Behavior Group, this program is now part of the Department of Organizational Behavior, School of Management, Case Western Reserve University. Masters degree programs in organization development or masters programs with concentrations in OD have been offered in recent years by several universities, including New York University, Brigham Young, Pepperdine, Loyola, Bowling Green, New Hampshire, Central Washington University, Columbia, and Case Western Reserve and Sheffield Polytechnic in England. The American University and NTL Institute jointly offer a masters degree program in Human Resource Development. The John F. Kennedy University and NTL cosponsor a masters program which has organization development and change as a major component. Many other major universities, if not most, now have graduate courses directly bearing on organization development, including UCLA, Stanford, Harvard, University of Southern Califiornia, Hawaii, Oklahoma, Colorado, Indiana, and Purdue, and in England, such courses are found at the University of Manchester Institute of Science and Technology and the University of Bath.[86]

This rapid growth in OD interest and attention has been given impetus by NTL's Program for Specialists in Organization Development (originally called PSOTD), discussed earlier in this chapter. PSOD started as an intensive, four-week session held in the summer at Bethel and was partly an outgrowth of an Organization Intern Program that had included some OD training. PSOD subsequently became a two-week program for managers/practitioners with several years of professional experience. Other NTL programs include Process Consultation, Team Building, A Socio-Technical Approach to Designing High Performing Systems, and Strategic Management and OD. Other professional programs in OD have been or are now being offered in the United States, Canada, the United Kingdom, Australia, New Zealand, and elsewhere under the sponsorship of universities, foundations, professional associations, and other institutions.

SUMMARY

Organization development has emerged largely from applied behavioral sciences and has three major stems: the invention of the T-group and innovations in the application of laboratory training insights to complex organizations, the invention of survey feedback technology, and the emergence of action research. Parallel and linked to these stems was the emergence of the Tavistock sociotechnical and socioclinical approaches.

Key figures in this early history interacted with each other and across these stems and were influenced by concepts and experiences from a wide variety of disciplines and settings. These disciplines and settings included clinical and social psychology, family group therapy, ethnography, military psychology and psychiatry, the theater, general semantics, systems theory, mathematics and physics, philosophy, psychodrama, client-centered therapy, survey methodology, experimental and action research, personnel and industrial relations, organizational behavior, and general management theory.

The history of OD is emergent in that a rapidly increasing number of behavioral scientists and practitioners in organizations are building on the research and insights of the past as well as discovering the utility of some of the earlier insights. These efforts are now expanding and include a wide range of organizations, types of institutions, occupational categories, and geographical locations around the world.

In the chapters that follow, the assumptions, theory, and techniques of organization development will be examined in substantial depth along with some speculation as to its future viability.

NOTES

1. The phrase "group dynamics" was coined by Kurt Lewin in 1939. See Warrent Bennis, address to the Academy of Management, San Diego, California, August 3, 1981.

2. This and the next paragraph are based on Kenneth D. Benne, Leland P. Bradford, Jack R. Gibb, and Ronald O. Lippitt, eds., *The Laboratory Method for Changing and Learning: Theory and Application* (Palo Alto, Calif.: Science and Behavior Books, 1975), pp. 1–6; and Alfred J. Marrow, *The Practical Theorist: The Life and Work of Kurt Lewin* (New York: Basic Books, 1969), pp. 210–214. For additional history, see Leland P. Bradford, "Biography of an Institution," *Journal of Applied Behavioral Science,* 3 (April–June 1967), pp. 127–143; and Alvin Zander, "The Study of Group Behavior During Four Decades," *The Journal of Applied Behavioral Science,* 15 (July–September 1979), pp. 272–282. We are indebted to Ronald Lippitt for his correspondence, which helped to clarify this and the following paragraph.

3. Jerrold I. Hirsch, *The History of the National Training Laboratories 1947–1986* (New York: Peter Lang Publishing, 1987), pp. 17–18; and address by Ronald Lippitt, Academy of Management annual conference, Chicago, Illinois, August 1986.

4. Peter B. Smith, ed., *Small Groups and Personal Change* (London: Methuen & Co. 1980), pp. 8–9.

5. Robert Chin and Kenneth D. Benne, "General Strategies for Effecting Changes in Human Systems," in Warren G. Bennis, Kenneth D. Benne, and Robert Chin, eds., *The Planning of Change,* 2nd ed. (New York: Holt, Rinehardt and Winston, 1969), pp. 100–102.

6. Correspondence with Kenneth Benne. Raup was Benne's Ph.D. major professor at Columbia. Benne states that he was also influenced by Edward Lindeman.

7. Chin and Benne, op cit., p. 102.

8. Correspondence with Ronald Lippitt.

9. Conversation with Lee Bradford, conference on current theory and practice in organization development, San Francisco, March 16, 1978.

10. See, for example, S. R. Slavson, *An Introduction to Group Therapy* (New York: The Commonwealth Fund, 1943); and S. R. Slavson, *Creative Group Education* (New York: Association Press, 1937), especially Chapter 1.

11. Based largely on correspondence with Ronald Lippitt. According to Lippitt, as early as 1945 Bradford and Lippitt were conducting "three-level training" at Freedman's Hospital in Washington, D.C., in an effort "to induce interdependent changes in all parts of the same system." Lippitt also reports that Leland Bradford very early was acting on a basic concept of "multiple entry," that is, simultaneously training and working with several groups in the organization.

12. Correspondence with Robert Tannenbaum.

13. Tannenbaum correspondence; memordandum of May 12, 1952, U.S. Naval Ordnance Test Station from E. R. Toporeck to "Office, Division and Branch Heads, Test Department," and "Minutes, Test Department Management Seminar, 5 March 1953."

14. Robert Tannenbaum, Verne Kallajian, and Irving R. Weschler, "Training Managers for Leadership," *Personnel,* 30 (January 1954), p. 3.

15. Verne J. Kallejian, Irving R. Weschler, and Robert Tannenbaum, "Managers in Transition," *Harvard Business Review,* 33 (July–August 1955), pp. 55–64.

16. Tannenbaum correspondence.

17. Ibid.

18. Correspondence with Chris Argyris; and Chris Argyris, *Interpersonal Competence and Organizational Effectiveness* (Homewood, Ill.: Richard D. Irwin, 1962).

19. Argyris correspondence.

20. Chris Argyris, *Intervention Theory and Method* (Reading, Mass.: Addison-Wesley, 1970).

21. Argyris correspondence.

22. Donald D. Bowen, "Competence and Justice: A Conversation with Chris Argyris," p. 4.2 of a manuscript accepted for publication in the *1988 OD Annual.*

23. Argyris correspondence.

24. Ibid. Argyris' Ph.D. in organizational behavior may have been the first ever awarded.

25. Argyris correspondence.

26. See Richard Beckhard, W. Warner Burke, and Fred I. Steele, "The Program for Specialists in Organization Training and Development," p. ii, mimeographed paper (NTL Institute for Applied Behavioral Science, December 1967); and John Paul Jones, "What's Wrong with Work?" in *What's Wrong with Work?* (New York: National Association of Manufacturers, 1967), p. 8. According to correspondence with Rensis Likert, the link between McGregor and John Paul Jones occurred in the summer of 1957. Discussion took place between the two when Jones attended one of the annual two-week seminars at Aspen, Colorado, organized by Hollis Peter of the Foundation for Research on Human Behavior and conducted by Douglas McGregor, Mason Haire, and Rensis Likert.

27. Gilbert Burck, "Union Carbide's Patient Schemers," *Fortune,* 72 (December 1965), pp. 147–149. For McGregor's account, see "Team Building at Union Carbide," in Douglas McGregor, *The Professional Manager* (New York: McGraw-Hill, 1967), pp. 106–110.

28. See the Editor's Preface to Douglas McGregor, *The Professional Manager* (New York: McGraw-Hill, 1967), p. viii.

29. Conversation with George Strauss, Western Division of the Academy of Management conference, San Diego, California, March, 1985. For a brief overview of Rogers' life and career, see "Carl Rogers (1902–1987)," *American Psychologist,* 43: 127–128 (February 1988). Carl Rogers was also on the staff of several NTL president's labs in the early days. Seminar with Carl Rogers, Western Division of the Academy of Management conference, San Diego, California, March, 1985.

30. Douglas McGregor, *The Human Side of Enterprise* (New York: McGraw-Hill, 1960). For more on McGregor, see Marvin R. Weisbord, *Productive Workplaces* (San Francisco: Jossey-Bass Publishers, 1987), pp. 106–122.

31. This paragraph is based on interviews with Herbert Shepard, August 3, 1981. For a brief discussion of the career of Clarence Hicks, see Wendell French, *The Personnel Management Process,* 6th ed. (Boston: Houghton Mifflin, 1987), Chap. 2.

32. Much of the historical account in this paragraph and the following three paragraphs is based on correspondence and interviews with Herbert Shepard, with some information added from correspondence with Robert Blake.

33. Correspondence with Robert Blake and Herbert Shepard. For further reference to Murray Horwitz and Paul Buchanan, as well as to comments about the innovative contributions of Michael Blansfield, see Herbert A. Shepard, "Explorations in Observant Participation," in Bradford, Gibb, and Benne, eds., *T-Group Theory,* pp. 382–383. See also Marshall Sashkin, "Interview with Robert R. Blake and Jane Srygley Mouton," *Group and Organization Studies,* 3 (December 1978), pp. 401–407.

34. See Robert Blake and Jane Srygley Mouton, "The Instrumented Training Laboratory," in Irving R. Weschler and Edgar M. Schein, eds., *Selected Readings Series Five: Issues in Training* (Washington, D.C., National Training Laboratories, 1962), pp. 61–85. In this chapter, Blake and Mouton credit Muzafer and Carolyn Sherif with important contributions to early inter-

group experiments. Reference is also made to the contributions of Frank Cassens of Humble Oil and Refinery in the early phases of the Esso program. For a brief description of the development of the two-dimensional Managerial Grid, see Robert Blake and Jane Srygley Mouton, *Diary of an OD Man* (Houston, Gulf 1976), pp. 332–336.

35. Based on correspondence with Robert Blake. See also Robert R. Blake and Jane Srygley Mouton, "Why the OD Movement Is 'Stuck' and How to Break It Loose," *Training and Development Journal,* 33 (September 1979), pp. 12–20.

36. Blake correspondence.

37. Mouton corrrespondence.

38. Blake correspondence.

39. Ibid.

40. Ibid.

41. Correspondence with Richard Beckhard.

42. Ibid.

43. Based on Beckhard correspondence and other sources.

44. Interpretations of Blake correspondence, Shepard interview, Beckhard correspondence, and Larry Porter, "OD: Some Questions, Some Answers—An Interview with Beckhard and Shepard," *OD Practitioner,* 6 (Autumn 1974), p. 1.

45. Blake correspondence.

46. Jane Srygley Mouton and Robert R. Blake, "University Training in Human Relations Skills," *Selected Readings Series Three: Forces in Learning* (Washington, D.C.: National Training Laboratories, 1961), pp. 88–96, reprinted from *Group Psychotherapy,* 10 (1957), pp. 342–345.

47. Shepard and Blake correspondence.

48. Interview with Herbert Shepard, San Diego, California, August 3, 1981.

49. Beckhard correspondence.

50. Burck, "Union Carbide's Patient Schemers," p. 149.

51. Harry D. Kolb, "Introduction" to *An Action Research Program for Organization Improvement* (Ann Arbor, Mich.: Foundation for Research on Human Behavior, 1960), p. i. The phrase *organization development* is used several times in this monograph based on a 1959 meeting about the Esso programs and written by Kolb, Shepard, Blake, and others.

52. Based on Beckhard correspondence.

53. This history is based largely on correspondence with Rensis Likert and partially on "The Career of Rensis Likert," *ISR Newsletter,* Winter 1971; and *A Quarter Century of Social Research,* Institute for Social Research, 1971. See also Charles Cannell and Robert Kahn, "Some Factors in the Origins and Development of The Institute for Social Research, The University of Michigan," *American Psychologist,* 39: (November 1984), pp. 1256–1266.

54. "Rensis Likert," *ISR Newsletter,* p. 6.

55. Likert correspondence. Floyd Mann later became the first director of the Center for Research on the Utilization of Scientific Knowledge (CRUSK) when the center was established by ISR in 1964. See also Floyd C. Mann, "Studying and Creating Change," in Bennis, Benne, and Chin, eds., *Planning of Change,* pp. 605–613.

56. Mann, "Studying and Creating Change," p. 609.

57. Howard Baumgartel, "Using Employee Questionnaire Results for Improving Organizations: The Survey (Feedback) Experiment," *Kansas Business Review,* 12 (December 1959), pp. 2–6.

58. Likert correspondence.

59. Marrow, *The Practical Theorist,* p. 164. This book, about the life and work of Kurt Lewin, is rich with events that are important to the history of OD.

60. Likert correspondence.

61. Argyris correspondence.

62. Likert correspondence.

63. H. V. Dicks, *Fifty Years of the Tavistock Clinic* (London: Routledge & Kegan Paul, 1970), pp. 1, 32.

64. Based on Ibid., pp. 5, 7, 133, 140; and Robert DeBoard, *The Psychoanalysis of Organizations* (London: Tavistock 1978), pp. 35–43.

65. Eric Trist and Marshall Sashkin, "Interview," *Group & Organization Studies,* 5 (June 1980), pp. 150–151.

66. Ibid., p. 155.

67. The previous three paragraphs are based largely on ibid., pp. 144–151. The brief statement about action research is also partly based on Alfred J. Marrow, "Risks and Uncertainties in Action Research," *Journal of Social Issues* 20, No. 3 (1964), p. 17.

68. Bennis address, Academy of Management, August 3, 1981.

69. Argyris correspondence.

70. Stephen R. Michael, "Organizational Change Techniques: Their Present, Their Future," *Organizational Dynamics,* 11 (Summer 1982), p. 77.

71. Interview with Sam Shirley, February 4, 1982; correspondence with Sheldon A. Davis; Sheldon A. Davis, "An Organic Problem-Solving Method of Organizational Change," *Journal of Applied Behavioral Science,* 3 (November 1, 1967), pp. 3–21; and the case study of the TRW Systems Group in Gene Dalton, Paul Lawrence, and Larry Greiner, *Organizational Change and Development* (Homewood, Ill.: Irwin-Dorsey, 1970), pp. 4–153.

72. Correspondence with Sam Shirley; and interview with Sam Shirley, Western Division, Academy of Management, Big Sky, Montana, March 25, 1988.

73. Shirley interview.

74. Mel R. Spehn, "Reflections on the Organizational Effectiveness Center and School," mimeographed paper, compiled in the summer/fall of 1985, Fort Ord, California, p. 3.

75. Ibid., p. 11.

76. See Eva Schindler-Rainman, "Community Development Through Laboratory Methods," in Benne, Bradford, Gibb, eds.; and Lippitt, *Laboratory Method of Changing and Learning,* pp. 445–463.

77. Shepard correspondence. Starting in 1967, Herbert Shepard was involved in the applications of OD to community problems in Middletown, Connecticut.

78. See Scott Myers, "Overcoming Union Opposition to Job Enrichment," *Harvard Business Review,* 49 (May–June 1971), pp. 37–49; and Robert Blake, Herbert Shepard, and Jane Mouton, *Managing Intergroup Conflict in Industry* (Houston: Gulf, 1964), pp. 122–138.

79. Shepard correspondence.

80. Correspondence with W. Warner Burke and memoranda and attendance lists pertaining to 1967–1969 Network meetings furnished by Burke.

81. For example, the following topics were included in the program of the 1965 convention: "Strategies for Organization Improvement: Research and Consultation," "Managerial Grid Organization Development," and "The Impact of Laboratory Training in Research and Development Environment," *American Psychologist,* 20 (July 1965), pp. 549, 562, 565.

82. Frank Friedlander and L. Dave Brown, "Organization Development," *Annual Review of Psychology,* 25 (1974), pp. 313–341.

83. Clay Alderfer, "Organization Development," *Annual Review of Psychology,* 28 (1977), pp. 197–223.

84. Michael Beer and Anna Elise Walton, "Organizational Change and Development," *Annual Review of Psychology,* 38 (1987), pp. 339–367.

85. Claude Faucheux, Gilles Amada, and André Laurent, "Organizational Development and Change," *Annual Review of Psychology,* 33 (1982), pp. 343–370.

86. D. D. Warrick, ed., *OD Newsletter,* OD Division, Academy of Management, Spring 1979, p. 7.

4

UNDERLYING ASSUMPTIONS AND VALUES

Implicit in the preceding chapters and throughout the book are a number of underlying assumptions and values that we should now make explicit. These assumptions, which we believe are basic to most organization development activities, relate to people as individuals, to people as group members and as leaders, and to people as members of total organizational systems. The following appear to be some of the basic assumptions underlying organization development efforts and, in general, are congruent with the theories of Mayo, Roethlisberger and Dickson, Rogers, Maslow, McGregor, Likert, Mann, Argyris, Schein, Bennis, Benne, Sheats, and others.[1] The assumptions seem to us to be reasonable ones, at least for free, democratic, and relatively egalitarian societies.

ASSUMPTIONS ABOUT PEOPLE AS INDIVIDUALS

We think that organization development efforts make two basic assumptions about people. One has to do with personal growth and the other with constructive contributions.

The first assumption about people is that most individuals have drives toward personal growth and development if provided an environment that is both supportive and challenging. Most people want to become more of what they are capable of becoming.

The second assumption, related to the first, is that most people desire to make, and are capable of making, a higher level of contribution to the attainment of organizational goals than most organizational environments will permit. A tremendous amount of constructive energy can be tapped if organizations recognize this, for example, by asking for and acting on suggestions to solve problems. Frequently, however, organizational members learn that what they thought would be seen as helpful is self-defeating in the sense that these efforts are not rewarded and may be penalized. For example, lateral communications between peers in two different departments in attempts to solve some problem may be squelched by one of the superiors' adherence to some principle about the chain of command. As another example, suggestions for change from production employees may be seen and dismissed as typical griping from people "who can't possibly see the whole picture" or who are "always complaining about something."

Assumptions that people have drives toward personal growth and development and toward constructive contribution differ markedly from more traditional views about people. As Tannenbaum and Davis state it,

> The traditional view of individuals is that they can be defined in terms of given interests, knowledge, skills and personality characteristics: they can gain new knowledge, acquire additional skills, and even at times change their interests, but it is rare that people really change. This view, when buttressed by related organizational attitudes and modes, insures a relative fixity of individuals, with crippling effects.[2]

Thus, one can view people as fixed entities, or one can view them as potentially "in process" or in "the process of becoming."[3] The latter assumption underlies many OD interventions—many of which are aimed at unleashing drives toward personal growth and contribution or are aimed at modifying organizational constraints that are having a dampening or throttling effect.

ASSUMPTIONS ABOUT PEOPLE IN GROUPS AND ABOUT LEADERSHIP

The importance of the work team has long been recognized, and the significance of the "informal" part of group life has received considerable attention since the Hawthorne studies of the late 1920s and early 1930s.[4] Extensive knowledge about group dynamics and collaborative ways of managing group culture, however, has had a more recent origin. In particular, the laboratory training movement of post-World War II has contributed to this knowledge. The following are some assumptions growing mainly out of this recent history.

The first assumption is that one of the most psychologically relevant reference groups for most people is the work group, including peers and the superior. What goes on in the work team, especially at the informal level, has great significance for feelings of satisfaction and competence.

A related assumption is that most people wish to be accepted and to interact cooperatively with at least one small reference group, and usually with more than one group, that is, the work group, the family, and so forth. Furthermore, most people are capable of greatly increasing their effectiveness and of helping their reference groups to solve problems. From our experience, most work groups have only begun to utilize their resources for effective collaboration. Stating the case negatively, a great deal of energy is expended sub rosa on such issues as inclusion-exclusion, unclear communications, ineffective feedback, and suppressing productivity if there is no collaborative effort to examine and manage such dimensions.

A third assumption is that for a group to optimize its effectiveness, the formal leader cannot perform all the leadership and maintenance functions in all circumstances at all times; hence group members must assist each other with effective leadership and member behaviors. For many managers and groups, these are difficult patterns from which to extricate themselves and frequently require a change in perspective on the part of both the manager and the total group. For example, if the manager begins to realize that improvements in unit functioning really require fuller participation on the part of all subordinates, the norms of the group may need to be examined to legitimatize such participation. To illustrate, the current norms may call for deference to one or two more vocal members, or the norm may be to avoid issues facing the total unit in order to concentrate efforts on solving narrower problems where there is a more immediate payoff.

A fourth assumption is that suppressed feelings and attitudes adversely affect problem solving, personal growth, and job satisfaction. The culture in most groups and organizations tends to suppress the expression of feelings and attitudes that people have about each other and their behaviors—both positive and negative—and about where they and their organizations are heading. An emphasis on ''rationality'' seems to assume that emotions and attitudes are best handled by repressing them—that feelings, in particular, are taboo. Of course, what happens is that feelings are expressed covertly instead of openly. For example, we have probably all been to meetings in which we have felt unduly limited in what we could say and have approached others afterward to express our authentic feelings about what was going on and about the decisions that were made. As a consequence, we have consciously or inadvertently set in motion forces that mitigated or thwarted the apparent action steps that were planned. This does not mean that the expression of feelings per se will always be helpful or that individuals and groups immediately have the skill to manage this organizational underworld of sentiments. The development of such skill requires much learning, and much of it together in the group that wishes to improve its performance. Viewing feelings as data important to the organization, however, coupled with the development of group skills in dealing with feelings, tends to open up many avenues for improved goal setting, leadership, communications, conflict resolution, problem solving, between-group collaboration, and morale.

A fifth assumption is that the level of interpersonal trust, support, and cooperation is much lower in many groups and organizations than is either necessary or desirable, in spite of drives toward these same qualities. Typically a number of forces contribute to such situations, including an absence of viewing feelings as important data, lack of group problem-solving skills, and leadership styles that reinforce dysfunctional competition. As one example, in an organization where norms result in a suppression of positive sentiments between people, thus leaving the bulk of evaluative statements to be in a critical mode, organizational members will feel unsupported and will tend to be guarded in their interchange with others. As another example, if the prevailing leadership style emphasizes one-on-one communications and political maneuvering behind closed doors, a highly competitive, mistrusting kind of climate tends to be spawned.

A sixth assumption about people in groups is that the solutions to many attitudinal and motivational problems in organizations are transactional. That is, such problems have the greatest chance of constructive solution if all parties in the system or subsystem alter their mutual relationships. The question becomes, not How can A get B to perform better? but *How can A and B work together to modify their interactions toward the goal of B becoming more effective and A and B becoming more mutually effective?* Frequently, the challenge is broader, to include *How can persons C, D, and E support and assist in these changes?*

Thus the unit for attention becomes a system larger than one individual—the group. This is not to deny the importance of the individual but to stress the significance of the interactional nature of human relationships in the organizational setting. As Peters and Waterman state in *In Search of Excellence,* ''Small groups are, quite simply, the basic organizational building blocks of excellent companies.''[5]

ASSUMPTIONS ABOUT PEOPLE IN ORGANIZATIONAL SYSTEMS

A number of ideas or assumptions about people in systems more complex than groups also underlie organization development efforts. Some of these assumptions follow, and others will be elaborated upon in subsequent chapters.

In recent years it has frequently been observed that organizations tend to be characterized by overlapping work groups, with the superior and others serving, in Likert's terminology, as ''linking pins.''[6] (See Figure 4-1.[7]) Thus a manager is a member of at least two work teams—as the superior in one and as a subordinate and peer in another.

This leads to an assumption relative to OD that we believe to be true: the interplay of the dynamics of these work teams, as conveyed by the ''linking pin'' incumbents, has a powerful effect on the attitudes and behavior of people in both groups. In particular, the leadership style and the climate of the higher team tend to get transmitted to the lower teams. Conditions of trust, support, openness, and teamwork tend to influence the style of managers lower on the hierarchy and rub off onto their subordinates. Similarly, conditions of mistrust, political infighting, guardedness, and lack of cooperation tend to get transmitted both upward and downward and tend to influence attitudes and interactions at those levels.

This assumption extends to committees or task forces that draw members from several work groups. The culture of these temporary work teams carries over into the culture of the more permanent work teams, and vice versa. The creation of what Zand

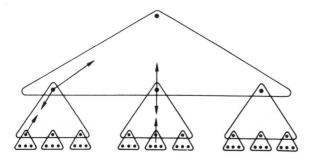

(The arrows indicate the linking pin function)

Figure 4-1 The Linking Pin Function. Source: Rensis Likert, *New Patterns of Management,* New York: McGraw-Hill Book Company, 1961. Used with permission.

calls "collateral organizations" (see Chapter 14), which are designed in part to influence the broader culture of the organization, is based on the same assumption.

A second assumption about human dynamics in organizations is that "win-lose" conflict strategies between people and groups, in which one comes off the triumphant winner and the other the defensive loser, while realistic and appropriate in some situations, are not optimal in the long run to the solution of most organizational problems. If the struggle is between two managers, subordinates get drawn into the fray in subtle ways, if no more than through their withholding of information from the "enemy" group or remaining silent rather than expressing their real opinion on some issue. Most organizational problems can better be approached in terms of "how can we all win?"

And finally, there are at least two assumptions made that relate to the complexities and difficulties involved in helping make major shifts in the culture of an organization. One is that it takes time and patience, and the key movers in an OD effort need to have a relatively long-range time perspective. The other is that improved performance stemming from organization development efforts needs to be sustained by appropriate changes in the appraisal, compensation, training, staffing, task, and communications subsystems—in short, in the total human resources sytem. (The latter assumption is a complex topic and is discussed in Chapter 16, System Ramifications and New Demands.)

ASSUMPTIONS THAT RELATE TO VALUES IN THE CLIENT ORGANIZATION

A basic assumption that most OD practitioners seem to make in engaging with a client is that members of the system, in general, place value in collaborative effort and in the end products of the system. It is essential, obviously, that some values must be held in common between organizational members if conflict-resolving and group problem-solving techniques are to be useful; otherwise people or groups tend to resort to raw power. To state the case negatively, organization development strategies will be unsuccessful to the degree that system members place no value on the goals of the organization and/or have some ideological commitment to chronic dissension and turmoil, anarchy, hate, violence, or destruction. This is not to say that organization development has no role in the management of dissent. It can play a major role in clarifying and resolving issues, but it will not work if people are not willing to try to work together to solve problems.

A further, and related, basic assumption underlying organization development activities is that value is placed on welfare of all system members, particularly by the people having the most power over others. This assumption is the most basic and perhaps the most obvious one of all, but it needs to be made explicit. OD programs are aimed at improving the welfare and quality of work life for all contributing members of the organization. They are neither a method for giving tools of manipulation or exploitation to any group (say, the managerial group), nor are they a method for improving the welfare of one group at the expense of other groups. The degree to which both these assumptions hold true relative to the culture of the organization needs to be sensed early in any organization development effort, and any serious incongruities should be worked out between consultant and client, or the relationship should be terminated.

VALUE AND BELIEF SYSTEMS OF BEHAVIORAL SCIENTIST CHANGE AGENTS

While some would argue that scientific inquiry is value free, other argue that *all* research is value laden.[8] In any event, it seems to us that the *applications* of science have value connotations. From our experience, applied behavioral scientists in the organization development field tend to have several values in common relative to their practice. We do not assume, of course, that they are a completely homogeneous group.

One value, to which many behavioral scientist-change agents tend to give high priority, is that the needs and aspirations of human beings are the reasons for organized effort in society. They tend, therefore, to be developmental in their outlook and concerned with the long-range opportunities for the personal growth of people in organizations.

This orientation creates a self-fulfilling prophecy. The belief that people are important tends to result in their being important. The belief that people can grow and develop in terms of personal and organizational competency tends to produce this result. Thus, values and beliefs can be self-fulfilling, and the question becomes, "What do you choose to want to believe?" While this position can be naive in the sense of not seeing the real world, nevertheless, behavioral scientist-change agents—these authors at least—tend to place a value on optimism. It is a kind of optimism that says people, in collaboration with others, can do a better job of goal setting, diagnosing and solving problems, and implementing plans.[9]

A second value that tends to be held by change agents is that working and life can become richer and more meaningful, and organized effort more effective and enjoyable, if feelings and sentiments are permitted to be a more legitimate part of the culture of organizations. This value, of course, like any other, can be held in excess with a lack of attention to organizational realities. For example, the OD consultant may be overly zealous in promoting openness in a conflict situation. A reality may be that the reward system rewards winners of such struggles regardless of the human resources wasted in the process, and that it is the reward system that needs changing before there is any hope that the conflict will diminish.

A third value that tends to be held by change agents is a commitment to both action and research broadly conceived, which can include inquiry and examination into the nature of change processes and the effectiveness of interventions. Although many change agents are perhaps overly action oriented in terms of the utilization of their time, as a group they are paying more and more attention to research and to the examination of ideas and the building of theory.

Finally, a value frequently attributed to applied behavioral scientists is a presumed value placed on democratization of organizations or on "power equalization." The latter has been defined as "a reduction in differences in power, status and influence between superiors and subordinates."[10]

While most would probably place high value on humanizing the work place and on a democratic-participative way of life, our distinct impression is that most are not on an excursion to reduce or neutralize the power of owners of managers. The goal they have is to utilize human resources more effectively and thus to increase the power of everybody, including the boss, at least in the sense of increased authority based on technical and human relations competence.[11]

This is where we are on these issues. As organization development consultants, we do not see our role as power equalizers or power dismantlers. We do, however, believe that most organizations can profitably learn to be more responsive to organizational members and constituencies and that all parties concerned can learn to be more skillful in this responsiveness. This means that many managers need to augment the authority of their positions with additional skills and that more resources will have to be allocated at all levels to training in group dynamics, conflict resolution, collaborative problem solving, and the organization development process generally.

Parenthetically, it should be added that it is important that behavioral scientist-change agents make their values and beliefs visible to both themselves and their clients. Neither party can learn to trust the other adequately without such exposure—hidden agendas handicap both trust building and mutual learning. Perhaps more pragmatically, organization development change efforts tend to fail if strategies or techniques are applied unilaterally and without open collaboration.[12]

SUMMARY

Organization development activities rest on a number of assumptions about people as individuals, in groups, and in total systems, about the transactional nature of organization improvement, and about values. These assumptions tend to be developmental and optimistic, while acknowledging the realities of the exercise of power on and within organizations. Assumptions and values held by change agents need to be made explicit, both for enhancing working relationships with clients and for continuous testing through practice and research.

Some assumptions stem from a "systems" view of organizations. In the next chapter, we will elaborate upon some of these systems concepts.

NOTES

1. See, for example, Elton Mayo, *The Social Problems of an Industrial Civilization* (Cambridge, Mass.: Harvard University Press, 1945); F. J. Roethlisberger and W. J. Dickson, *Management and the Worker* (Cambridge, Mass.: Harvard University Press, 1939); Carl R. Rogers, *Counseling and Psychotherapy* (Boston: Houghton Mifflin, 1942); Abraham Maslow, *Motivation and Personality,* 2nd ed. (New York: Harper & Row, 1970); Douglas McGregor, *The Professional Manager* (New York: McGraw-Hill, 1967); Rensis Likert, *The Human Organization: Its Management and Value* (New York: McGraw-Hill, 1967); Floyd C. Mann, "Studying and Creating Change," in Warren Bennis, Kenneth Benne, and Robert Chin, eds., *The Planning of Change* (New York: Holt, Reinhart and Winston, 1961); Chris Argyris, *Integrating the Individual and the Organization* (New York: John Wiley, 1964); Edgar H. Schein and Warren G. Bennis, *Personal and Organizational Change Through Group Methods* (New York: John Wiley, 1965); and Kenneth D. Benne and Paul Sheats, "Functional Roles of Group Members," *Journal of Social Issues,* 4 (Spring 1948), pp. 41–49.

2. Robert Tannenbaum and Sheldon Davis, "Values, Man and Organizations," *Industrial Management Review,* 10 (Winter 1969), pp. 68–70. See also O'Toole's list of Motorola's assumptions about employees in contrast to "Old Guard" assumptions. James O'Toole, *Vanguard Management: Redesigning the Corporate Future* (Garden City, N.Y.: Doubleday & Company, Inc., 1985), pp. 97–98.

3. See Gordon W. Allport, *Becoming* (New Haven, Conn.: Yale University Preess, 1955).

4. For the major work growing out of these studies, see Roethlisberger and Dickson, *Management and the Worker.*

5. Thomas J. Peters and Robert H. Waterman, Jr., *In Search of Excellence: Lessons from America's Best-Run Companies* (New York: Harper & Row, 1982), p. 126. See also Harold J. Leavitt, "Suppose We Took Groups Seriously. . ." in Eugene L. Cass and Frederick G. Zimmer, eds., *Man and Work in Society* (New York: Van Nostrand Reinhold Company, 1975), pp. 67–77.

6. See Rensis Likert, *New Patterns of Management* (New York: McGraw-Hill, 1961), p. 113.

7. This figure is from ibid., p. 133. Used with permission of McGraw-Hill Book Company.

8. See George S. Howard, "The Role of Values in the Science of Psychology," *American Psychologist,* 40 (March 1985), pp. 255–265. See also Leonard Krasner and Arthur C. Houts, "A Study of the 'Value' Systems of Behavioral Scientists," *American Psychologist,* 39 (August 1984), pp. 840–850.

9. See also Dov Eden, "OD and Self-Fulfilling Prophecy: Boosting Productivity by Raising Expectations," *The Journal of Applied Behavioral Science,* 22: (No. 1, 1986), pp. 1–13.

10. Jean M. Bartunek and Christopher B. Keys, "Power Equalization in Schools Through Organization Development," *Journal of Applied Behavioral Science,* 18 (November 2, 1982), p. 171.

11. For a discussion of "authority of competence" and "authority of person," see Robert L. Peabody, "Perceptions of Organizational Authority: A Comparative Analysis," *Administrative Science Quarterly,* 6 (March 1962), p. 470.

12. Margulies and Raia recommend that OD professionals become more assertive in their roles as "values advocates." Newton Margulies and Anthony P. Raia, "Some Reflections on the Values of Organizational Development," *Academy of Management OD Newsletter,* (Winter 1988), pp. 1, 9–11.

5

RELEVANT SYSTEMS CONCEPTS

We have already used the word *system* and would like to elaborate on the concept because it has considerable utility in helping to pose questions about organization development and in planning change strategies. Although a system view of organizations and change will be drawn upon throughout this book, we try to be explicit about its relevance in this chapter. We first look at some definitions and descriptions and then move on to a further discussion of the relevance of these ideas to organization development.

THE CONCEPT OF SYSTEM

Fagen defines *system* as "a set of objects together with relationships between the objects and between their attributes."[1] Von Bertalanffy refers to a system as a set of "elements standing in interaction."[2] Kast and Rosenzweig define system as "an organized, unitary whole composed of two or more interdependent parts, components, or subsystems, and delineated by identifiable boundaries from its environmental suprasystem."[3]

Thus, *system* denotes interdependency or interaction of components or parts, and an identifiable wholeness or gestalt. Organizations are systems, and the aspects of interdependency and interaction of components and of wholeness are very important dimensions in organization development, as we will see later.

Additional Characteristics of Systems

Other dimensions of systems are also relevant. Systems in operation (active systems), such as organizations, can be viewed as a linkage of *input* flows (energy, materials, or information) from *sources* in the external environment, a transforming mechanism (a machine or a technical-human organization), and flows of *outputs* or *outcomes,* provided to *users.* The system may include one or more *feedback* mechanisms for self-regulation. For example, signals from the internal or external environment that the output is substandard could result in changes in either the transforming mechanism or the inputs, or both (see Figure 5–1).

Each of these components needs to be effectively managed and linked if there is to be a healthy organization. For example, to focus most attention on the technical-human organization (transforming mechanism) and to ignore how customers or clientele are reacting to the product (user-output relationship) can lead to serious consequences. We have seen how lack of attention by the American automobile industry to public interest in economy cars led to lost opportunity for many years. We recall a top executive of a major automobile corporation saying some years ago that Volkswagen owners ''were crazy''; a few years later American automobile manufacturers were spending billions to catch up with German and Japanese manufacturers of economy cars.

Similarly, to focus on seeking sources of funding (input) or to concentrate on marketing (output) to the extent of ignoring the effectiveness of the technical-human organization can also have disastrous results. As an illustration, we have seen a chief executive of a private organization almost destroy it by spending almost all his energy on external matters while paying inadequate attention to the quality of internal communications and administration. As a consequence, all his key subordinates were frustrated, were often in serious conflict with each other, and harbored a growing disillusionment with his leadership. Both illustrations are examples of inadequate attention to feedback mechanisms and to managing the interrelationships of system components.[4]

To elaborate further, while systems differ in the degree to which they are in an open versus a closed state, organizations and subparts of organizations are essentially

Figure 5–1   A System in Interaction With Its Environment

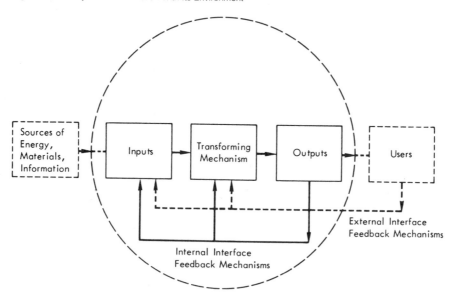

open systems in that they exist in interdependent, exchange relationships with their environments. The more effectively these exchange relationships—that is, the interfaces—are managed in terms of utilizing inputs, the less the system is subject to *entropy,* that is, running down, becoming marginal or obsolete, or going out of existence. In the illustration of the automobile company, the external interface was not being managed properly. In the illustration of the chief executive, the internal interfaces between organizations subsystems—between himself and the board of directors, between himself and his staff, and between departments—were being ignored.

ORGANIZATIONS DESCRIBED IN SYSTEMS TERMINOLOGY

Although it is very helpful to view subunits of organizations—for example, departments and divisions—as subsystems, we also find it useful to think of organizations as consisting of a number of significant interacting variables that cut across or are common to all subunits. These variables have to do with goals, tasks, technology, human-social organization, structure, and external interface relationships. Thus we can visualize organizations as consisting of a goal subsystem, a task subsystem, a technological subsystem, a human-social subsystem, a structural subsystem, and an external interface subsystem.[5] (See Figure 5-2.) All can be influenced by OD efforts, although, in a sense, the human-social subsystem is the initial change target, as we will see later.

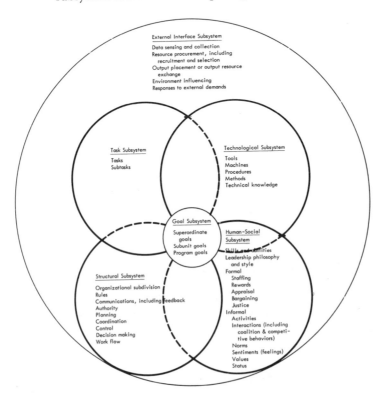

Figure 5-2 Major Organizational Subsystems

This way of viewing the organization is more elaborate than the ideas implicit in Figure 5-1, but it can include them all. For example, the concept of feedback is included in Figure 5-2 in the notion of the external interface system, and in the notion of the internal communications subsystem. (What is a "system" or a "subsystem" is purely relative and depends upon at what level of abstraction or level of complexity one is focusing one's analysis.)

To elaborate on this way of viewing organizations, the *goal subsystem* consists of one or more (usually several) interrelated superordinate objectives or goals, usually set forth in the organization's charter or mission statement, plus the subgoals of units and programs stemming from or forming the superordinate goals. Although corporate goals are frequently reported in terms of profit objectives, even a superficial probing finds most business executives talking about the production of particular kinds of goods or services at a profit. Most are very conscious of the importance of satisfying certain customer or client needs if they are to satisfy their own. Furthermore, significant aspects of the goal system are the subunit or program goals that either stem from or act interdependently with overall goals.[6] The interrelationship between these levels of goals typically is an area of considerable tension in organizations and requires extensive managing. Thus the goal subsystem is usually highly complex.

The *technological subsystem* consists of tools, machines, procedures, methods, and technical knowledge. In essence, this subsystem consists of the artifacts and knowledge that have been assembled to produce an end product, and it stems largely from the goal subsystem.

The *task subsystem* consists of the subdivision of the total work to be performed into those tasks and subtasks that need to be accomplished by organization members to produce the end product. The actual tasks to be done are highly dependent upon the technological subsystem. For example, the kinds of machines or tools used will extensively influence the tasks to be performed.

The *structural subsystem* is highly influenced by the technological subsystem and consists of task groupings, such as units, departments, or divisions. Interrelated with such task groupings is the design of the work flow, that is, where a partially completed product goes next, and so forth. Also included in the structural subsystem are work rules, such as beginning and ending hours; the authority system, for example, who reports to whom, and who can exercise sanctions toward whom; and procedures and practices relative to communicating, planning, coordination, control, and decision making. These three subsystems—technological, task, and structural—are obviously highly interdependent.

The *human-social subsystem* can be viewed as consisting of four aspects: the *skills and abilities* of organizational members, the *leadership philosophy and style*, a *formal* subsystem, and an *informal* subsystem. Skills and abilities are included because the capabilities of organization members pervade all organizational subsystems. While leadership philosophy and style can be considered one aspect of skills and abilities, we choose to separate out these dimensions because they are so highly interrelated with such matters as the way decisions are made and the degree of concern for human values expressed in the organization. By formal subsystem is meant personnel subsystems, such as staffing (assignment, transfer, promotion, separation), rewards (financial and otherwise), and appraisal (performance review and the communication of the review); bargaining subsystems (formalized collective bargaining or quasi-bargaining relationships); and the system of organizational justice (mechanisms for equitable treatment and for remedying wrongs, for example, appeal systems). The informal subsystem consists of nonprogrammed activities and interactions, including resistant behaviors and coalition and competitive behaviors; group norms, sentiments (feelings); values; and status.

The *external interface subsystem* consists of data sensing and gathering (e.g., market or public reaction surveys); resource procurement (e.g., recruitment and selection, and purchasing); output placement or exchanges of outputs for resources; environment influencing (e.g., advertising, public relations, lobbying, pollution control); and responses to external demands. The latter has recently become a very conspicuous and impactive aspect of organizational life. The incidents are too numerous to recount: governmental requirements about hiring, promotion, and compensation practices; deregulation; picketing of business firms and of conventions; partial consumer boycotts; and the like. How all these kinds of interface problems are managed can have important consequences for the success, health, or viability of an organization.

RELEVANCE TO ORGANIZATION DEVELOPMENT: ADDITIONAL COMMENTS

The preceding discussion of systems concepts and a systems view of organizations leads to several generalizations about organization development. First, *because organizational subsystems exist in a highly interdependent state, systemwide changes may occur by introducing changes in any one of these subsystems.* Thus, OD interventions need to be based on a diagnosis of the consequences throughout the system of different options open to the change agent and key clients.

Second, *the initial vehicle for organization development efforts—for improvements in any or all of the organizational subsystems—tends to be an intervention in the human-social and the structural subsystems.* That is, perceptions and sentiments of organizational members are tapped relative to problems they see in the organization, and in this process the communications and perhaps even the authority and control subsystems are altered. A prior condition may be some change in leadership philosophy or style.

As a third generalization, *there is an immediate interrelated impact between the human-social and the structural subsystems.* For example the moment that group members start trying to understand the norms under which they have been operating, their communications and probably their decision making will be affected. When a manager begins to listen to and understand feelings, the authority structure begins to shift. Reciprocally, the outcome of a manager altering his or her communications style to a more inquiring and understanding-seeking stance is likely to be a positive shift in subordinate feelings.

And fourth, *while the initial vehicle for organization development efforts tends to be an intervention in the human-social and the structural subsystems, there is likely to be either a direct or an indirect confrontation of the goal, task, technological, and external interface systems, plus the human-social and the structural subsystems themselves.* For example, unit or organizational goals are frequently reviewed and modified in "team-building" sessions. Action planning pertaining to goals was explicit in all the illustrations provided in Chapter 1.

Further, the external interface subsystem is frequently examined in OD efforts. In Illustration 1 there was a review of customer relationships. In some OD efforts, key people involved in the interface are brought together to work on mutual problems with the help of a third party. For example, manufacturers and salespeople from one organization may be brought together to meet with key people from a customer organization.

Although extensive technological changes are typically not made directly through OD interventions, team member reactions to obstacles in carrying out tasks may result in changes in procedures or equipment (technological subsystem). For example, in the instance of Illustration 1 Chapter 1, action plans that emerged from the workshop included changing procedures having to do with customer complaints. In Illustration 3, hazardous work practices were analyzed and modified. In Illustration 5 ("Departure from Tradition in a Division of a Large Corporation"), action steps included adding direct telephone lines between plants to avoid switchboard delays. In Illustration 8, mechanical and maintenance problems were analyzed and corrected.

Indirectly, the task subsystem is always modified in OD efforts. For example, in Illustration 7 ("A New Plant Manager"), the very fact that subordinate managers were involved in group sessions served to alter the mix of tasks and the nature of their jobs. Very simply, the planning and decision-making components were being enlarged. More directly, the task subsystem is frequently altered through an exploration of group members' expectations of each other. This occurred in Illustrations 4 and 5 and in Illustration 6 ("Organizational Improvement in an Indian Tribe").

Thus, organization development efforts may be somewhat more of a total or gestalt kind of consulting than has sometimes been recognized. It does not suffice, for example, to say that OD focuses on "human relations" or "interpersonal relations" unless, of course, the consultant's style or the client's needs keep the change effort in these realms.

Indicative of this gestalt approach is a fairly common question asked by change agents in the data gathering phase of an organization development intervention: "What do you see as getting in the way of getting the job done the way you would like to see it get done?" The responses can pertain to any one of the organizational subsystems as described in Figure 5-2. We should, however, recognize the "set" that respondents will have; if there has been appropriate prework, a change agent will be perceived as an organizational facilitator, not as a technological expert.

To elaborate, the change agent may assist a unit in facing up to and making decisions about technology but will tend to stay out of making technological or other prescriptions. The change agent may, however, suggest additional options for consideration if the problem area is within his or her area of expertise. A major trap for the OD consultant is to permit the client to place the consultant in the role of the expert who is supposed to solve problems *for* the organization. The OD consultant is likely to lose effectiveness quickly if he or she gets into this bind. (See Chapter 17 for a further discussion of this point.)

As a concluding generalization, the question of *whether to embark on an OD effort is to raise the question of whether to increase the extent and quality of system openness.* Whereas all organizations are open systems, they do differ markedly in the degree to which relevant (or potentially relevant) data are shared between people and between subparts of the system. A central issue in organizational life is the degree to which members of the organization are permitted to communicate fully with each other about their perceptions of and their feelings about the various organizational subsystems and the degree to which such communications are facilitated. This issue is at the heart of organization development: *the decision to explore the usefulness of an OD strategy is to decide to examine the wisdom of enlarging the sharing of data by organization members in strategy formulation, problem diagnosis, action planning, and implementation.* And since fuller information and more complete understanding lead to more mutual influence, the issue becomes one of whether or not the key power figures wish to enlarge the domain of mutual influence within the organization.

At another level is the issue of the *quality* of system openness and the quality of the feedback mechanisms. In particular, to what degree is the OD effort to become truly collaborative? The more secret or unilateral the efforts, the more manipulative; the more open and truly participative, the more the efforts are nonmanipulative and the more viable the intervention is likely to be. But openness can be either constructive or destructive. Are the feedback mechanisms developmental or are they punitive and reductive? Thus, both the extent and the quality of system openness are important issues in OD, as will be implicit throughout this book.

SUMMARY

The concept of system, which is a major assumption in organization development efforts, denotes interdependency of components and an identifiable wholeness or gestalt.

Organizations can be viewed as consisting of goal, task, technological, human-social, structural, and external interface subsystems existing in a state of dynamic interdependence. Such concepts as interface, entropy, feedback, and openness are useful in understanding organizations and in raising issues relative to improvement strategies. For example, issues pertaining to both the extent and the quality of organizational feedback mechanisms are important.

The initial vehicles for organization development efforts tend to be the human-social and the structural subsystems, that is, the communications and feedback systems and the attitude and sentiment components of the informal system. However, these become vehicles for confronting problems in any of the major organizational subsystems. The OD process sets off interdependent changes in the human-social and the structural subsystems, and quite likely in all the major organizational subsystems. The OD consultant concentrates on facilitating problem solving relative to these subsystems and avoids being placed in the role of advisor-expert except in matters of procedure relative to the OD process itself.

NOTES

1. See A. D. Hall and R. E. Fagen, "Definition of a System," *General Systems,* Yearbook of the Society for the Advancement of General Systems Theory, 1 (1956), pp. 18–28.

2. Ibid., pp. 1–10.

3. Fremont E. Kast and James E. Rosenzweig, *Organization and Management: A Systems Approach,* 4th ed. (New York: McGraw-Hill, 1985), p. 15.

4. O'Toole refers to the importance of "stakeholder symmetry." His is a similar notion—that all of the component parts must be attended to and all of the constituencies "simultaneously served." James O'Toole, *Vanguard Management: Redesigning the Corporate Future* (Garden City, N.Y.: Doubleday & Company, Inc., 1985), pp. 42–46.

5. This view of an organization is congruent with the models described by Leavitt and Seiler. The former views industrial organizations as complex systems with four major "interacting variables": task, structural, technological, and human; the latter views organizations as sociotechnical systems comprised of four major variables: human, technological, organizational, and social. See Harold J. Leavitt, "Applied Organizational Change in Industry: Structural, Technological and Humanistic Approaches," in James G. March, ed., *Handbook of Organizations* (Chicago: Rand McNally, 1965), pp. 1144–1145. Katz and Kahn refer to production or technical, maintenance, supportive, adaptive, and managerial subsystems. See Daniel Katz and Robert L. Kahn, *The Social Psychology of Organizations,* 2nd ed. (New York: John Wiley, 1978), Chap. 3.

6. To be more specific, we can also think about goals in terms of a descending level of abstraction, for example, end-result, strategic, tactical, and program goals.

6

OPERATIONAL COMPONENTS

the nature of organization development

Organization development, defined in Chapter 2, was differentiated from other organizational and educational interventions as a unique process for improving organizational functioning. In this chapter and the next, we continue and extend that earlier discussion by focusing attention on the nature of OD. The efficacy of organization development is due largely to the nature of the OD process itself. The nature of OD—what it is, what it tries to accomplish, what characteristics and components it has, and what its theoretical underpinnings are—that is the scope of this discussion.

The nature of OD could be presented in several ways. As shown in Figure 6-1, we have chosen to characterize it in terms of the foundations of the OD process and the *components of the OD process in operation*. The outer ellipse describes the foundation characteristics we consider important; the inner ellipse describes the basic components or operations found in any OD program. We will discuss the operational components of OD in this chapter (the inner ellipse) and the characteristics and foundations of the OD process in the next chapter (the outer ellipse).

There are three basic components of the OD process in operation; any OD program will contain these elements of *diagnosis, action,* and *process maintenance*. In the next chapter the major characteristics and the theoretical underpinnings of organization development are explored; these might be considered the foundation upon which the process is built. The characteristics we want particularly to emphasize are that organization development is an ongoing interactive process, is data based (built on an action research model), is experience based, is goal oriented, constitutes a normative-reeducative strategy of changing, is both a form of and a result of applied behavioral science, uses a systems approach, has a work team emphasis, and uses a participation/empowerment

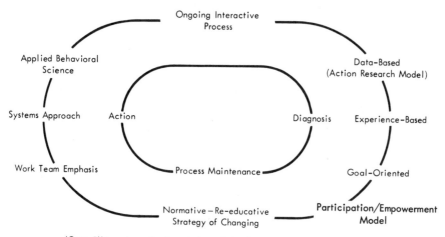

(Outer Ellipse shows the Foundations of the OD Process; Inner Ellipse shows the Components of the OD Process in Operation)

Figure 6-1 The Nature of Organization Development

model. Some facets of the characteristics are treated more extensively in other sections of the book, but we deal with them all in Chapter 7 to show the broad base of organization development as a process of planned change.

OVERVIEW OF THE OPERATIONAL COMPONENTS
OF ORGANIZATION DEVELOPMENT

Implementation of an OD program requires attention to three operations that we call the basic components or elements of an OD program in operation: the diagnostic component, representing a continuous collection of system data, focuses on the total system, its subsystems, and system processes; the action (or intervention) component consists of all the activities of consultants and system members designed to improve the organization's functioning;[1] and the process-maintenance component encompasses the activities oriented toward the maintenance and management of the OD process itself. The first two elements relate to the OD process vis-à-vis the organization; the third element relates to the OD process vis-à-vis itself.

Figure 6-2 shows what we mean when we describe the OD process in terms of diagnosis, action, and process-maintenance components.

The first step in organization development is to diagnose the state of the system: What are its strengths? What are its problem areas? As we indicated in the preceding chapter, the system can be conceptualized as having various subsystems, such as the goal, task, technological, structural, human-social, and external interface subsystems. The diagnosis (step 1) will focus on any or all of these subsystems. From the diagnosis comes identification of strengths and problem areas. Action plans are then developed to correct the problem areas and maintain the areas of strength. These action plans usually result from various interventions that constitute the OD technology. Interventions have been

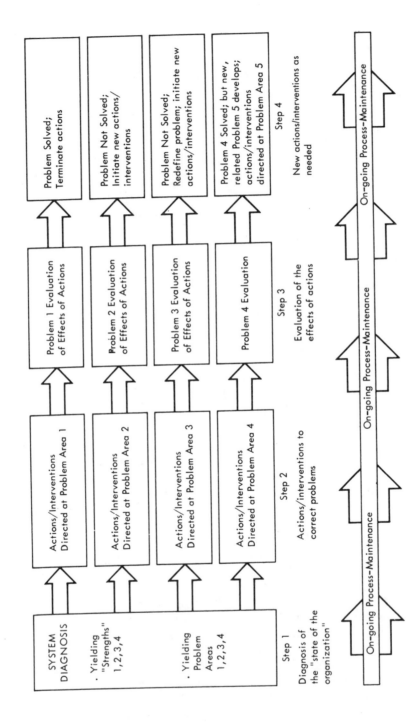

Figure 6-2 Components of the OD Process: Diagnosis, Action, Process Maintenance

developed to correct problems at the levels of individual effectiveness, team effectiveness, intergroup relations, and so forth and also to correct problems at the levels of the various subsystems, such as human-social, goal, and structural. Step 2 then consists of actions and interventions to correct specific problems. Step 3 consists of fact-finding concerning the results of the corrective action taken. Did the actions have the desired effects? Is the problem solved? If the answer is yes, the organization members move on to new and different problems; if the answer is no, the organization members initiate new action plans and interventions to correct the problem (step 4). Often when problems remain unsolved after an initial attack on them, steps 3 and 4 entail redefining and reconceptualizing the problem areas. There may be steps 5, 6, 7, and so on for some problems, but further steps are just iterations of the basic sequence of diagnosis-action-evaluation-action.

During the entire sequence attention must be paid simultaneously to the OD process itself. Energy is expended to ensure that the program is supported by the organization members, that the program is relevant to the organization's priority concerns, and that the program is making discernible progress.

THE DIAGNOSTIC COMPONENT: DIAGNOSING THE SYSTEM AND ITS PROCESSES

Organization development is at heart an action program based on valid information about the status quo, current problems and opportunities, and effects of actions as they relate to goal achievement. An OD program thus starts with diagnosis and continuously employs data collecting and data analyzing throughout. The requirement for diagnostic activities—activities designed to provide an accurate account of things as they really are—stems from two needs: the first is to know the state of things or "what is"; the second is to know the effects or consequences of actions.

The importance of diagnostic activities is emphasized by Beckhard as follows:

> The development of a strategy for systematic improvement of an organization demands an examination of the present state of things. Such an analysis usually looks at two broad areas. One is a diagnosis of the various subsystems that make up the total organization. These subsystems may be natural "teams" such as top management, the production department, or a research group; or they may be levels such as top management, middle management, or the work force.
>
> The second area of diagnosis is the organization processes that are occurring. These include decision-making processes, communications patterns and styles, relationships between interfacing groups, the management of conflict, the setting of goals, and planning methods.[2]

Table 6-1 shows how one would proceed to diagnose a system and its subsystems (the whole and its subunits). For each of the major targets or subsystems in an organization, the typical information desired and common methods of obtaining the information are given. The OD practitioner may be interested in all these target groups or in only one or two of them; he or she may work with one subsystem during one phase of the program and other subsystems during subsequent phases. Frequently, the improvement

Table 6–1 Diagnosing Organizational Subsystems

DIAGNOSTIC FOCUS OR TARGET	EXPLANATION AND IDENTIFYING EXAMPLES	TYPICAL INFORMATION SOUGHT	COMMON METHODS OF DIAGNOSIS
The total organization (having a common "charter" or mission and a common power structure)	The total system is the entity assessed and analyzed. The diagnosis might also include, if relevant, extrasystem (environmental) organizations, groups, or forces, such as customers, suppliers, and governmental regulations. Examples are a manufacturing firm, a hospital, a school system, a department store chain, or a church denomination.	What are the norms ("cultural oughts") of the organization? What is the organization's culture? What are the attitudes, opinions, and feelings of system members toward various "cognitive objects" such as compensation, organization goals, supervision, and top management? What is the organization climate—open vs. closed, authoritarian vs. democratic, repressive vs. developmental, trusting vs. suspicious, cooperative vs. competitive? How well do key organizational processes, such as decision making and goal setting, function? What kind and how effective are the organization's "sensing mechanisms" to monitor internal and external demands? Are organization goals understood and accepted?	Questionnaire surveys are most popular with a large organization. Interviews, both group and individual, are useful for getting detailed information, especially if based on effective sampling techniques. A panel of representative members who are surveyed or interviewed periodically is useful to chart changes over time. Examination of organizational "potsherds"—rules, regulations, policies, symbols of office and/or status, etc., yields insight into the organization's culture. Diagnostic meetings held at various levels within the organization yield a great amount of information in a short time period.
Large subsystems that are by nature complex and heterogeneous	This target group stems from making different "slices" of the organization, such as by hierarchical *level*, *function*, and geographical *location*. Two criteria help to identify this set of subsystems: first they are viewed as a subsystem by themselves or others; and second, they are heterogeneous in makeup, that is, the members have some things in common, but many differences from each other, too. Examples would be the middle-management group, consisting of managers from diverse	All of the above, plus: How does this subsystem view the whole and vice versa? How do the members of this subsystem get along together? What are the unique demands of this subsystem? Are organization structures and processes related to the unique demands? Are there "high" and "low" subunits within the subsystem in terms of performance? Why? What are the major problems confronting this subsystem and its subunits? Are the subsystem's goals compatible with organization goals?	If the subsystems are large or widely dispersed, questionnaire and survey techniques are recommended. Interviews and observations may be used to provide additional supporting or hypothesis-testing information.

Subsystem type	Description	Diagnostic questions	Methods
	functional groups; the personnel department members of an organization that has widely dispersed operations with a personnel group at each location; everyone in 1 plant in a company that has 10 plants; a division made up of several different businesses.	Does the heterogeneity of role demands and functional identity get in the way of effective subsystem performance?	Typical methods include the following: individual interviews followed by a group meeting to review the interview data; short questionnaires; observation of staff meetings and other day-to-day operations; and a family group meeting for self-diagnosis.
Small subsystems that are simple and relatively homogeneous	These are typically formal work groups or teams that have frequent face-to-face interaction. They may be permanent groups, temporary task forces, or newly constituted groups (e.g., the group charged with the "start-up" of a new operation, or the group formed by an acquisition or merger). Examples are the top-management team, any manager and his or her key subordinates, committees of a permanent or temporary nature, task force teams, the work force in an office, the teachers in a single school, etc.	The questions on culture, climate, attitudes, and feelings are relevant here, plus: What are the major problems of the team? How can team effectiveness be improved? What do people do that gets in the way of others? Are member/leader relations those that are desired? Do individuals know how their jobs relate to group and organizational goals? Are the group's working processes, i.e., the way they get things done as a group, effective? Is good use made of group and individual resources?	
Small, total organizations that are relatively simple and homogeneous	An example would be a local professional organization. Typical problems as seen by officers might be declining membership, low attendance, or difficulty in manning special task forces.	How do the officers and the members see the organization and its goals? What do they like and dislike about it? What do they want it to be like? What is the competition like? What significant external forces are impacting on the organization?	Questionnaires or interviews are frequently used. Descriptive adjective questionnaires can be used to obtain a quick reading on the culture, "tone," and health of the organization. Diagnostic family group meetings can be useful.
Interface or intergroup subsystems	These consist of subsets of the total system that contain members of two subsystems, such as a matrix organizational structure requiring an individual or a group to have two reporting lines. But more often this	How does each subsystem see the other? What problems do the two groups have in working together? In what ways do the subsystems get in each other's way? How can they collaborate to improve the perform-	Confrontation meetings between both groups are often the method for data gathering and planning corrective actions. Organization mirroring meetings are used when three or more groups are involved. Inter-

Table 6-1 *(cont.)*

	target consists of members of one subsystem having common problems and responsibilities with members of another subsystem. We mean to include subsystems with common problems and responsibilities such as production and maintenance overlaps, marketing and production overlaps.	ance of both groups? Are goals, subgoals, areas of authority and responsibility clear? What is the nature of the climate between the members? What do the members want it to be?	views of each subsystem followed by a "sharing the data" meeting or observation of interactions can be used.
Dyads and/or triads	Superior/subordinate pairs, interdependent peers, linking pins—i.e., persons who have multiple group memberships—all these are subsystems worthy of analysis.	What is the quality of the relationship? Do the parties have the necessary skills for task accomplishment? Are they collaborative or competitive? Are they effective as a subsystem? Does the addition of a third party facilitate or inhibit their progress? Are they supportive of each other?	Separate interviews followed by a meeting of the parties to view any discrepancies in the interview data are often used. Checking their perceptions of each other through confrontation situations may be useful. Observation is an important way to assess the dynamic quality of the interaction.
Individuals	Any individual within the organization, such as president, division heads, key occupants of positions in a work flow process, e.g., quality control, R&D. In school systems, this would be students, teachers, or administrators.	Do people perform according to the organization's expectations? How do they view their place and performance? Do certain kinds of problems typically arise? Do people meet standards and norms of the organization? Do they need particular knowledge, skills, or ability? What career development opportunities do they have/want/need? What pain are they experiencing?	Interviews, information derived from diagnostic work team meetings, or problems identified by the personnel department are sources of information. Self-assessment growing out of team or subsystem interventions is another source.
Roles	A role is a set of behaviors enacted by a person as a result of his occupying a certain position within the organization. All persons in the organization have roles requiring certain	Should the role behaviors be added to, subtracted from, or changed? Is the role defined adequately? What is the "fit" between the person and role? Should the role performer be given	Usually information comes from observations, interviews, role analysis technique, a team approach to "management by objectives." Career planning activities yield this information

	behaviors, such as the secretaries, production supervisors, accountants.	special skills and knowledge? Is this the right person for this role?	as an output.
Between organization systems constituting a suprasystem	An example might be the system of law and order in a region, including local, county, state, federal police or investigative and enforcement agencies, courts, prisons, parole agencies, prosecuting officers and grand juries. Most such suprasystems are so complex that change efforts tend to focus on a pair or a trio of subparts.	How do the key people in one segment of the suprasystem view the whole and the subparts? Are there frictions or incongruities between subparts? Are there high-performing and low-performing subunits? Why?	Organizational mirroring, or developing lists of how each group sees each other, is a common method of joint diagnosis. Questionnaires and interviews are useful in extensive long-range interventions.

strategy (the overall OD intervention strategy) calls for concentrating on different organizational targets in a planned sequence. For example, the program may start at an important subsystem, move to another subsystem, and then extend to the total organization; or the initial focus could be on the total organization and then move to selected subsystems. Some of the critical issues and dimensions concerning how, when and where to begin the OD program will be covered in later chapters.

An alternative way to conceptualize the diagnostic components emphasizes the organization's principal processes rather than its primary target groups. Such a scheme is presented in Table 6–2 showing the principal organization processes, the typical desired information concerning the processes, and the common methods of obtaining the information.

In practice the OD consultant works from both tables simultaneously. Although interested in some specific target group from Table 6–1 and the information about that group, the consultant is also interested in the processes found in that group and would rely on Table 6–2. Organizational processes are the *what* and the *how* of the organization, that is, What is going on? and How is it being accomplished? To know about the organization's processes is to know about the organization in its dynamic and complex reality. Organization development practitioners typically pay special attention to the processes listed in Table 6–2 because of their centrality for effective organization functioning, because of their ubiquitous nature in organizations, and because significant organizational problems often stem from them. Careful examination of the two tables will give a good sense of the inner workings of an OD program and its thrusts, emphases, and mechanics.

These tables are intended as heuristic tools for diagnosing organizations, their processes, and their subunits. For example, say the vice president of a large heterogeneous division composed of several different businesses with multiple manufacturing and marketing organizations is worried about decreasing profitability. The questions the vice president needs answers to are those listed for the total organization and large subsystems from Table 6–1, as well as questions about organizational processes such as goal setting, decision making, technology, and strategic management from Table 6–2. This knowledge would likely be gained in the diagnostic phase of an OD effort sponsored by the vice president.

Continual diagnosis is thus a necessary ingredient of any planned change effort. Such diverse activities as getting rich, managing your time, and losing weight, for example, all begin with an audit of "what is"—the status quo—and then require continual monitoring of the changing status quo over time. From a comparison of "what is" with "what should be" comes a discovery of the gap between actual and desired conditions. Action plans are then developed to close the gap between the actual and the desired conditions; and the effects (consequences) of these action plans are continuously monitored to measure progress or movement toward the goal.[3] Diagnostic activities are therefore basic to all goal-seeking behaviors.

Organization development, with its emphasis on moving the organization from "what is" to "what should be," requires continuous generation of system data.[4] In this regard, Argyris states that the consultant ("interventionist" in his terms) has three "primary intervention tasks": to help the client system generate valid data; to enable

Table 6-2 Diagnosing Organizational Processes

ORGANIZATIONAL PROCESS	IDENTIFYING REMARKS AND EXPLANATION	TYPICAL INFORMATION SOUGHT	COMMON METHODS OF DIAGNOSIS
Communications patterns, styles and flows	Who talks to whom, for how long, about what? Who initiates the interaction? Is it two-way or one-way? Is it top-down; down-up; lateral?	Is communication directed upward, downward, or both? Are communications filtered? Why? In what way? Do communications patterns "fit" the nature of the jobs to be accomplished? What is the "climate" of communications? What is the place of written communications vs. oral?	Observations, especially in meetings; questionnaires for large-sized samples; interviews and discussions with group members—all these methods may be used to collect the desired information. Analysis of videotaped sessions by all concerned is especially useful.
Goal setting	Setting task objectives and determining criteria to measure accomplishment of the objectives takes place at all organizational levels.	Do they set goals? How is this done? Who participates in goal setting? Do they possess the necessary skills for effective goal setting? Are they able to set long-range and short-range objectives?	Questionnaires, interviews, and observation all afford ways of assessing goal-setting ability of individuals and groups within the organization.
Decision making, problem solving, and action planning	Evaluating alternatives and choosing a plan of action are integral and central functions for most organization members. This includes getting the necessary information, establishing priorities, evaluating alternatives, and choosing one alternative over all others.	Who makes decisions? Are they effective? Are all available sources utilized? Are additional decision-making skills needed? Are additional problem-solving skills needed? Are organization members satisfied with the problem-solving and decision-making processes?	Observation of problem-solving meetings at various organizational levels is particularly valuable in diagnosing this process. Analysis of videotaped sessions by all concerned is especially useful.
Conflict resolution and management	Conflict—interpersonal, intrapersonal, and intergroup—frequently exists in organizations. Does the organization have effective ways of dealing with conflict?	Where does conflict exist? Who are the involved parties? How is it being managed? What are the system norms for dealing with conflict? Does the reward system promote conflict?	Interviews, third-party observations, and observation meetings are common methods for diagnosing these processes.
Managing interface relations	Interfaces represent these situations wherein two or more groups (sub-	What is the nature of the relations between two groups? Are goals clear?	Interviews, third-party observations, and observation of group meetings are

Table 6–2 (cont.)

	systems) face common problems or overlapping responsibility. This is most often seen when members of two separate groups are interdependently related in achieving an objective but have separate accountability.	Is responsibility clear? What major problems do the two groups face? What structural conditions promote/inhibit effective interface management?	common methods for diagnosing these processes.
Superior-subordinate relations	Formal hierarchical relations in organizations dictate that some people lead and others follow: these situations are often a source of many organizational problems.	What are the extant leadership styles? What problems arise between superiors and subordinates?	Questionnaires can show overall leadership climate and norms. Interviews and questionnaires reveal the desired leadership behaviors.
Technological and engineering systems	All organizations rely on multiple technologies—for production and operations, for information processing, for planning, for marketing, etc., to produce goods and services.	Are the technologies adequate for satisfactory performance? What is the state of the art and how does this organization's technology compare with that? Should any changes in technology be planned and implemented?	Generally this is not an area of expertise of the OD consultant. He or she must then seek help from "experts" either inside the organization or outside. Interviews and group discussions focused on technology are among the best ways to determine the adequacy of technological systems. Sometimes outside experts conduct an audit and make recommendations; sometimes inside experts do so.
Strategic management and long-range planning	Monitoring the environment, adding and deleting "products," predicting future events, and making decisions that affect the long-term viability of the organization must occur for the organization to remain competitive and effective.	Who is responsible for "looking ahead" and for making long-range decision? Do they have adequate tools and support? Have recent long-range decisions been effective? What is the nature of current and future environmental demands? What are the unique strengths and competencies of the organization? What are the threats to the organization?	Interviews of key policy-makers, group discussions, and examination of historical records give insights to this dimension.

the client system to have free, informed choice; and to help the client system generate internal commitment to the choices made.[5] Argyris says: "One condition that seems so basic as to be defined axiomatic is the generation of *valid information*. Without valid information it would be difficult for the client to learn and for the interventionist to help. . . . Valid information is that which describes the factors, plus their interrelationships, that create the problem for the client system."[6]

Granted that diagnosis is a sine qua non of effective organization development, two issues remain. First, is the diagnosis systematically planned and structured in advance so that it follows an extensive category system and structured question format, or is the diagnosis more emergent—following the data wherever they may lead? Second, what diagnostic categories are to be used? Practice varies widely on these two dimensions. We tend to be about in the middle of the "structured in advance—emergent" continuum. We have some structured questions but follow up on leads as they develop in the course of the diagnosis. We also tend to use the diagnostic categories of Tables 6–1 and 6–2 because we focus on system and subsystem cultures and processes.

Roger Harrison uses somewhat different categories (see Figure 6–3) and an emergent diagnostic approach.[7] In his words, "I approach the system with my antennae waving, and as data are produced I probably slot them into these different categories; and then if one or another of them seems predominant as a focus for the system members, then that's the one I'm likely to use as entry."[8]

Probably the most thorough and systematic diagnostic activities in OD are done as a part of Grid OD, the six-phase organization development program used by Robert Blake and Jane Mouton.[9] (See Chapter 13 for a discussion of this approach.) In addition to being thorough, Blake and Mouton extend the diagnostic categories to include financial considerations, general business strategy, and general business logic. In their view a corporation has six major areas of activities—human resources, financial management, operations (production/manufacturing), marketing, research and develpoment, and corporate. Each of these areas must be managed effectively if the corporation is to achieve corporate excellence, and each of these areas is measured/assessed in depth and detail. This extension of diagnosis to the business logic of the organization, in addition to the more usual focus of most OD practitioners on the human and social dynamics of the organization, represents a significant positive feature of Grid OD.

Finally, in an OD program, not only are the *results* of diagnostic activities important but *how the information is collected* and *what is done with the information* are also significant aspects of the process. There is active collaboration between the OD practitioner and the organization members about such issues as what target groups are to be diagnosed, how the diagnosis is best accomplished, what processes and dynamics should be analyzed, what is to be done with the information, how the data will be worked with, and how the information will be used to aid action planning. Usually information is collected through a variety of methods—interviews, observations, questionnaires, and organization records. Information is generally considered to be the property of those persons who generated it; the data serve as the foundation for planning actions. This is basically an action research model consisting of the following steps: (1) data collection, (2) data feedback to the people who supplied the data, (3) identification of problem areas based on the data, (4) planning corrective action steps, (5) implementing the action steps, and (6) collecting data to

> **Information System**
>
> Modes of communication
> (written, group, individual, etc.)
> Informal groupings
> Information channels

> **Technical System**
>
> Work process—technology
> and organization of tasks
> Responsibility and authority
> for specific things
> Types of decisions which are
> made

> **Points of Entry**
>
> System members' own change
> and improvement goals
> Role conflicts and concerns
> of members
> Members' blocks to job
> effectiveness
> Conflicting goals of
> subsystems
> Satisfaction of members with
> their jobs
> Performance evaluation and
> appraisal of organizational
> units
> Performance evaluation and
> appraisal of individuals

> **Power System**
>
> Formal authority structure
> Informal reward system
> Responsibility and authority
> for major types of decisions
> Types of decisions
> Types of decisions which are
> made

> **System Objectives**
>
> Goals of system
> Priorities among system
> objectives
> Goals of subsystems:
> especially those which
> conflict

> **Ideology**
>
> Organizational culture:
> norms and values of
> system members
> Control systems

Harrison's categories were derived from his response to a portion of the Hornstein and Tichy "Change Agent Survey" questionnaire which instructed respondents to: (1) indicate what information (from a list including such things as formal reward structure, goals, control system, individual satisfactions, etc.) they would seek in order to diagnose and understand an organization; and (2) arrange the items into categories.

Figure 6–3 Harrison's Model for Organizational Diagnosis: Categories and Subcategories

Source: Reproduced by special permission from *The Journal of Applied Behavioral Science,* "An interview with Roger Harrison," by Noel Tichy, Vol. 9, No. 6, p. 707. Copyright 1973 NTL Institute for Applied Behavioral Science.

evaluate the effects of the actions. Therefore the diagnostic component and the action component are intimately related in organization development.

THE ACTION COMPONENT: INTERVENING IN THE CLIENT SYSTEM

As we have seen, organization development may be viewed as a process designed to improve an organization's adapting, coping, problem-solving, and goal-setting processes. The assumptions are made that the organization is not doing these processes as well as it could or should be doing them and that the organization can improve. Improvement requires, first, knowing what processes are inadequate—gained through diagnosis— and, second, doing something to make the inadequate processes more effective— accomplished by taking corrective actions. Taking corrective actions is achieved through activities in the client system called *interventions,* which we define in Chapter 9 as *"sets of structured activities* in which selected organizational units (target groups or individuals) engage with a task or sequence of tasks where the task goals are related *directly or indirectly to organizational improvement."*

To intervene in the client system is to interpose or interject activities into the normal activities of the organization in such a way that the intervention activities are done *in addition to* the normal activities or are done *instead of* the normal activities. An example of an "in addition to" intervention would be for a staff group to include a "process critique" at the end of each staff meeting. This simply means that a few minutes are set aside to look at "how we worked"—the process—during the meeting. Critiquing "how we worked" can enable the group to correct any deficient processes and become more effective in its deliberations. An example of an "instead of" intervention would be getting a key service department of an organization to hold an "organization mirroring" workshop with its user-clients to determine how the clients view the services provided and how they want the services changed or improved. In this case, instead of the normal activities of begging, cajoling, or coercing the user-clients to utilize the staff services, a problem-solving workshop called the organization mirror is convened in which the clients give feedback to the service group regarding services and a two-way dialogue is established between service providers and service users. Such a meeting would probably not be a normal activity in the organization.

The range of OD interventions is quite extensive. Structured activities have been developed to solve most organizational problems. For example, there are interventions that focus on most of the target groups in Table 6-1 and most of the organizational processes of Table 6-2. Thus, if problems exist in a particular organizational system or subsystem or in a particular organizational process, intervention activities can be initiated to remedy the problems. An inventory of OD interventions is given in Chapters 9 through 14.

A well-designed OD program unfolds according to a strategy or game plan, called the *overall OD strategy.* This strategy may be planned in advance or may emerge over time as events dictate. The strategy is based on answers to such questions as the following: What are the overall change/improvement goals of the program? What parts of the organization are most ready and receptive to the OD program? What are the key leverage points (individuals and groups) in the organization? What are the most pressing problems of the client organization? What resources are available for the program in terms of client time and energy and internal and external facilitators? Answers to these questions lead the practitioner to develop a game plan for where to intervene in the system, what to do, the sequencing of interventions, and so forth.

It can be seen that planning actions, executing actions, and evaluating the consequences of actions are an integral and essential part of organization development. This emphasis on action planning and action taking is a powerful feature of OD and, in some respects, is a distinguishing one. In many traditional educational and training activities, learning and action taking are separated in that the knowledge and skills are "learned" in one setting, say, in a classroom, and are then taken back to the organization with the learner being admonished to practice what he or she has learned, that is, to take actions. This artificial separation is minimized in most OD interventions in several ways. First, in many intervention activities there are two goals: a learning or educational goal and an accomplishing-a-task goal. Second, OD problem-solving interventions tend to focus on real organization problems that are central to the needs of the organization rather than on hypothetical, abstract problems that may or may not fit the members' needs. Third, OD interventions utilize several learning models, not just one. Let us examine these three points in more detail.

The dual aspect of OD interventions can be clarified with an illustration. Let us say that the top executives of an organization spend three days together in a workshop in which they do the following things: (1) explore the need for and desirability of a long-range strategic plan for the organization; (2) learn how to formulate such a strategy by analyzing other strategies, determining what the strategic variables are, being shown a sequence of steps for preparing a comprehensive plan, and so forth; and (3) actually make a three-year strategic plan for the organization.[10] This intervention combines the dual features of learning and action: the executives engaged in activities in which they learned about strategic planning, and they then generated a strategy. In some OD interventions, the "learning aspect" predominates, and in others, the "action aspect" predominates; but both aspects are present in most interventions.

Organization development interventions tend to focus on real problems rather than on abstract problems. The problems facing organization members are real, not hypothetical; the problems members get rewarded for solving are real, not hypothetical; and the problems central to the needs of organization members are real, not hypothetical. Developing the skills and knowledge to solve real problems as they arise in their "natural state" means that the educational problem of "transfer of learning" from one situation to another is minimized (although the problem of generalization, that is, knowing the appropriate times and places to apply this particular set of skills and knowledge, is still present.)

An additional feature of working on real problems as found in some OD interventions is that the real set of individuals involved in the problem is the group that the problem solvers work with. For example, in a human relations class, if a manager were having trouble understanding and working with disadvantaged subordinates, he or she would perhaps "role play" the situation with the instructor or fellow students. In OD the manager would probably interact with the disadvantaged employees with whom he or she was having difficulties—but would do so in carefully structured activities that have a high probability of resulting in learning for both parties and a high probability of being a ''success experience'' for both parties.

Organization development programs rely on several learning models. For example if ''learning how to'' do something precedes ''doing'' it, then we have a somewhat traditional approach to learning that most people are familiar with. If the ''doing'' precedes the ''learning how to,'' then we have a ''deficiency'' model of learning in which the learning comes primarily from critiquing the actions after the fact to see how they could have been done differently and, presumably, better. Both models are viable learning modes, and both are used extensively in organization development. Even the traditional model of ''learning how to'' and ''doing'' becomes nontraditional as performed in OD, however, since the OD approach would be for a formal work team to be learning and doing *together* with the help of a change agent.

Action programs in OD are closely linked with explicit goals and objectives. Careful attention is given to the problem of translating goals into observable, explicit, and measurable actions or behaviors, and equal care is given to the related problem of ensuring that actions are relevant to and instrumental for goal attainment. Such questions as the following thus become an integral part of organizational life: How does this action relate to the goal we have established? What are the action implications of that goal for me, my subordinates, my group? When we say we want to achieve a certain goal, what do we really mean by that, in measurable terms? Given several alternative forms of action, which one seems most appropriate to achieve the goal we have set?

Diagnosis, action taking, and goal setting are inextricably related in an OD program. Diagnostic activities are precursors to action programs; that is, fact-finding is done to provide a foundation for action. Actions are continuouly evaluated for their contribution to goal accomplishment. Goals are continuously evaluated in terms of their appropriateness—whether or not they are attainable and whether or not they can be translated into action programs. Organization development is a continuous process of the cycling of setting goals and objectives, collecting data about the status quo, planning and taking actions based on hypotheses and on the data, and evaluating the effects of action through additional data collection.

THE PROCESS-MAINTENANCE COMPONENT: MAINTAINING AND MANAGING THE OD PROCESS ITSELF

Just as OD practitioners apply behavioral science principles and practices to ongoing complex systems to improve the system's functioning, ideally they apply these same principles and practices to their own work. The OD process and the practitioner group typically model the techniques being proposed for the organization; both the program and the practitioners practice what they preach. Diagnosing and evaluating are an integral part of managing the OD process, similarly so is treating the organization from a systems viewpoint with the OD program being a component force within a wider field of system forces. Practitioners would find the client system probably resisting their teaching and preaching about the desirability and feasibility of managing interpersonal conflict if it were known that conflict was not being managed within the OD group; teaching others to manage against measurable objectives would appear hollow if the OD group did not know where it was going and how; reverberations will occur throughout the total organization as a result of an OD program in one subsystem and this fact must be taken into account.

Among other things, managing the OD process means actively seeking answers to the following questions:

> Are we being timely and relevant in our interventions?
>
> Are our activities producing the effects we intended and wanted? If not, why not; if so, why?
>
> Is there continued "ownership," that is, involvement, commitment, and investment, in the program by the clients?
>
> What are the total system ramifications of our efforts? Did we anticipate these? Are any of the ramifications undesirable? If yes, what do we do about them?
>
> What about the culture of our own OD group? Must it be changed in any way? Are we solving problems effectively, managing against clearly understood goals, and modeling the kind of interpersonal climate we think is desirable in an organization?

To summarize, the process-maintenance element is designed to accomplish several objectives: to model self-analysis and self-reflection as means of self-improvement; to model the action research principles of goal setting coupled with data feedback loops to guide and evaluate actions; to work to ensure ownership of the interventions and the entire program by organization members; to model the ability to detect and cope with problems and opportunities in the internal and the external environment; to test the effectiveness of interventions by utilizing feedback from the system; to test for relevancy of the program to the organization's needs; to test for timeliness of interventions; and to ensure that intended and unintended consequences do not obviate the organization's and the OD program's goals.

The importance of this component can hardly be overstated. Managing the OD process effectively can spell the difference between success and failure for the improvement effort. This component, maintenance and management of the OD process, may help to explain why there are many aborted OD efforts and few long-range, successful ones. The practicing-what-you-preach aspect probably contributes significantly to bringing about real, genotypic, lasting change in the organization instead of apparent, phenotypic, or "pasted on" change. In later chapters we pay considerable attention to the problems that can arise in OD programs as well as to issues and dimensions related to sound maintenance of the process.

OD, ACTION RESEARCH, AND THE ANALYSIS OF DISCREPANCIES

Diagnosis, action taking, and process maintenance have been emphasized as major operational components of organization development programs, and the central role of problem solving in OD has been described. OD is much more than just problem solving, but certainly such activities are of paramount importance.

A useful underlying model for this discussion of problem solving could be termed discrepancy analysis—examination of the discrepancies or gaps between what is happening and what should be happening and discrepancies between where one is and where one wants to be. Discrepancies, therefore, define both problems and goals. Discrepancies require *study* (diagnosis and planning) and *action* if the gaps are to be eliminated. We believe that a good part of OD is problem solving, hence, discrepancy analysis. Action research (explored in Chapter 8) describes an iterative problem-solving process that is essentially discrepancy analysis and linking that to action taking. Any manager's primary task is essentially discrepancy analysis—the study of problems and opportunities (goals) or the study of the discrepancies between where one is and where one wants to be. Organization development provides technologies for studying and closing gaps.

This simple but powerful analytical model is presented clearly and effectively by Charles Kepner and Benjamin Tregoe in *The Rational Manager*.[11] Their ideas have been translated into training seminars to improve problem-solving and decision-making skills. Kepner and Tregoe state, ''The problem analyzer has an expected standard of performance, a 'should' against which to compare actual performance....A problem is a deviation from a standard of performance.''[12] According to these authors, a problem is a gap; problem solving is discovering the *cause* of the gap; decision making is discovering a *solution*—a set of actions—to close the gap.

In *Analyzing Performance Problems,* Robert Mager and Peter Pipe use a discrepancy or gap model to great advantage.[13] Beginning with a ''performance discrepancy,'' they show how to discover the source of the discrepancy and how to correct it. By focusing first on precisely defined performance discrepancies, then determining whether or not the cause is related to a skill deficiency, they show how performance problems can be quickly analyzed and corrected. The basic model is discrepancy analysis. This method of analyzing performance discrepancies is readily applicable to many day-to-day problems found in organizations.

In *The New Science of Management Decision,* Herbert Simon proposed a discrepancy model of problem analysis.[14] He stated that a problem is a deviation from an expected standard and a cause of a problem is a *change* of some sort. Simon's conclusions were derived from his studies of human cognitive processes and computer science. His model is one of analyzing gaps. Kepner and Tregoe call Simon's book ''the best statement of problem-solving theory to be found in the literature on the subject.''[15]

Goals also represent gaps—gaps between where we are and where we want to be. Goal setting is the process of defining or imposing a gap; goal accomplishment is made possible by taking actions to close the gap.

We have said that organization development is more than just problem solving and goal seeking. But a large part of any OD program is devoted to these two critical activities. The discrepancy analysis approach is a fruitful way in which to conceptualize problems and goals.

SUMMARY

We have identified three major components of an operational OD program as follows: the diagnostic component; the intervention, or action-taking, component; and the OD process-maintenance component. All three components are necessary for success. The diagnostic component has two facets: finding out about the state of the system and evaluating the effects of remedial action plans. The action/intervention component represents the range of OD interventions designed to improve the functioning of the organization. The process-maintenance component directs attention to keeping the process itself viable and relevant. Finally, it has been suggested that there is considerable value in conceptualizing problems and goals within a framework of discrepancy analysis, where gaps between where one is and where one wants to be are examined and systematically eliminated.

NOTES

1. In fact, all three components represent actions or interventions in the system and thus fall into an action category. Diagnostic activities, for example, have a powerful "action impact" on an organization. We have artificially separated the three components here for analytical purposes only.

2. Richard Beckhard, *Organization Development: Strategies and Models* (Reading, Mass.: Addison-Wesley, 1969), p. 26. Beckhard's use of subsystem synonymously with *subunit* is congruent with our usage in Chapter 5. However, we develop a supplemental conceptual scheme in that chapter that also permits viewing the organization in terms of subsystems that are common to all subunits: goal, technological, task, structural, human-social, and external interface.

3. This "actual condition" versus "ideal condition" discrepancy model is an integral feature of Kurt Lewin's force field analysis [Kurt Lewin, *Field Theory in Social Science* (New York: Harper & Bros., 1951)] and appears, in fact, to be basic to all human goal-seeking and problem-solving activities. See, for example, George A. Miller, Eugene Galanter, and Karl H. Pribram, *Plans and the Structure of Behavior* (New York: Holt, Rinehart and Winston, 1960).

4. The movement of the organization from "what is" to "what should be" is the explicit underlying dynamic in Grid OD. See Robert R. Blake and Jane Srygley Mouton, *Corporate Excellence Through Grid Organization Development* (Houston: Gulf, 1968).

5. Chris Argyris, *Intervention Theory and Method: A Behavioral Science View* (Reading, Mass.: Addison-Wesley, 1970).

6. Ibid., pp. 16–17.

7. Noel Tichy, "An Interview with Roger Harrison," *Journal of Applied Behavioral Science* 9, No. 6 (1973), pp. 701–711. This figure is taken from page 707 and is used by permission.

8. Ibid., pp. 706, 708.

9. Robert R. Blake and Jane Srygley Mouton, *Building a Dynamic Corporation Through Grid Organization Development* (Reading, Mass.: Addison-Wesley, 1969); and R. R. Blake and J. S. Mouton, *Corporate Excellence Diagnosis: The Phase 6 Instrument* (Austin, Tex.: Scientific Methods, 1968).

10. Actually, in a real strategy planning session steps 1 and 2 might take place during the first session, with that session concluding with some "homework" assignments to the members in order that the necessary information for the strategy plan could be available. Then, in a second session, step 3 would be finalized. This kind of separation in time is not the artificial one just described but, rather, a separation in time designed to facilitate step 3.

11. Charles H. Kepner and Benjamin B. Tregoe, *The Rational Manager* (New York: McGraw-Hill, 1965). This book is highly recommended for OD practitioners.

12. Ibid., p. 44.

13. Robert F. Mager and Peter Pipe, *Analyzing Performance Problems or "You Really Oughta Wanna"* (Belmont, Calif.: Fearon, 1970).

14. Herbert A. Simon, *The New Science of Management Decision* (New York: Harper & Row, 1960).

15. Kepner and Tregoe,, *The Rational Manager,* p. 252.

7

CHARACTERISTICS
AND FOUNDATIONS
OF THE OD PROCESS

the nature of organization development

Examining the basic components of an OD program in operation afforded one look at the nature of organization development. In this chapter OD is examined from additional perspectives—call them underlying characteristics, distinguishing features, foundations, or theoretical and practice underpinnings. These perspectives show different facets of the OD process that, taken together, give organization development its unique stamp.

In this chapter OD is characterized in several different ways—as a process, as a form of applied behavioral science, as normative change, as incorporating a systems approach to organizations, as similar to and based on an action research (data-based) model, as an experience-based learning mode, as emphasizing goals and objectives, as concentrating on intact work teams as the primary instruments for organization improvement, and as using a participation/empowerment model. These different aspects of OD serve as the foundation upon which the process is built, and the foundation has played a significant role in shaping the practice of organization development.

OD IS AN ONGOING INTERACTIVE PROCESS

One understands much about the nature of OD by viewing it as an ongoing interactive process. A *process* is an identifiable flow of interrelated events moving over time toward some goal or end.[1] In the OD process, the identifiable flow of interrelated events consists of interventions in the client system and responses to the interventions. Behind the pattern is the overall OD strategy directing the selection, timing, and sequencing of intervention activities; this strategy ties the individual events together into a coherent, directed thrust. In practice, an initial strategy will be formulated, and this will be modified and changed as events and experience suggest emergent directions and emergent problems.

But the essential point in calling OD a process is to characterize it as a dynamic, moving, changing thing. People learn new skills and forget old ones; the structure of the organization changes, and then another change is put on top of that; problems are solved and new ones develop; a sick subsystem gets well and a heretofore healthy one develops bad symptoms. There are good days and bad days for the OD program as well as successes and failures. Thus it is imperative that organization development be viewed as a dynamic process for changing dynamic systems. Neither human systems (organizations) nor planned change processes (OD) are static phenomena; they are in constant flux and flow.

Another facet of OD as a process is that the process of improving organizations may be a process of "becoming"—of approaching some end state without ever reaching it in the usual sense of "arriving." Although most pepole would generally agree about whether one organization is "better" or "worse" than another in terms of organizational effectiveness, there is less agreement on when an organization has "arrived" and lack of agreement on the indicators used to signal that arrival. This is not to say that OD practitioners do not know where they are going and what they are trying to achieve, because that is not so; but it is to say that at this stage in the art and the science of organization development projections about the goals of the OD effort serve primarily as guides or heuristic servomechanisms rather than as definitive descriptions of an end state.

The ongoing process nature of OD implies that it is not to be regarded as a one-shot solution to organizational problems, but more as a "growing toward" greater effectiveness through a *series* of intervention activities over a period of time. Managing and directing the change of an organization's culture and processes does not happen overnight; a more realistic time estimate is several years. Isolated changes, such as in specific individual behaviors, organizational reporting relationships, and policies and procedures, can often be effected quickly. But changing the *culture* of a work team or a department or an entire organization is a long-term, involved process. The culture is the bedrock or source of the system's strengths and weaknesses. It is the culture that must be altered if permanent improvement is to take place. And culture change requires persistence, a considerable investment of energy, and time.

Regarding this point, differing estimates of how long the process will probably take may lead to problems between practitioners and organization members in that members may want and expect immediate results and may get discouraged when they are not forthcoming. On the other hand, a trap into which practitioners can fall is to raise members' expectations, either deliberately or inadvertently, for quick, easy solutions to problems and then not be able to produce results. At the other end of the spectrum, the practitioner may emphasize the long-term nature of OD to the point that the prospective client gets frightened away with visions of being locked for years into some kind of mysterious program that may or may not work. Successful OD efforts can start with small beginnings and without long-range commitments, providing that expectations are realistic. Viewing the program as an ongoing process can allow both client and consultant to take a few initial steps and then to evaluate these outcomes before committing themselves to a long-term contract.

The interactive nature of the process also implies a series of actions and reactions, initiated activities, and the responses to these activities. Organizational behavior is incredibly complex, and probably the only adequate way to conceptualize it is through an interaction theory of social behavior. But as Bennis, Schein, Berlew, and Steele indicate, we have no such theory in the social sciences at this time.[2] Viewing the OD process as a complex series of interactions promotes a better understanding of organizational dynamics, even though no comprehensive theory exists to help explain the phenomena. The interactive nature of the OD process, however, does suggest the necessity for effective feedback loops for monitoring the reactions to interventions, the readiness of subsystems for change, and emergent problems and new directions.

Finally, organization development is a process in the sense that in OD *how* things are done is as important as *what* is done. That is, the *process* of the OD program—how it is done—is as important as the *content* of the OD program—what is done. This may be a relatively little understood feature of OD to those pepole who are newly exposed to it. But it is an essential characteristic based on the following reasoning. Broadly speaking, the goals of organization development are to improve the organizational functioning in two ways: first, to solve existing problems and correct existing deficiencies in the organization's culture and processes and, second, to instill in the client system the capabilities for *future* problem solving, self-renewing, and culture managing (without the aid or presence of the OD consultant). Almost all forms of consultation address the first goal; OD is one of the few consulting approaches that addresses both the first and the second goals. The first goal can be attained by appropriate content—make the solutions relevant to the problems. The second goal can be attained by an intervention process done in such a way that the client system builds its own internal capacities and skills. This is achieved by designing interventions so they have a skill-building or skill-learning component in addition to the problem-solving component directed to the immediate problem. Diagnostic skills and action-taking skills are the skills learned from the interventions. This attention to the process of intervening in the client system is an important foundation of organization development.

OD IS A FORM OF APPLIED BEHAVIORAL SCIENCE

An OD program applies the scientific and practice principles from several behavioral sciences: social psychology, social anthropology, sociology, psychiatry, economics, and political science. The OD practitioner is neither magician nor charlatan; he or she is simply translating what is known about people and organizations as found in behavioral science knowledge into applicable programs of actions. In fact, this section could be titled ''demythologizing organization development'' because we wish to show that OD is not a mysterious and magical spell cast upon an organization by the incantations of a behavioral scientist ''change agent.'' Quite to the contrary, practitioners base their diagnoses and actions on the known, lawful-patterned events and dynamics that help explain individual, group, and organization behavior. Knowledge of these lawful patterns comes primarily from personality theory, social psychology, group dynamics, and organization theory, typically coupled with knowledge about theory and practice regarding adult education, planned change, systems theory, and a dash of operations research. Another definition of OD could be "OD is the application of behavioral science knowledge, practices, and skills in ongoing systems in collaboration with system members."

A conventional distinction is usually made between (1) "pure" or basic science, the object of which is knowledge for its own sake, and (2) "technology," applied science, or practice, the object of which is knowledge to solve practical, pressing problems.[3] Greenwood discusses the activities of the practitioner as follows: "The problem that confronts a practitioner is customarily a state of disequilibrium that requires rectification. The practitioner examines the problem situation, on the basis of which he or she prescribes a solution that, hopefully, reestablishes the equilibrium, thereby solving the problem. This process is customarily referred to as diagnosis and treatment."[4] Both diagnosis and treatment consist of observing a situation, and on the basis of selected variables, placing it in a classification scheme or typology. The diagnostic typology allows the practitioner to know what category of situation he or she has examined; the treatment typology allows the practitioner to know what remedial efforts to apply to correct the problem. On this point, Greenwood states:

> The diagnostic and treatment typologies are employed together. Each type description of the diagnostic typology contains implications for a certain type of treatment. The practitioner uses treatment as the empirical test of his diagnosis, success corroborating the diagnosis, failure negating it and thus requiring rediagnosis. The principles of diagnosis and of treatment constitute the principles of practice, i.e., with their elaborations and implications constitute practice theory.[5]

It is from this "practice theory" that the OD practitioner works: first diagnosing the situation, then selecting and implementing treatments based on the diagnosis, and finally evaluating the effects of the treatments.

Organization development is both a result of applied behavioral science and a form of applied behavioral science; perhaps more accurately, it is a program of applying behavioral science to organizations. Figure 7–1 shows some of the inputs to applied behavioral science. The two bottom inputs, behavioral science research and behavioral science theory, are intended to represent contributions from "pure" or basic science; the two top inputs, practice research and practice theory, are intended to represent contributions from "applied" science.

Some examples of contributions from these four sources that are relevant for applying behavioral science in organization development are the following:

Contributions from behavioral science theory are these:

> The importance of social norms in determining perceptions, motivations, and behaviors (Sherif)
>
> The role or an exchange theory of behavior that postulates that people tend to exchange approximately equivalent units to maintain a balance between what is given and received (Gouldner, Homans)
>
> The importance of the existing total field of forces in determining and predicting behavior (Lewin)
>
> The relevance of role theory in accounting for stability and change in behavior (G. H. Mead)

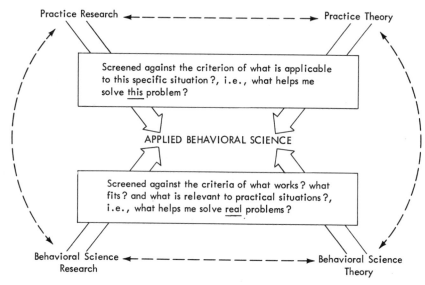

Figure 7–1 Composition of Applied Behavioral Science

The role and importance of activities, interactions, and sentiments as explanatory concepts for elementary social behavior (Homans)

The possibilities inherent in views of motivation different from those provided by older theories (McGregor, Herzberg, Maslow)

The importance of individual goal setting for increasing productivity and improving performance (Locke)

The place of social learning theory, general theories of learning, effects of reward and punishment, attitude change theories, and so on in understanding organizational behavior (Bandura, Skinner, McGuire)

Contributions from behavioral science research are these:

Studies on the causes, conditions and consequences of induced competition on behavior within and between groups (Sherif and Blake and Mouton)

Results on the effects of cooperative and competitive group goal structures on behavior within groups (Deutsch)

Studies on the effects of organizational and managerial climate on leadership style (Fleishman, Schein)

Studies on the variables relevant for organizational health (Likert)

Studies showing the importance of the social system in relation to the technical system (Trist and Bamforth)

Results from studies on different communication networks (Leavitt), causes and consequences of conformity (Asch), group problem solving (Kelley and Thibaut), and group dynamics (Cartwright and Zander)

Contributions from practice theory are these:

Implications from the theory and practice of the laboratory training method (Bradford, Benne, and Gibb)

Implications from theories of group development (Schutz and Bennis and Shepard)

New dimensions in the helping relationship and specifically the client-consultant relationship (Rogers)

Codification of the practice of management (Drucker)

New ideas about the education process (Dewey)

The concept of ''management by objectives'' (Drucker, McGregor)

Implications of social learning theory and behavior modeling for supervisor training (Goldstein and Sorcher)

Explorations in intervention theory and method (Argyris)

Developments in consultation typologies and theory (Blake and Mouton)

Implications and applications from theories of *planned change* (Lippitt, Watson, and Westley; Bennis, Benne, and Chin)

Contributions from practice research are these:

Studies showing that feeding back survey research data can bring about organization change (Mann, Likert, Baumgartel)

Results indicating the importance of the informal work group on individual and group performance (Roethlisberger and Dickson)

Results showing the efficacy of grid organization development in large organizations (Blake, Mouton, Barnes, and Greiner)

Results documenting improved organizational performance and improved organization climate stemming from a long-term OD effort in a manufacturing firm (Marrow, Bowers, and Seashore)

Results showing the complexity of intraorganizational communication and interaction patterns on job performance (Whyte)

Results showing the ability of behavior modeling training to improve supervisory human relations skills (Latham and Saari) and organizational effectiveness (Porras)

Results from the action research studies in Chapter 8 showing how to change organizational practices[6]

These contributions are not meant to be exhaustive, but only to show some of the sources and kinds of information/knowledge that OD practitioners, as applied behavioral scientists, bring to the organizational setting.

OD IS A NORMATIVE-REEDUCATIVE STRATEGY OF CHANGING

Since organization development is a process for improving organizational effectiveness, this implies doing things differently and better, and this means changing some features of the organization (usually its processes and culture). OD is a program of planned change, but not a program of change for change's sake. To some people, change is a defense-provoking word; to others, change is a panacea for all problems. We agree with neither of these views. Instead we subscribe to the belief that change, when it is desired by the people who will be affected, and when it opens up alternatives of action rather than closing off alternatives, and when it seems to incorporate choices of action that in other situations have been demonstrated to be good ones or that by generally enlightened criteria (say, for example, the scientific method) are considered good ones—then we believe that change is indicated as a desirable action step. OD is not a broadside attack on the values held by individuals, organizations, or a society, but it does represent a value framework, much of which was discussed in the chapter on assumptions and values in OD. For example, OD practitioners are not interested in changing people's values about religion, politics, marriage, the nation, and so forth; but they would try to change people's values in the direction of belief in the worth of the individual, belief in the dysfunctional aspects of many zero-sum games in the organization, belief that participation in decisions promotes feelings of self-worth, and the like. In addition, most OD practitioners would make known to clients their value systems and would permit the client to accept or reject them.

But organization development does involve change, and it rests on a particular strategy of changing that has implications for practitioners and organization members alike. Chin and Benne describe three types of strategies for changing.[7] First there are the empirical-rational strategies, based on the assumptions that people are rational, will follow their rational self-interest, and will change if and when they come to realize the change is advantageous to them. The second group of strategies are the normative-reeducative strategies, based on the assumptions that norms form the basis for behavior and change comes through a reeducation process in which old norms are discarded and supplanted by new ones. The third set of strategies constitutes the power-coercive strategies, based on the assumption that change is compliance of those with less power to the desires of those with more power. Evaluated against these three change approaches, OD is clearly seen to fall within the normative-reeducative category, although in some senses, it may represent a combination of the normative-reeducative with the empirical-rational. The nature of this second change strategy is indicated by Chin and Benne:

> A second group of strategies we call normative-reeducative. These strategies build upon assumptions about human motivation different from those underlying the first. The rationality and intelligence of men are not denied. Patterns of action and practice are supported by sociocultural norms and by commitments on the part of individuals to these norms. Sociocultural norms are supported by the attitude and value systems of individuals—normative outlooks which undergird their commitments. Change in a pattern of practice or action, according to this view, will occur only as the persons involved are brought to change their normative orientations to old patterns and develop commitments to new ones. And changes in normative orientations involve changes in attitudes, values, skills, and significant relationships, not just changes in knowledge, information, or intellectual rationales for action and practice.[8]

An illustration may clarify these three strategies of changing. Suppose that the Salk polio vaccine has just been invented, tested, and cleared for public use and that you are in charge of disseminating it to the public. Your procedure would depend upon which strategy of changing you believed in. If you espoused the empirical-rational theory of changing, then you would assume that all rational, self-interested people (and that is everyone, just about) would use the vaccine if only they had information and knowledge about its availability and its efficacy. Your program, therefore, would be to disseminate the knowledge and information. As a consequence, everyone would take the vaccine, since it would be in his or her best interests.

On the other hand, if you held a normative-reeducative belief about changing, you would do additional things. While you would not disbelieve or disregard people's intelligence, rationality, and self-interest, you would also believe that many behaviors are rooted in sociocultural norms, values, and beliefs that must be changed for them to accept and use the vaccine. Some of these beliefs might be that "all new drugs are dangerous until they have been on the market for 10 years"; "My neighbor, Mrs. Jones, isn't going to use the vaccine, and neither am I since she's always right about these things"; "Well, no one in my family has ever had polio, so I'm not afraid of getting it and don't need to be vaccinated." Holding to the second strategy of changing, you would assume that norms and values had to be changed, in addition to making the information available to the public. You would mount both an education campaign about the new drug and a reeducation campaign to change some norms and values.

If you held to a power-coercive strategy of changing, your task would be straightforward: you would pass a law stating that all persons must get vaccinated, and you would ensure and enforce compliance to the law. If you had the power to pass the law, and power to enforce the law, the people would take the vaccine.

The point here is that there are different strategies for effecting change, and OD is based primarily on a normative-reeducative one and secondarily on a rational-empirical one. Focusing on the normative-reeducative strategy for change, as practiced in an organization development program, the following implications are associated with that change strategy: the *client* defines what changes and improvements he or she wants to make, rather than the change agent; the change agent attempts to intervene in a mutual, collaborative way with the client as they together define problems and seek solutions; anything hindering effective problem solving is brought to light and publicly examined, that is, doubts, anxieties, and negative feelings are surfaced for "working through"; the methods and knowledge of the behavioral sciences are used as resources by both change agents and clients; and solutions to problems are not a priori assigned to greater technical information or knowledge but may reside in values, attitudes, relationships, and customary ways of doing things.[9] The desire for and the form of reeducation are decisions for the client to make; implementing the reeducation chosen by the client is the work of the practitioner. These are far-reaching implications for OD for several reasons: they significantly dictate practitioner values and behaviors; they give the clients considerable choice and control over the situation; they impel a collaborative effort rather than a "doing something to" effort; and they lead to more options and alternatives rather than fewer ones for both the client and the practitioner.

Our definition of organization development refers to improving and managing the organization's culture—a clear reference to sociocultural norms and to the normative nature of the change process. Burke and Hornstein emphasize the normative nature of OD even more in their definition:

> Organization development is a process of planned change. It involves change of an organization's culture from one which avoids an examination of social processes in organizations, especially decision making, planning and communications, to one which institutionalizes and legitimizes this examination.[10]

These authors assert that the initial focus of OD is normative change and that individual change is merely a by-product. The nature of the change in the culture indicated by Burke and Hornstein is congruent with our definition and with those of others. These changes are not of the nature to affront, belittle, coerce, or harass individuals' personally held, deep-seated values but relate more to norms, attitudes, and values about how to get the organizational mission accomplished.

Warren Bennis, in a discussion on the characteristics of organization development, comments on the normative aspect of this process as follows:

> Change agents share a set of *normative goals* based on their philosophy. . . . Most commonly sought are:
>
> 1. Improvement in interpersonal competence.
> 2. A shift in values so that human factors and feelings come to be considered legitimate.
> 3. Development of increased understanding between and within working groups in order to reduce tensions.
> 4. Development of more effective "team management," i.e., the capacity. . . for functional groups to work more competently.
> 5. Development of better methods of "conflict resolution." Rather than the usual bureaucratic methods which rely mainly on suppression, compromise, and unprincipled power, more rational and open methods of conflict resolution are sought.
> 6. Development of organic rather than mechanical systems. This is a strong reaction against the idea of organizations as mechanisms which managers "work on," like pushing buttons.[11]

Bennis likewise emphasizes the educational nature of OD: "Organization development (OD) is a response to change, a complex educational strategy intended to change the beliefs, attitudes, values, and structure of organizations so that they can better adapt to new technologies, markets, and challenges, and the dizzying rate of change itself."[12]

Although a normative-reeducative strategy of changing is most characteristic of the OD process, there is a rational-empirical aspect to it also. Many of the objectives of OD interventions have an appeal as being "obviously" a better way. For example, it is often intrinsically satisfying to learn to manage conflict well, or to learn to make better decisions, or to learn to manage against clearly defined objectives. Clients often know there must be better ways of doing things and have the strong desire to identify these better ways, but they have never been presented with the information and knowledge. Once given the knowledge, there is immediate changeover to new ways of managing and new ways of behaving. From our experience, much change does occur in organization development through the processes described in the rational-empirical strategy for changing.

OD VIEWS ORGANIZATIONS FROM A SYSTEMS APPROACH

Systems concepts relevant to organization development were discussed in Chapter 5, so we will touch on them only briefly here. A systems approach views and emphasizes organizational phenomena and dynamics in their interrelatedness, their connectedness, their interdependence, and their interaction. This is the perspective we believe is useful for understanding organizational life. As Chin says of the systems approach: "The analytic model of system demands that we treat the phenomena and the concepts for organizing the phenomena as if there existed organization, interaction, interdependency, and integration of parts and elements. Systems analysis assumes structure and stability within some arbitrarily sliced and frozen time period."[13]

Several consequences of viewing organizations from this perspective have value and functionality for applying behavioral science to organization development.

First, issues, events, forces, and incidents are not viewed as isolated phenomena; they occur in relation to other events, issues, phenomena. Understanding only the single phenomenon and not understanding it in relation to other phenomena is to have only a half understanding.

Second, a systems approach encourages analysis of events in terms of multiple causation rather than single causation. The real world is complex; events in it are complex. It is probably a more accurate description of reality to posit multiple causes to events; this is facilitated by the systems approach.

Third, and this is taken from Kurt Lewin's field theory in social psychology, the field of forces at the time of the event are the relevant forces for analysis.[14] This dictum moves the practitioner away from an analysis of historical events and forces to an examination of the contemporary events and forces—to a more existential vantage point.

Fourth, one cannot change one part of a system without influencing other parts in some ways. A related point to this one is that the systems viewpoint inclines the practitioner to anticipate multiple effects rather than single effects. These effects show up in other parts of the system and also in "surprises" in the part of the system with which he or she is working. Anticipating multiple causes and multiple effects, a viewpoint practiced by OD practitioners, takes many of the surprises out of organizational dynamics.

The fifth and final point is that if one wants to change a system, one changes the system, not just its component parts. Organization development is the development of a system, not only of the parts of a system. Blake and Mouton address this issue:

> Organization development means development of the organization. Because of the history of education, training and development in industry, the inclination on seeing the word organization before development is to think and substitute for it the word individual. If the reader does this, he will miss the deeper implication of what is presented. The reason is that he will fail to comprehend how deeply the culture of a corporation controls the behavior of all of its individuals. While the ultimate objective of organization development is to liberate all of the individuals within it, so that they will be free, participative, and contributive to problem solving, in order to achieve corporate purposes of profitability, this objective cannot be reached until the constraints that operate within the corporation's culture have been studied and deliberately rejected. The key difference between individual and organization development will be found in this proposition.[15]

Additional systems concepts are presented in other parts of this book, but we wanted to emphasize that a systems approach is one of the foundations of organization development. When practitioners started viewing organization change from a systems approach, a significant step was taken toward the invention of organization development. In the chapter on OD history, it was pointed out that shifting attention from individuals to intact work teams "permitted OD to come into focus." Such a shift was basically a move to a systems approach to effecting organization change.

OD IS A DATA-BASED APPROACH TO PLANNED CHANGE

A data-based model, the action research model, underlies sound OD programs and is a significant facet of the nature of organization development. The action research model is discussed in Chapter 8, but we want to make a few comments here. Many OD interventions are designed either to generate data or to plan actions based on data. A key value inculcated in organization members is a belief in the validity, desirability, and usefulness of *data about the system itself,* specifically, data about the system's culture and processes.

The data-based nature of organization development has some features that distinguish it from other data-based change activities. Some of the characteristics and their implications are the following. First, strong emphasis is placed on the value of data in the OD process, perhaps stronger than that in most change programs. As a consequence of this, organization members learn how to collect, work with, and utilize data for problem solving in the organization. Second, in OD programs, specific kinds of data are preferred over others. For example, data about the organization's human and social processes would usually be used more than technical data, financial data, market information, and the like. Third, in OD programs, the data usually "belong to" and are used by the people who generated them. This means that an attitude survey, for example, is not conducted just so that top management can study the results; rather it is conducted so that the contributors at all levels may have an accurate picture of the situations they confront and may then plan action programs to capitalize on the positive attributes and eradicate the negative attributes. The data are public; the data are the property of all organization members; the data are a springboard to action. Fourth, the contradictory data or the discrepancy data are viewed as "nuggets" rather than as nuisances in OD programs. They point the way to differences in perceptions, motivations, attitudes, and so forth that often, once discovered, can lead to breakthroughs in improving the organization's effectiveness. For example, if one hierarchical level views the compensation plan as fair and equitable and another level views it as unjust and unfair (and if neither of these levels knew the other felt that way), then the finding of this nugget can point toward action plans to decide what to do about the discrepancy. Fifth, in OD programs, feelings toward "facts" tend to shift from viewing facts as either "good" or "bad" to looking at the consequences or functionality/dysfunctionality of the facts. For example, a particular leadership style, highly authoritarian, may be a fact. The important thing about this fact is not to label it as good or bad, but to understand the conditions under which it is functional for certain results and dysfunctional for other results. This is, then, a shift from *evaluating* data to *describing* data—a subtle but important difference. When data are described, people tend to become less defensive about them, compared with when they are evaluated. A sixth point is that in OD programs data tend to be used as aids to problem solving rather than as "clubs" to enforce certain behaviors. One of the goals of organization development is to build the climate in the system to the point where data are used not to punish people but to aid them in problem solving. Seventh, the strong data base used in organization development is similar to that of the scientific method, in the sense that decisions are made increasingly on the basis of empirical facts rather than on power, position, tradition, persuasion, and so forth. As a final note, the data used in the OD process stem from the stated needs and problems of the system members, that is, they are data to supply answers to central needs of the organization and its members.

OD IS EXPERIENCE BASED

The experience-based nature of the OD process derives from an underlying belief of most OD practitioners that people learn how to do things by doing them. And they learn about organizational dynamics by experiencing them and reflecting on the experience. These beliefs are based on tenets of the laboratory training movement. People learn about the need to manage conflict when they experience the deleterious effects of conflict; people learn to make decisions by making some and then evaluating them. When people are engaged in real experiences, they are engaged with their minds, emotions, strivings— their whole beings. There are no artificial separations engendered, say, by memorizing something so that at some future time one may act in a certain way.

Instead of treating hypothetical problems and abstract organizational issues, OD interventions tend to focus on the real behavior of individuals and groups, tend to try to solve real problems, and tend to derive generalizations about organizational dynamics inductively from experience. Then more general theory input, knowledge building, and skill building are overlaid on the experience base as needed.

Experience-based learning calls not just for exposure to an experience but also for reflection about the experience. Organizational members experience something through an activity, then reflect on that experience to derive learnings and generalizations about the phenomenon. Many OD interventions call for scheduling reflection time after an activity, during which the participants examine such issues as the following: What were the causal relationships we found in this activity? What were the things we appeared to do right in this task? What things hindered our reaching our goals? What can we learn from this experience that may apply to future experiences and tasks? This constant questioning and reflecting is itself related to the goal of increasing people's ability to "learn how to learn." Essentially the concept of learning how to learn refers to having an experimental/inquiry attitude "set" that the individuals take into all their experiences; they continually examine their own experiences in order that they may learn and change and grow.

Many OD practitioners have also worked extensively with laboratory training methods and procedures. The laboratory training approach to learning is heavily dependent upon experiential learning—learning about something by experiencing it and then reflecting on the experience. Experiential learning methods appear to be particularly efficacious for learning about human and social relations, that is, increasing interpersonal skills, learning about small group dynamics, and so forth. When experiential methods were applied to other task areas, such as planning, goal setting, and decision making, they were found to be equally potent for learning. Various kinds of experiential learning exercises are used in organization development, and this experience-based component is thus another cornerstone in the foundation.

OD EMPHASIZES GOAL SETTING AND PLANNING

It has been said before, but we want to say again, that goal setting and planning are important features of the OD process. The OD process has goals, specifically those of improving, in various ways, the functioning of the organization. One of the ways in which OD programs facilitate organizational improvement is through emphasizing the importance of goals and plans and structuring learning activities designed to improve goal-setting and planning skills. Beckhard addresses this issue as follows: "One of the major assumptions underlying organization development efforts and much managerial strategy today is the need to assure that organizations are managing against goals. Healthy organizations tend to have goal-setting at all levels."[16]

Both organizations and individuals need to manage their affairs against goals—explicit, measurable, obtainable goals. To help achieve this for the organization, OD interventions may be directed toward examination of the planning function, strategy-making processes, and goal-setting processes at the individual, group, and organizational levels. To help achieve this for the individual, OD interventions are directed toward the activities just mentioned and may also devote time to a series of activities called "life-and career-planning" exercises. Career development and life-planning activities are those in which individuals work on clarifying their life and career objectives and goals and determine how they can achieve them. In addition, when management by objectives is a part of an OD program, work teams with their immediate superiors learn to set realistic objectives that will be periodically reviewed. In this way individuals develop goal-setting abilities.

The power of goals to affect performance is highlighted by the goal-setting theory of Edwin Locke, which states that hard, specific goals, if accepted by the individual, will lead to increased performance.[17] Specifically, hard specific goals are associated with greater performance more often than are vague goals, no goals, and "do your best" goals. Dozens of laboratory and field studies provide evidence for the validity of goal-setting theory.[18] Hard, specific goals direct, focus, and energize behavior. Goal setting and management by objectives are thus important antecedents of individual effectiveness.

The importance of goal setting in OD programs, at both the individual and the organizational levels, probably represents a response to changes in the culture of organizations in this country in the last decade or two. It used to be that goal setting and planning were the sole function of the top echelons of the organization, while the functions of the lower echelons were to carry out the plans and help reach the objectives. It is now believed that wider participation in goal setting leads to a greater utilization of an organization's resources, human and technical, and results in significantly better plans. In addition, the plans that have been the contribution of many people at all levels of the organization probably have more chance of being realistic and attainable and also have some built-in support for carrying them out. But individuals and groups at lower organizational levels often did not have the skills necessary to do good plan making, since they had never been called upon to do so. OD interventions directed toward learning and practicing these skills attempt to meet this need of the organization and its members.

The Blake and Mouton *Grid Organization Development model* is particularly relevant for teaching goal-setting and planning abilities. In this six-phase model, phase 4 consists of the top management team studying the properties of an "ideal strategic corporate model"—what properties a corporation should optimally possess if it is to maximize its goals. This is followed by analyzing the organization to see where it falls short of the ideal model. Phase 5 consists of developing implementation tactics for converting the organization from what it is and has been to what it should become as an ideal corporation. The paradigm first teaches the characteristics and properties of a desirable ideal organization, then measures the real organization against that ideal, then develops implementation procedures for moving from "what we are now" to "what we want to be."[19]

The goal-setting and planning interventions concentrate on the following major skills and abilities: (1) learning to set goals and objectives, (2) learning to translate goals into actions and procedures for achieving them, and (3) learning how to plan and make decisions to facilitate goal attainment. (In a sense, this third point is a restatement of the first two points.) What we mean by goals and plans can best be shown by calling on writings from the fields of management and administration. Koontz and O'Donnell describe the planning function as follows:

> Plans involve selecting enterprise objectives and departmental plans and programs, and determining ways of reaching them. Plans thus provide a rational approach to preselected objectives.... Planning is deciding in advance what to do, how to do it, when to do it, and who is to do it.... Planning is an intellectual process, the conscious determination of courses of action, the basing of decision on purpose, facts, and considered estimates.[20]

The relation between planning and goals is suggested by Kast and Rosenzweig as follows:

> Basically, goals are plans expressed as results to be achieved. In this broad sense, goals include objectives, purposes, missions, deadlines, standards, targets, quotas, etc. Goals represent not only the end point of planning but the end toward which the other managerial activities, such as organizing and controlling, are aimed.[21]

Thus the emphasis on goal setting and planning in the OD process began as a response to the needs of organizations to have these skills available to all levels of the organization. Now the importance of "managing against objectives" and its positive consequences for better effectiveness are recognized as important in their own right. It is this belief that makes this feature another of the foundations of organization development.

OD ACTIVITIES FOCUS ON INTACT WORK TEAMS

A fundamental belief in organization development is that the organization does its work through work teams of a variety of kinds and natures. A second fundamental belief is that changing the culture, processes, relationships, and ways of performing tasks within these teams is a way to achieve permanent and lasting improvement in the organization. From a historical point of view, it was probably a realization of these two beliefs and the actions on them taken by Blake, Mouton, Shepard, Horowitz, McGregor, and others that gave birth to what we now know as organization development. The capacity for learning and change that comes from working with intact organizational teams can never be captured by the more traditional "stranger-type" learning activities.

Many different kinds of teams have salience and significance for the organizational members and for the OD practitioners. The potency and ability to make things happen by having intact work teams work together to improve their team effectiveness is frankly astounding compared with working with a group of individuals who are organizationally irrelevant to each other. This is true for a number of reasons, some of which are the following. First, much individual behavior is rooted in the sociocultural norms and values of the work team. If the team, as a team, changes those norms and values, the effect on individual behavior is immediate and lasting. Second, the intact work team possesses the "reality configuration of relationships" that the individuals must in fact accommodate to and learn to utilize and cope with. This is to say that many of the "significant others" of the individual's work world are in the work group. Effective (or ineffective) relationships with these people can have far-reaching effects on the individual's performance and behavior. Third, the "reality configuration of organizational dynamics" that the individuals must accommodate to are found in the work team. By this we mean that the work team is the source of most of the individual's knowledge about organizational processes such as communications, decision making, and goal setting. These are the processes that most influence the individual's behavior. Fourth, it is commonly believed that many of the individual's needs for social interaction, status, recognition, and respect are satisfied by his or her work group, consisting of both peers and superior. Any process that improves the work team's processes or task performance will thus probably be related to central needs of the individual members. We believe work teams are the basic building blocks of organizations; if work teams function well, individuals and the total organization will function well.

In our experience, most OD programs rely heavily on interventions designed to improve work team relationships, processes, and task performance. In the Grid approach to organization development, for example, phase 1 concentrates on learning about managerial style and interpersonal competence for individual managers; then phase 2 moves immediately into improving the work team culture and processes through activities in intact work teams.[22]

While working with intact groups to improve their functioning can be a powerful instrumentality for organizational change, it can also do considerable damage to the team if the activities are poorly conceived or poorly executed. Because the work team is so important to the individual, doing anything to destroy the relationships or to impair the processes or the ability for task performance can cause a profound and disastrous effect. This is another reason why we believe that an external change agent should be involved in the early stages of an OD program. There are numerous tales within the OD trade of calamitous effects in team-building sessions—some of these are true, but many of them are mythical. Team sessions are complex affairs, and a professional should be present to ensure that they go right.

OD USES A PARTICIPATION/EMPOWERMENT MODEL

One of the most pervasive and far-reaching foundations of organization development is its use of a participation/empowerment model. "Getting everybody into the act" is both a hallmark of OD and a strategy of empowerment. Participation in OD programs is not restricted to "elites" or "the top people" only; it is extended broadly and deeply into the organization. A number of reasons account for this pillar of OD practice.

Research on group dynamics began in the 1940s and achieved exponential growth in the 1950s and 1960s.[23] This research demonstrated that involvement and participation in affairs directly affecting them were: desired by most people, had the ability to energize greater performance, released latent knowledge and skills in people, produced better solutions to problems, greatly enhanced acceptance of decisions, worked to overcome resistance to change, increased commitment to the organization, reduced stress levels, and generally made people feel better about themselves and their worlds.[24] Participation is a powerful elixir—it not only makes people feel better, it dramatically improves individual and organizational performance. Active involvement is more effective than passive involvement. Participation is superior to nonparticipation.

Participation empowers people. To empower someone is to give him or her power. How is empowerment accomplished? Through the ability to participate and the ability to influence. Participation thus incorporates dimensions of empowerment. And empowerment in turn enhances performance and a sense of individual well-being. "Empowerment" has only recently become a popular term in the organizational literature, but it highlights the critical interface between the individual and the organization.[25] Participation, as practiced in organization development, enhances empowerment.

A rule of thumb regarding problem solving in OD is: "Involve all those who are part of the problem or part of the solution." Implementing this rule has been shown to produce better diagnoses and better solutions. This rule promotes an expanded participation method of problem solving. Another rule of thumb in OD is: "Have decisions made by those who are closest to the problematic situation." This rule pushes decision making lower in the organization, treats those closest to the problem as the relevant experts, and gives more power to more people. This rule of thumb likewise reflects a participation/empowerment model.

Susan Jackson found that increasing the amount of participation (by increasing the number of staff meetings per month) in an outpatient hospital significantly increased perceptions of perceived influence and significantly reduced perceptions of role conflict and role ambiguity.[26] Erez and Arad explored participation in goal setting in a laboratory experiment to tease out the causal components of participation. They examined three factors: the social factor of group discussion (versus no discussion), the motivational factor of direct involvement (versus no involvement), and the cognitive or increased information factor (versus no information) for their effects on a number of dependent variables. They found that the social and motivational factors of participation positively increased performance quantity, incidental learning, goal acceptance, group commitment, and satisfaction, while the motivational and cognitive factors significantly increased performance quality.[27] Participation works—it is, *sui generis,* a powerful force for increased effectiveness.

Many OD interventions capitalize on the power of participation. Activities such as quality circles, collaborative MBO, team building, intergroup team building, collateral organizations, and the like all specifically extend participation and empowerment throughout the organization.

SUMMARY

In this chapter we have continued to present our conception of the nature of organization development. In Chapter 6 OD as an operational process was seen to possess three basic components: the diagnostic, the action (or intervention), and the process-maintenance components, although we said that, in effect, all these components are interventions into the client system. In this chapter the foundations or building blocks characterizing the OD process have been explicated. Organization development was seen to have the following characteristics: it is an ongoing process; it is a form of applied behavioral science; it constitutes a normative-reeducative strategy for changing; it utilizes a systems approach; it is a data-based problem-solving model; it reflects an experience-based learning model; it emphasizes goal setting and the planning function; it involves intact work teams; and it utilizes a participation/empowerment model.

These foundations suggest an important conclusion: OD is the confluence of several diverse streams, all of which define the organization development process. Organization development is not one or two of these, but the result of all of these. Organization development represents the process emerging from the coming together at this point in time of the foundations—and each of these foundations was itself the result of diverse streams from earlier theories and earlier practices.

REFERENCES

ARGYRIS, C. *Intervention Theory and Method: A Behavioral Science View.* Reading, Mass.: Addison-Wesley, 1970.

ASCH, S. "Studies of Independence and Conformity: A Minority of One Against a Unanimous Majority," *Psychological Monograph,* 70, No. 9 (1956).

BANDURA, A. *Social Learning Theory.* Englewood Cliffs, N.J.: Prentice-Hall, 1977.

BAUMGARTEL, H. "Using Employee Questionnaire Results for Improving Organizations: The Survey 'Feedback' Experiment." *Kansas Business Review,* 12 (December 1959), pp. 2-6.

BENNIS, W. G., and H. A. SHEPARD. "A Theory of Group Development." *Human Relations,* 9, No. 4 (1956), pp. 415-438.

———, K. D. BENNE, and R. CHIN, eds. *The Planning of Change.* New York: Holt, Rinehart and Winston, 1961.

BLAKE, R. R., and J. S. MOUTON. *Consultation.* Reading, Mass.: Addison-Wesley, 1976.

———. "Conformity, Resistance, and Conversion." In I. A. Berg and B. M. Bass, eds., *Conformity and Deviation,* pp. 1-37. New York: Harper & Row, 1961.

———, J. S. MOUTON, L. B. BARNES, and L. E. GREINER. "Breakthrough in Organization Development." *Harvard Business Review,* 42 (November-December 1964), pp. 133-135.

BRADFORD, L. P., J. R. GIBB, and K. D. BENNE, eds. *T-Group Theory and Laboratory Method.* New York: John Wiley, 1964.

CARTWRIGHT, D., and A. ZANDER. *Group Dynamics* (2nd ed.). New York: Harper & Row, 1960.

DEUTSCH, M. "A Theory of Cooperation and Competition." *Human Relations,* 2, No. 2 (1949), pp. 129-152.

DEWEY, J. *How We Think* (rev. ed.). New York: Heath, 1933.

DRUCKER, P. F. *The Practice of Management.* New York: Harper & Row, 1954.

FLEISHMAN, E. A. "Leadership Climate, Human Relations Training and Supervisory Behavior." *Personnel Psychology,* 6 (Summer 1953), pp. 205-222.

GOLDSTEIN, A. P., and SORCHER, M. *Changing Supervisor Behavior.* New York: Pergamon Press, 1974.

GOULDNER, A. W. "The Norm of Reciprocity: A Preliminary Statement." *American Sociological Review,* 25 (April 1960), pp. 161-178.

HERZBERG, F., B. MAUSNER, and B. SNYDERMAN. *The Motivation to Work.* New York: John Wiley, 1959.

HOMANS, C. G.   *The Human Group*. New York Harcourt, Brace & World, 1950.
———, *Social Behavior: Its Elementary Forms*. New York: Harcourt, Brace & World, 1961.
KELLEY, H. H., and J. W. THIBAUT.   "Group Problem Solving." In G. Lindzey and E. Aronson, eds., *Handbook of Social Psychology* (2nd ed.), Vol. IV, pp. 1–101. Reading, Mass.: Addison-Wesley, 1969.
LATHAM, L. P., and SAARI, L. M.   "The Application of Social Learning Theory to Training Supervisors Through Behavior Modeling." *Journal of Applied Psychology*, 64 (1979), pp. 239–246.
LEAVITT, H. J.   "Some Effects of Certain Communication Patterns on Group Performance." *Journal of Abnormal and Social Psychology*, 46 (January 1951), 38–50.
LEWIN, K.   *Field Theory in Social Science*. New York: Harper & Bros., 1951.
LIKERT, R.   *New Patterns of Management*. New York: McGraw-Hill, 1961.
LIPPITT, R., J. WATSON, and B. WESTLEY.   *The Dynamics of Planned Change*. New York: Harcourt, Brace & World, 1958.
LOCKE, E. A.   "Toward a Theory of Task Motivation and Incentives." *Organizational Behavior and Human Performance*, 3 (1968), pp. 157–189.
MCGREGOR, D. M.   *The Human Side of Enterprise*. New York: McGraw-Hill, 1960.
MCGUIRE, W. J.   "The Nature of Attitudes and Attitude Change." In G. Lindzey and E. Aronson, eds., *Handbook of Social Psychology* (2nd ed.), vol. III, pp. 136–314. Reading, Mass.: Addison-Wesley, 1969.
MANN, F. C.   "Studying and Creating Change." In W. G. Bennis, K. D. Benne, and R. Chin, *The Planning of Change*, pp. 605–613. New York: Holt, Rinehart and Winston, 1961.
MARROW, A. J., D. G. BOWERS, and S. E. SEASHORE.   *Management by Participation*. New York: Harper & Row, 1967.
MASLOW, A.   *Motivation and Personality*. New York: Harper & Row, 1964.
MEAD, G. H.   *Mind, Self, and Society*. Chicago: University of Chicago Press, 1934.
PORRAS, J. I., K. HARGIS, K. J. PATTERSON, D. G. MAXFIELD, N. ROBERTS, and R. J. BIES.   "Modeling-Based Organizational Development: A Longitudinal Assessment," *The Journal of Applied Behavioral Science*, Vol. 18, No. 4, 1982, pp. 433–446.
ROETHLISBERGER, F. J., and W. J. DICKSON.   *Management and the Worker*. Cambridge, Mass.: Harvard University Press, 1956.
ROGERS, C. R.   *Client-Centered Therapy*. Boston: Houghton Mifflin, 1951.
SCHEIN, E.   *Organizational Culture and Leadership*. San Francisco: Jossey-Bass, 1985.
SCHUTZ, W.   *FIRO: A Three-Dimensional Theory of Interpersonal Behavior*. New York: Holt, Rinehart and Winston, 1958.
SHERIF, M.   *The Psychology of Social Norms*. New York: Harper & Bros. 1936.
———, O. J. HARVEY, B. J. WHITE, W. R. HOOD and C. SHERIF.   *Intergroup Conflict and Cooperation: The Robbers Cave Experiment*. Norman, Okla.: University Book Exchange, 1961.
SKINNER, B. F.   *About Behaviorism*. New York: Alfred A. Knopf, 1974.
TRIST, E. L., and K. W. BAMFORTH.   "Some Social and Psychological Consequences of the Longwall Method of Coal-Getting." *Human Relations*, 4, No. 1 (1951), pp. 1–38.
WHYTE, W. F.   *Human Relations in the Restaurant Industry*. New York: McGraw-Hill, 1948.

NOTES

1. Wendell French, *The Personnel Management Process*, 5th ed. (Boston: Hougton Mifflin, 1982), p. 39.
2. W. G. Bennis, E. H. Schein, D. E. Berlew, and F. I. Steele, *Interpersonal Dynamics* (Homewood, Ill,: Dorsey, 1964), pp. 2–3.
3. Robert K. Merton and Daniel Lerner, "Social Scientists and Research Policy," in W. G. Bennis, K. D. Benne, and R. Chin, eds., *The Planning of Change* (New York: Holt, Rinehart and Winston, 1961), pp. 53–69.

4. Ernest Greenwood, "The Practice of Science and the Science of Practice," in Bennis, Benne, and Chin, eds., *The Planning of Change,* p. 78.

5. Ibid., p. 79.

6. See the end of chapter references for the contributions of each of these authors.

7. R. Chin and K. Benne, "General Strategies for Effecting Changes in Human Systems," in W. G. Bennis, K. D. Benne, R. Chin, and K. E. Corey, eds., *The Planning of Change,* 3rd ed. (New York: Holt, Rinehart and Winston, 1976), pp. 22–45.

8. Ibid., p. 23

9. Based on a discussion in Chin and Benne, "General Strategies," pp. 32–33.

10. W. W. Burke and H. A. Hornstein, *The Social Technology of Organization Development* (Washington, D.C.: NTL Institute for Applied Behavioral Science Learning Resources Corporation, 1971), p. 1.

11. Warren Bennis, *Organization Development: Its Nature, Origins, and Prospects* (Reading, Mass.: Addison-Wesley, 1969), p. 15.

12. Ibid., p. 2.

13. Robert Chin, "The Utility of System Models and Developmental Models for Practitioners," in Bennis, Benne, and Chin, eds., *The Planning of Change,* 2nd ed., pp. 299–300.

14. Kurt Lewin, *Field Theory in Social Science* (New York: Harper & Bros., 1951).

15. R. R. Blake and J. S. Mouton, *Building a Dynamic Corporation Through Grid Organization Development* (Reading, Mass.: Addison-Wesley, 1969), p. vi.

16. Richard Beckhard, *Organization Development: Strategies and Models* (Reading, Mass.: Addison-Wesley, 1969), p. 35.

17. Edwin A. Locke, "Toward a Theory of Task Motivation and Incentives," *Organizational Behavior and Human Performance,* 3 (1968), pp. 157–189.

18. Edwin A. Locke, "The Ubiquity of the Technique of Goal Setting in Theories and Approaches to Employee Motivation," *Academy of Management Review,* 3 (1978), pp. 594–601.

19. Blake and Mouton, *Building a Dynamic Corporation,* p. 16.

20. Harold Koontz and Cyril O'Donnell, *Principles of Management,* 4th ed. (New York: McGraw-Hill, 1968), p. 81.

21. Fremont E. Kast and James E. Rosenzweig, *Organization and Management* (New York: McGraw-Hill, 1974), pp. 439–440.

22. Blake and Mouton, *Building a Dynamic Corporation,* p. 16.

23. See Dorwin Cartwright, "Achieving Change in People: Some Applications of Group Dynamics Theory," *Human Relations,* Vol. 4, No. 4, 1951, pp. 381–392.

24. J. E. McGrath, *Groups: Interaction and Performance,* (Englewood Cliffs, N.J.: Prentice-Hall, 1984).

25. See R. M. Kanter, *The Changemasters,* (New York: Simon and Schuster, 1983); and Tom Peters, *Thriving on Chaos,* (New York: Alfred A. Knopf, 1988).

26. Susan E. Jackson, "Participation in Decision Making as a Strategy for Reducing Job-Related Strain," *Journal of Applied Psychology,* Vol. 68, No. 1, 1983, pp. 3–19.

27. Miriam Erez and Revital Arad, "Participative Goal-Setting: Social, Motivational, and Cognitive Factors," *Journal of Applied Psychology,* Vol. 71, No. 4, 1986, pp. 591–597.

8

ACTION RESEARCH AND ORGANIZATION DEVELOPMENT

A basic model underlying most organization development activities is the action research model—a data-based, problem-solving model that replicates the steps involved in the scientific method of inquiry. Three processes are involved in action research: data collection, feedback of the data to the clients, and action planning based on the data.[1] Action research is both an *approach* to problem solving—a model or a paradigm—and a problem-solving *process*—a series of activities and events.

We examine the action research model in this chapter for two main reasons: first, to show the importance of action research as an underpinning for OD; and second, to explain what action research is. After a brief overview of the concept, action research is examined from two different perspectives—that of a problem-solving process and that of a problem-solving approach. Next the history and different kinds of action research are explored, followed by a discussion of its role and use in organization development.

A BRIEF INTRODUCTION TO ACTION RESEARCH

Action research is research on action with the goal of making that action more effective. Action refers to programs and interventions designed to solve a problem or improve a condition. It was Kurt Lewin, the consummate applied social scientist, who proposed the concept of action research as we are using it here. Lewin was an academician who was also interested in solving social problems. Deutsch describes the impetus for action research as follows:

As a citizen deeply sensitive to the world in which he lived, aware of the personal tragedies caused by oppression and prejudice, Lewin devoted much of his scientific work to furthering the understanding of the practical day-by-day problems of modern society. His book, *Resolving Social Conflicts* (1948), presents many of his sociopsychological analyses which deal with such important social problems as the effects of prejudice, methods of facing oppression, conflict in industry, conflict in marriage, morale in time of war, and methods of changing prejudiced groups. Lewin felt that the social scientist could not only contribute to the solution of social problems but also that the study of attempts to produce change in social conditions would make possible scientific insight into social processes which might not otherwise be attainable. These feelings led Lewin to stimulate an interest in action research . . . . [2]

Lewin believed that *research on action programs,* especially social change programs, was imperative if progress was to be made in solving social problems. Action research, as a proposed new methodology, would address several needs simultaneously: the pressing need for greater knowledge about the causes and dynamics of social ills; the need to understand the laws of social change; the need for greater collaboration and joint inquiry between scientists and practitioners; the need for "richer" data about real world problems; the need to discover workable, practical solutions to problems; and the need to discover general laws explaining complex social phenomena. Lewin wrote of the need for action research as follows:

> The research needed for social practice can best be characterized as research for social management or social engineering. It is a type of action-research, a comparative search on the conditions and effects of various forms of social action, and research leading to social action . . . .
> This by no means implies that the research needed is in any respect less scientific or "lower" than what would be required for pure science in the field of social events. I am inclined to hold the opposite to be true. [3]

There is a strong family resemblance between action research and organization development, as we shall see in this chapter.

ACTION RESEARCH AS A PROCESS

Action research may be described as a process, that is, as an ongoing series of events and actions. Used in this way, we define *action research* as follows: action research is the process of systematically collecting research data about an ongoing system relative to some objective, goal, or need of that system; feeding these data back into the system; taking actions by altering selected variables within the system based both on the data and on hypotheses; and evaluating the results of actions by collecting more data. This definition characterizes action research in terms of the activities comprising the process: first, a static picture is taken of an organization; on the basis of "what exists," hunches and hypotheses suggest actions; these actions typically entail manipulating some variables in the system that are under the control of the action researcher (this often means doing something differently from the way it has always been done); later, a second static picture is taken of the system to examine the effects of the action taken. These steps are the same steps we have described as being what the OD practitioner does when he or she attempts to improve an organization's functioning via organization development.

Several authors have noted the importance of viewing action research as a process. Stephen Corey, an early advocate of action research in education, states that ''The process by which practitioners attempt to study their problems scientifically in order to guide, correct, and evaluate their decisions and actions is what a number of people have called action research.''[4] Elsewhere Corey defines action research more in terms of a practitioner's tool: ''Action research in education is research undertaken by practitioners in order that they may improve their practices.''[5] In a study of the Tremont Hotel in Chicago, William F. Whyte and Edith L. Hamilton described their work as follows:

> What was the project? It was an action-research program for management. We developed a process for applying human relations research findings to the changing of organization behavior. The word *process* is important, for this was not a one-shot affair. The project involved a continuous gathering and analysis of human relations research data and the feeding of the findings into the organization in such a way as to change behavior.[6]

This study by Whyte and Hamilton is a particularly cogent example of the role of action research in improving an organization. Although the study itself was conducted in 1945 and 1946—before the term *organization development* was introduced—it would be considered an OD program today, even though it was based solely on an action research model.

In Figure 8–1 French presents a diagram of the process of action research as it relates to organization development.[7] His diagram points up the iterative or cyclical nature of the process. He clarifies the model as follows:

> The key aspects of the model are *diagnosis, data gathering, feedback to the client group, data discussion and work by the client group, action planning, and action.* The sequence tends to be cyclical, with the focus on new or advanced problems as the client group learns to work more effectively together.[8]

Action research is a process in two different ways: it is a sequence of events and activities *within* each iteration (data collection, feedback and working the data, and taking action based on the data); and it is a *cycle* of iterations of these activities sometimes treating the same problem through several cycles and sometimes moving to different problems in each cycle. Both aspects point up the ongoing nature of action research.

ACTION RESEARCH AS AN APPROACH

Action research may also be described as an approach to problem solving, thus suggesting its usefulness as a model, a guide, or a paradigm. Used in this way, *action research* may be defined as follows: action research is the application of the scientific method of fact-finding and experimentation to practical problems requiring action solutions and involving the collaboration and cooperation of scientists, practitioners, and laypersons. The desired

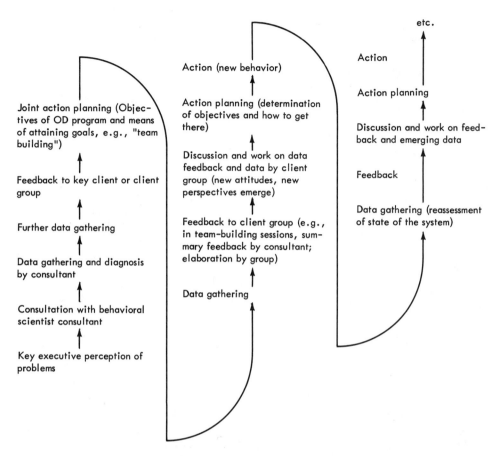

Figure 8-1 An Action Research Model for Organization Development. *Source:* Copyright 1969 by the Regents of the University of California. Reprinted from *California Management Review,* Vol. XII, No. 2, p. 26, Figure 1. By permission of the Regents.

outcomes of the action research approach are solutions to the immediate problems and a contribution to scientific knowledge and theory. Viewing action research from this perspective points up additional features that are important.

Action research was the conceptual model for an early organization improvement program in a series of oil refineries. Herbert Shepard, one of the behavioral scientists involved in that program, defines the nature of action research as follows:

> The action-research model is a normative model for learning, or a model for planned change. Its main features are these. In front of intelligent human action there should be an objective, be it ever so fuzzy or distorted. And in advance of human action there should be planning, although knowledge of paths to the objective is always inadequate. Action itself should be taken a step at a time, and after each step it is well to do some fact-finding. The fact-finding may disclose whether the objective is realistic, whether it is nearer or more distant than before, whether it needs alteration. Through fact-finding, the present situation can be assessed, and this information, together with information

about the objective, can be used in planning the second step. Movement toward an objective consists of a series of such cycles of planning–acting–fact-finding–planning.[9]

Shepard diagrams his concept of the action research model as shown in Figure 8–2.[10]

Shepard highlights the relations among goals (objectives), planning, and action in his diagram—a point we think is a very important feature of action research. And both he and French emphasize that action research is research inextricably linked to action; furthermore, it is research with a purpose, that is, to guide present and future action.

In an action research approach, the role of the consultant/change agent takes on a special form, as shown by Shepard:

> The role is to help the manager plan his actions and design his fact-finding procedures in such a way that he can learn from them, to serve such ends as becoming a more skillful manager, setting more realistic objectives, discovering better ways of organizing. In this sense, the staff concerned with follow-up are research consultants. Their task is to help managers formulate management problems as experiments.[11]

By viewing action research as an approach to problem solving we have noted the following features: the normative nature of this model, the importance and centrality of goals and objectives, and the different role requirements of the consultant/change agent vis-à-vis the clients. Three additional features deserve discussion: first, the elements of the action research model that link it to the scientific method of inquiry, second, the collaborative relation among scientists, practitioners, and laypersons that often is a component of action research, and third, the increased richness of the knowledge that can be derived from action research programs.

The paradigm for problematical inquiry that serves both as the model for the scientific method and as the model for action research was introduced by the philosopher John Dewey in his book *How We Think.*[12] He identified the following five phases of reflective thinking: suggestion, intellectualization, hypothesizing, reasoning, and testing the hypothesis by action. This approach to problem solving is translated into the scientific

Figure 8–2   Action Research Model. *Source:* Herbert A. Shepard, "An Action Research Model" in *An Action Research Program for Organization Improvement,* Ann Arbor, Mich.: Foundation for Research on Human Behavior, 1960. Used with permission.

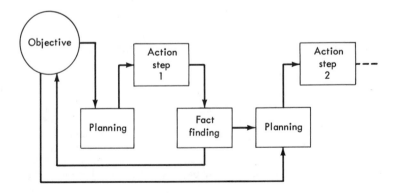

method steps as follows. First, the scientist is confronted with a *problem, obstacle, or new idea* that he or she wants to understand (Dewey's suggstion phase). The scientist identifies the problem, intellectualizes about it (what we usually call "thinking"), and arrive's at the point where an *hypothesis* about the problem can be formulated. (An *hypothesis* is a conjectural statement positing the relations between two or more phenomena, usually referred to as a "cause" and an "effect.") The next step, a critical one, consists of the scientist *reasoning or deducing the consequences of the hypothesis.* The final step consists of *observing, testing, or experimenting* to see if the relation between the two phenomena expressed in the hypothesis is verified or disconfirmed.[13]

These steps for the scientific method are identical with the steps outlined by Corey for action research:

> The significant elements of a design for action research are
>
> 1. The identification of a problem area about which an individual or a group is sufficiently concerned to want to take some action.
> 2. The selection of a specific problem and the formulation of a hypothesis or prediction that implies a goal and a procedure for reaching it. This specific goal must be viewed in relation to the total situation.
> 3. The careful recording of actions taken and the accumulation of evidence to determine the degree to which the goal has been achieved.
> 4. The inference from this evidence of generalizations regarding the relation between the actions and the desired goal.
> 5. The continuous retesting of these generalizations in action situations.
>
> If the problem under attack is one of concern to many people, or if it is likely that the experiment will affect many people, the action research should involve these people. It then becomes *cooperative* action research.[14]

An example applying action research to a typical organizational problem might be helpful. Suppose that the problem is unproductive staff meetings—they are poorly attended, members express low commitment and involvement in them, and they are generally agreed to be unproductive. Suppose also that you are the manager in charge of both the meetings and the staff and that you desire to make the meetings a vital, productive instrument for your organization. Following the action research model, the first step is to gather data about the status quo. Assume that this has been done and that the data suggest the meetings are generally disliked and regraded as unproductive. The next step is to search for causes of the problem and to generate one or more hypotheses from which you deduce the consequences that will allow the hypotheses to be tested. Say you come up with the following four hypotheses. Note the very important feature that an action research hypothesis consists of two aspects: a goal and an action or procedure for achieving that goal.

1. Staff meetings will be more productive if I solicit and use agenda topics from the staff rather than have the agenda made up just by me.
2. Staff meetings will be more productive if I rotate the chair of the meeting among the staff rather than my always being chairperson.
3. Staff meetings will be more productive if we have them once a week instead of twice a week.

4. I have always run the staff meetings in a brisk "all-business no-nonsense" fashion; perhaps if I encourage more discussion and am more open about how I am reacting to what is being said, then staff meetings will be more productive.

Each of these action research hypotheses has a goal, or objective (better staff meeting productivity), and each has an action, or procedure, for achieving the goal. Additional work would be done to clarify and specify the goal and the actions in more detail, and then the hypotheses would be systematically tested (implemented) one at a time and evaluated for their effects through data collection.

Another distinguishing feature of action research is collaboration between individuals inside the system—clients—and individuals outside the system—change agents or researchers. Havelock, for example, defines action research as

> the collaboration of researcher and practitioner in the diagnosis and evaluation of problems existing in the practice setting. . . . It provides the cooperating practitioner system with scientific data about its own operation which may be used for self-evaluation.[15]

Elsewhere Havelock discusses "collaborative action inquiry," which

> is similar to "action research." However, this model places greater emphasis on service to the practitioner system and on the collaborative teaming of research and practitioner. The inquiry team collaborates on defining goals, on all phases of the research, and on change strategies.[16]

Almost all authors stress the collaborative nature of action research, with some seeing it as the primary reason for the model's efficacy.[17]

It is a widely held belief that people tend to support what they have helped to create. Such a belief is highly congruent with the collaborative aspect of the action research model and impels practitioners and researchers alike to cooperate extensively with client system members. Such a point of view implies that the client system members and the researcher should jointly define the problems they want to address, should define the methods used for data collection, should identify the hypotheses relevant to the situations, and should evaluate the consequences of actions taken. We believe this collaborative ingredient of action research is particularly important in organization development.

As scientists and laypersons work together to understand and change a problematic condition, that joint inquiry process typically yields rich data and insights about the phenomenon of interest. The problem is a real one, not hypothetical; the actors know more about the situation than the outsiders do; and the actors have a vested interest in getting to the true facts since they will benefit from the solution. As Shani and Bushe observe: "It is the development of high-quality relations between action researchers and organizational members that creates access to important information that otherwise might not be available to outsiders. . . ."[18] As Deutsch observes, this was an appealing characteristic of action research for Kurt Lewin:

> In addition to the value that action research might have for social agencies, Lewin felt that linking research to social action might give the social scientist access to basic social processes which he would otherwise be unable to study. Furthermore, Lewin's orienta-

tion to dynamics in individual and group psychology led him to the conclusion that change studies are necessary to reveal underlying processes. Since the social scientist is rarely in the position to create social change on his own initiative, he has much to gain through cooperation with social agencies that attempt to produce social and community change.[19]

Because the data available in action research are so rich, this adds to the value of action research as a problem-solving approach.

THE HISTORY, USE, AND VARIETIES OF ACTION RESEARCH

John Dewey translated the scientific method of problem solving into terms understandable by practitioners and laypersons, and these seminal ideas were incorporated into action research several years later. The origin of action research can be traced to two independent sources. One source, John Collier, was a man of practical affairs; the other, Kurt Lewin, was a man of science. John Collier was commissioner of Indian Affairs from 1933 to 1945, a role in which he had to diagnose problems and recommend remedial programs for the improvement of race relations. Collier found that effecting changes in ethnic relations was an extremely difficult process and required *joint effort* on the part of the scientist (researcher), the administrator (practitioner), and the layperson (client).

> Principle seven I would call the first and the last: that research and then more research is essential to the program, that in the ethnic field research can be made a tool of action essential to all the other tools, indeed, that it ought to be the master tool. But we had in mind a particular kind of research, or, if you will, particular conditions. We had in mind research impelled from central areas of needed action. And since action is by nature not only specialized but also integrative to more than the specialities, our needed research must be of the integrative sort. Again, since the findings of the research must be carried into effect by the administrator and the layman, and must be criticized by them through their experience, the administrator and the layman must themselves participate creatively in the research, impelled as it is from their own area of need.[20]

Collier called this form of research *action research.* Taking effective actions requires research directed to important practical problems, and the solutions must be relevant and feasible. To be able to implement a good action plan also requires cooperation of the client. Action research seemed to afford a means to mesh these diverse elements.

The other major source for theory and practice of action research, Kurt Lewin, was a social psychologist who was profoundly interested in applying social science knowledge to help solve social problems. In the mid-1940s and early 1950s, Lewin and his students conducted action research projects in many different behavioral domains: Lewin applied action research principles to inter-group relations and to changing eating habits; Lippitt and Lippitt and Radke applied the tool to an extensive community relations project; Bavelas conducted an action research project on leadership training; Coch and French applied the model to studying resistance to change in an industrial plant.[21] As Lewin succinctly stated the issue, "No action without research, and no research without action."

Lewin's work with social agency practitioners engaged in eradicating prejudice led him to conclude that research to help the practitioner was imperative. His answer to the need was action research. Only by conducting research could action people generate standards by which to measure progress. Speaking to this problem he said,

> In a field that lacks objective standards of achievement, no learning can take place. If we cannot judge whether an action has led forward or backward, if we have no criteria for evaluating the relation between effort and achievement, there is nothing to prevent us from making the wrong conclusions and to encourage the wrong work habits. Realistic fact-finding and evaluation is a prerequisite for any learning. Social research should be one of the top priorities for the practical job of improving inter-group relations.[22]

For the Lewin group, action research represented a linking of experimentation and application, and at the same time, people of science and people of action. As an example Lippitt, in the preface to his book on community action research, states: "Bringing together in a single cooperative adventure the skills and resources of both men of science, and men of action, this project is an example of 'action research.'"[23]

Other noteworthy action research projects may be found in the literature.[24] Whyte and Hamilton studied the effects of human relations practices in a large hotel; Elliott Jaques used the action research model in effecting change in the culture of a factory in England; Cyril Sofer applied the methods in three diverse organizations undergoing change for which he was a researcher-consultant; Floyd Mann and Seashore and Bowers applied the methods to industrial plants undergoing changes in leadership; Shepard, Katzell, and others, working at a large refinery, used action research to effect a planned change program; Morse and Reimer's field experiment investigating leadership styles and participation in an insurance company is an example of action research; and Miles, Hornstein, Callahan, Calder, and Schiavo used action research to investigate the processes of self-renewal in a school system. Abraham Shani, writing in 1981, found over 100 published reports of action research projects and over 100 theoretical statements about this methodology. Shani found that many of these action research efforts were linked to OD programs.[25]

The payoff from a good action research project is high: practical problems get solved, a contribution is made to theory and to practice in behavioral science, and greater understanding grows among scientist, practitioner, and layperson. Some varieties of action research emphasize one kind of payoff over others, as we see in the next section.

Action research projects may be directed toward diverse goals, thereby giving rise to several variations of the model. Lewin, for example, suggested two broad categories of action research: the investigation of general laws and the diagnosis of a specific situation.[26] The study of general laws leads to contributions to theory and practice, and to generalizations about natural phenomena; the diagnosis of a specific situation leads to solving immediate, practical problems.

Raymond Katzell, in the refinery action research project, suggested three types of situations in which the research consultant staff were providing data feedback to managers: the first situation was described as "adventitious," that is, the research group happened to have already collected data that turned out to be quite useful to someone at a later time; the second situation represented data collection on a refinerywide basis of a preplanned, systematic nature, that is, a periodic pulse taking of the organization; the third situation was to work intensively with a small "demonstration" group, continuously collecting data on all sorts of topics and feeding them back to the group as they were needed.[27] The second situation is often found in programs involving surveys taken, say, annually. In this situation it is possible to measure changes in various parts of the organization over time. The third situation is also found in organization development programs where a team of consultants has time and energy to spend on researching the consequences of behaviors within a small group with whom they are working intensively.

Chein, Cook, and Harding enumerate four varieties of action research—diagnostic, participant, empirical, and experimental.[28] In *diagnostic action research,* the scientist enters a problem situation, diagnoses it, and makes recommendations for remedial treatment to the client. The recommendations are intuitively derived, not pretested, and usually come from the scientist's experience or knowledge. Often the recommendations are not put into effect by the client group. This gave rise to a second kind of action research, *participant action research,* in which the people who are to take action are involved in the entire research and action process from the beginning. This involvement both facilitates a carrying out of the actions once decided upon and keeps the recommended actions feasible and workable.

Empirical action research is that in which the actor keeps a systematic, extensive record of what he or she did and what effects it had. This is similar to the practitioner's keeping a day-to-day diary. Limitations of this method are the difficulties found in any clinical data collecting: the actor may have too few experiences to draw from; he or she may encounter situations too divergent from one another to compare them; the situation may be unique and may not permit generalizations; the actor may lack objectivity in evaluating his or her own performance; and there are difficulties inherent in being both researcher and change agent simultaneously.

> A fourth variety of action research, the *experimental,* is controlled research on the relative effectiveness of various action techniques. There is almost always more than one possible way of trying to accomplish something. The problem is to find which is the best. This is research *on* action in the strictest sense of both words.[29]

These authors indicate that experimental action research may make the greatest contribution to the advancement of scientific knowledge, but at the same time it is the most difficult to accomplish. The experimental nature of the research permits definitive testing of hypotheses and that is good. Controlling conditions to the extent that the hypothesis is tested in exactly the same way over several situations is difficult to do, however, when clients want immediate answers to pressing problems. In situations like these, the research aspects of the project often become subordinated to the problem-solving/remedial treatment requirements of the situation.

Organization development practitioners typically utilize participant action research and, occasionally, experimental action research. The participant model is highly congruent with current OD practices, and the experimental model, while being congruent, is simply harder to implement. In this regard, we maintain that the practice of organization development itself is in a sense a result of the experimental action research model, in that certain kinds of interventions (actions and hypotheses) were found to be effective by practitioners for achieving organization improvement and they were kept in the repertoire, while other interventions were found to be ineffective and were dropped from use.

Argyris promotes action research under the label of "action science" and he believes action science (action research) is more appropriate and effective for the study of social change and social action than is "normal science."[30] He criticizes traditional scientific methods for focusing on trivial problems, distorting human subjects and researchers alike, generating unrealiable data, and being generally unable to answer questions about everyday life. According to Argyris, Lewin's action research was characterized by six features: "...(1) it was problem-driven, (2) it was client-centered, (3) it challenged the status quo and was simultaneously concerned with (4) producing empirically disconfirmable propositions that (5) could be systematically interrelated into a theory designed to be (6) usable in everyday life...."[31] All six characteristics should be present in action research programs but often are not. Specifically, researchers become overly client-centered and focus only on action, not research; they do not define problems from the perspective of the client; they do not study the processes of their own interventions; they neglect to test hypotheses; and they continue to work within the paradigm of "normal science." Given these shortcomings, there should be a return to pure action research. And the use of action science will prove to be a better method for studying complex social situations, Argyris believes. Action science appears to be similar to experimental action research as identified by Chein, Cook, and Harding.

WHEN AND HOW TO USE ACTION RESEARCH
IN ORGANIZATION DEVELOPMENT

The OD process is basically an action research program in an organization designed to improve the functioning of that organization. Effective improvement programs almost always require a data base, that is, they rely on systematically obtained empirical facts for planning action, taking action, and evaluating action. Action research supplies an approach and a process for generating and utilizing information about the system itself that will provide a base for the action program.

The collaborative inquiry feature of action research suggests to practitioners and laypersons alike the desirability for jointly determining central needs, critical problems, and hypotheses and actions. The potential experimental nature of actions inherent in action research provides a different "set" for managers as they try to solve problems, that is, viewing problems in cause-effect terms and viewing solutions to problems as only one action hypothesis from a range of several. The systematic collection of data about variables related to the organization's culture and testing the effects of managerial actions on these variables offers a new tool for understanding organizational dynamics. All these features fit with a program to improve the organization.

Two recent examples will show how action research is used in organization development. Gavin conducted a comprehensive survey feedback program in a mining company of approximately 400 employees in the southwestern United States.[32] In several respects the OD program was a success—it was well received by the hourly employees and many key managers; it led to the solution of many immediate problems; and it led to numerous long-term organizational changes that increased the effectiveness of the mine. And in several respects it was a failure—increasing lack of trust of the consultants by some managers led to increasingly strained relations between higher management and the consultant team which led to the premature termination of the program. But Gavin and his doctoral students had conceptualized the project from the beginning as an action research project, not just an OD effort using survey feedback methodology. Therefore they simultaneously studied the effects of the OD program, their own intervention's processes and dynamics, and the changing client-consultant relations over time. The result was a rich case study yielding vital new information about both research and practice.

Shani and Eberhardt conducted an action research project at a medical rehabilitation hospital designed to improve the effectiveness of health care teams.[33] Patient care was provided by clinical teams comprised of professionals from many different medical specialties. Some teams were more effective than others. What caused the differences? How could less effective teams be made more effective? As one can imagine, the causes, correlates, and conditions of health care team effectiveness are complex and multifaceted. The expertise and cooperation of organization members were needed to discover the causal mechanisms and to plan and implement changes. The authors established a "parallel organization" consisting of a steering committee to guide the project and a study group to do the work. Shani and Eberhardt define a parallel organization as "...an institutionalized supplemental organizational form coexisting alongside the formal,"[34] and argue that such vehicles are particularly valuable for conducting action research programs. The parallel organization defined the data needs, conducted several iterations of data collection and making sense of the information, formulated hypotheses to be tested, and suggested alternatives for future steps to the hospital management. A major conclusion was that the action research approach yields better, richer information than the usual methods of social science research.

The natures of organization development and action research are very similar. They are both variants of applied behavioral science; they are both action oriented; they are both data based; they both call for close collaboration between insider and outsider; and they are both problem-solving social interventions. This is why we believe a sound organization development program rests on an action research model.

SUMMARY

Two philosophical and pragmatic values underlie action research. The first value is that action plans and programs designed to solve real problems should be based on valid public data generated collaboratively by clients and consultants. This belief calls for actions to be based on diagnostic research—an *action-should-follow-research* mode of thinking. Or, to state it another way, diagnose the problem situation and base action plans on that diagnosis. The second value is that action in the real world should be accompanied by research on that action so that we can build up a cumulative body of knowledge and theory of the effects of various actions directed to solving real-world problems—a *research-should-follow-action* mode of thinking. Only if we systematically evaluate (do research on) actions can we know what the real effects of these actions are. And only if we systematically and cumulatively build a body of knowledge can we build better social science theories.

Thus actions to solve real-world problems offer a unique opportunity for both the scientist-researcher and the administrator-layperson if the problems are approached from the standpoint of the action research model: the administrator's problems will be solved and the scientist's quest for theory and empirical validation of theory will be furthered. The applied behavioral science discipline of organization development is a fertile ground for action research projects.[35] We predict an increasing payoff from the use of experimental action research in OD.

NOTES

1. Richard Beckhard, *Organization Development: Strategies and Models* (Reading, Mass.: Addison-Wesley, 1969), p. 28.

2. Morton Deutsch, "Field Theory in Social Psychology," in *The Handbook of Social Psychology,* Gardner Lindzey and Elliott Aronson, eds., 1968, Vol. 1, pp. 412–487. This quotation is from p. 465.

3. Kurt Lewin, "Frontiers in Group Dynamics," *Human Relations,* Vol. 1, No. 2, 1947, pp. 150–151.

4. Stephen M. Corey, *Action Research to Improve School Practices* (New York: Bureau of Publications, Teachers College, Columbia University, 1953), p. 6.

5. Ibid., p. 141.

6. William F. Whyte and Edith L. Hamilton, *Action Research for Management* (Homewood, Ill.: Irwin-Dorsey, 1964), pp. 1–2.

7. Wendell French, "Organization Development Objectives, Assumptions, and Strategies," *California Management Review,* 12 (Winter 1969), pp. 23–34.

8. Ibid., p. 26.

9. Herbert A. Shepard, "An Action Research Model," in *An Action Research Program for Organization Improvement* (Ann Arbor: The Foundation for Research on Human Behavior, University of Michigan, 1960), pp. 33–34.

10. Figure 8–2 is from Herbert A. Shepard, "An Action Research Model," in *An Action Research Program for Organization Improvement* (Ann Arbor: The Foundation for Research on Human Behavior, 1960), p. 33, and is used with permission.

11. Ibid., p. 34

12. John Dewey, *How We Think,* rev. ed. (New York: Heath, 1933).

13. Based on a discussion in Fred N. Kerlinger, *Foundations of Behavioral Research,* 2nd ed. (New York: Holt, Rinehart and Winston, 1973), pp. 11–15.

14. Corey, *Action Research to Improve School Practices,* pp. 40–41.

15. Ronald G. Havelock, *Planning for Innovation Through Dissemination and Utilization of Knowledge* (Ann Arbor: Institute for Social Research, University of Michigan, 1969), pp. 9–33.

16. Ibid.

17. In this regard, the work of Collier (cited later in this chapter), Corey, and Lippitt (cited later) indicates a heavy emphasis on the importance of collaboration between all the individuals affected by a change project of this nature. And in a more recent article on action research and OD, client-consultant collaboration is cited as one of the basic processes of the action research model. Mark A. Frohman, Marshall Sashkin, and Michael J. Kavanagh, "Action-Research as Applied to Organization Development," *Organization and Administrative Sciences,* 7, Nos. 1 and 2 (Spring-Summer 1976), pp. 129–161.

18. Abraham B. Shani and Gervase R. Bushe, "Visionary Action Research: A Consultation Process Perspective," *Consultation,* Vol. 6, No. 1, (Spring 1987) p. 8.

19. Deutsch, "Field Theory in Social Psychology," pp. 465–466.

20. John Collier, "United States Indian Administration as a Laboratory of Ethnic Relations," *Social Research,* 12 (May 1945), pp. 275–276.

21. The relevant sources for Lewin's work are as follows: Kurt Lewin, "Action Research and Minority Problems," *Journal of Social Issues,* 2, No. 4 (1946), pp. 34–46; *Resolving Social Conflicts* (New York: Harper & Bros., 1948); in addition, Ronald Lippitt, *Training in Community Relations* (New York: Harper & Row, 1951); Ronald Lippitt and Marion Radke, "New Trends in

the Investigation of Prejudice,'' *Annals of the American Academy of Political and Social Science,* 244 (March 1946), pp. 167–176; and Lester Coch and J.R.P. French, Jr., ''Overcoming Resistance to Change,'' *Human Relations,* 1 (1948), pp. 512–532.

22. Lewin, ''Action Research and Minority Problems,'' p. 35.

23. Lippitt, *Training in Community Relations,* p. ix.

24. Whyte and Hamilton, *Action Research for Management;* Elliott Jaques, *The Changing Culture of a Factory* (New York: Dryden Press, 1952); Cyril Sofer, *The Organization from Within* (Chicago: Quadrangle Books, 1962); Floyd Mann, ''Studying and Creating Change: A Means to Understanding Social Organization,'' in C. M. Arensberg et al., eds., *Research in Industrial Human Relations* (New York: Harper & Row, 1957); and S. E. Seashore and D. G. Bowers, *Changing the Structure and Functioning of an Organization,* Monograph No. 33 (Ann Arbor: Survey Research Center, University of Michigan, 1963). Herbert A. Shepard and Raymond A. Katzell are two of the writers for the book *An Action Research Program for Organization Improvement.* Also see Nancy Morse and E. Reimer, ''The Experimental Change of a Major Organizational Variable,'' *Journal of Abnormal and Social Psychology,* 52 (January 1956), pp. 120–129; and Matthew Miles, Harvey Hornstein, Daniel Callahan, Paula Calder, and R. Steven Schiavo, ''The Consequences of Survey Feedback: Theory and Evaluation,'' in Warren Bennis, Kenneth Benne, and Robert Chin, eds., *The Planning of Change,* 2nd ed. (New York: Holt, Rinehart and Winston, 1969), pp. 457–468.

25. A. B. Shani, *Understanding the Process of Action Research in Organizations: A Theoretical Perspective.* Unpublished doctoral dissertation, Case Western Reserve University, Cleveland, Ohio, 1981.

26. Lewin, ''Action Research and Minority Problems,'' pp. 34–46.

27. Raymond Katzell, ''Action Research Activities at One Refinery,'' in *An Action Research Program for Organization Improvement,* pp. 37–47.

28. Isadore Chein, Stuart Cook, and John Harding, ''The Field of Action Research,'' *American Psychologist,* 3 (February 1948), pp. 43–50.

29. Ibid., p. 48.

30. C. Argyris, R. Putnam, and D. M. Smith, *Action Science* (San Francisco: Jossey-Bass, 1985). C. Argyris, *Inner Contradictions of Rigorous Research* (New York: Academic Press, 1980). C. Argyris and D. A. Schön, *Theory in Practice* (San Francisco: Jossey-Bass, 1974).

31. Chris Argyris, ''Action Science and Intervention,'' *The Journal of Applied Behavioral Science,* Vol. 19, No. 2 (1983), pp. 115–140. This quotation is from p. 115.

32. James F. Gavin, ''Survey Feedback: The Perspectives of Science and Practice,'' *Group and Organization Studies,* Vol. 9, No. 1 (March 1984), pp. 29–70.

33. Abraham B. Shani and Bruce J. Eberhardt, ''Parallel Organization in a Health Care Institution,'' *Group and Organization Studies,* Vol. 12, No. 2 (June 1987), pp. 147–173.

34. Ibid., p. 150.

35. See Frohman, Sashkin and Kavanagh, ''Action-Research as Applied to Organization Development,'' pp. 129–161. Also Michael Peters and Viviane Robinson, ''The Origins and Status of Action Research,'' *The Journal of Applied Behavioral Science,* Vol. 20, No. 2 (1984), pp. 113–124.

9

OD INTERVENTIONS—
AN OVERVIEW

The term *OD interventions* refers to the range of planned programmatic activities clients and consultants participate in during the course of an organization development program. These activities are designed to improve the organization's functioning through enabling organization members better to manage their team and organization cultures. OD interventions constitute the continually evolving technology—the methods and techniques—of the practice of organization development. Knowing the OD intervention armamentarium and knowing the rationale underlying the use of different interventions contributes substantially to understanding the philosophy, assumptions, nature, and processes of organization development. In these six chapters on interventions, we examine the techniques that apply behavioral science theory and practice to changing and improving ongoing systems. In this chapter we look at issues, definitions, rationale, and several classification schemata related to interventions. In Chapters 10 through 14 we extend the discussion by examining the current inventory of OD interventions.

A DEFINITION OF OD INTERVENTIONS

The term *intervention* is currently used in several different ways. On the one hand, this seems to be due to confusion and lack of definition; on the other hand, it is due to the fact that it quite accurately refers to several orders of meaning in terms of level of abstraction. Is an OD intervention something that someone does to an organization, or is it something that is going on, that is, an activity? It is both. We prefer, however, that emphasis be placed on the activity nature of interventions; interventions are "things that happen," activities, in an organization's life.

One use of the term that is common with practitioners and laypersons alike is that an intervention is something that the outside consultant does to the client system. The major shortcomings of this definition are, first, that it does not provide for the client system doing something to itself without the assistance of an external, or even internal, consultant, and, second, it denies the joint collaboration that takes place between consultant and client. In OD programs, individuals and units within the organization often initiate activities designed to improve their functioning on their own. These activities can constitute OD interventions.

The term is often used to refer to any learning technique or method available to the practitioner. Thus, any one of the extant methods available, what Burke and Hornstein call "the social technology of OD,"[1] is an intervention according to this use. (These techniques are available both to the client system and to consultants.) This is probably the most common use, and it is an appropriate one. The technology of OD consists of educational activities, methods, and techniques; some "things to do" and "things to be sure not to do"; questionnaires, observation and interview schedules, and so forth. Any of these is appropriately considered an intervention when it is used to bring about organization improvements.

Common usage also finds the term applied to the following different levels of activities:

> A single task, say, a two-hour decision-making exercise.
>
> A sequence or series of related tasks designed around some theme or objective; for example, Beckhard's *confrontation meeting* is a series of tasks designed to surface an organization's major problems, determine the priorities for solving the problems, and assign responsibilities for actions.[2]
>
> A "family" of activities that is related but may be quite different; for example, the set of activities called team-building interventions is a wide variety of diverse activities all designed to improve a team's effectiveness as a unit, and the activities may relate to ways to perform the task better or to ways to improve the relations between the team members.
>
> The overall plan for relating and integrating the organization improvement activities that an organization might be engaged in over a period of years (this is generally referred to as the *intervention strategy,* the *strategy of intervention,* or the *OD strategy* of the organization development program).

All these are correct uses of the term *intervention,* but they relate to different levels of abstraction and can thus be confusing at times.

Finally, to give our definition of the term, OD interventions are *sets of structured activities* in which selected organizational units (target groups or individuals) engage in a task or a sequence of tasks where the task goals are related directly or indirectly to organizational improvement. Interventions constitute the action thrust of organization development; they "make things happen" and are "what's happening."

The OD practitioner is a professional versed in the theory and practice of organization development. The practitioner brings four sets of attributes to the organizational setting: a set of values; a set of assumptions about people, organizations, and interpersonal relationships; a set of goals and objectives both for the practitioner and for the organization and its members; and a set of structured activities that are the *means* to implementing the values, assumptions, and goals. These activities are what we mean by the word *interventions*.

A BRIEF WORD ABOUT THE NATURE OF OD INTERVENTIONS

In the chapter on the nature of organization development, the characteristics, nature, and scope of OD interventions were discussed in relation to the OD process. Many of the characteristics ascribed to OD inhere also in OD interventions. The foundations and characteristics of the OD process are given there as follows: it is data based and experience based, with emphasis on action, diagnosis, and goal setting; it frequently utilizes work teams as target groups; it rests on a system approach and a participation/empowerment approach to organizations; it is a normative-reeducative strategy of changing; and it is an ongoing process. In this section we deal explicitly with OD interventions, covering some new materials and some old materials in a new way.

OD interventions are structured activities of selected target groups. Some ''secrets'' of OD are contained in this statement, because there are ''better'' ways and ''worse'' ways to structure activities for learning and change to take place. Organization development practitioners know how to structure activities in the ''better'' ways through attending to the following points:

1. Structure the activity so that the relevant people are there. The relevant people are those affected by the problem or the opportunity. For example, if the goal is improved team effectiveness, have the whole team engage in the activities. If the goal is improved relations between two separate work groups, have both work groups present. If the goal is to build some linkages with some special group, say, the industrial relations people, have them there and have the linking people from the home group there. This preplanning of the group composition is a necessary feature of properly structuring the activity.

2. Structure the activity so that it is (a) problem oriented or opportunity oriented and (b) oriented to the problems and opportunities generated by the clients themselves. Solving problems and capitalizing on opportunities are involving, interesting, and enjoyable tasks for most people, whether it is due to a desire for competence or mastery (as suggested by White),[3] or a desire to achieve (as suggested by McClelland),[4] or whatever. This is especially true when the issues to be worked on have been defined by the client. There is built-in support and involvement, and there is a real payoff when clients are solving issues that they have stated have highest priority.

3. Structure the activity so that the goal is clear and the way to reach the goal is clear. Few things demotivate an individual as much as not knowing what he or she is working toward and not knowing how what the individual is doing contributes to goal attainment. Both these points are part of structuring the activity properly. (Parenthetically, the goals will be important goals for the individuals if point 2 is followed.)

4. Structure the activity so that there is a high probability of successful goal attainment. Implicit in this point is the warning that expectations of practitioners and clients should be realistic. But more than that, manageable, attainable objectives once achieved produce feelings of success, competence, and potency for the people involved. This, in turn, raises aspiration levels and feelings of self- and group-worth. The task can still be hard,

complicated, taxing—but it should be attainable. And if there is failure to accomplish the goal, the reasons for this should be examined so they can be avoided in the future.

5. Structure the activity so that it contains both experience-based learning and conceptual/cognitive/theoretical-based learning. New learnings gained through experience are made a permanent part of the individual's repertoire when they are augmented with conceptual material that puts the experience into a broader framework of theory and behavior. Relating the experience to conceptual models, theories, and other experiences and beliefs helps the learning to become integrated for the individual.

6. Structure the climate of the activity so that individuals are "freed up" rather than anxious or defensive. Setting the climate of interventions so that people expect "to learn together" and "to look at practices in an experimenting way so that we can select better procedures" is what we mean by climate setting.

7. Structure the activity so that the participants learn both how to solve a particular problem and "learn how to learn" at the same time. This may mean scheduling in time for reflecting on the activity and teasing out learnings that occurred; it may mean devoting as much as half the activity to one focus and half to the other.

8. Structure the activity so that individuals can learn about both *task* and *process.* The task is what the group is working on, that is, the stated agenda items. The term *process,* as used here, refers to *how* the group is working and *what else is going on* as the task is being worked on. This includes the group's processes and dynamics, individual styles of interacting and behaving, and so on. Learning to be skillful in both of these areas is a powerful tool. Activities structured to focus on both aspects result in learnings on both aspects.

9. Structure the activity so that individuals are engaged as whole persons, not segmented persons. This means that role demands, thoughts, beliefs, feelings, and strivings should all be called into play, not just one or two of these. Integrating disparate parts of individuals in an organizational world where differentiation in terms of roles, feelings, and thoughts is common probably enhances the individual's ability to cope and grow.

These features are integral characteristics of OD interventions and also of the practitioner's practice theory of organization development. Little attention is given to characteristics of structuring activities in the literature, but knowledge of them helps to take some of the mystery out of interventions and may also help people who are just beginning to practice OD.

A different approach to the nature of OD interventions is provided by Robert Blake and Jane Mouton, who list the major interventions in terms of their underlying themes.[5] They describe the following kinds of interventions:

1. *Discrepancy intervention,* which calls attention to a contradiction in action or attitudes that then leads to exploration.

2. *Theory intervention,* where behavioral science knowledge and theory are used to explain present behavior and assumptions underlying the behavior.

3. *Procedural intervention,* which represents a critiquing of how something is being done to determine whether the best methods are being used.

4. *Relationship intervention,* which focuses attention on interpersonal relationships (particularly those where there are strong negative feelings) and surfaces the issues for exploration and possible resolution.

5. *Experimentation intervention,* in which two different action plans are tested for their consequences before a final decision on one is made.

6. *Dilemma intervention,* in which an imposed or emergent dilemma is used to force close examination of the possible choices involved and the assumptions underlying them.

7. *Perspective intervention,* which draws attention away from immediate actions and demands and allows a look at historical background, context, and future objectives in order to assess whether or not the actions are "still on target."

8. *Organization structure intervention,* which calls for examination and evaluation of structural causes for organizational ineffectiveness.

9. *Cultural intervention,* which examines traditions, precedents, and practices—the fabric of the organization's culture—in a direct, focused approach.

These different kinds of interventions suggest the range of different ways the OD practitioner can intervene in the client system. They also suggest the underlying dynamics of interventions.

Blake and Mouton have continued to examine and refine the nature of interventions and have proposed a theory and typology for the entire consultation field.[6] The typology, called the Consulcube®, is a 100-cell cube depicting virtually all consultation situations. The cube is built on three dimensions. The first dimension is what the consultant *does,* that is, what kind of intervention the consultant uses. There are five basic types of interventions—*acceptable* (the consultant gives the client a sense of worth, value, acceptance, and support); *catalytic* (the consultant helps the client generate data and information in order to restructure the client's perceptions); *confrontation* (the consultant points out value discrepancies in the client's beliefs and actions); *prescription* (the consultant tells the client what to do to solve the problem); and *theories and principles* (the consultant teaches the client relevant behavioral science theory so that the client can learn to diagnose and solve his or her own problems).

The second dimension is the *focal issues* causing the client's problems. Four focal issue categories are identified: power-authority, morale/cohesion, norms/standards of conduct, and goals/objectives.

The third dimension of the cube is the units of change that are the target of the consultation. Five units are proposed: individual, group, intergroup, organization, and larger social systems such as a community or even a society.

Five kinds of interventions, four different focal issues, and five different units of change are thus seen to encompass the range of consultation possibilities. Blake and Mouton's Consulcube represents a major contribution in the development of a theory of consultation and intervention. It is a contribution that clarifies the role of organization development and the different interventions that make up the OD technology.

A similar rubric, called the "OD Cube," has been proposed by Richard Schmuck and Matthew Miles.[7] This cube classifies OD interventions based on three dimensions: the diagnosed problems, the focus of attention, and the mode of intervention. The OD Cube is shown in Figure 9-1. It is also a road map for understanding most of the OD interventions discussed in this book.

THE MAJOR FAMILIES OF OD INTERVENTIONS

Not all OD programs contain all the possible intervention activities, but a wide range of activities is available to the practitioner. As we see it, the following are the major "families" or types of OD interventions.

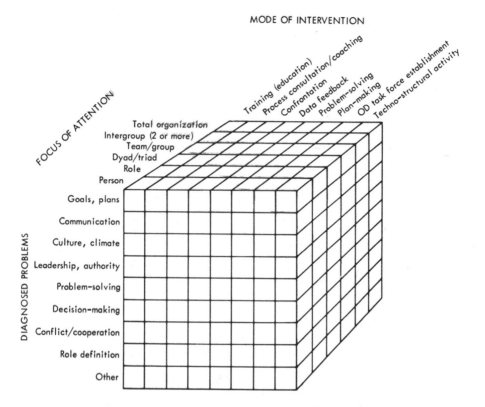

Figure 9–1 The OD Cube: A Scheme for Classifying OD Interventions. *Source:* Richard A. Schmuck and Matthew B. Miles, eds., *OD in Schools,* La Jolla, Calif.: University Associates, Inc., 1971. Used with permission.

1. *Diagnostic Activities:* Fact-finding activities designed to ascertain the state of the system, the status of a problem, the "way things are." Available methods range from projective devices such as "build a collage that represents for you your place in this organization" to the more traditional data collection methods of interviews, questionnaires, surveys, and meetings.

2. *Team-Building Activities:* Activities designed to enhance the effective operation of system teams. They may relate to task issues, such as the way things are done, the needed skills to accomplish tasks, the resource allocations necessary for task accomplishments; or they may relate to the nature and quality of the relationships between the team members or between members and the leader. Again, a wide range of activities is possible. In addition, consideration is given to the different kinds of teams that may exist in the organization, such as formal work teams, temporary task force teams, newly constituted teams, and cross-functional teams.

3. *Intergroup Activities:* Activities designed to improve effectiveness of interdependent groups. They focus on joint activities and the output of the groups considered as a single system rather than as two subsystems. When two groups are involved, the activities are generally designated intergroup or interface activities; when more than two groups are involved, the activities are often called *organizational mirroring.*

4. *Survey Feedback Activities:* Related to and similar to the diagnostic activities mentioned in that they are a large component of those activities. However, they are important enough in their own right to be considered separately. These activities center on actively working the data produced by a survey and designing action plans based on the survey data.

5. *Education and Training Activities:* Activities designed to improve skills, abilities, and knowledge of individuals. There are several activities available and several approaches possible. For example, the individual can be educated in isolation from his or her own work group (say, in a T-group comprised of strangers), or one can be educated in relation to the work group (say, when a work team learns how better to manage interpersonal conflict). The activities may be directed toward technical skills required for effective task performance or may be directed toward improving interpersonal competence. The activities may be directed toward leadership issues, responsibilities and functions of group members, decision making, problem solving, goal setting and planning, and so forth.

6. *Technostructural or Structural Activities:* Activities designed to improve the effectiveness of the technical or structural inputs and constraints affecting individuals or groups. The activities may take the form of (a) experimenting with new organization structures and evaluating their effectiveness in terms of specific goals or (b) devising new ways to bring technical resources to bear on problems. In Chapter 14 we discuss these activities and label them "structural interventions," defined as "the broad class of interventions or change efforts aimed at improving organization effectiveness through changes in the task, structural, and technological subsystems." Included in these activities are certain forms of job enrichment, management by objectives, sociotechnical systems, collateral organizations, and physical settings interventions.

7. *Process Consultation Activities:* Activities on the part of the consultant that "help the client to perceive, understand, and act upon process events which occur in the client's environment."[8] These activities perhaps more accurately describe an approach, a consulting mode in which the client is given insight into the human processes in organizations and taught skills in diagnosing and managing them. Primary emphasis is on processes such as communications, leader and member roles in groups, problem solving and decision making, group norms and group growth, leadership and authority, and intergroup cooperation and competition.

8. *Grid Organization Development Activities:* Activities invented and franchised by Robert Blake and Jane Mouton, which constitute a six-phase change model involving the total organization.[9] Internal resources are developed to conduct most of the programs, which may take from three to five years to complete. The model starts with upgrading individual managers' skills and leadership abilities, moves to team improvement activities, then to intergroup relations activities. Later phases include corporate planning for improvement, developing implementation tactics, and concluding with an evaluation phase assessing change in the organization culture and looking toward future directions.

9. *Third-Party Peacemaking Activities:* Activities conducted by a skilled consultant (the third party), which are designed to "help two members of an organization manage their interpersonal conflict."[10] They are based on confrontation tactics and an understanding of the processes involved in conflict and conflict resolution.

10. *Coaching and Counseling Activities:* Activities that entail the consultant or other organization members working with individuals to help them (a) define learning goals, (b) learn how others see their behavior, and (c) learn new modes of behavior to see if these help them to achieve their goals better. A central feature of this activity is the nonevaluative feedback given by others to an individual. A second feature is the joint exploration of alternative behaviors.

11. *Life- and Career-Planning Activities:* Activities that enable individuals to focus on their life and career objectives and how they might go about achieving them. Structured activities

lead to production of life and career inventories, discussions of goals and objectives, and assessment of capabilities, needed additional training, and areas of strength and deficiency.

12. *Planning and Goal-Setting Activities:* Activities that include theory and experience in planning and goal setting, utilizing problem-solving models, planning paradigms, ideal organization versus real organization "discrepancy" models, and the like. The goal of all of them is to improve these skills at the levels of the individual, group, and total organization.

13. *Strategic Management Activities:* Activities that help key policymakers reflect systematically on their organization's basic mission and goals and environmental demands, threats, and opportunities and engage in long-range action planning of both a reactive and proactive nature. These activities direct attention in two important directions: outside the organization to a consideration of the environment, and away from the present to the future.

Each of these families of interventions has many activities and exercises included in it. They all rely on inputs of both conceptual material and actual experience with the phenomenon being studied. Some of the families are directed toward specific targets, problems, or processes. For example, the team-building activities are specific to intact work teams, while the life-planning activities are directed to individuals, although this latter activity takes place in group settings. Some interventions are problem specific: examples of this are the third-party peacemaking activities and the goal-setting activities. Some activities are process specific, that is, specific to selected processes: an example of this is the intergroup activities in which the processes involved in managing interfaces are explored.

Additional interventions used in OD exist and are discussed in the following chapters. Examples of important interventions that in themselves do not constitute a family are the confrontation meeting, sensitivity training, force-field analysis, the role analysis technique (RAT), quality circles, responsibility charting, Gestalt OD (the application of Gestalt therapy techniques to organization problems), behavior modeling, and transactional analysis (TA). There are also several approaches to organization improvement based on theoretical formulations, such as Lawrence and Lorsch's contingency theory and Likert's System 4 Management theory. These theory-based interventions are usually considered to be OD interventions.

Most of these OD interventions have been around for many years. Team building, survey feedback, education and training activities, technostructural activities, and Grid OD have been widely used and are highly regarded. But new interventions are continually being developed, and surges of popularity cause certain interventions to rise to prominence for a time. In the last 10 years, there has been a substantial interest shown in sociotechnical systems interventions, "Japanese management" technologies (especially quality circles), and strategic management methodologies. Many sociotechnical systems programs also go under the label quality of work life (QWL) programs. They are discussed in Chapter 14. Quality circles are used extensively in Japan (millions of Japanese workers meet weekly to discuss quantity and quality of production and exchange ideas about ways to improve performance). This technique is becoming increasingly popular in the United States; it is discussed in Chapter 14. Strategic management techniques are still being developed, but several current models of interventions are discussed in Chapter 13.

SOME CLASSIFICATION SCHEMATA FOR OD INTERVENTIONS

Several ways of classifying OD interventions have alrady been discussed: the families of interventions represent one approach; Blake and Mouton's nine intervention types and their Consulcube represent additional views; and Schmuck and Miles's OD Cube represents yet another way to order and classify OD interventions. In this section we wish to construct some classification schemata showing interventions from various perspectives. Our purpose in doing this is to impart a better working knowledge of the different interventions and their dynamics so that we can better accomplish our objective of examining OD from a kaleidoscopic rather than from a microscopic point of view.

One way to gain a perspective of OD interventions is to form a typology of interventions based on the following questions: (1) Is the intervention directed primarily toward individual learning, insight, and skill building or toward group learning? (2) Does the intervention focus on *task* or *process* issues? (Task is what is being done; process is how it is accomplished, including how people are relating to each other and what processes and dynamics are occurring.) A four-quadrant typology constructed by using these two questions is shown in Figure 9-2.

This classification method presents one approximation of the categories of various interventions; it is difficult to assign the interventions precisely because a single intervention may have the attributes of more than one of the quadrants. Interventions simply are not mutually exclusive; there is great overlap of emphasis and the activity will frequently focus on, say, task at one time and process at a later time. Generally, however, the interventions may be viewed as belonging predominantly in the quadrant in which they are placed. It is thus possible to see that the interventions do differ from each other in terms of major emphases.

Another way to view interventions is to see them as *designated to improve the effectiveness of a given organizational unit*. Given different organizational targets, what interventions are most commonly used to improve their effectiveness? This is shown in Figure 9-3.

Examination of Figures 9-2 and 9-3 reveals redundancy and overlap in that specific interventions and activities appear in several classification categories. This may be confusing to the reader who is new to organization development, but it nevertheless reflects the use to which various interventions are put. Perhaps a positive feature of the redundancy is that it suggests patterns among the interventions that the practitioner knows but that may not be readily apparent to the layperson.

Another means of categorizing the OD interventions is to determine the underlying causal mechanisms of the intervention that probably are the source of its efficacy. This method is more controversial in that different authors might hypothesize different causal dynamics. Several causal mechanisms inherent in OD interventions may lead to change and learning. These causal mechanisms are found to greater and lesser degrees in different interventions, and it is probable that their efficacy therefore rests on different causes. Some features of different interventions that may be causally related to learning and change follow.

1. *Feedback.* This refers to learning new data about oneself, others, group processes, or organizational dynamics—data that one did not previously take active account of. Feedback refers to activities and processes that "reflect" or "mirror" an objective picture

Individual vs. Group Dimension

	Focus on the Individual	Focus on the Group
Focus on Task Issues	Role analysis technique Role negotiation technique Education: technical skills; also decision making, problem solving, goal setting, and planning Career planning Grid OD phase 1 (see also below) Some forms of job enrichment and Management by Objectives (MBO) Behavior modeling (see also below)	Technostructural changes Survey feedback (see also below) Force field analysis Team-building sessions with task emphasis Responsibility charting Intergroup activities Grid OD phases 2, 3 (see also below) Some forms of sociotechnical systems Quality circles
Focus on Process Issues	Life planning Process consultation with coaching and counseling of individuals Education: group dynamics, planned change Stranger T-groups Third-party peacemaking Grid OD phase 1 Gestalt OD Transactional analysis Behavior modeling	Survey feedback Team-building sessions with process emphasis Intergroup activities Process consultation Family T-group Grid OD phases 2, 3

Task vs. Process Dimension

Figure 9-2 OD Interventions Classified by Two Independent Dimensions: Individual-Group and Task-Process

of the real world. Awareness of this "new information" may lead to change if the feedback is not too threatening. Feedback is prominent in such interventions as process consultation, organization mirroring, sensitivity training, coaching and counseling, and survey feedback.

2. *Awareness of Changing Sociocultural Norms or Dysfunctional Present Norms.* Often people modify their behavior, attitudes, values, and so on when they become aware of changes in the norms that are helping to determine their behavior. Thus, awareness of new norms has change potential because the individual will adjust his or her behavior to bring it in line with the new norms. The awareness that "this is a new ball game" or that "we're now playing with a new set of rules" is here hypothesized to be a cause of changes in individual behavior. Also awareness of dysfunctional present norms can serve as an incentive to change. When people sense a discrepancy between the outcomes their present norms are causing and the desired outcomes they want, this can lead to change. This causal mechanism is probably operating in team building and intergroup team-building activities as well as in Likert's System 4 Mangement programs.

3. *Increased Interaction and Communication.* Increasing interaction and communication between

Target Group	Types of Interventions
Interventions designed to improve the effectiveness of INDIVIDUALS	Life-and career- planning activities Role analysis technique Coaching and counseling T-group (sensitivity training) Education and training to increase skills, knowledge in the areas of technical task needs, relationship skills, process skills, decision making, problem solving, planning, goal-setting skills Grid OD phase 1 Some forms of job enrichment Gestalt OD Transactional analysis Behavior modeling
Interventions designed to improve the effectiveness of DYADS/TRIADS	Process consultation Third-party peacemaking Role negotiation technique Gestalt OD Transactional analysis
Interventions designed to improve the effectiveness of TEAMS & GROUPS	Team building — Task directed — Process directed Grid OD phase 2 Family T-group Responsibility charting Process consultation Role analysis technique "Start-up" team-building activities Education in decision making, problem solving, planning, goal setting in group settings Some forms of job enrichment and MBO Sociotechnical systems and Quality of Work Life programs Quality circles Force field analysis
Interventions designed to improve the effectiveness of INTERGROUP RELATIONS	Intergroup activities — Process directed — Task directed Organizational mirroring (three or more groups) Structural interventions Process consultation Third-party peacemaking at group level Grid OD phase 3 Survey feedback
Interventions designed to improve the effectiveness of the TOTAL ORGANIZATION	Technostructural activities such as collateral organizations, sociotechnical systems, and organizational restructuring Confrontation meetings Strategic planning/strategic management activities Grid OD phases 4, 5, 6 Survey feedback Interventions based on Lawrence and Lorsch's contingency theory Interventions based on Likert's Systems 1 — 4 Physical settings

Figure 9–3 Typology of OD Interventions Based on Target Groups

individuals and groups may in and of itself effect changes in attitudes and behavior. Homans, for example, suggests that increased interaction leads to increased positive sentiments.[11] Individuals and groups in isolation tend to develop "tunnel vision" or "autism," according to Murphy.[12] Increasing communication probably counteracts this tendency. Increased communication allows one to check one's perceptions to see if they are socially validated and shared. This mechanism underlies almost all OD interventions. The rule of thumb is: Get people talking and interacting in new, constructive ways and good things will result.

4. *Confrontation.* This term refers to surfacing and addressing differences in beliefs, feelings, attitudes, values, or norms to remove obstacles to effective interaction. Confrontation is a process that actively seeks to discern real differences that are "getting in the way," surface those issues, and work on the issues in a constructive way. Many obstacles to growth and learning exist; they continue to exist when they are not actively looked at and examined. Confrontation underlies most conflict resolution interventions such as intergroup team building, third-party peacemaking, and role negotiation.

5. *Education.* This refers to activities designed to upgrade (a) knowledge and concepts, (b) outmoded beliefs and attitudes, and (c) skills. In organization development the education may be directed toward increasing these three components in several content areas: task achievement, human and social relationships and behavior, organiational dynamics and processes, and processes of managing and directing change. Education has long been an accepted change technique. Education is the primary causal mechanism in behavior modeling, force-field analysis, transactional analysis, and life- and career-planning.

6. *Participation.* This refers to activities which increase the number of people who are allowed to be involved in problem solving, goal setting, and the generation of new ideas. Participation has been shown to increase the quality and acceptance of decisions, to increase job satisfaction, and to promote employee well-being. Participation is a principal underlying mechanism of quality circles, collateral organizations, quality of work life (QWL) programs, Likert's System 4 Management, team building, survey feedback, and Beckhard's Confrontation Meeting. It is likely that participation plays a role in most OD interventions.

7. *Increased Accountability.* This refers to activities that clarify who is responsible for what and that monitor performance related to those responsibilities. Both of these features must be present for accountability to enhance performance. OD interventions that increase accountability are the role analysis technique, responsibility charting, Gestalt OD, life- and career-planning, quality circles, and MBO.

Another convenient classification method is to categorize OD interventions into those that focus on team improvement (Chapter 10), improving intergroup relations (Chapter 11), personal, interpersonal, and group processes (Chapter 12), comprehensive or total organization interventions (Chapter 13), and structural interventions (Chapter 14). This method is similar to the typology based on target groups presented in Figure 9–3 but separates out the "process" and "structural" interventions for special attention.

In addition to knowledge about various interventions and knowledge about the appropriateness and timeliness of interventions, the OD practitioner is cognizant of the many dimensions inherent in each particular activity. Since an intervention contains the possibility for going in many directions, the practitioner attends to the range of alternatives in his or her own inputs. For example, in a team-building meeting, the practitioner will have various dimensions in mind that guide his or her inputs and contributions. These dimensions can be explained through looking at the questions the practitioner may be considering:

> We are dealing with individual behavior right now; how can this learning be translated to learning for the group?
>
> We are dealing with group phenomena right now; how can this learning be translated to learning for the individuals?
>
> We are focusing on task competencies and requirements; how do these relate to process issues and understanding of the group's dynamics?
>
> We have just learned about a phenomenon by experiencing it; what theoretical or conceptual material would augment this learning?
>
> We are dealing with issues and forces impinging on this group from outside the group; what activities must be designed to facilitate more appropriate handling of these interface issues?
>
> We are dealing with an old problem in a new way; does that signal a change in the sociocultural norms of this group, and are the members aware of it?
>
> We are diagnosing areas of interpersonal and intergroup conflict; what interventions are appropriate to deal with these issues?

The practitioner also possesses a set of guidelines to be used for choosing and sequencing interventions. Michael Beer suggests the following "decision rules":

> These decision rules . . . can help a change agent focus on the relevant issues in making decisions about how to integrate a variety of interventions. They are rules for managing the implementation process.
>
> 1. *Maximize diagnostic data.* In general, interventions that will provide data needed to make subsequent intervention decisions should come first. This is particularly true when change agents do not know much about the situation. Violation of this rule can lead to choosing inappropriate interventions.
> 2. *Maximize effectiveness.* Interventions should be sequenced so that early interventions enhance the effectiveness of subsequent interventions. For example, interventions that develop readiness, motivation, knowledge, or skills required by other interventions should come first. Violation of this rule (leapfrogging) can result in interventions that do not achieve their objectives, regression, and the need to start a new sequence of interventions.
> 3. *Maximize efficiency.* Interventions should be sequenced to conserve organizational resources such as time, energy, and money. Violation of this rule will result in overlapping interventions or in interventions that are not needed by certain people or parts of the organization.
> 4. *Maximize speed.* Interventions should be sequenced to maximize the speed with which ultimate organizational improvement is attained. Violation of this rule occurs when progress is slower than is necessary to conform to all the other rules.
> 5. *Maximize relevance.* Interventions that management sees as most relevant to immediate problems should come first. In general, this means interventions that will have an impact on the organization's performance or task come before interventions that will have an impact on individuals or culture. Violation of this rule will result in loss of motivation to continue with organization development.
> 6. *Minimize psychological and organizational strain.* A sequence of interventions should be chosen that is least likely to create dysfunctional effects such as anxiety, insecurity, distrust, dashed expectations, psychological damage to people, and unanticipated

and unwanted effects on organizational performance. Violating this rule will lower people's sense of competence and confidence and their commitment to organizational improvement.[13]

SUMMARY

In this chapter we have taken an overview of OD interventions—the sets of structured activities in which selected organizational units (target groups or individuals) engage with a task or a sequence of tasks where task goals are related directly or indirectly to organizational improvement. Different definitions of OD interventions were discussed. The nature of interventions and several classifications of them were presented to gain a picture of interventions from several different perspectives. In the next several chapters OD interventions are described in greater detail in an inventory of most of the extant techniques and methods used in organization development.

NOTES

1. W. W. Burke and H. A. Hornstein, *The Social Technology of Organization Development* (Washington, D.C.: NTL Learning Resources Corporation, 1971), p. 1.

2. Richard Beckhard, "The Confrontation Meeting," *Harvard Business Review,* 45 (March–April 1967), pp. 149–153.

3. R. W. White, "Motivation Reconsidered: The Concept of Competence," *Psychological Review,* 66 (1959), pp. 297–334.

4. D. C. McClelland, J. W. Atkinson, R. A. Clark, and E. L. Lowell, *The Achievement Motive* (New York: Appleton-Century-Crofts, 1953).

5. Robert R. Blake and Jane S. Mouton, *The Managerial Grid* (Houston: Gulf, 1964), pp. 281–283.

6. Robert R. Blake and Jane S. Mouton, *Consultation* (Reading, Mass.: Addison-Wesley, 1976).

7. Richard A. Schmuck and Matthew B. Miles, eds., *Organizational Development in Schools* (Palo Alto, Calif.: National Press Books, 1971), p. 8. Used by permission.

8. E. H. Schein, *Process Consultation* (Reading, Mass.: Addison-Wesley, 1969), p. 9. See also E. H. Schein, *Process Consultation Volume I* (Reading, Mass.: Addison-Wesley, 1988).

9. R. R. Blake and J. S. Mouton, *Building a Dynamic Corporation Through Organization Development* (Reading, Mass.: Addison-Wesley, 1969). This book is a treatise showing how grid organization development programs operate.

10. R. E. Walton, *Interpersonal Peacemaking: Confrontation and Third-Party Consultation* (Reading, Mass.: Addison-Wesley, 1969), p. 1. This entire book is devoted to an explication of this specialized intervention technique. See also R. E. Walton, *Managing Conflict,* 2nd ed. (Reading, Mass.: Addison-Wesley, 1987).

11. George C. Homans, *The Human Group* (New York: Harcourt, Brace & Co., 1950).

12. G. Murphy, "The Freeing of Intelligence," *Psychological Bulletin,* 42 (1945), pp. 1–19.

13. From *Organization Change and Development* by Michael Beer. Copyright © 1980 by Scott, Foresman and Company. Reprinted by permission.

10

TEAM INTERVENTIONS

a descriptive inventory of OD interventions

In Chapters 10 through 14 we examine in detail the intervention activities utilized to develop an organization. These activities are the techniques and methods designed to change the culture of the organization, move it from "where it is" to "where it wants to be," and generally enable the organization members to improve their practices so that they may better accomplish their goals.[1] The nature of these interventions and a preliminary look at the different types of methods have already been presented. In this chapter we want to present descriptions, goals, and mechanics of the various technical tools of OD practitioners that are directed toward improving the performance of intact work teams within the organization.

TEAMS AND WORK GROUPS:
STRATEGIC UNITS OF ORGANIZATION

Collaborative management of the work team culture is a fundamental emphasis of organization development programs. This reflects the assumption that in today's organizations much of the work is accomplished directly or indirectly through teams. This also reflects the assumption that the work team culture exerts a significant influence on the individual's behavior. Usually, the techniques and the theory for understanding and improving team processes come from the laboratory training movement coupled with research in the area of group dynamics. An appreciation of the importance of the formal work team as a determinant of individual behavior and sentiments has come from cultural anthropology, sociology, organization theory, and social psychology.

Among those writers who have directed attention to the importance of team functioning are Rensis Likert, Chris Argyris, and Douglas McGregor.[2] Likert suggests that organizations are best conceptualized as systems of interlocking groups, as we indicated in Chapter 4, Underlying Assumptions and Values. These work groups are connected by *linking pins*—indivudals who occupy memberships in two groups (as a subordinate in one group and a boss in the other). It is through these interlocking groups that the work of the organization gets done. The key reality seems to be that individuals in organizations function not so much as *individuals* alone but as *members* of groups or teams. For an individual to function effectively, frequently a prerequisite is that the team must be functioning effectively.[3]

Another key reality is that individual behavior usually reflects the work team culture. The *culture* of a work group or organization consists of the prevailing pattern of beliefs, sentiments, norms, practices, and so forth, that individuals subscribe to and use as guides to behavior. Work groups and organizations have distinct cultures, and often the work culture is the most important one for the individual. The recognition of the importance of teams and work groups for determining both individual and organizational effectiveness was a crucial step in the emergence of the theory and practice of OD.

Douglas McGregor identified some of the characteristics of a well-functioning effective group as follows:

> The atmosphere tends to be relaxed, comfortable, and informal
>
> The group's task is well understood and accepted by the members
>
> The members listen well to each other; there is a lot of task-relevant discussion in which most members participate
>
> People express both their feelings and ideas
>
> Conflict and disagreement are present but are centered around ideas and methods, not personalities and people
>
> The group is self-conscious about its own operation
>
> Decisions are usually based on consensus, not majority vote
>
> When actions are decided upon, clear assignments are made and accepted by the members[4]

When these conditions are met, it is likely that the team is successfully accomplishing its mission and simultaneously satisfying the personal and interpersonal needs of its members.

Teams and work groups are thus considered to be fundamental units of organizations and also key leverage points for improving the functioning of the organization. Several different interventions have been developed to make teams more effective.

TEAM-BUILDING INTERVENTIONS

Probably the most important single group of interventions in OD are the team-building activities the goals of which are the improvement and increased effectiveness of various teams within the organization. Some interventions focus on the family group, an intact, permanent work team composed of a boss and subordinates; other interventions focus on special teams such as "start-up" teams, newly constituted teams due to mergers or organization structure changes, task forces, and committees. The team-building interventions are typically directed toward four major substantive areas: diagnosis, task accomplishments, team relationships, and team and organization processes. These separate thrusts are diagrammed in Figure 10-1.

Let us examine several of these interventions as they might be conducted with a family group. The major actors are a consultant, who is not a member of the group (the *third party*), the group leader, and the group members.

THE FAMILY GROUP DIAGNOSTIC MEETING

The purpose of the family group diagnostic meeting is to conduct a general critique of the performance of the group, that is, to take stock of "where we are going" and "how we are doing," and to surface and identify problems so that they may be worked on. Typically the leader and the consultant discuss the idea first, and if it appears that a genuine need for a diagnostic meeting exists, the idea is put to the group for their reactions. The leader may structure his or her testing for the group's reaction in the form of the following questions: What problems do we have that we should work on? How are we doing

Figure 10-1   Varieties of Team-Building Interventions

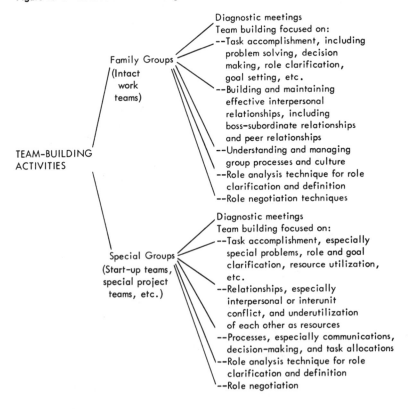

in regard to our assigned tasks? How are our relationships with each other? What opportunities should we be taking advantage of? What are we doing right and wrong?

If it is decided to conduct the family group diagnostic meeting, after some thinking about their own performance, the group assembles for a half-day or a day meeting. There are several ways of getting the diagnostic data out, that is, to make the information public:

> A total-group discussion involving everyone making individual contributions to the total assemblage
>
> Subgrouping, which involves breaking down into smaller groups where a more intensive discussion takes place, then the subgroups reporting back to the total group
>
> Pairing of two individuals who interview each other or who simply discuss their ideas with each other, each pair then reporting back to the total group

When the data are shared throughout the group, the next steps consist of discussing the issues, grouping the issues in terms of themes (say, planning problems, interface problems, goal ambiguity problems), and getting a preliminary look at the next action steps. The next action steps may call for a family team-building meeting, may assign different persons to task groups to work on the problems, or may include a number of other strategies that involve moving from the diagnostic data to corrective action taking. It should be noted however that the primary focus of the family group diagnostic meeting is to surface issues and problems that should be worked on and to decide *how* to take action steps. Taking action is generally a postmeeting activity or an activity for subsequent team meetings.

The family group diagnostic meeting permits a group to critique itself and to identify its strengths and problem areas, and it allows everyone to participate in generating the necessary data. The data then form the basis for planning future actions. Such a meeting requires only a minimal expenditure of time. Semiannual diagnostic meetings afford an excellent method for staying on top of problems. A key secret to the success of a short diagnostic meeting is the realization by all participants that the meeting is for the purpose of identifying problems, not solving problems.

Diagnostic meetings for newly constituted groups, say, task forces or new teams resulting from mergers or acquisitions, are similar in form and function to the family group diagnostic meeting. These meetings may have to be held more frequently to stay ahead of the problems. Furthermore, linking diagnostic meetings with problem-solving sessions or team-building sessions may be indicated for newly constituted teams.

THE FAMILY GROUP TEAM-BUILDING MEETING

The family group team-buildng meeting has the goal of improving the team's effectiveness through better management of task demands, relationship demands, and group processes. It is an inward look by the team at its own performance, behavior, and culture for the purposes of dropping out dysfunctional behaviors and strengthening functional ones. The group critiques its performance, analyzes its way of doing things, and attempts to develop strategies to improve its operation. Sometimes the purpose of the meeting is a special agenda item, such as developing the group's performance goals for the coming year. Often the purpose of the meeting is for the more general charge expressed in the questions: How can we build ourselves into a better functioning team? and How can we do the job better?

The family group team-building session is usually initiated by the manager in consultation with the third party. The idea is then tested for reactions with the group. (Conversely, the group may initiate the idea and take it to the boss if they sense pressing problems that need examination and solution.) A good length of time for the meeting is anywhere from one to three days. The session should be held away from the work place.

The usual practice for these sessions is to have the consultant interview each of the group members and the leader prior to the meeting, asking them what their problems are, how they think the group functions, and what obstacles are getting in the way of the group performing better. These interview data are categorized into themes by the consultant, who presents the themes to the group at the beginning of the meeting. The group examines and discusses the issues, ranks them in terms of their importance, examines the underlying dynamics of the problems, begins to work on solutions to the problems, and establishes some action steps to bring about the changes deemed desirable. It is imperative to have follow-up meetings to determine whether the action steps that were outlined were taken and to determine whether or not they had the desired effects. This is the flow of events for the family group team-building meeting. But let us look closer at the components.

The meeting may be called for a special purpose, such as a new member coming into the group, an organization structure change, or planning for the next year; or it may primarily be devoted to maintaining and managing the group's culture and processes. If it is a special-purpose meeting, time should still be allocated to an examination and critique of the group's dynamics.

As mentioned above, it is often desirable for the consultant to interview the entire group, using an open-ended approach, such as ''What things do you see getting in the way of this group being a better one?'' This procedure introduces the consultant to the group members and allows the consultant to assess commitment to the team-building session. The consultant decides in advance and informs the interviewees whether or not the information each gives will be considered public or confidential. There seem to be advantages and disadvantages to either approach. For example, if the information in the interviews is confidential, the interviewees may be more candid and open than they will be if they know the information is public. On the other hand, treating the information as public data helps to set a climate of openness, trust, and constructive problem solving. If the information is considered confidential, the consultant is careful to report the findings in a general way that does not reveal the sources of information. Other ways the agenda items for the meeting are developed are through such devices as the family group diagnostic meeting or through a survey.

The consultant presents the interview results in terms of themes. When everyone has understood the themes, these are ranked by the group in terms of their importance, and the most important ones form the agenda for the meeting. In the course of the meeting, much interpersonal and group process information will be generated, and that may be examined too. The group thus works on two sets of items: the agenda items and the items that emerge from the interactions of the participants.

As important problems are discussed, alternatives for action are developed. Generally, the team-building meeting involves deciding on action steps for remedying problems and setting target dates for *"who* will do *what when."*

Significant variations of the team-building session entail devoting time to problem-solving methods, planning and goal-setting methods, conflict resolution techniques, and the like. These special activities are usually initiated in response to the needs demonstrated or stated by the group. The consultant often makes conceptual inputs (lectures or lecturettes) or structures the situation so that a particular problem or process is focused on and highlighted. A wide variety of exercises may be interspersed into the three-day meeting, depending upon the problems identified and the group phenomena that emerge. (Illustration 6 in Chapter 1 describes some of these specialized activities that facilitate or build upon the emerging issues in a team-building meeting.)

Figure 10–1 suggests that team-building sessions may be directed toward problem solving for task accomplishment, examining and improving interpersonal relationships, or managing the group's culture and processes. It may be that one of these issues is the principal reason for holding the team-building meeting. For example, suppose that the meeting is designed as a team problem-solving session to examine the impact on the team of a new function or task being added to the group's work requirements. Even in this case a portion of the session will probably be reserved for reflecting on *how* the team is solving its problems, that is, critiquing the group's processes. In this way the team becomes more effective at both the task level and the process level.

Richard Beckhard lists, in order of importance, the four major reasons or purposes involved in having teams meet other than for the sharing of information: (1) to set goals and/or priorities. . .(2) to analyze or allocate the way work is performed. . .(3) to examine the way a group is working, its processes (such as norms, decision making, communications). . .and (4) to examine relationships among the people doing the work.[5] He notes that often all four items will be covered in a single team-building session, but it is imperative that the *primary* goal be clear and accepted by all. It is especially important that the leader and the consultant agree on the primary goal. Often the consultant will have a priority list of items that are inverse to those just given—from relationships among people as most important, to the way the group works together as next most important, to the work itself next, and to goals and priorities as least important. Lack of agreement on the primary goal can lead to wasted energy and a generally unproductive and frustrating team-building session. We agree with Beckhard when he states that the consultant should help to implement the group leader's goals for the session, not the consultant's goals.

Bell and Rosenzweig relied heavily upon team-building workshops in an OD program in a municipal government organization and came to the following assessment:

> Our experience leads us to the tentative conclusion that some relatively simple notions underlie success, namely:
>
> 1. Get the *right people* together for
> 2. A *large block of uninterrupted time*
> 3. To work on *high-priority problems or opportunities* that
> 4. *They have identified* and that are worked on
> 5. In *ways that are structured* to enhance the likelihood of
> 6. *Realistic solutions and action plans* that are

7. *Implemented* enthusiastically and
8. *Followed up* to assess actual versus expected results.[6]

These authors comment on the overall nature of team-building sessions as follows:

> We have come to believe strongly that initial improvement efforts should be task oriented rather than focused on interpersonal relations. It is usually safer, less resisted, and more appropriate in terms of the problems and opportunities identified by the client. We have tended not to focus on team building per se; rather, we find that it occurs as a natural by-product of learning to solve problems in a group setting. However, we don't avoid interpersonal or team ineffectiveness issues if they are getting in the way of effective and efficient problem solving.[7]

When a team engages in problem-solving activities directed toward task accomplishment, the team members *build something together*. It appears that the act of building something together also builds a sense of camaraderie, cohesion, and *esprit de corps*. The major ingredients involved in a team's building something together are probably the eight steps identified by Bell and Rosenzweig.

In our own consulting we have increasingly come to designate these sessions as "team-building problem-solving workshops"—a clear signal to us and the client that *both* building a more effective team and solving priority problems constitute the business at hand. We consider team-building problem-solving interventions to be a cornerstone of the OD technology.

An example of a team-building program might be helpful. The top management team of a quasi-governmental agency decided collectively that they "needed help to become more goal-directed and effective." They interviewed several consultants and selected one who the Executive Director (the boss) and the team felt was most appropriate for them, their organization, and their problems. At a meeting the consultant explained the team-building problem-solving process, how it would be conducted, and what could be expected of the consultant and the team. Questions were answered; mutual expectations were established.

The consultant then interviewed all team members in confidential interviews to gain an understanding of the strengths and weaknesses of the team and the organization. When the interviews were completed, the consultant met with the Executive Director to give him an overview of the interview results. While maintaining confidentiality, the consultant described the issues uncovered in the interviews and solicited the Executive Director's reaction which was that the diagnosis agreed with his own perceptions. Let us explain why we include this step since not all OD practitioners give a preliminary overview to the team leader. We include this step for several reasons: so the leader will not be surprised (and possibly defensive) at the first team-building meeting; so that the leader is forewarned if he or she is viewed as a "problem;" so that we can gauge the leader's willingness to address the problems identified; and so that the leader can be coached to respond constructively to the array of problems. The leader is not allowed to censor problems or to delete problems from the agenda. This step is a useful one, in our view, in that it helps to build a foundation of trust and openness between the key client and the consultant. (The team had been informed that this step would occur.)

The next event was the first meeting, an all-day, off-site workshop. The Executive Director opened the meeting with remarks that established a constructive, optimistic climate. Next the consultant presented the strengths and problem areas found in the interviews and asked the team to prioritize the problem areas in terms of importance and urgency. The rest of that day was spent exploring the three highest priority problems and developing action steps to correct the problems. Four subsequent all-day meetings were held at intervals of three or four weeks until the original problem agenda was worked through. This schedule allowed enough time between meetings to implement action steps, while at the same time keeping the level of momentum and energy high. At the fifth meeting the team decided to hold quarterly team-building meetings to monitor progress and to address and solve new problems. Three quarterly meetings were held with the consultant present and later meetings were held without him. This is a typical team-building intervention sequence of activities and events.

An excellent statement of the team-building process is found in William Dyer's *Team Building: Issues and Alternatives.*[8] He describes team building as a data gathering, diagnostic, action planning, and action taking process conducted by intact work teams. He says of the process,

> One underlying assumption rgarding teams in organizations is that resources are available in the individuals in the work unit. They have the capability to address and deal with the above questions, [issues of declining performance] and the problems behind the questions, if given the time, encouragement, and freedom needed to work honestly toward solutions. Team development in its best sense is creating the opportunity for people to come together to share their concerns, their ideas, and their experiences, and to begin to work together to solve their mutual problems and achieve common goals.[9]

The basic building blocks of organizations are teams, and one of the basic building blocks of organization development is team building.

ROLE ANALYSIS TECHNIQUE INTERVENTION

The role analysis technique (RAT)* intervention is designed to clarify role expectations and obligations of team members to improve team effectiveness. In organizations individuals fill different specialized roles in which they manifest certain behaviors. This division of labor and function facilitates organization performance. Often, however, the role incumbent may not have a clear idea of the behaviors expected of him or her by others and, equally often, what others can do to help the incumbent fulfill the role is not understood. Ishwar Dayal and John M. Thomas developed a technique for clarifying the roles of the top management of a new organization in India.[10] This technique is particularly applicable for new teams, but it may also be helpful in established teams where role ambiguity or confusion exists. The intervention is predicated on the belief that consensual determination of role requirements for team members, consisting of a joint building

*Our colleague Charles Hosford suggests the more euphonic label role analysis process (RAP) for this procedure.

of the requirements by all concerned, leads to more mutually satisfactory and productive behavior. Dayal and Thomas call the activity the *role analysis technique.*

In a structured series of steps, role incumbents, in conjunction with team members, define and delineate role requirements. The role being defined is called the *focal role.* In a new organization, it may be desirable to conduct a role analysis for each of the major roles.

The first step consists of an analysis of the focal role initiated by the focal role individual. The role, its place in the organization, the rationale for its existence, and its place in achieving overall organization goals are examined along with the specific duties of the office. The specific duties and behaviors are listed on a chalkboard and are discussed by the entire team. Behaviors are added and deleted until the group and the role incumbent are satisfied that they have defined the role completely.

The second step examines the focal role incumbent's expectations of others. The incumbent lists his or her expectations of the other roles in the group that most affect the incumbent's own role performance, and these expectations are discussed, modified, added to, and agreed upon by the entire group.

The third step consists of explicating others' expectations and desired behaviors of the focal role, that is, the members of the group describe what they want from and expect from the incumbent in the focal role. These expectations of others are discussed, modified, and agreed upon by the group and the focal role person.

Upon conclusion of this step, the focal role person assumes responsibility for making a written summary of the role as it has been defined; this is called a *role profile* and is derived from the results of the discussions in steps 1 through 3. Dayal and Thomas describe the role profile as follows: "This consists of (a) a set of activities classified as to the prescribed and discretionary elements of the role, (b) the obligation of the role to each role in its set, and (c) the expectations of this role from others in its set. Viewed in toto, this provides a comprehensive understanding of each individual's 'role space.'"[11]

The written role profile is briefly reviewed at the following meeting before another focal role is analyzed. The accepted role profile constitutes the role activities for the focal role person.

This intervention can be a nonthreatening activity with high payoff. Often the mutual demands, expectations, and obligations of interdependent team members have never been publicly examined. Each role incumbent wonders why "the other guy" is "not doing what he is supposed to," while in reality all the incumbents are performing as they think they are supposed to. Collaborative role analysis and definition by the entire work group not only clarifies who is to do what but ensures commitment to the role once it has been clarified.

From our experience, this procedure can be shortened if there is already high visibility and understanding of the current activities of various role incumbents. For example, if one of the problems facing an organization is confusion over the duties of the board of directors and the president or the executive director, the following sequence can be highly productive. (This technique was used in Illustration 6 of Chapter 1.) This occurred in a workshop setting involving the board, the president, and the key subordinates.

1. With the board listening, the president and his staff members discuss this question: "If the board were operating in an optimally effective way, what would they be doing?"
2. During this discussion, responses are made visible on a chalkboard or on large newsprint, and disagreements are recorded.
3. After 45 minutes or so, the list is modified on the basis of general consensus of the total group.
4. The procedure is repeated, but this time the president listens while staff and board members discuss the question, "If the president were operating in an optimally effective way, what would he be doing?" Again, responses are made visible during the discussion. The president responds, and then there is an attempt at consensus.

As with the longer technique, this procedure helps to clarify role expectations and obligations and frequently leads to some significant shifts in the whole network of activities of the management group, including the board. For example, we have seen this procedure result in boards shifting their activities almost exclusively to policy determination, pulling away from previously dysfunctional tinkering with day-to-day operating problems, and delegating operations to the president and the staff.

A ROLE NEGOTIATION TECHNIQUE

When the causes of team ineffectiveness are based on people's behaviors that they are unwilling to change because it would mean a loss of power or influence to the individual, a technique developed by Roger Harrison called "role negotiation" can often be used to great advantage.[12]

> Role negotiation intervenes directly in the relationships of power, authority, and influence within the group. The change effort is directed at the work relationships among members. It avoids probing into the likes and dislikes of members for one another and their personal feelings about one another.[13]

The technique is basically an imposed structure for controlled negotiations between parties in which each party agrees in writing to change certain behaviors in return for changes in behavior by the other. The behaviors relate to the job. Specifically, I ask you to change some of your behaviors so that I can do my job more effectively; and you ask me to change some of my behaviors so that you can do your job more effectively. Harrison states that the technique rests on one basic assumption: "*Most people prefer a fair negotiated settlement to a state of unresolved conflict,* and they are willing to invest some time and make some concessions in order to achieve a solution."[14]

The role negotiation technique usually takes at least one day to conduct. A two-day session with a follow-up meeting a month later is best. We will outline the steps of the technique as given by Harrison.[15] The first step is *contract setting.* Here the consultant sets the climate and establishes the ground rules: we are looking at work behaviors, not feelings about people; be specific in stating what you want others to *do more of* or do better, to *do less of* or stop doing, or *maintain unchanged;* all expectations and demands must be *written;* no one is to agree to changing any behavior unless there is a quid pro quo in which the other must agree to a change also; the session will consist of individuals negotiating with each other to arrive at a *written contract* of what behaviors each will change.

The next step is *issue diagnosis.* Individuals think about how their *own effectiveness* can be improved if others change their work behaviors. Then each person fills out an Issue Diagnosis Form for every other person in the group. On this form the individual states what he or she would like the other to do more of, do less of, or maintain unchanged. These messages are then exchanged among all members, and the messages received by each person are written on a chalkboard or newsprint for all to see.

The next step is the *influence trade* or negotiation period, in which two individuals discuss the *most important* behavior changes they want from the other and the changes they are willing to make themselves. A quid pro quo is required in this step: each person must give something in order to get something. Often this step is demonstrated by two individuals with the rest of the group watching. Then the group breaks into negotiating pairs. "The negotiation process consists of parties making contingent offers to one another such as "If you do X, I will do Y.' The negotiation ends when all parties are satisfied that they will receive a reasonable return for whatever they are agreeing to give."[16] All agreements are written, with each party having a copy. The agreement may be published for the group to see or may not. The influence trade step is concluded when all the negotiated agreements have been made and written down. It is best to have a follow-up meeting to determine whether the contracts have been honored and to assess the effects of the contracts on effectiveness.

In our view Harrison's role negotiation technique is an effective way of bringing about positive improvement in a situation where power and influence issues are working to maintain an unsatisfactory status quo. We have used this technique successfully with several groups and have found that it is an intervention that leads to improved team functioning. It is based on the fact that frequently individuals must change their work behaviors for the team to become more effective.

RESPONSIBILITY CHARTING

In work teams decisions are made, tasks are assigned, and individuals and small groups accomplish the tasks. This is easily described on paper, but in reality a decision to have someone do something is somewhat more complex than it appears because there are in fact multiple actors involved in even the simplest task assignment. There is the person who does the work, one or more people who may approve or veto the work, and persons who may "contribute" in some way to the work while not being responsible for it. The issue is, *Who is to do what, with what kind of involvement by others?*

A recently developed technique called *responsibility charting* helps to clarify who is responsible for what on various decisions and actions.[17] It is a simple, relevant, and very effective technique for improving team functioning. Richard Beckhard and Reuben Harris explain the technique as follows:

> The first step is to construct a grid; the types of decisions and classes of actions that need to be taken in the total area of work under discussion are listed along the left-hand side

of the grid, and the actors who might play some part in decision making on those issues are identified across the top of the grid....

The process, then, is one of assigning a behavior to each of the actors opposite each of the issues. There are four classes of behavior:

1. *Responsibility* (R)—the responsibility to initiate action to ensure that the decision is carried out. For example, it would be a department head's responsibility (R) to initiate the departmental budget.
2. *Approval required, or the right to veto* (A-V)—the particular item must be reviewed by the particular role occupant, and this person has the option of either vetoing or approving it.
3. *Support* (S)—providing logistical support and resources for the particular item.
4. *Inform* (I)—*must be* informed and, by inference, cannot influence.[18]

A fifth behavior (or nonbehavior) is noninvolvement of a person with the decision; this is indicated on the chart with a dash (—). One type of responsibility chart is in Figure 10–2.

Responsibility charting is usually done in a work team context. Each decision or action is discussed and responsibility is assigned. Next, approval-veto, support, and inform functions are assigned. Beckhard and Harris offer some guidelines for making the technique more effective. First, assign responsibility to only one person. That person initiates and then is responsible and accountable for the action. Second, avoid having too many people with an approval-veto function on an item. That will slow down task accomplishment or will negate it altogether. Third, if one person has approval-veto involvement on most decisions, that person could become a bottleneck for getting things done.

Figure 10–2   Responsibility Chart. *Source:* Richard Beckhard and Reuben T. Harris, *Organizational Transitions: Managing Complex Change,* © 1977. Addison-Wesley, Reading, Mass., Figure 6.1. Reprinted with permission.

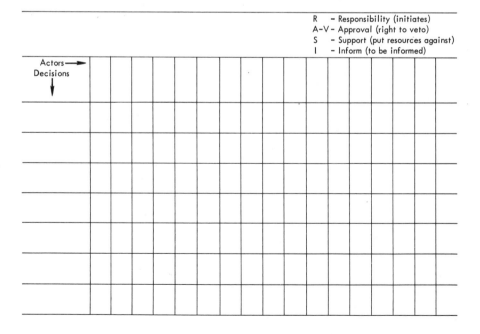

Fourth, the support function is critical. A person with a support role has to expend resources or produce something that is then used by the person responsible for the action. This support role and its specific demands must be clarified and clearly assigned. And, finally, the assignment of functions (letters) to persons at times becomes difficult. For example, a person may want A-V on an item, but not really need it; a person may not want S responsibility on an item, but should have it; or two persons each want R on a particular item, but only one can have it.

A responsibility charting session can quickly identify who is to do what on new decisions as well as help to pinpoint reasons why old decisions are not being accomplished as desired. Responsibility charting is a good intervention to use to improve the task performance of a work team.

THE FORCE FIELD ANALYSIS TECHNIQUE

The oldest intervention in the OD practitioner's kit bag is the Force Field Analysis, a device for *understanding* a problematic situation and *planning corrective actions.* This technique rests on several assumptions: the present state of things (the current condition) is a quasi-stationary equilibrium representing a resultant in a field of opposing forces. A desired future state of affairs (the desired condition) can only be achieved by dislodging the current equilibrium, moving it to the desired state, and stabilizing the equilibrium at that point. To move the equilibrium level from the current to the desired condition the field of forces must be altered—by adding driving forces or by removing restraining forces.

This technique was first proposed by Kurt Lewin in 1947.[19] It is essentially a vector analysis—an analytical tool learned in first-year engineering classes. But the genius of Lewin was to apply the device to social problems, social equilibria, and social change. Lewin proposed that social phenomena—productivity of a factory, morale on a sports team, level of prejudice in a community, and so forth—could best be understood as *processes* being influenced by social forces and events. Furthermore, social phenomena tend to stabilize at equilibrium points because opposing forces come into balance over time.[20] The Force Field Analysis involves the following steps:

Step 1.   Decide upon a problematic situation you are interested in improving, and carefully and completely describe the current condition. What is the "status quo"? What is the current condition? Why do you want it changed?

Step 2.   Carefully and completely describe the desired condition. Where do you want to be? What is the desired state of things?

Step 3.   Identify the forces and factors operating in the current "force field." Identify the driving forces pushing in the direction of the desired condition; identify the restraining forces pushing away from the desired condition. Identification and specification of the force field should be thorough and exhaustive so that a picture of why things are as they are becomes clear.

Step 4.   Examine the forces. Which ones are strong, which are weak? Which forces are susceptible to influence, which are not? Which forces are under your control, which are not? (Important individual forces could themselves be subjected to a Force Field Analysis in order to understand them better.)

Step 5.   Strategies for moving the equilibrium from the current condition to the desired condition are the following: add more driving forces; remove restraining forces; or do both. Lewin advises against simply adding new driving forces because that may increase resistance and tension in the situation. Therefore, in this step one selects several important, adaptable restraining forces and develops action plans to remove them from the field of forces. As restraining forces are removed, the equilibrium shifts toward the desired condition. New driving forces may also be proposed and action plans developed to implement them.

Step 6.   Implement the action plans. This should cause the desired condition to be realized.

Step 7.   Describe what actions must be taken to stabilize the equilibrium at the desired condition and implement those actions.

An example of the Force Field Analysis is shown in Figure 10–3. Assume that the management team of Plant X is concerned about excessive turnover and wants to correct that situation. They generate the following Force Field Analysis:

Figure 10–3   Force Field Analysis of a Turnover Problem at Plant X

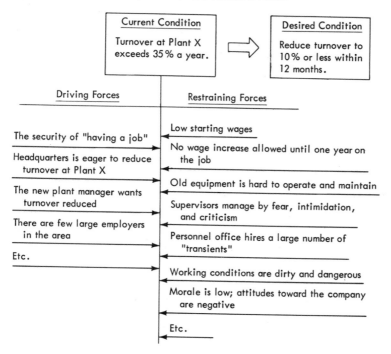

Mapping the field of forces in this way permits the management team of Plant X to understand the multiple facets of the problem. They would next decide which restraining forces should be removed and develop action plans to initiate those changes.

This technique is excellent for diagnosing change situations. We label it a team intervention (although it is also a tool for individuals) because it can be so powerful and exciting when used by groups. Group analysis typically yields a comprehensive understanding of what is happening to cause the problem and what must be done to correct it.

The Force Field Analysis is an old and valued friend of the OD practitioner.

A GESTALT ORIENTATION TO TEAM BUILDING

A form of team building that focuses more on the individual than the group is the Gestalt approach to OD. The major advocate of this orientation is Stanley M. Herman, a management and OD consultant to TRW Systems and other organizations; the approach rests on a form of psychotherapy developed by Frederick S. "Fritz" Perls called Gestalt therapy.[21] Gestalt therapy is based on the belief that persons function as whole, total organisms. And each person possesses positive and negative characteristics that must be "owned up to" and permitted expression. People get into trouble when they get fragmented, when they do not accept their total selves, and when they are trying to live up to the demands ("shoulds") of others rather than being themselves. Robert Harman lists the goals of Gestalt therapy as awareness, integration, maturation, authenticity, self-regulation, and behavior change.[22] Basically, one must come to terms with oneself, must accept responsibility for one's actions, must experience and live in the "here and now," and must stop blocking off awareness, authenticity, and the like by dysfunctional behaviors.

Stanley Herman applies a Gestalt orientation to organization development, especially in working with leader-subordinate relations and team building. The primary thrust is to make the *individual* stronger, more authentic, and more in touch with the individual's own feelings; building a better team may result, but it is not the primary desired outcome. As Herman says,

> My objective here is not to provide instruction on making the organization culture safer, more pleasant or easier for the individual, but rather to help the individual recognize, develop and experience his own potency and ability to cope with his organization world, whatever its present condition. Further, I would like to encourage him to discover for himself his own unique wants of that environment and his capacity to influence and shape it in ways that get him more of what he wants.[23]

To do this people must be able to express their feelings fully, both positive and negative. They must "get in touch" with "where they are" on issues, relations with others, and relations with selves. They must learn to "stay with" transactions with others and work them through to resolution rather than suppressing negative feelings or cutting off the transactions prematurely. They must learn to accept the polarities within themselves—weakness-strength, autocratic-democratic urges, and so forth.

The Gestalt OD practitioner fosters the expression of positive and negative feelings, encourages people to stay with transactions, structures exercises that cause individuals to become more aware of what they want from others, and pushes toward greater authenticity for everyone. The Gestalt OD practitioner often works within a group setting, but the focus is usually on individuals.

Use of the Gestalt orientation to OD is not widespread. An interesting book by Herman and Korenich gives a theoretical framework, examples, and exercises for Gestalt OD, and this intervention may become more popular in organization development.[24]

We are somewhat ambivalent about the Gestalt orientation to OD. On the one hand, better individual functioning is a laudable goal and deserves support. On the other hand, this is an intervention of considerable "depth" and one that people might not choose to expose themselves to—they may believe they are being coerced into a therapeutic situation that they would prefer to avoid. One thing is certain: the Gestalt orientation to team building should not be used except by practitioners trained in this method.

A FINAL COMMENT ON TEAMWORK

The reason team building produces such powerful positive results is because it is an intervention in harmony with the nature of organizations as social systems. Under a system of division of labor, parts of the total organizational task are assigned to teams; and then that team assignment is broken down and assigned to individuals. In most cases individual members of the team are *interdependently related* to each other and must coordinate and integrate individual efforts in order to achieve successful task accomplishment. Conceptualizing the team as the relevant system rather than individuals was the profound insight developed by early OD pioneers such as Blake, Shepard, Mouton, and McGregor: the team is the relevant unit for making individuals more effective. (See Chapter 3 for this history.) The efficacy of team building confirms the validity of that view.

A new conceptualization has evolved in recent years that likewise has validity, efficacy, and implications for practice. That idea is this: on many projects the relevant "team" (or system) includes persons outside the functional unit; the relevant system is a cross-funtional team. The criterion is still the same—identifying those persons who are *interdependently related* in the successful accomplishment of the task. For example, in the development of the new Saturn automobile at General Motors cross-functional teams were used from the outset. Rather than have one functional team (say, design) do its work and then "throw the plans over the wall" to the next functional team (say, production), cross-functional teams provided oversight throughout the entire project.[25] In his latest book, *Thriving On Chaos,* Tom Peters advocates increasing the use of cross-functional teams so that American industry can compete successfully in today's fast-paced environment.[26] Increasingly, the *relevant system* for making individuals effective and for facilitating task accomplishment includes cross-functional representation.

SUMMARY

In this chapter we have examined the major sets of activities that constitute team-building interventions and their rationales. The interventions to be described in Chapter 12 are closely related to the activities found in team-building, team diagnosis, and role analysis interventions. Those interventions are more narrowly focused, but they also utilize the medium of the small group.

It is probable that if it were not for the interventions directed to improving intergroup relations (see Chapter 11) or interventions directed to improving the total organization (see Chapters 13 and 14); there would not be such a discipline as OD today; there would instead only be an expanded "small-group" discipline. We want to underscore that while the small group or team is an entry point in most OD strategies, and while ongoing attention to team effectiveness is a sine qua non for successful OD efforts, achieving total organizational improvement is possible only by going beyond the level of the team.

NOTES

1. Detailed discussions of interventions can be found in several sources. The most complete treatments are given in J. K. Fordyce and R. Weil, *Managing WITH People: A Manager's Handbook of Organization Development Methods* (Reading, Mass.: Addison-Wesley, 1971); E. F. Huse and T. G. Cummings, *Organization Development and Change,* 3rd ed., (St. Paul, Minn.: West Publishing Company, 1985); W. Warner Burke, *Organization Development,* (Boston: Little, Brown and Co., 1982); and Michael Beer, "The Technology of Organization Development," in Marvin D. Dunnette, ed., *Handbook of Industrial and Organizational Psychology* (Chicago: Rand McNally, 1976), pp. 937–993. Additional sources are Richard Beckhard, *Organization Development: Strategies and Models* (Reading, Mass.: Addison-Wesley, 1969); and W. W. Burke and H. A. Hornstein, *The Social Technology of Organization Development* (Washington, D.C.: NTL Learning Resources Corporation, 1971).

2. R. Likert, *New Patterns of Management* (New York: McGraw-Hill, 1961), C. Argyris, *Integrating the Individual and the Organization* (New York: John Wiley, 1964); and D. McGregor, *The Human Side of Enterprise* (New York: McGraw-Hill, 1960).

3. Likert, *New Patterns of Management.*

4. McGregor, *Human Side of Enterprise.*

5. Taken from Richard Beckhard, "Optimizing Team-Building Efforts," *Journal of Contemporary Business,* Vol. 1, No. 3 (Summer 1972), pp. 23–32. This list of goals is on page 24.

6. Cecil Bell, Jr., and James Rosenzweig, "Highlights of an Organization Improvement Program in a City Government," in W. L. French, C. H. Bell, Jr., and R. A. Zawacki, eds., *Organization Development: Theory, Practice, and Research* (Dallas: Business Publications, 1978).

7. Ibid.

8. William G. Dyer, *Team Building: Issues and Alternatives* (Reading, Mass.: Addison-Wesley, 1977). See also W. Brendan Reddy and Kaleel Jamison, *Team Building* (Alexandria, Va.: NTL Institute for Applied Behavioral Science; and San Diego: University Associates, 1988).

9. Dyer, *op. cit.,* p. 41.

10. I. Dayal and J. M. Thomas, "Operation KPE: Developing a New Organization," *Journal of Applied Behavioral Science,* 4, No. 4 (1968), pp. 473–506. The present discussion is based on this article.

11. Ibid., p. 488.

12. Roger Harrison, "When Power Conflicts Trigger Team Spirit," *European Business,* Spring 1972, pp. 27–65.

13. Ibid., p. 58.

14. Ibid., p. 58. [Harrison's emphasis.]

15. These steps are paraphrased from ibid., pp. 59–63.

16. Ibid., p. 63.

17. See Richard Beckhard and Reuben T. Harris, *Organizational Transitions: Managing*

Complex Change (Reading, Mass.: Addison-Wesley, 1977), pp. 76–82.

18. Ibid., p. 76.

19. Kurt Lewin, "Frontiers in Group Dynamics: Concept, Method, and Reality in Social Science; Social Equilibria and Social Change," Human Relations, Vol. 1, No. 1, June 1947, pp. 5–41.

20. See the following articles in *The Planning of Change,* W. G. Bennis, K. D. Benne, and R. Chin, eds., (New York: Holt, Rinehart and Winston, 1964): "The Utility of System Models and Developmental Models for Practitioners" by Robert Chin, pp. 201–214; "Force Field Analysis Applied to a School Situation" by David H. Jenkins, pp. 238–244.

21. F. Perls, R. Hefferline, and P. Goodman, *Gestalt Therapy* (New York: Julian Press, 1951). See also F. Perls, *Gestalt Therapy Verbatim* (Lafayette, Calif.: Real People Press, 1969).

22. Robert L. Harman, "Goals of Gestalt Therapy," *Professional Psychology,* May 1974, pp. 178–184.

23. Stanley M. Herman, "A Gestalt Orientation to Organization Development," in W. Warner Burke, ed., *Contemporary Organization Development: Conceptual Orientations and Interventions* (Washington, D.C.: NTL Institute for Applied Behavioral Science, 1972), pp. 69–89. This passage is taken from page 70.

24. Stanley M. Herman and Michael Korenich, *Authentic Management: A Gestalt Orientation to Organizations and Their Development* (Reading, Mass.: Addison-Wesley, 1977).

25. This was described in the symposium "The Role of OD in General Motors' Saturn Project" at the 1987 Academy of Management Annual Meeting in New Orleans, October 11, 1987.

26. Tom Peters, *Thriving On Chaos,* (New York: Alfred A. Knopf, 1988).

11

INTERGROUP INTERVENTIONS

a descriptive inventory of OD interventions

When there is tension, conflict, or competition among groups, some very predictable things happen: each group sees the other as an ''enemy'' rather than as a neutral object; each group describes the other in terms of negative stereotypes; interaction and communication between the two groups decrease, cutting off feedback and data input between them; what intergroup communication and interaction does take place is typically distorted and inaccurate; each group begins to prize itself and its products more positively and to denigrate the other group and its products; each group believes and acts as though it can do no wrong and the other group can do no right; under certain circumstances the groups may commit acts of sabotage (of various kinds) against the other group.[1] Most people are aware of the existence of considerable intergroup conflict in organizations, and most people are aware of the patterns of behavior of groups in conflict. But few people know ways to alleviate the conflict to avoid the consequences of the conflict.

Several strategies for reducing intergroup conflict have been identified in the literature. They include a ''common enemy'' (an outside object or group that both groups dislike, which brings the groups closer together); increasing the interaction and communication among the groups (increased interaction under favorable conditions tends to be associated with increased positive feelings and sentiments); finding a supraordinate goal (a goal that both groups desire to achieve but that neither can achieve without the help of the other); rotating the members of the groups; and instituting some forms of training.[2] Even knowing these strategies for reducing intergroup conflict may not be very helpful—the questions still remain, How can we *implement* conflict-reducing mechanisms? and How do we *begin?*

In this chapter we examine the technology that has been developed to reduce intergroup conflict and to enhance intergroup relations. Because of the magnitude of intergroup problems in organizations, these interventions are very important ones. In addition, the development of techniques to improve subsystems larger than single teams marked a significant step toward being able to improve total systems.

INTERGROUP TEAM-BUILDING INTERVENTIONS

The focus of this team-building group of OD interventions is on improving intergroup relations. The goals of these activities are to increase communications and interactions between work-related groups, to reduce the amount of dysfunctional competition, and to replace a parochial independent point of view with an awareness of the necessity for interdependence of action calling on the best efforts of both groups. It is not uncommon for a significant amount of dysfunctional energy to be spent in competition, misunderstanding, miscommunication, and misperception between groups. Organizational reward structures often encourage such behavior through emphasis on unit goal attainment as contrasted with total-organization goal attainment. Organization development methods provide ways of increasing intergroup cooperation and communication, as we see in this series of interventions.

One set of activities developed by Blake, Shepard, and Mouton is widely applicable to situations where relations between groups are strained or overtly hostile.[3] The steps are these:[4]

Step 1. The leaders of the two groups (or the total membership) meet with the consultant and are asked if they think the relations between the two groups can be better and are asked if they are willing to search for mechanisms or procedures that may improve intergroup relations. Their concurrence that they are willing to search for ameliorative mechanisms is all that they are asked to commit themselves to at that time. If they agree to do this, the following activities take place.

Step 2. The intergroup intervention per se begins now. The two groups meet in separate rooms and build two lists. In one list they give their thoughts, attitudes, feelings, and perceptions of the other group—what the other group is like, what it does that gets in their way, and so on. In the second list the group tries to predict what the other group is saying about them in its list—that is, they try to anticipate what the other group dislikes about them, how the other group sees them and so on. Both groups build these two lists.

Step 3. The two groups come together to share with each other the information on the lists. Group A reads its list of how it sees Group B and what it dislikes about Group B. Group B reads its list of how it sees Group A and what it dislikes about it. The consultant imposes the rule that there will be no discussion of the items on the lists and limits questions to clarifying the meaning of the lists only. Next, Group A reads its list of what it expected Group B would say about it, and Group B reads its list of what it thought Group A would say about it.

Step 4. The two groups return to their separate meeting places and are given two tasks. First, they react to and discuss what they have learned about themselves and the other group. It typically happens that many areas of disagreement and friction are discovered to rest on misperceptions and miscommunication; these are readily resolved through the information sharing of the lists. The differences between the two groups are seen not to be as great as was imagined, and the problems between them are seen to be fewer than imagined. After this discussion, the group is given a second task: to make a list of the priority issues that still need to be resolved between the two groups. The list is generally much smaller than the original list. Each group builds such a list.

Step 5. The two groups come back together and share their lists with each other. After comparing their lists, they then together make one list containing the issues and problems that should be resolved. They set priorities on the items in terms of importance and immediacy. Together they generate action steps for resolving the issues and assign responsibilities for the actions. "Who will do what when" is agreed upon for the most important items. That concludes the intervention.

Step 6. As a follow-up to the intergroup team-building activity, it is desirable to have a meeting of the two groups or their leaders to determine whether the action steps have in fact occurred and to assess how the groups are doing on their action plans. This ensures that the momentum of the intergroup intervention is not lost.

This procedure can also be used with large groups drawn from two very large populations. For example, after an expression of interest by parole officers and police officers in improving mutual understanding and relationships, we spent an evening with the two groups in an exercise called Project Understanding. By coincidence, members of the two groups happened to be attending workshops the same week at the same conference center. We simply divided the two large populations into small groups and paired off these small groups and conducted an exercise almost identical to the sequence given. Tentative action recommendations were posted in the large general session room for informal perusal during a social activity which followed.

A slightly modified version of this procedure is presented by Fordyce and Weil based on their experiences at TRW Systems.[5] In this version, two groups that have decided to work on improving their intergroup relations come together for the intergroup team-building meeting and are separated into two meeting rooms. Each group is assigned the task of building three lists as follows:

1. A "positive feedback" list containing the things the group values and likes about the other group
2. A "bug" list containing the things the group does not like about the other group
3. An "empathy" list containing a prediction of what the other group is saying in its list

The two groups come together, and spokespeople for the groups read their lists. Questions are limited to issues of clairification only; discussion of the items is disallowed.

At this point, instead of breaking into separate groups again, the total group together builds an agenda or a master list of the major problems and unresolved issues between the two groups. The issues are ranked in terms of importance.

Subgroups are formed containing members from each group and are given the task of discussing and working on each item. The subgroups all report back to the total group.

On the basis of the information from the subgroups, the work on the issues that has been going on, and the total information shared by the two groups, the participants now build a list of action steps for improving intergroup relations and commit themselves to carrying out the actions. For each of the action steps, people are assigned specific responsibilities and an overall schedule of completion for the action steps is recorded.

We have found that it is possible to work simultaneously with *three* groups in these kinds of intergroup activities, without the participants (or the consultants) finding the procedure too confusing. For example, in working with the key people in one Indian tribal organization, we requested each of three groups to develop lists about the other two groups plus themselves and to share the results in the total group. More specifically, the tribal council (one of the three groups) was requested to develop the following lists:

  I. How the tribal council sees the tribal staff
     A. Things we like about the tribal staff
     B. Concerns we have about the tribal staff
 II. What we (the tribal council) predice the tribal staff will say about us
III. How the tribal council sees the Community Action Program (CAP) staff
     A. Things we like about the CAP staff
     B. Concerns we have about the CAP staff
 IV. What we (the tribal council) predict the CAP staff will say about us.

Concurrently, the tribal staff and the CAP staff developed comparable lists reflecting their perceptions of the other two groups and their predictions of what would be said about them.

These kinds of activities have been found to bring about better intergroup relations. It has empirically been shown time and again, in diverse situations, that in a relatively short time period (say, a day) these structured intergroup activities can result in improved intergroup relations. The intergroup problems and frictions are decreased or resolved, and intergroup communication and interaction are increased.

ORGANIZATION MIRROR INTERVENTIONS

The *organization mirror* is a set of activities in which a particular organizational group, the host group, gets feedback from representatives from several other organizational groups about how it is perceived and regarded. This intervention is designed to improve the relationships between groups and increase the intergroup work effectiveness. It is different from the intergroup team-building intervention in that three or more groups are involved, representatives of other work-related groups typically participate rather than the full membership, and the focus is to assist the host unit that requested the meeting.[6]

The flow of events is as follows: an organizational unit that is experiencing difficulties with units to which it is work related may ask key people from those other units to come to a meeting to provide feedback on how they see the host unit. The consultant often interviews the people attending the meeting before the meeting takes place in order to get a sense of the problems and their magnitude, to prepare the participants, and to answer any questions that the participants may have.

After opening remarks by the manager of the host group, in which he or she sets the climate by stating that the host group genuinely wants to hear how the unit is perceived, the consultant feeds back to the total group information from the interviews. The outsiders "fishbowl" to discuss and explore the data presented by the consultant. (A fishbowl is a group seating and talking configuration in which there is an inner circle of chairs for people who talk and an outside circle of observers and noninteractors.) The fishbowl allows the invited participants to talk about the host unit in a natural, uninterrupted way while the host group members listen and learn. Following this, the host group members fishbowl and talk about what they have heard, ask for any clarification, and generally seek to understand the information they have heard. There may at this point be a general discussion to ensure that everyone understands what is being said, but at this time the participants do not start to work on the problems that have been uncovered.

For actually working on the problems, subgroups composed of both host group members and invited participants are formed. The subgroups are asked to identify the most important changes that need to be made to improve the host unit's effectiveness. After the small groups have identified the key problems, the total group convenes to make a master list to work out specific action plans for bringing about the changes deemed most important. The total group hears a summary report from each subgroup. Action plans are firmed up, people are assigned to tasks, and target dates for completion are agreed upon. This concludes the organization mirror intervention, but a follow-up meeting to assess progress and to review action steps is strongly recommended.

In a short period of time an organizational unit can get the feedback it needs to improve its relations with significant work-related groups. The organization mirror intervention provides this feedback effectively. It is imperative that following the meeting the host group in fact implement the action plans that were developed in the meeting.

SUMMARY

Intergroup team building and the organization mirror are the two major interventions that have been developed to improve intergroup relations. They both work, that is, they actually reduce intergroup conflict and improve intergroup relations.

Why these interventions work is not very well understood. But the underlying dynamics that cause these techniques to be efficacious are probably the following:

1. The interactions between the groups are *controlled* and a *structure is imposed to maintain control.* Control is imposed when the groups are asked to build the lists separately, when

they are permitted only minimal interaction at the early stages of the interventions, when they are not allowed to argue or defend positions on the lists, and when they are held to a lockstep procedure by the third-party consultant. Even having to build written lists rather than being allowed to talk between groups is a powerful form of control. These controls keep negative feelings and passions in check; any hostile feelings are not allowed to escalate.

2. The interventions are based on data, and the *data are complete and public*. When group A puts down *all* the things about group B that it dislikes, that gives group B a grasp of the scope of the problem issues and permits a *comprehensive understanding* of the differences and problems. Knowing the scope of the issues and having a comprehensive understanding of them is probably a necessary ingredient in making a group (or an individual) move from a defensive posture to a problem-solving stance. Suppose that group A is telling group B the things it does not like about group B. Someone introduces item 1. It is argued about, defended, rationalized, and so forth. Probably before there is any resolution on item 1 someone introduces item 2, which triggers a new round of argument and counterargument and probably no resolution. By the time items 3 and 4 have been tossed into the ring, most of the discussants will be frustrated, angry, and convinced that "*we* were right all along about *them*" and "*they* just don't understand *us*." When the problems are lobbed in like mortar shells, the group feels that it is under attack: its members are continually off balance; they feel their defense is necesary but is not very good, since it is a tactical one only; and they are hindered from building a strategy for defense, much less a strategy for problem solving or change.

   Making the data public seems to have its own important dynamic. There is a sense of "Finally, it's all out in the open." Instead of private gripes and complaints, rumors of which may get back to the offending party, now things are public and available to all. For joint problem solving to take place, all the actors who are part of the problem or part of the solution must share the same data. Making the data public is one way of making this happen. Another aspect of public data is that now the problems are clearly identified as specific problems; people now have something to work on—they know what expertise or resources must be brought to bear, and how to start to solve the problems. Furthermore, people are by nature problem solvers—once a specific problem is identified and made public, people just naturally start to "work it."

3. The early stages of these interventions—making lists and sharing them and using the fishbowl technique—lead the participants to *experience feelings of success in dealing with the other group*. Feelings of anxiety, apprehension, and hostility start to give way to feelings of competence and success as the early stages of the interventions produce better communication and understanding than the participants had expected. Nothing succeeds like success, and the early stages are usually perceived as a success experience by both groups. This leads to the optimistic realization that "We *can* work together with those people." Participants are watching for subtle cues of defensiveness, resistance to the data, stubbornness, and the like, and the controlled nature of the process makes most of these unnecessary. This starts building momentum for feelings of competence and success.

4. The *constructive, problem-solving tone* of the meetings, set by the leaders or the consultant, *carries a force of its own*. If people want to be negative, destructive, and defensive, they have to go against the tenor of the meeting. This is increasingly difficult to do if a clear problem-solving climate has been established.

There are no doubt other dynamics of the intergroup interventions, but those just listed indicate some of the reasons why such interventions usually work. The intergroup interventions are an important part of the OD practitioner's repertoire. They require some skill in their execution, but the process itself carries the brunt of the work in making them effective interventions.

NOTES

1. Research evidence for these statements comes from the following sources: M. Sherif and Carolyn Sherif, *Groups in Harmony and Tension* (New York: Harper & Row, 1953); and R. R. Blake and Jane S. Mouton, "Conformity, Resistance, and Conversion," in I. A. Berg and B. M. Bass, eds., *Conformity and Deviation* (New York: Harper & Row, 1961). For a succinct summary of this issue, see E. H. Schein, *Organizational Psychology,* 2nd ed. (Englewood Cliffs, N.J.: Prentice-Hall, 1970), Chap. 5.

2. Schein, *Organizational Psychology,* Chap. 5.

3. R. R. Blake, H. A. Shepard, and J. S. Mouton, *Managing Intergroup Conflict in Industry* (Houston: Gulf, 1965).

4. This discussion is based on R. Beckhard, *Organization Development: Strategies and Models* (Reading, Mass.: Addison-Wesley, 1969), pp. 33–35.

5. This discussion is taken from J. K. Fordyce and R. Weil, *Managing WITH People* (Reading, Mass.: Addison-Wesley, 1971), pp. 124–130.

6. Fordyce and Weil, in *Managing WITH People,* discuss this intervention in detail (pp. 101–105). We believe this technique was developed by the OD practitioners at TRW Systems.

12

PERSONAL, INTERPERSONAL, AND GROUP PROCESS INTERVENTIONS

a descriptive inventory of OD interventions

The activities described in this chapter are learning techniques directed toward individuals, dyads and triads, and groups. The central theme of the interventions is learning through an examination of underlying processes. In *process consultation,* an important genre of OD interventions, there is an almost exclusive focus on the diagnosis and management of personal, interpersonal, and group processes. Expertise in this area is essential for OD practitioners. *Third-party peacemaking* focuses on interpersonal conflict and the dynamics of cooperation and competition in sociations of two and three. *Sensitivity training,* the educational and social invention giving rise to the laboratory training movement, typically yields learnings about self, interpersonal relations, and group dynamics. We view sensitivity training as an important, but not prepotent, OD intervention technique. *Transactional analysis* (TA) can be a form of psychotherapy, a framework for analyzing interpersonal relations and transactions, or an educational intervention that is introduced into some OD programs. The focus is on the individual and the major benefits accrue to individuals, namely, enhanced individual functioning. But TA has also been used as a technique for team building. *Behavior modeling* is a training technique designed to increase effectiveness in problematic interpersonal situations. *Life- and career-planning* interventions are less process oriented than the other interventions in this chapter and reflect more a systematic approach to a substantive area that has heretofore received little attention. While these planning activities are intended to enhance individual functioning, the setting is generally the small group.

The interventions discussed in this chapter are important ones. Depending on the overall OD strategy, not all of them might be used in a particular OD program, but understanding the activities, and understanding when they are appropriate is necessary for client and consultant alike.

151

PROCESS CONSULTATION INTERVENTIONS

Process consultation (PC) represents an approach or a method for intervening in an ongoing system. The crux of this approach is that a skilled third party (consultant) works with individuals and groups to help them learn about human and social processes and learn to solve problems that stem from process events. This approach has been around a long time; many practitioners operate from this stance. Edgar Schein has pulled together the disparate practices and principles of process consultation in a comprehensive and coherent exposition.[1] In this book he also describes the role of PC in organization development.

Process consultation consists of many different interventions; it is not any single thing the consultant does. The paramount goal of PC is stated by Schein as follows:

> The job of the process consultant is to help the organization to solve its own problems by making it *aware of organizational processes,* of the consequences of these processes, and of the mechanisms by which they can be changed. The ultimate concern of the process consultant is the organization's capacity to do for itself what he has done for it. Where the standard consultant is more concerned about passing on his knowledge, the process consultant is concerned about passing on his skills and values.[2]

Some particularly important organizational processes are communications, the roles and functions of group members, group problem solving and decision making, group norms and group growth, leadership and authority, and intergroup cooperation and competition.[3] The PC consultant works with the organization, typically in work teams, and helps them to develop the skills necessary to diagnose and solve the process problems that arise.

Schein describes the kinds of interventions he believes the process consultant should make:

1. Agenda-setting interventions, consisting of:
   —Questions which direct attention to interpersonal issues.
   —Process-analysis periods.
   —Agenda review and testing procedures.
   —Meetings devoted to interpersonal process.
   —Conceptual inputs on interpersonal-process topics.
2. Feedback of observations or other data, consisting of:
   —Feedback to groups during process analysis or regular work time.
   —Feedback to individuals after meetings or after data-gathering.
3. Coaching or counseling of individuals [see discussion following].
4. Structural suggestions:
   —Pertaining to group membership.
   —Pertaining to communication or interaction patterns.
   —Pertaining to allocation of work, assignment of responsibility, and lines of authority.[4]

In Schein's view, the process consultant would most often make interventions in that same order: agenda setting, feedback of observations or other data, counseling and coaching, and, least likely, structural suggestions. Specific recommendations for the solution of substantive problems are not listed because to Schein such interventions violate the underlying values of the PC model in that the consultant is acting as an expert rather than as a resource.[5]

In *coaching and counseling interventions,* which may be considered either as a part of PC or as a set of interventions in their own right, the consultant is placed in the role of responding to such questions from groups or individuals as "What do you think I should do in this instance to improve my performance?" "Now that I can see some areas for improvement, how do I go about changing my behavior?"

Schein sees the consultant's role in coaching and counseling situations to be the following: "The consultant's role then becomes one of adding alternatives to those already brought up by the client, and helping the client to analyze the costs and benefits of the various alternatives which have been mentioned."[6] Thus the consultant, when counseling either individuals or groups, continues to maintain the posture that real improvements and changes in behavior should be those decided upon by the client. The consultant serves to reflect or mirror accurate feedback, to listen to alternatives and suggest new ones (often through questions designed to expand the client's horizons), and to assist the client in evaluating alternatives for feasibility, relevance, and appropriateness.

The basic congruence between theories of counseling and the theory of process consultation is pointed out by Schein: "In both caes it is essential to help the client improve his ability to observe and process data about himself, to help him accept and learn from feedback and to help him become an active participant with the counselor/consultant in identifying and solving his own problems."[7]

The process consultation model is similar to team-building interventions and intergroup team-building interventions except that in PC greater emphasis is placed on diagnosing and understanding process events. Furthermore, there is greater emphasis on the consultant being more nondirective and questioning as he or she gets the groups to solve their own problems.

THIRD-PARTY PEACEMAKING INTERVENTIONS

Third-party interventions into conflict situations have the potential to control (contain) the conflict or resolve it. R. E. Walton has presented a statement of theory and practice for third-party peacemaking interventions that is both important in its own right and important for its role in organization development.[8] His book is directed toward interpersonal conflict—understanding it and intervening in ways to control or resolve the conflict. This intervention technique is somewhat related to intergroup relations described in Chapter 11, but there are many unique aspects to conflict situations involving only two people. In this section, rather than describe specific interventions, we explicate some of the features of the theory presented by Walton.

A basic feature of third-party intervention is confrontation: the two principals must be willing to confront the fact that conflict exists and that it has consequences for the effectiveness of the two parties involved. The third party must know how, when, and where to utilize confrontation tactics that surface the conflict for examination.

The third party must be able to diagnose conflict situations, and Walton presents a diagnostic model of interpersonal conflict based on four basic elements: the conflict issues, the precipitating circumstances, the conflict-relevant acts of the principals, and the consequences of the conflict.[9] In addition, conflict is a cyclical process, and the cycles may be benevolent, malevolent, or self-maintaining. For accurate diagnosis it is particularly important to know the source of the conflict. Walton speaks to this issue:

> A major distinction is drawn between substantive and emotional conflict. *Substantive issues* involve disagreements over policies and practices, competitive bids for the same resources, and differing conceptions of roles and role relationships. *Emotional issues* involve negative feelings between the parties (e.g., anger, distrust, scorn, resentment, fear, rejection).[10]

This distinction is important for the third-party consultant in that substantive issues require problem-solving and bargaining behaviors between the principals, while emotional issues require restructuring perceptions and working through negative feelings.

Intervention tactics for the third party consist of structuring confrontation and dialogue between the principals. Many choice points exist for the consultant. Walton lists the ingredients of productive confrontation:

1. mutual positive motivation [both parties are disposed to attempt to resolve the conflict]
2. balance in the situational power of the two principals [power parity is most conducive to success]
3. synchronization of their confrontation efforts [initiatives and readiness to confront should occur in concert between the two parties]
4. appropriate pacing of the differentiation and integration phases of a dialogue [time must be allowed for working through of negative feelings and clarification of ambivalent or positive feelings]
5. conditions favoring openness in dialogue [norms supporting openness and reassurance for openness should be structured for the parties]
6. reliable communicative signs [making certain each can understand the other]
7. optimum tension in the situation [there should be moderate stress on the parties][11]

Most of these ingredients are self-explanatory, but some elaboration may be helpful on the differentiation and integration phases. In the differentiation phase of conflict, the principals clarify the differences that divide them and sort out the negative feelings they have; in the integration phase, the principals seek to clarify their commonalities, the positive feelings or ambivalence that may exist, and the commonality of their goals.

The third party will intervene directly and indirectly in facilitating dialogue between the principals. Examples of direct interventions would be interviewing the principals before a confrontation meeting, helping to set the agenda, attending to the pace of the dialogue, and refereeing the interaction; examples of more subtle interventions of the third party would be setting the meeting on neutral turf, setting time boundaries on the interaction, and the like.

Third-party intervention into interpersonal conflict situations requires a highly skilled professional or a highly skilled layperson who understands the dynamics of conflict. This intervention should not be undertaken by a novice in human and social processes of organizations.

SENSITIVITY TRAINING LABORATORIES

Sensitivity training laboratories were a cornerstone of early organization development efforts. These are used less frequently now as interventions, but they are still an important OD technique. The reduction in the use of sensitivity training (or T-groups, *T* for *training*) is not due to its lack of effectiveness or its appropriateness for OD, but rather more to its being supplanted by such interventions as team building and process consultation. T-groups are still an excellent learning and change intervention, particularly for the personal growth and development of the individual.

A T-group is an unstructured, agendaless group session for about 10 to 12 members and a professional "trainer" who acts as catalyst and facilitator for the group. The data for discussion are the data provided by the interaction of the group members as they strive to create a viable society for themselves. Actions, reactions, interactions, and the concomitant feelings accompanying all of these are the data for the group. The group typically meets for three days up to two weeks. Conceptual material relating to interpersonal relations, individual personality theory, and group dynamics is a part of the program. But the main learning vehicle is the group experience.

Learnings derived from the T-group vary for different individuals, but they are usually described as learning to be more competent in interpersonal relationships, learning more about oneself as a person, learning how others react to one's behavior, and learning about the dynamics of group formation and group norms and group growth. Benne, Bradford, and Ronald Lippitt list the goals of the laboratory method as follows:

1. One hoped-for outcome for the participant is increased awareness of and sensitivity to emotional reactions and expression in himself and in others. . . . .

2. Another desired objective is greater ability to perceive and to learn from the consequences of his actions through attention to feelings, his own and others'. Emphasis is placed on the development of sensitivity to cues furnished by the behavior of others and ability to utilize "feedback" in understanding his own behaviors.

3. The staff also attempts to stimulate the clarification and development of personal values and goals consonant with a democratic and scientific approach to problems and personal decision and action. . . .

4. Another objective is the development of concepts and theoretical insights which will serve as tools in linking personal values, goals, and intentions to actions consistent with these inner factors and with the requirements of the situation. . . . One important source of valid concepts is the findings and methodologies of the behavioral sciences. . . .

5. All laboratory programs foster the achievement of behavioral effectiveness in transactions with one's environment. . . . The learning of concepts, the setting of goals, the clarification of values, and even the achievement of valid insight into self, are sometimes far ahead of the development of the performance skills necessary to expression in actual social transactions. For this reason laboratory programs normally focus on the development of behavioral skills to support better integration of intentions and actions.[12]

The T-group is a powerful learning laboratory where individuals gain insights into the meaning and consequences of their own behavior, the meaning and consequences of others' behaviors, and the dynamics and processes of group behavior. These insights are coupled with growth of skills in diagnosing and taking more effective interpersonal and group action. Thus the T-group can give the individuals the basic skills necessary for more competent action taking in the organization.

Uses of T-groups in OD are varied, but they are particularly appropriate to introduce key members of the organization to group methods and they are appropriate to give a basic skill level relevant to group and individual dynamics to individuals. In addition, the T-group may be constituted in several different ways depending on the desired outcome. There are "cousin" laboratories consisting of people from the same organization but who do not have direct working relationships with each other and in fact may not know each other. A different configuration is the "cluster" lab consisting of persons from different parts of the organization similar to the cousin labs, but each group also has "clusters" of work-related people—a 12-person group may have three separate groups of four persons each who are related in their work in the organization. Another possibility is the "family T-group" in which the intact work team undergoes a T-group experience together.[13] Finally, individuals from an organization may attend a "stranger" lab composed of people from other organizations.

Many people think that organization development means putting everyone in the organization through a T-group. This is not correct. The T-group is only one technique out of many available to the OD practitioner. And laboratory training, while appropriate in some situations, is not the basic thrust or modality of OD.

TRANSACTIONAL ANALYSIS

Transactional analysis (TA) began as a form of psychotherapy but has increasingly been used as an educational technique. It was developed primarily by Eric Berne and was popularized in his book *Games People Play*.[14] Transactional analysis is a valuable tool both for disturbed people and for healthy individuals. Its use in OD is mainly as an educational intervention, and in this sense it is directed toward the healthy "uncertified normals" who people most organizations. Training seminars containing theory and practice related to TA are the usual mode of introducing the technique into organizations. Individuals attend the seminars either with other nonwork-related persons or with persons from their own work group.

Huse describes TA as follows:

> Transactional analysis focuses on such areas as the structure of the personality (structural analysis), the way in which people interact (transactional analysis), or the way in which people structure their time (time structuring), and the roles that people learn to play in life.[15]

Structural analysis in TA postulates that the personality is made up of three *ego states:* the *Parent,* the *Adult,* and the *Child.* Individuals are always acting out of one of these three ego states. The *Parent* ego state is gained from one's real parents; it reflects an ego state of superiority, authority, being right, judging others, and the like. The *Adult* ego state reflects maturity, objectivity, problem solving, logic, and rationality. This ego state represents the capacity for mature, wholesome commerce with the world. The *Child* ego state is gained from one's experiences as a child when one is dependent, rebellious, and perhaps inadequate.

Analysis of the transactions or communications between people is a major aspect of TA. Transactions can be (1) complementary, (2) crossed, or (3) ulterior. *Complementary* transactions are those in which messages from one ego state are responded to with messages from an appropriate ego state. These parallel transactions can be Adult-Adult, Parent-Child, Parent-Parent, and so forth; the response is natural and expected. *Crossed* transactions are those in which messages from one ego state are responded to with messages from an inappropriate or unexpected ego state. Examples would be an Adult-Child transaction or a Parent-Adult transaction. The response is not to the same ego states the sender is in. Crossed transactions make people feel angry, hurt, and put down. *Ulterior* transactions are those in which the messages do not mean what they literally convey; the apparent, surface ego states implied by the message are not the real ego states directing the messages. These are often seen in flirtation games. An example would be ''come let me show you the barn,'' says the cowboy. ''Why, I've always been interested in rural architecture,'' replies the female visitor. Interpersonal relations and communication are vastly improved when ulterior and crossed transactions are decreased and complementary transactions are increased.

There are six basic ways to structure time: withdrawal, rituals, pastimes, games, activities, and authenticity.[16] Games are often destructive sets of interpersonal encounters; they stem from pathology and cause the individual to avoid intimacy and authenticity. Authenticity is mature, meaningful, intimate contact with others. *Script analysis* is the analysis of the patterns and roles—the basic themes—that one plays out throughout one's lifetime.

How does Transactional Analysis relate to OD? People are trained in seminars to identify dysfunctional life scripts, time structuring, games, and crossed and ulterior transactions in themselves and others so that they may enjoy better relations with themselves and others. The assumption is made that this knowledge will make them more effective in their organizational roles and personal lives. Lyman Randall, an OD and TA practitioner with American Airlines, defines OD from a TA perspective:

> Organization development is an evolving set of specific activities designed and implemented to achieve the following: (a) To maximize Adult-Adult transactions between individuals. (b) To give an OK to the Natural Child in individuals to participate in transactions with others. (c) To identify and untangle quickly crossed transactions between people. (d) To minimize destructive game playing among people and between work groups. (e) To maximize authentic encounters (intimacy) between individuals. (f) To develop administrative systems, policies, and work climate that support the preceding objectives.[17]

Transactional Analysis is best thought of as only one part of a larger OD program where it is used in conjunction with other interventions. It is primarily directed to individuals and teams in the organization, usually through the vehicle of seminars and practice sessions. Anecdotal evidence from the many organizations using this intervention suggests that it makes individuals more effective in their job-related interactions with others.

BEHAVIOR MODELING

Behavior modeling is a training technique designed to improve interpersonal competence. It is not an OD intervention per se, but we believe it should be added to the OD practitioner's repertoire because it is such an effective tool, and because problems with interpersonal relations are common in organizations. For improving interpersonal skills, behavior modeling is the intervention of choice.

Based on Albert Bandura's Social Learning Theory and utilizing procedures developed by Goldstein and Sorcher, behavior modeling has been shown to be an excellent way to make first-line supervisors more effective (Latham and Saari) and to improve organizational performance (Porras et al.).[18] The basic premise of Social Learning Theory is that for persons to engage successfully in a behavior, they (1) must perceive a link between the behavior and certain outcomes; (2) must desire those outcomes (called positive valence); and (3) must believe they can do it (called self-efficacy).[19] For example, many first-line supervisors find it difficult to discipline employees. To learn this behavior they must see a link between successful disciplining and desired outcomes (like favorable recognition from superiors or less hassle from subordinates) and must come to believe they can do it. This latter belief can be instilled by viewing a model similar to them being successful, by discovering the specific behavioral skills that led to success, and by practicing the skills until they too are proficient. This is the methodology of behavior modeling.

A simple problem-solving model underlies most behavior modeling training. Porras and Singh describe it as follows:

> The problem-solving approach, a rather straightforward one consisting of three phases—problem identification, problem-solving, and implementation, consisted of five behavioral skills:
>
> 1. Behavior description. The ability to describe behavior of self or others in specific concrete terms and to avoid generalizations or inferences drawn from observed behaviors.
> 2. Justification. The ability to clearly explain the impact of an observed behavior on the individual, the observer, or the organization.
> 3. Active listening. The ability to accurately reflect both content and feelings of another's communication.
> 4. Participative problem-solving. The ability to involve another, meaningfully and appropriately, in the process of solving a work-related problem.
> 5. Positive reinforcement. The ability to compliment another in a sincere and authentic manner.[20]

The steps involved in behavior modeling are simple. First determine the most pressing problems facing a target group, say, first-line supervisors. These usually consist of such issues as counseling the poor performer, correcting absenteeism, encouraging the average performer, correcting unsafe work behavior, and so forth. Training modules for each of about 10 problems are developed, the core of which are videotapes showing a person (model) correctly handling the situation. The specific behaviors exhibited by the model that cause success are highlighted as ''learning points''—typically these are the behavioral skills mentioned by Porras and Singh. Weekly training sessions of four hours each are scheduled for each module for groups of approximately 10 participants.

At the training sessions the problem situation is announced and briefly discussed. Participants then observe a videotape in which the model (who looks similar to them) successfully solves the problem by enacting specific behavioral skills. The trainees discuss the behavioral skills and then *role play the situation* receiving *feedback from the group and the trainer* on their performances. Role playing continues until each participant successfully masters all the specific skills. Participants then commit to practicing the new skills on the job in the coming week. At the beginning of the next session participants report on how their new skills worked on the job. If necessary, additional practice is held to ensure mastery of the skills. Then a new problem is addressed, the model is observed on videotape, and role playing and feedback occur until all participants learn how to solve the new problem.

Behavior modeling works; it teaches the skills and behaviors needed to deal with interpersonal problems. It should be in the practitioner's kit bag.

LIFE- AND CAREER-PLANNING INTERVENTIONS

Managing against objectives is important for individual effectiveness as well as for organizational effectiveness. A series of interventions focuses on the life goals and the career goals of individual organization members so that they may better exert control over their own destinies. The interventions focus on past, present, and future. The tasks are completed by individuals and then are discussed in small groups. The sequence of steps enables individuals to come to grips with the following issues:

1. An assessment of life and career paths up to this point, noting highlights, particularly important events, choice points, strengths, and deficiencies
2. A formulation of goals and objectives related to both desired life style and career path—these are future-oriented goals
3. A realistic plan for achieving the goals and moving systematically toward goal accomplishment; that is, the goals are specified, action steps needed to reach the goals are determined, and a schedule of target dates is established for measuring progress

Generally, life planning and career planning are done concurrently because career planning is but one subset of life planning.

One series of life- and career-planning exercises is shown in the discussion that follows. Herbert A. Shepard is generally acknowledged as the author and originator of these exercises, and the role of these interventions in organization development programs is due primarily to him.

Life Goals Exercise

I. First Phase
    A. Draw a straight horizontal line from left to right to represent your life span. The length should represent the totality of your experience and future expectations.
    B. Indicate where you are now.
    C. Prepare a life inventory of important ''happenings'' for you, including the following:
        1. Any peak experiences you have had.

    2. Things which you do well.

    3. Things which you do poorly.

    4. Things you would like to stop doing.

    5. Things you would like to learn to do well.

    6. Peak experiences you would like to have.

    7. Values (e.g., power, money, etc.) you want to achieve.

    8. Things you would like to start doing now.

  D. Discussions in subgroups.

II. Second Phase

  A. Take 20 minutes to write your own obituary.

  B. Form pairs. Take 20 minutes to write a eulogy for your partner.

  C. Discussions in subgroups.[21]

Additional approaches exist to get the individual thinking about his or her life and career trajectory and to provide data that may be shared in small-group discussion. For example, the outline of activities suggested by Fordyce and Weil has the following steps.[23] First, individuals working in small groups are asked to make a "collage"—a symbolic representation of their lives constructed out of art materials, old magazines and newspapers, and the like; these are posted on the walls for later discussion. Second, individuals write two letters, the instructions for which are as follows:

> Now imagine that you have died ten years from now. Write a letter from one of your best friends to another good friend, telling about you and your life. What do you *want* him to be able to say about you? Next, imagine you have been killed in an auto accident next week. Now write a similar letter. What would he be likely to say about you?[23]

At this point, the group discusses the collages and letters of each individual, giving the individual the chance to get feedback from the rest of the group about their reactions and also allowing the group to learn more about each other. This third set of public sharing serves to prepare the members for the next step, consisting of building a "life inventory," similar to the one just described. After the preparation of the life inventory, each individual prepares a career inventory by writing answers to questions like the following: What facets of work (my career up to this point) do I like most, least? What do I think are my best skills, abilities,and talents that I bring to the work situation? What kinds of rewards do I seek from my job—money, status, recognition, being a part of a team? What new career areas do I want to pursue? What new skills do I need to develop for the new career areas? These inventories are shared and discussed within the group. As a final step, individuals set down a plan of action steps for achieving the goals they have identified.

Life- and career-planning activities may take only a day; but sometimes an entire week can be spent generating data about oneself, analyzing the data both individually and in groups, and formulating clear goals and action plans for achieving them. These activities have great meaning for organization members and are particularly helpful for individuals who feel that they are in a rut, who are contemplating a career change, or who have seldom introspected about their own life-style and career pattern.

SUMMARY

In this chapter we have examined a variety of interventions that, taken together, considerably expanded the repertoire of the organization development practitioner. They apply to different situations, different configurations of actors, and different problem areas. They are used as components of an OD program, not the entire program. When used in conjunction with a careful diagnosis, these personal, interpersonal, and group process interventions have proved helpful in furthering individual and organizational functioning.

NOTES

1. E. H. Schein, *Process Consultation: Its Role in Organization Development* (Reading, Mass.: Addison-Wesley, 1969). The discussion is based on this source.

2. Ibid., p. 135.

3. Ibid., p. 13.

4. Ibid., pp. 102–103.

5. Ibid., p. 103.

6. Ibid., p. 116.

7. Ibid., p. 116.

8. R. E. Walton, *Interpersonal Peacemaking: Confrontations and Third Party Consultation* (Reading, Mass.: Addison-Wesley, 1969).

9. Ibid., p. 71.

10. Ibid., p. 73.

11. Ibid. This list is taken from page 94; our interpretation is shown in brackets; Walton's discussion of the list is on pages 94–115.

12. K. D. Benne, L. P. Bradford, and R. Lippitt, "The Laboratory Method," in L. P. Bradford, J. R. Gibb, and K. D. Benne, eds. *T-Group Theory and Laboratory Method* (New York: John Wiley, 1964), pp. 15–44. This quotation, pp. 16–17.

13. Based on discussions in J. K. Fordyce and R. Weil, *Managing WITH People* (Reading, Mass.: Addison-Wesley, 1971), pp. 109–113.

14. Eric Berne, *Games People Play* (New York: Grove Press, 1964). See also Thomas A. Harris, *I'm OK—You're OK: A Practical Guide to Transactional Analysis* (New York: Harper & Row, 1967).

15. Edgar F. Huse, *Organization Development and Change* (St. Paul, Minn.: West Publishing, 1975), p. 283.

16. Muriel James and Dorothy Jongeward, *Born to Win: Transactional Analysis with Gestalt Experiments* (Reading, Mass.: Addison-Wesley, 1971), p. 56. See also David D. Bowen and Raghu Nath, *Academy of Management Review,* January 1978, pp. 79–89.

17. Lyman K. Randall, "Red, White and Blue TA at 600 MPH," in Dorothy Jongeward and contributors, *Everybody Wins: Transactional Analysis Applied to Organizations* (Reading, Mass.: Addison-Wesley, 1973), pp. 123–146. This quotation is from page 137.

18. See Albert Bandura, *Social Learning Theory,* (Englewood Cliffs, NJ: Prentice-Hall, 1977); A. P. Goldstein and M. Sorcher, *Changing Supervisor Behavior,* (New York: Pergamon, 1974); G. P. Latham and L. M. Saari, "Application of Social-Learning Theory to Training Supervisors Through Behavioral Modeling," *Journal of Applied Psychology,* Vol. 64, 1979, pp. 239–246; and J. I. Porras, K. Hargis, K. J. Patterson, D. C. Maxfield, N. Roberts, and R. J. Bies, "Modeling-Based Organizational Development: A Longitudinal Assessment," *The Journal of Applied Behavioral Science,* Vol. 18, No. 4., 1982, pp. 433–446.

19. Bandura, ibid.

20. J. I. Porras and J. V. Singh, "Alpha, Beta, and Gamma Change in Modeling-Based Organization Development," *Journal of Occupational Behavior,* Vol. 7, 1986, pp. 9–23. This quotation is from page 11.

21. These are representative of the life-planning exercises used in NTL Institute programs for the training of OD practitioners. See also Gordon Lippitt, "Developing Life Plans," *Training and Development Journal,* May 1970, pp. 2–7.

22. Based on a discussion in Fordyce and Weil, *Managing with People,* pp. 131–133.

23. Ibid., p. 131.

13

COMPREHENSIVE INTERVENTIONS

a descriptive inventory of OD interventions

Some OD interventions are sufficiently comprehensive to be categorized as total organizational interventions. In increasing order of comprehensiveness are the *confrontation meeting, strategic management activities, survey feedback,* and *Grid OD.* The confrontation meeting has a total organization quality because it simultaneously involves all the top managers of an organization. Strategic management usually involves the top executives and managers. Survey feedback typically involves all the employees of an organization (or a major subdivision), as well as managers, and includes two major phases. Grid OD, seen in its entirety, can involve all employees at all levels and has several distinct phases spanning several years. In addition, we wish to examine two theory-based approaches to organization development that, while not being interventions per se, nevertheless constitute systematic guidelines for improving organizational effectiveness. These approaches are based on the *System 4 Management* theory of Rensis Likert and the *contingency theory* of Paul Lawrence and Jay Lorsch. Both approaches are considered by many authors to be part of the theory and practice of OD.

THE CONFRONTATION MEETING

The *confrontation meeting,* developed by Richard Beckhard, is a one-day meeting of the entire management of an organization in which they take a reading of their own organizational health.[1] In a series of activities, the management group generates information about its major problems, analyzes the underlying causes, develops action plans to correct the problems, and sets a schedule for completed remedial work. This intervention is an important one in organization development; it is a quick, simple, and reliable way in which

163

to generate data about an organization and to set action plans for organizational improvement. Beckhard says of the confrontation meeting:

> Experience shows that it is appropriate where
>> There is a need for the total management group to examine its own workings.
>> Very limited time is available for the activity.
>> Top management wishes to improve the conditions quickly.
>> There is enough cohesion in the top team to ensure follow-up.
>> There is real commitment to resolving the issue on the part of top management.
>> The organization is experiencing, or has recently experienced, some major change.[2]

The steps involved in the confrontation meeting are as follows.[3]

Step 1. Climate Setting (45 to 60 minutes). The top manager introduces the session by stating his or her goals for the meeting, citing the necessity for free and open discussion of issues and problems, and making it clear that individuals will not be punished for what they say. This is generally followed by a statement from the consultant regarding the importance of communication within the organizations, the practicability of organization problem solving, and the desirability of addressing and solving organizational problems.

Step 2. Information Collecting (1 hour). Small groups of seven or eight members are formed on the basis of heterogeneity of composition; that is, there is a maximum of people from different functional areas and working situations on each team. The only rule is that bosses and subordinates not be put together on the same team. The top-management group meets as a separate group during this time. The charge to all the groups is as follows:

> Think of yourself as an individual with needs and goals. Also think as a person concerned about the total organization. What are the obstacles, "demotivators," poor procedures or policies, unclear goals, or poor attitudes that exist today? What different conditions, if any, would make the organization more effective and make life in the organization better?[4]

The groups work on this task for an hour and recorder/reporters list the results of the discussion.

Step 3. Information Sharing (1 hour). Reporters from each small group report the group's complete findings to the total group and these are placed on newsprint on the walls. The total list of items is categorized, usually by the meeting leader, into a few major categories that may be based on type of problem (e.g., communications problems), type of relationship (e.g., troubles with top management), or type of area (e.g., problems with the accounting department).

Step 4. Priority Setting and Group Action Planning (1 hour and 15 minutes). This step typically follows a break during which time the items from the lists are duplicated for distribution to everyone. In a 15-minute general session, the meeting leader goes through the list of items and puts a category assignment on each one so that everyone has his or her own copy of the categorized items. Next the participants form into functional, natural work teams reflecting the way they are organized in the organization. Each group is headed by the top manager in the group. The groups are asked to respond to a three-part charge, that is, to do three tasks. First, they are to identify and discuss the issues and problems related to their area, decide on the priorities of these problems, and determine early action steps to remedy the problems that they are prepared to commit themselves (in the total group) to work on. Second, they are asked to identify the problems they think should be the priority issues for top management. Third, they are to determine how they will communicate the results of the confrontation meeting to their subordinates. This completes the confrontation meeting for all the managers except for the top management group.

Step 5. Immediate Follow-up by Top Team (1 to 3 hours). The top-management team meets after the rest of the participants have left to plan first follow-up action steps and to determine what actions should be taken on the basis of what they have learned during the day. These follow-up action plans are communicated to the rest of the management group within several days.

Step 6. Progress Review (2 hours). A follow-up meeting with the total management group is held four to six weeks later to report progress and to review the actions resulting from the confrontation meeting.

This is the flow of activities for the confrontation meeting. It is an excellent way to get fast results leading toward organization improvement. Beckhard believes that the confrontation meeting provides a quick and accurate means for diagnosing organizational health, promotes constructive problem identification and problem solving, enhances upward communication within the organization, and increases involvement and commitment to action on the part of the entire managerial group.[5] We agree with his assessment.

STRATEGIC MANAGEMENT ACTIVITIES

Most OD programs and interventions are directed toward the internal workings of the organization. Team development, managing intergroup relations, clarifying roles, and solving problems at all levels of the organization—these are primarily inward-looking activities. In the last decade, there has been a growing awareness of the importance of the external environment and the necessity for monitoring and maneuvering within that environment. With this awareness has come the realization that organization development must develop and provide outward-looking interventions for organization members—activities directed toward environmental analysis and strategic planning.

Recent research and theory, especially in the field of business policy, have led to the development of the concept of ''strategic management.'' Strategic management can be defined as the development and implementation of the organization's ''grand design'' or overall strategy in relation to its current and future environmental demands. The concept is described by Schendel and Hofer as follows: ''There are six major tasks that comprise the strategic management process: (1) goal formulation; (2) environmental analysis; (3) strategy formulation; (4) strategy evaluation; (5) strategy implementation; and (6) strategic control.''[6] These six components of the process are assumed to be related as shown in Figure 13-1.

Developing organizational goals is the first step, followed by an assessment of the constraints and opportunities afforded by the environment. Two environments are relevant: the present environment and the future environment. The present environment can be monitored directly; constraints and opportunities of the future environment must be predicted. Strategic plans, derived from goals and environmental analysis, are then developed, implemented, and monitored for results. It is generally assumed that some ''dominant coalition'' of key decision makers in the organization is responsible for the strategic management process.

Several OD interventions directed toward strategic planning have been around for a long time. These include goal-setting activities, Beckhard's Confrontation Meeting, and phases 4, 5, and 6 of Blake and Mouton's Grid OD. In phase 4 of a Grid program, for example, organization members build an Ideal Strategic Corporate Model, and in later stages they develop action plans to achieve that model.

Figure 13-1 An Overview of the Strategic Management Process. *Source:* Dan Schendel and Charles W. Hofer, *Strategic Management: A New View of Business Policy and Planning*, p. 15. Copyright © 1979 by Little, Brown and Company (Inc.). Reprinted by permission.

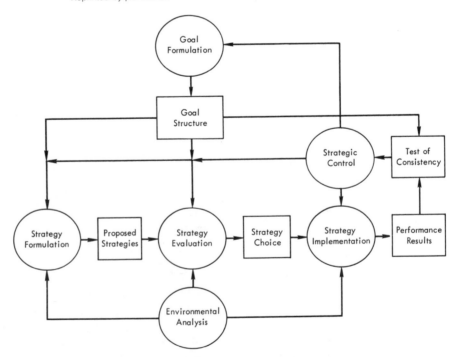

Some recent strategic planning techniques will be described here. One technique, used by our colleague Charles E. Summer who conducts strategic planning activities with organizations, is based on four questions:

1. What is your present strategy?
2. What are the opportunities and threats to that strategy?
3. What are your strengths and weaknesses to meet those threats and opportunities?
4. What kind of future policies must you adopt to avoid the threats and maximize your strengths?[7]

A top-management team will work for six months to a year answering these four questions. Meetings are held every one or two months; extensive data collection and analysis take place between meetings. It can be seen that the first question requires an in-depth analysis of what the organization is currently doing or what it thinks it is doing. The second question directs attention to the external environment and to forces that may affect the organization's ability to compete and remain viable. The third question starts to mesh organizational capabilities with environmental demands. The fourth question addresses the actions and changes needed to allow the organization to operate as desired in the future.

A strategic planning technique developed by Thomas Rogers[8] uses a series of two-day meetings with the top policymakers. After several "warm-up" questions to get everyone focused on long-range patterns within the organization and within the environment, the group addresses the question, What business are we in? The answers are worked into a *mission statement* for the organization. The next step is to identify and analyze the various "domains" or environmental segments that make demands on the organization. Rogers says that "A major premise about domains is that organizations do not exist independently, but in an interactive state with the various bodies they affect and are affected by. Four basic domains are suppliers, consumers, competition, and regulators."[9] The steps involved in analyzing domains are (1) to identify the various domains, (2) to identify the current demands of the domains, (3) to identify the current responses of the organization to those demands, (4) to predict future domain demands and future organizational responses, and (5) to identify ideal or desired domain demands and ideal responses. Action planning and implementation designed to act on the environment to bring about desired conditions are then initiated.

Open Systems Planning (OSP) is a technique developed by Charles Krone, G. K. Jayaram, and others[10] to assess the environment in a systematic way. Here the top team develops a number of "scenarios." The Present scenario is a description of the expectations and demands of environmental domains and internal groups and subgroups, along with a description of the current response to those demands. The Realistic Future scenario projects what the future demand picture is likely to be and what the future response pattern is likely to be *if the organization makes no adaptive changes.* This extrapolation is likely to highlight impending undesirable events if the organization simply maintains the status quo. Next an Idealistic Future scenario is developed that describes what an ideal or desired demand system would be like and identifies what actions would have to be taken by the organization to cause the desired state to exist. These needed actions are then analyzed for feasibility and costs. Open Systems Planning thus helps decision makers to move back and forth from present to future and from "what is" to "what should be." These word pictures make salient the need for organizational adaptation and change and lead to action planning and implementation.

Beckhard and Harris propose a seven-step strategic planning process for organizations undergoing major transitions.[11] Their approach assumes organizations are open systems that must respond to multiple demands from multiple sources. The first step in their procedure is to determine the core mission of the organization—its reason for being or purpose. Step two maps the current demand system—what groups and organizations are making what demands on the organization? Step three maps the current response system—what the organization is doing to respond to contemporary demands. Step four maps the demand system that is projected to exist in the future three or four years hence— what the likely future demands will be and from whom, assuming that the organization continues on its current path. Step five asks the executives to identify the *desired* state of affairs they would like to see exist in three or four years. Comparisons between the data generated in steps four and five suggest discrepancies that must be corrected if the desired state is to become reality. Step six consists of planning the necessary actions for achieving the desired state—articulating the specific actions that must be taken to ensure the desired state is achieved. Step seven examines feasibility, cost-effectiveness, and intended and unintended consequences of the action plans generated in step six. Having the top executives and managers of an organization work through this process in a systematic way increases the likelihood that the desired future state will become reality, according to Beckhard and Harris.

We believe organization development practitioners need to become experts in strategic management *processes* and need to have more than just a cursory knowledge of strategic management *content*. Excellent sources for content are Michael Porter's books, *Competitive Strategy* and *Competitive Advantage*[12] and Benjamin Trego and John Zimmerman's *Top Management Strategy*.[13] Porter, an academic, has summarized, synthesized, and extended the field of strategic management. Tregoe and Zimmerman are practitioners who have worked with hundreds of top management teams helping them to develop strategic plans for their organizations. The works of the OD practitioners cited in this section and also material in the Tregoe and Zimmerman book give valuable insights for structuring strategic management processes for success.

Zand wrote in 1984 that there is considerable separation and often conflict between strategic management people and OD people in organizations.[14] As a result, strategic planning and implementation suffer. Zand calls for closer cooperation between these two fields which should be highly complementary. Greiner and Schein challenge OD practitioners to become more involved in the strategic management process—both to improve these activities in organizations and to build a power base for the practitioner.[15] We agree with all these authors: there needs to be a concerted effort on the part of OD theorists and practitioners to improve and expand the contribution organization development makes to the strategic management process.

We end this discussion of strategic management with an observation by Richard Beckhard:

> The autonomy of organizations is fast becoming a myth. Organization leaders are increasingly recognizing that the institutions they manage are truly *open* systems. Improve-

ment strategies based on looking at the internal structure, decision making, or intergroup relationships exclusively are an incomplete method of organization diagnosis and change strategy. A more relevant method for today's environment is to start by examining how the organization and its key subsystems relate to the different environments with which the organization interfaces.[16]

SURVEY FEEDBACK

An important and widely used intervention for organization development rests on the process of systematically collecting data about the system and feeding back the data for individuals and groups at all levels of the organization to analyze, interpret the meaning of, and design corrective action steps upon. These activities—which have two major components, the use of an attitude survey and the use of feedback workshops—are called *survey feedback*.

An attitude survey, if properly used, can be a powerful tool in organization improvement. Most attitude surveys are not used in an optimal way—at the maximum, most give top management some data for changing practices or provide an index against which to compare trends. At the minimum, they are filed away with little of consequence resulting. (See Figure 13–2 for a comparison of two approaches to the use of attitude surveys—the traditional approach and the survey feedback approach.) Symptomatic of the lack of knowledge about how to use surveys effectively is the fact that most textbooks on personnel management do not refer to systematic data feedback in connection with their use for organization improvement. Those texts that do comment on feedback do so in a most cursory way. For us, data collection is only part of the process; appropriate feedback is an equally significant aspect.

Research at the Institute for Social Research at the University of Michigan indicates that if the survey is to be optimally useful, the following steps must occur.[17]

Step 1. Organization members at the top of the hierarchy are involved in the preliminary planning.

Step 2. Data are collected from all organization members.

Step 3. Data are fed back to the top executive team and then down through the hierarchy in functional teams. Mann refers to this as an "interlocking chain of conferences."[18]

Step 4. Each superior presides at a meeting with his or her subordinates in which the data are discussed and in which (a) subordinates are asked to help interpret the data, (b) plans are made for making constructive changes, and (c) plans are made for the introduction of the data at the next lower level.

Step 5. Most feedback meetings include a consultant who has helped prepare the superior for the meeting and who serves as a resource person.

The conclusions regarding the usefulness of survey feedback grew out of a four-year program with a large organization. In the first phase, data were gathered from some

	Traditional Approach	Survey Feedback or OD Approach
Data collected from:	Rank and file, and maybe supervisors	Everyone in the system or subsystem
Data reported to:	Top management, department heads, and perhaps to employees through newspaper	Everyone who participated
Implications of data are worked on by:	Top management (maybe)	Everyone in work teams, with workshops starting at the top (all superiors with their subordinates)
Third-party intervention strategy:	Design and administration of questionnaire, development of a report	Obtaining concurrence on total strategy, design and administration of questionnaire, design of workshops, appropriate interventions in workshops
Action planning done by:	Top management only	Teams at all levels
Probable extent of change and improvement:	Low	High

Figure 13-2 Two Approaches to the Use of Attitude Surveys

8,000 employees throughout the company (1948). Comparable data were gathered two years later (1950) from the eight accounting departments, involving 800 employees and 78 supervisors. In this second phase, four of the eight departments carried on feedback activities as described earlier; two departments served as control groups with nothing further done after one all-department meeting; and two departments were eliminated from the design because of changes in key personnel. Two years later (1952), another survey was made and the researchers found that "more significant positive changes occurred in employee attitudes and perceptions in the four experimental departments than in the two control departments."[19] In particular, important changes occurred relative to how employees felt about "(1) the kind of work they do (job interest, importance, and level of responsibility); (2) their supervisor (ability to handle people, give recognition, direct their work, and represent them in handling complaints); (3) their progress in the company; and (4) their group's ability to get the job done."[20]

From our experience, feedback workshops take on many of the characteristics of team-building sessions but are less likely to deal with interpersonal matters. However, they frequently focus on leadership style or on matters pertaining to cooperation and teamwork. For example, the following two items were included in a questionnaire used by one of the authors:

Management sidesteps or evades things that bother people on the job

Strongly agree	Agree	Undecided	Disagree	Strongly disagree

There is good cooperation and teamwork in my work group

Strongly agree	Agree	Undecided	Disagree	Strongly disagree

In this questionnaire, items were included pertaining to "Organizational Climate," "Pay and Benefits," "Relations with Other Units," "Communications," "Supervisor/Employee Relations," "Performance Counseling," "My Job," "Pressure of Work," "Management by Objectives," "Opportunities for Personal Growth and Advancement," and "Training."

This kind of attitude survey, coupled with a series of workshops involving work teams at successively lower levels of the organization, can be used to create action plans and change across a wide range of variables in the social, structural, goal, and task subsystems of an organization. We think this approach has exciting possibilities because, in the words of Baumgartel (also quoted in Chapter 3), "*it deals with the system of human relationships as a whole. . . and it deals with each manager, supervisor, and employee in the context of his own job, his own problems, and his own work relationships.*"[21] This is the thrust that permeates most OD activities and is one of the dimensions that differentiates OD from traditional interventions in organizations.

A closer look at some of the underlying dynamics of survey feedback reveals why it works. The survey feedback technique is essentially a procedure for giving objective data about the system's functioning to the system members so that they can change or improve selected aspects of the system. The objective data are obtained by a survey; working with the data to improve the organization is done in feedback sessions. Frank Neff describes these feedback sessions as follows:

> This procedure, which has been called "feedback," was originally developed by Floyd C. Mann. It starts with the assumption that the organization is hierarchically structured. This structure can be thought of as a pyramid of "organizational families." Each family is composed of a supervisor and the people who report to him, starting with the president and going down through the "link-pins" (member of one family, head of the next lower) the first line supervisor and his subordinates. The information about the study unit (company, department, etc.) goes first to the head of that unit and then to his "family." Then the "family members" take the data to the subordinate family of which they are "heads." Through a series of conferences at each level, data are presented and discussed, down through this hierarchy of "families."[22]

The leaders of each work group guide the feedback presentation, the discussion, the diagnosis of problems based on the data, and the building of action steps to solve the problems. Usually a behavioral scientist consultant works with the leader, acting as a resource and facilitator.

Neff states that for organization improvement (change) to take place, three things must happen. First, the work group must *accept the data as valid*. Often people are defensive and resistant to data about their own organization. This must be overcome. Second, the work group must *accept responsibility* for the part they play in the problems identified. The leader plays a very important role in this regard—he or she should "model" behaviors indicating that the problem is "owned" by the leader and the group. Third, the work group must commit itself to *solving problems;* that is, its members must commit themselves to doing something about the problems. In summary, the work group must accept the data from the survey as valid, must accept responsibility for the problems identified, and must start solving the problems.

Bowers and Franklin state that the rationale for survey feedback, or what they also call "survey-guided development," is based on a model that views people as rational, cognitive, information processing individuals. Furthermore, when there are differences between a person's perceptions, these differences act as sources of motivation. New information leads to new perceptions that may be in conflict with old perceptions. In this way, new information becomes a force for changing perceptions and actions. Another basic assumption of survey-guided development is that human behavior is goal-seeking or goal-oriented. Bowers and Franklin describe how the goal-seeking process works:

> at least four elements are involved: (1) a model, (2) a goal, (3) an activity, and (4) feedback. The model is a mental picture of the surrounding world, including not only structural properties, but cause-and-effect relations. It is built by the person(s) from past accumulations of information, stored in memory. From the workings of the model and from the modeling process which he employs, alternative possible future states are generated, of which one is selected as a *goal.* At this point what is called the "goal selection system" ends and what is known as the "control system" *per se* begins. *Activities* are initiated to attain the goal, and *feedback,* which comes by some route from the person's environment, is used to compare, confirm, adjust, and correct responses by signaling departures from what was expected. [23]

A well-designed survey helps organization members to develop valid models of how organizations work and also provides information (feedback) about progress toward the goal.

Survey feedback has been shown to be an effective change technique in OD. In a longitudinal study evaluating the effects of different change techniques in 23 different organizations, survey feedback was found to be the most effective change strategy when compared with interpersonal process consultation, task process consultation, and laboratory training. [24] These results may be somewhat misleading, however, in that the survey feedback programs may have been more comprehensive than the other programs and the positive results may reflect the superiority of more comprehensive programs compared with less comprehensive ones. On the other hand, survey feedback is a cost-effective means of implementing a comprehensive program, thus making it a highly desirable change technique.

RENSIS LIKERT'S SYSTEM 4 MANAGEMENT

The survey feedback approach is closely related to a larger theory of management developed by Rensis Likert called System 4 Management.[25] System 4 Management provides some of the theoretical foundation for survey feedback, and survey feedback techniques are used as a part of System 4 interventions.

Likert's lifelong thrust has been that of building a scientifically based theory of management. He has collected data from hundreds of different organizations and from these data has constructed the System 4 Management theory, named after an ideal model of how to run the organization. Four different broad styles of management have been identified by Likert as forming a continuum, with autocratic, task-centered leadership at one end and democratic, participative, employee-centered leadership at the other. The autocratic end of the continuum represents System 1; the democratic end of the continuum represents System 4. Likert labels these systems as follows: System 1 is exploitative-authoritative; System 2 is benevolent-authoritative; System 3 is consultative; and System 4 is participative group. The type of management system prevalent in any organization can be determined by having the organization members complete questionnaires describing the organization's processes and climate.

Likert has consistently found that the most effective organizations show System 4 characteristics and the least effective organizations show System 1 and System 2 characteristics. Since effectiveness and System 4 Management go together, the implications for organization improvement are straightforward: move the management style of the organization from where it is (System 1 or 2) to System 4 and keep it at System 4. This is done by having the leaders manifest democratic, participative leadership styles while focusing on goal attainment, and also by building intact work groups into more effective teams.

A number of organizations have used the System 4 Management theory to guide their organization development efforts. A comprehensive organization change project involving the Weldon Company, a sleepwear manufacturing company, is one of the best OD programs reported in the literature.[26] In this project, massive changes were made in the organization work flow, incentive and reward systems, training programs, leadership styles, and utilization of all employees as resources for expertise. The results were impressive and significant: improvement in almost all aspects of the organization's functioning were reported and maintained over time.[27]

System 4 Management was also used to turn a General Motors assembly plant that had been a "loser" into a "winner." As reported by William Dowling, training sessions to inculcate the Likert theory, team-building sessions starting at the top of the organization and moving to lower levels, improved information and communication flows to the hourly employees, changes in the first-line supervisor's job, increased participation in job changes by the hourly employees, some newly constituted cross-functional teams, and new approaches to goal setting—all were used in this program that lasted several years.[28] Operating efficiency improved, grievances decreased, waste costs decreased, and other indicators showed impressive improvement.

We believe that Likert's theory is basically correct, that it can be translated into organization development interventions and programs, and that it represents a significant contribution both to management theory and to the theory of planned change. A theory-guided approach to organization development allows organization members and practitioners alike to have a cognitive map or model of the change process and the change goals.

GRID ORGANIZATION DEVELOPMENT

Perhaps the most thoroughgoing and systematic organization development program is that designed by Robert R. Blake and Jane S. Mouton, *Grid Organization Development.*[29] In a six-phase program lasting about three to five years, an organization can move systematically from the stage of examining managerial behavior and style to the development and implementation of an "ideal strategic corporate model." The program utilizes a considerable number of instruments, enabling individuals and groups to assess their own strengths and weaknesses; it focuses on skills, knowledge, and processes necessary for effectiveness at the individual, group, intergroup, and total-organization levels. The organizational program is conducted by internal members who have been pretrained in Grid concepts.

Basic to the Grid OD program are the concepts and methods of the Managerial Grid, also developed by Blake and Mouton, a two-dimensional schematic for examining and improving the managerial practices of individual managers.[30] One dimension underlying this diagnostic questionnaire is "concern for people"; the other dimension is "concern for production." The most effective managers are those who score high on both of these dimensions—a 9,9 position. A 9,9 management style is described as follows: "Work accomplishment is from committed people; interdependence through a 'common stake' in organization purpose leads to relationships of trust and respect."[31]

The relation between the Managerial Grid diagnostic questionnaire and Grid OD is explained by Blake and Mouton: "The single most significant premise on which Grid Organization Development rests is that the 9,9 way of doing business is acknowledged universally by managers as the soundest way to manage to achieve excellence."[32] As used in the Grid OD process, the managerial Grid questionnaire becomes one vehicle for individuals and groups to examine and explore their styles and modify prevailing practices.

Behavioral science concepts and rigorous business logic are combined in the Grid OD program's six phases. These phases are described as follows.[33]

Prephase 1. Before an organization (usually a business corporation) begins a Grid organization development program, selected key managers who will later be instructors in the organization attend a Grid Seminar. In this week-long experience-based laboratory, managers learn about Grid concepts, assess their own styles using the Managerial Grid questionnaire and the two-dimensional schematic, develop team action skills, learn problem-solving and critiquing skills, work at improved communication skills, and learn to analyze the culture of a team and of an organization. Learning takes place through the use of instruments, study team projects which are judged for adequacy, critiquing of individual and team performance, and conceptual inputs.

After several managers have gone to a Grid Seminar, some might go on to advanced Grid courses or for further exposure to the Grid OD approach. At a Grid OD Seminar, participants are taught the materials involved in phase 2 to 6. They learn both what the Grid OD program is all about and how to conduct it in their own company.

Another advanced course is the Instructor Development Seminar, in which participants actually learn to conduct an in-company phase 1 Grid Seminar. Training these managers in the various seminars accomplishes two things: the managers learn how to conduct a Grid OD program in their own organization, and they can also evaluate the Grid approach to determine whether or not they think it is a good idea for their organization to embark on such a course of action.

If, at this point, the company decides to implement a Grid organization development program, it might conduct a *pilot* phase 1 program for volunteer managers. If the result of this is a "go" signal, then phase 1 begins.

Phase 1: The Managerial Grid. In this phase, a Grid Seminar, conducted by in-company managers, is given to all the managers of the organization. The focus of the training is similar to that just described: attention is given to assessing an individual's managerial styles; problem-solving, critiquing, and communication skills are practiced; the skills of synergistic teamwork are learned and practiced. In this phase, managers learn to become 9,9 managers.

Phase 2: Teamwork Development. The focus of this phase is work teams in the organization. The goal is *perfecting* teamwork in the organization through analysis of team culture, traditions, and the like and also developing skills in planning, setting objectives, and problem solving. Additional aspects of this phase include feedback given to each manager about his or her individual and team behavior; this critique allows the manager to understand how others see his or her strengths and weaknesses in the team's working.

Working on teamwork is done in the context of actual work problems. The problems and issues dealt with are the real ones of the team. In this process of phase 2, individuals learn how to study and manage the culture of their work teams.

Phase 3: Intergroup Development. The focus of this phase is intergroup relations, and the goal of this phase is to move groups from their ineffective, often win-lose *actual* ways of relating between groups toward an *ideal* model of intergroup relations. The dynamics of intergroup cooperation and competition are explored. Each group separately analyzes what an ideal relationship would be like; these are shared between groups. Action steps to move toward the ideal are developed and assigned to individuals. The phase thus includes building operational plans for moving the two groups from their actual state to an ideal state of intergroup relations.

The phase consists of teams convening, in twos, to work on the issues stated above. Not all teams would pair with all others; only teams that have particularly important interface relationships do so. Often only selected members of the teams take part in the exercises and activities. These are the people who are closely work related with the other team.

Phase 4: Developing an Ideal Strategic Corporate Model. In this phase the focus shifts to corporate strategic planning, with the goals being to learn the concepts and the skills of corporate logic necessary to achieve corporate excellence. The top-management group engages in the strategy planning activities of this phase, although their plans and ideas are tested, evaluated, and critiqued in conjunction with other corporate members. The charge to the top-management group is to design an ideal strategic corporate model that would define what the corporation would be like if it were truly excellent. Fact-finding, technical inputs and so on may be contributed from all persons in the organization.

Using the comparisons of ideal corporate logic versus real corporate logic, the top-management team is better able to recognize what aspects of the culture must be changed to achieve excellence.

In a process that may take up to a year, the top executives build the ideal strategic corporate model *for their particular organization.* This is the model used in the next phase.

Phase 5: Implementing the Ideal Strategic Model. In several different steps, the organization seeks to implement the model of corporate excellence developed in phase 4. To execute the conversion to the ideal strategic model, the organization must be reorganized. Logical components of the corporation are designated (these might be profit centers, geographical locations, product lines, etc.). Each component appoints a planning team whose job is to examine every phase of the component's operation to see how the business may be moved more in line with the ideal model. Every concept of the ideal strategic corporate model is studied by the planning team for its implications for the component. In addition, a phase 5 coordinator is appointed to act as a resource to the planning teams.

The planning teams thus conduct ''conversion studies'' to see how the components must change to fit the ideal strategic corporate model. An additional planning team is formed and is given the charge of designing a headquarters that would operate effectively and yet keep overhead to a minimum. After the planning and assessment steps are completed, conversion of the organization to the ideal condition is implemented.

Phase 6: Systematic Critique. In this phase the results of the Grid OD program, from prephase 1 to postphase 5, are measured. Systematic critiquing, measuring, and evaluating lead to knowledge of what progress has been made, what barriers still exist and must be overcome, and what new opportunities have developed that may be exploited. This phase is begun after phase 5 is going well and is beginning to convert the organization well along toward the ideal model. Taking stock of where the corporation has been, how far it has come, and where it currently is thus represents a ''new beginning'' from which to continue striving toward corporate excellence.

Grid organization development is an approach to organization improvement that is complete and systematic and difficult. Does it work? Blake, Mouton, Barnes, and Greiner evaluated the results of a Grid OD program conducted in a large plant that was part of a very large multiplant company. The 800 managers and staff personnel of the 4,000-person work force at the plant were all given training in the Managerial Grid and Grid OD concepts. Significant organizational improvements showed up on such ''bottom-line'' measures as greater profits, lower costs, and less waste.[34] Managers themselves, when asked about their own effectiveness and that of their corporation, likewise declared that changes for the better had resulted from the program.

THE CONTINGENCY THEORY OF LAWRENCE AND LORSCH

On the basis of research comparing effective and ineffective business organizations in three different industries, Paul Lawrence and Jay Lorsch of the Harvard Business School concluded that *different external environments required different organization structures* and that effective organizations had a good "fit" between structure and environment while ineffective organizations did not.[35] The external environment is the world the organization must operate in. Environments can be certain or uncertain; that is, they can be predictable or not, and they can be diverse or homogeneous. For example, the environment of the plastics industry is highly uncertain and diverse; the environment of the container industry is certain and homogeneous. Organization structure refers to how the work is divided up and how the different groups in the organization—for example, manufacturing, research and development, and marketing—relate to one another. The appropriate structure for any organization is *contingent* upon the environment the organization is operating in.

Specifically, the environment determines requirements for *differentiation* within and among work units (departments), and *integration* within and among work units. *Differentiation* is defined as "*the difference in cognitive and emotional orientation among managers in different functional departments.*"[36] Lawrence and Lorsch measured four dimensions on which managers can have different orientations; orientation toward particular goals, time orientation, interpersonal orientation, and formality of structure. Different work units will differ and should differ in their orientations to these four dimensions, depending on the environment. *Integration* is defined as "*the quality of the state of collaboration that exists among departments that are required to achieve unity of effort by the demands of the environment.*"[37] Different environments require (1) different amounts of integration and (2) integration between different work units.

Contingency theory carries implications for organization effectiveness and, by extension, implications for organization development. According to contingency theory, if one wants to improve the effectiveness of an organization, one must ensure that there is the right "fit" between organization structure—as indicated by differentiation and integration—and the environment. In general, certain and homogeneous environments require less differentiation and integration, while uncertain and diverse environments require more differentiation and integration. The steps to improve organization functioning using contingency theory are the following: first, measure the key constructs or variables—environment, differentiation, and integration; second, assess the fit between the organization structure variables and the environment; and, third, make the necessary adjustments in the organization structure variables to improve the goodness of fit with the environment.

Contingency theory is very popular with management and organization theorists and is becoming increasingly popular with OD practitioners. Although specific interventions to implement the contingency theory have not been formally developed, ad hoc interventions have been used in the several OD programs based on the theory. To implement contingency theory, differentiation must be either increased or decreased and/or integration must be either increased or decreased, depending on the environment. Usually the focus of attention is on achieving more integration or on achieving integration between selected work units. The interventions to achieve this have been cross-functional task forces, project teams, matrix team arrangements, and the like. These *structural* changes are sufficient to cause changes in the amount and quality of integration.

Lawrence and Lorsch's contingency theory was used to guide the OD efforts in the Electronic Products Division of the Corning Glass Works Corporation.[38] The theory was translated into the following implications: "A business that is cyclical, unpredictable, and rapidly changing calls for an organization characterized by a high degree of integration and the formulation of decisions as close to the point of execution as possible."[39] The implications were translated into the following activities: intergroup confrontation meetings were held between work units; the marketing department people were given roles as "integrators" between other work units; project teams were formed, made up of middle-level managers from different functional units, and the teams were assigned the task of developing new products. Later some "super" project teams were established. The results, after some difficulties, were positive: more new products were introduced in one year than had been introduced in the previous five years. Much of the credit was given to the OD program, which was predicated on the contingency theory of Lawrence and Lorsch.

SUMMARY

In this chapter we have examined OD interventions of a comprehensive nature. These interventions differ in scope, but they can all be applied to changing the total organization. Generally speaking, the interventions discussed in this chapter rest on more solid theoretical bases than do many of the other OD interventions.

NOTES

1. Richard Beckhard, "The Confrontation Meeting," *Harvard Business Review,* 45 (March–April 1967), pp. 149–155.
2. Ibid., p. 150.
3. This discussion represents paraphrasing, ibid., p. 154.
4. Ibid., p. 154.
5. Ibid., p. 153.
6. Dan E. Schendel and Charles W. Hofer, eds., *Strategic Management* (Boston: Little, Brown, 1979), p. 14.
7. Charles E. Summer, *Strategic Behavior in Business and Government* (Boston: Little, Brown, 1980), chap. 10.
8. Thomas H. Rogers, "Strategic Planning: A Major OD Intervention," in *American Society for Training and Development,* ASTD Publications, 1981, pp. 50–55.
9. Ibid., p. 52.
10. See Charles Krone, "Open Systems Redesign," in John Adams, ed., *Theory and Management in Organization Development: An Evolutionary Process* (Roslyn, Va.: NTL Institute, 1974); and G. K. Jayaram, "Open Systems Planning," in W. G. Bennis, K. D. Benne, R. Chin, and K. Cory, eds. *The Planning of Change,* 3rd ed. (New York: Holt, Rinehart and Winston, 1976), pp. 275–283. This discussion is based primarily on Jayaram's article.
11. R. Beckhard and R. T. Harris, *Organizational Transitions: Managing Complex Change,* (Reading, Mass.: Addison-Wesley, 1977).
12. Michael Porter, *Competitive Strategy,* (New York: The Free Press, 1980), and *Competitive Advantage,* (New York: The Free Press, 1985).
13. B. B. Tregoe and J. W. Zimmerman, *Top Management Strategy,* (New York: Simon and Schuster, 1980).
14. Dale E. Zand, "Organization Development and Strategic Management," *OD Newsletter,* Winter, 1984, pp. 1, 6–7.

15. Larry E. Greiner and Virginia E. Schein, "A Revisionist Look at Power and OD," *The Industrial-Organizational Psychologist,* 1988, Vol. 25, No. 2, pp. 59–61.

16. Richard Beckhard, "Strategies for Large System Change," in K. Benne, L. Bradford, J. Gibb, and R. Lippitt, eds., *Laboratory Method of Changing and Learning* (Palo Alto, Calif.: Science and Behavior Books, 1975). p. 231.

17. Floyd C. Mann, "Studying and Creating Change," in W. G. Bennis, K. D. Benne, and R. Chin, eds., *The Planning of Change* (New York: Holt, Rinehart and Winston, 1961), pp.605–613.

18. Ibid., p. 609.

19. Ibid., p. 611.

20. Ibid., p. 611.

21. Howard Baumgartel, "Using Employee Questionnaire Results for Improving Organizations: The Survey 'Feedback' Experiment," *Kansas Business Review,* 12 (December 1959), p. 6. [Baumgartel's emphasis.]

22. Frank W. Neff, "Survey Research: A Tool for Problem Diagnosis and Improvement in Organizations," in A. W. Gouldner and S. M. Miller, eds., *Applied Sociology* (New York: Free Press, 1966), pp. 23–38. This quotation is from page 28.

23. David G. Bowers and Jerome L. Franklin, "Survey-Guided Development: Using Human Resources Measurement in Organizational Change," *Journal of Contemporary Business,* 1, No. 3 (Summer 1972), pp. 43–55. This passage is taken from page 48.

24. David G. Bowers, "OD Techniques and Their Results in 23 Organizations: The Michigan ICL Study," *Journal of Applied Behavioral Science,* 9, No. 1 (1973), pp. 21–43.

25. See Rensis Likert's two major statements of the theory, *New Patterns of Management* (New York: McGraw-Hill, 1961), and *The Human Organization* (New York: McGraw-Hill, 1967). See also Rensis Likert and Jane Gibson Likert, *New Ways of Managing Conflict* (New York: McGraw-Hill, 1976).

26. See Alfred Marrow, David Bowers, and Stanley Seashore, *Management by Participation* (New York: Harper & Row, 1967), for a full account of the program.

27. See ibid.; and also Stanley Seashore and David Bowers, "Durability of Organizational Change," *American Psychologist,* 25, No. 3, March, 1970, pp. 227–233.

28. William F. Dowling, "System 4 Builds Performance and Profits," *Organizational Dynamics,* 3, No. 3 (Winter 1975), pp. 23–38.

30. R. R. Blake and J. S. Mouton, *The Managerial Grid* (Houston: Gulf, 1964). See also *The New Managerial Grid* (Gulf, 1978).

31. Blake and Mouton, *Building a Dynamic Corporation,* p. 61.

32. Ibid., p. 63.

33. This discussion is based on ibid., pp. 76–109.

34. R. R. Blake, J. S. Mouton, L. B. Barnes, and L. E. Greiner, "Breakthrough in Organization Development," *Harvard Business Review,* 42 (November–December 1964), pp. 133–155.

35. Paul R. Lawrence and Jay W. Lorsch, *Organization and Environment* (Cambridge, Mass.: Harvard University Press, 1967).

36. Ibid., p. 11. [Lawrence and Lorsch's emphasis.]

37. Ibid., p. 11. [Lawrence and Lorsch's emphasis.]

38. See William F. Dowling, "The Corning Approach to Organization Development," *Organizational Dynamics,* Spring 1975, pp. 16–34, for an overview and evaluation of the Corning project. See also articles by practitioners involved in the project: Edgar F. Huse and Michael Beer, "Eclectic Approach to Organizational Development," *Harvard Business Review,* 49 (September–October 1971), pp. 103–112; and Michael Beer and Edgar F. Huse, "A System Approach to Organization Development," *Journal of Applied Behavioral Science,* 8, No. 1 (1972), pp. 79–101.

39. Dowling, "The Corning Approach to Organization Development," p. 24.

14

STRUCTURAL INTERVENTIONS AND OD

a descriptive inventory of OD interventions

In this chapter we will examine what we call "structural interventions," a shorthand term we will use for the broad class of interventions or change efforts aimed at improving organization effectiveness through changes in the task, structural, and technological subsystems (see Chapter 5, Relevant Systems Concepts). This class of interventions includes changes in how the overall work of the organization is divided into units, who reports to whom, methods of control, the spatial arrangements of equipment and people, work flow and procedures, and role definitions. In particular, we want to examine certain interventions that are frequently discussed in connection with OD: job enrichment, quality circles, management by objectives (MBO), sociotechnical systems, and a unique form of task force called the "collateral organization," as well as some interventions pertaining to "physical settings."

SUGGESTED CRITERIA FOR CONGRUENCY/ INCONGRUENCY WITH OD

Although changes in structure are frequent outcomes of an OD effort, most programs targeted from the outset at structural change are not OD as we have defined the field. Interventions such as job enrichment, MBO, the formation of work teams congruent with a particular technology, and changes in work rules are often applied without much diagnosis and planning and are often "installed" without participation of the relevant work groups and/or the job incumbents. In such cases there is an absence of most or all of the participant action research continuum of preliminary diagnosis, data gathering from client groups, data feedback to client groups, data exploration and depth diagnosis by client groups, and action planning and action by client groups. Furthermore, such structural interventions may or may not include other features that make up the *gestalt* we have called OD, such as the use of a facilitator or change agent and attention to system ramifications. Implicit in this statement is that *collaborative diagnosis* and *collaborative action planning* loom large in OD but may or may not be a feature in various versions of structural interventions.

Figure 14–1 delineates roughly various improvement strategies in terms of the extent to which they approximate the gestalt of ingredients we see in OD. These ingredients are represented by the right-hand side of the scale: a process and group emphasis; the use of a particular kind of action research model, including use of the facilitator role, extensive participation; and a heuristic, long-range approach to change. Obviously, a two-dimensional scale cannot adequately portray five dimensions, but this scale should provide some visualization of how various techniques tend to cluster along a scale based on an amalgamation of relatively mutually consistent variables.

The farther we move to the left-hand side of the scale, the more the emphasis is on tasks and on the individual, the more the consulting mode is of the "expert" variety, or "analysis for the top,"[1] the more the diagnosis and implementation are unilateral, and the more the change is a fairly immediate phenomenon. (Structural changes such as a unilateral job enrichment program may occur fairly quickly; structural changes growing out of OD interventions are likely to take more time.) Improvement techniques to the left of the scale, points 1 to 3, we see as generally incongruent with OD. (Traditional forms of MBO are farther toward the right than are unilateral versions of job enrichment because the former typically include subordinate-superior dialogue.) Items toward the middle of the scale, point 4, we see as generally congruent with OD. Some interventions, for example, the Rushton Mine experiment to be discussed later in the chapter, which include the concept of self-managed work teams, begin to have one or more OD-like features.

Items on points 5, 6, and 7 either are OD or are highly congruent with OD. Point 7 includes "comprehensive OD," by which we mean the utilization of a variety of types of OD interventions including team building, which are parts of an internally consistent, long-range improvement strategy. "Survey feedback plus other OD interventions" is essentially the same as comprehensive OD except that questionnaires are extensively used in contrast to interviews. The six phases of Grid OD, also at point 7 on the scale, have all the elements of comprehensive OD. Point 7 includes some quality of work life programs (QWL) because they include multiple forms of OD interventions. Indeed, some QWL programs are essentially synonymous with OD, and vice versa.

This does not mean that unilateral action, a focus on individuals or task dimensions, or an "analysis for the top" can never occur while an OD effort is evolving, but it does mean that if a major change effort having such features is being undertaken simultaneously with an OD effort, there is likely to be a great deal of confusion, resistance, and wasted effort. For example, attempting to launch a participative OD effort simultaneously with an autocratic version of an MBO effort will create a great deal of resistance and cynicism relative to one or both. And a history of unilaterally imposed change efforts will create resistance to any new efforts, participative or otherwise. We will now take a look at several structural change efforts in turn.

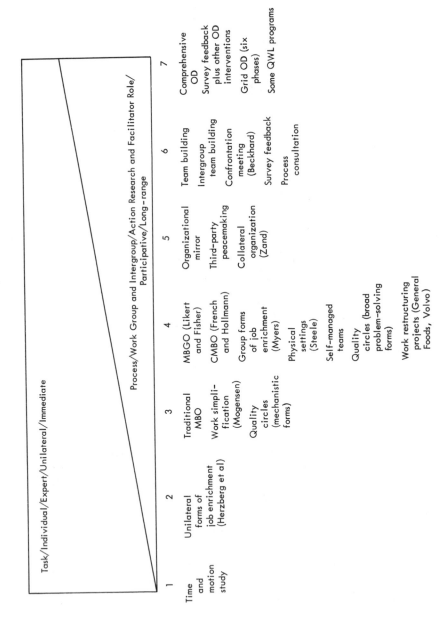

Figure 14-1 Emphases in Different Improvement Strategies

JOB DESIGN

The design of jobs, that is, intervening in the task subsystem, has been a popular domain of the consultant since the days of Frederick Taylor and the "scientific management" movement. In recent years the thrust of that movement has been reversed, with considerable attention being paid to "job enlargement" and, most recently, to "job enrichment." Both *can be,* but are not necessarily, congruent with organization development interventions. Even some offshoots of scientific management, such as work simplification, can be congruent with OD.

For clarification, a distinction needs to be made between (1) job enrichment, or vertical job enlargement, and (2) horizontal job enlargement. The latter simply adds activities, such as soldering three connections instead of one, whereas job enrichment (vertical job enlargement), as described by Myers, increases the proportion of planning and controlling components to the "doing" components of the job. (See Figure 14-2.[2])

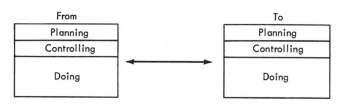

Figure 14-2   Job Enrichment (Vertical Job Enlargement)

In another significant work, Hackman and Oldham conceptualize job components differently, focusing on "skill variety," "task identity," "task significance," "autonomy," and "feedback from the job."[3] Frequent by-products of job enrichment efforts are either the elimination of a layer of supervision or a reconceptualization of the role of the supervisor.

Organization development activities inherently incorporate some job enrichment features, since the process clearly includes some additional subordinate planning and controlling, particularly in group situations, that were not present before. Paradoxically, however, the "doing" aspects of jobs may become narrower or more routine. For example, an office work team may recommend and plan the elimination of some tasks that have become unnecessary, thus reducing the variety of tasks or even the complexity of the jobs.

In what might be called a team problem-solving approach to job enrichment at Texas Instruments, these kinds of shifts in the planning, the controlling, and the doing aspects have occurred through the way the company has gone about the use of work simplification techniques, based on Allan Mogensen's pioneering concepts. Work simplification at TI has expanded on Mogensen's participative approach and has involved supervisors and subordinates in problem-solving meetings in which they explore ways to eliminate unncessary steps in production and to make tasks more efficient. In these meetings, work teams also decide who will perform which tasks, and they frequently divide up the work so that each member will have a mixture of challenging tasks along with the more repetitive tasks. And this process is supplemented by the work team's participating in goal setting.[4]

Relative to the dimensions in Figure 14-1, we find considerable use of the action research model in Myer's description of job enrichment at TI, including soliciting the employee's advice about the design of jobs and about their relationship to the larger task subsystem. Thus there is considerable team diagnosis and planning. Overall, the effort is highly congruent with OD and perhaps can be considered an OD intervention.

However, job enrichment activities are not necessarily congruent with organization development as we defined it. Herzberg and others, contrary to the practices at Texas Instruments cited, almost seem to say that job enrichment *should* be imposed from topside:

> So far as the process of job enrichment itself is concerned, experimental constraints in the studies dictated that there could be no participation by jobholders themselves in deciding what changes were to be made in their jobs. The changes nevertheless seemed to be effective. On the other hand, when people were invited to participate—not in any of the reported studies—results were disappointing. In one case, for example, a group of personnel specialists suggested fewer than 30 fairly minor changes in their jobs, whereas their managers had compiled a list of over 100 much more substantial possibilities.
>
> It seems that employees themselves are not in a good position to test out the validity of the boundaries of their jobs. So long as the aim is not to measure experimentally the effects of job enrichment alone, there is undoubtedly benefit in the sharing of ideas.[5]

Again referring to Figure 14–1, and if we limit our analysis to the two paragraphs quoted, we infer that there was very little use of a participative, action research model and a great deal of unilateral action. Before we would conclude that Herzberg's experiments were really all that unilateral, however, we would want to know much more about the preliminary stages of his job enrichment programs. More joint diagnosis and joint planning may be involved than is immediately evident. In some organizations, task specialization may have proceeded so far that a joint diagnosis of the problem may have been occurring in the informal system for some time, and a unilateral restructuring of jobs may be met with considerable relief.

Although we would hypothesize that a job enrichment effort growing out of an action research (OD) mode would usually have a much higher chance of success than a unilaterally planned and imposed one, our main purpose here has been to show that some job enrichment efforts may be highly congruent with organization development and some may not. It depends upon *what processes are used* in their adoption and utilization.[6]

QUALITY CIRCLES

The ''quality control circle'' or ''quality circle'' concept is similar to the group problem-solving, goal-setting form of job enrichment except that the primary focus tends to be on maintaining and enhancing product quality. The process is essentially the same.

Quality circles have been extensively used in Japan since the introduction of quality control techniques there in the 1950s and 1960s by Edward Deming and Joseph Juran of New York University and A. W. Feigenbaum of General Electric.[7] It is reported that Kaoru Ishikawa of Tokyo University integrated these techniques with the theories of American behavioral scientists such as Maslow, McGregor, and Herzberg, and thus, the quality circle was born.[8]

The Lockheed Missile and Space Company appears to be the first American firm to study the emerging Japanese approach and to implement an extensive program.[9]

Some 500 American firms were experimenting with quality circles as of 1980,[10] and the movement has grown rapidly since then, particularly in large firms. In 1985 it was estimated that over 90 percent of the Fortune 500 companies were utilizing quality circles, including such firms as Honeywell, Digital Equipment, TRW, and Westinghouse.[11]

Quality circles usually include a group of 7 to 10 employees from a unit (or across units) who have volunteered to meet together regularly to analyze and make proposals about product quality and other problems. Recommendations are forwarded to a coordinating or steering committee; meetings are typically held once a week for an hour on company time. Usually the meetings are chaired by a supervisor, but the circles are sometimes chaired by an employee elected from the group. Leaders are encouraged to create a high degree of participation within the group.

Prior to the formation of quality circles, those supervisors who have volunteered to participate are trained by quality control experts and facilitators in such matters as quality control concepts, including the necessary statistical tools, in leading participative group discussions, and in group dynamics and communications skills. In turn, the supervisors, with the help of facilitators, train those subordinates who volunteer to participate. The facilitators also help each circle in its linking with other groups and with the overall coordinating committee. Groups are encouraged to use experts from within the organization when their specialities are relevant and are frequently authorized by management to make changes without higher authority whenever feasible. Once or twice a year, a member of higher management meets with each group.[12]

Favorable results have generally been reported in the popular and technical media. In the first three years of Lockheed's experimentation with the process, the company was reported to have saved six dollars for every one it spent on the process, and defects in manufacturing declined by two-thirds. Morale and job satisfaction among participants were reported to have increased.[13] At Nippon Kokon K.K., where thousands of employees are involved in quality control circles, savings were reported of some $86 million in one year, stemming from suggestions emerging from the groups.[14]

Favorable results have also been reported through the use of cross-functional (or multi-functional) quality circle teams at such organizations as Ford and IBM. The latter has an extensive program using ''Process Improvement Teams'' whose members are drawn from multiple functions.[15]

Congruence between OD and major dimensions of quality circles is apparent. To the extent that subordinates are working with supervisors in participative group settings or in multi-functional teams on mutually identified problems, there is a use of a facilitator and attention to group dynamics and interpersonal communications skills, the process is highly congruent with OD. Even more congruence is present in those circumstances in which there is participative diagnosis and problem solving of a broader nature than focusing solely on quality control matters and in which intergroup issues are worked both horizontally and vertically in the organizational hierarchy.

In some companies, quality circles are more mechanistic than we have described in the sense that there is high emphasis on statistical techniques, almost exclusive focus on quality, little attention to group process, and meetings are ''run by the book.'' These forms of quality circles we see as less congruent with OD (see Figure 14–1), but they can be modified, of course, to be more congruent.[16]

MBO AND APPRAISAL

To be congruent with the OD effort, goal-setting and performance review processes should have a team thrust and should be both participative and transactional. By *participative and transactional* we mean that in goal setting, subordinates should have meaningful ways to provide inputs; and in reviewing performance, a collaborative examination of the major significant forces in the situation needs to be made, including the superior's and the team's impact on the subordinate's performance, not just an appraisal of the subordinate's performance. In addition to being different on the unilateral-participative scale, various MBO programs can also be differentiated as to whether they reinforce a team leadership style or a one-on-one style.

In their more congruent forms, MBO programs evolve from a collaborative organization diagnosis and are systems of joint target setting and performance review designed to increase a focus on objectives and to increase the frequency of problem-solving discussions between supervisors and subordinates and within work teams. (Such versions would be approximately in the middle of the scale shown in Figure 14–1.) In their least congruent forms, MBO programs are unilateral, autocratic mechanisms designed to force compliance with a superior's directives and, in the process, reinforce a one-on-one leadership mode. (Such versions would be on the left-hand side of the scale in Figure 14–1; most versions are probably at about point 2 or 3.)

Our hunch is that many MBO programs are imposed by line managers or promoted by personnel/human resources departments without much diagnosis of the problem to be solved. If there is some diagnosis, we suspect it is a diagnosis made by a very few people. Furthermore, our impression is that most MBO programs do not use a team approach, that they do not provide for sufficient acknowledgment of the interdependency between jobs, and that rather than helping examine team culture, they tend to intensify dysfunctional competition within teams.[17]

If an MBO effort is to avoid some of these deficiencies, and if it is to avoid being punitive or overly constraining, we think it should include such ingredients as the following. We call this "Collaborative Management by Objectives" or CMBO:[18]

1. A collaborative diagnosis of organizational problems, from which it is concluded that a collaborative MBO effort would be functional.
2. Increased skills in interpersonal communications and group processes. (This will be crucial to the team aspects of this approach.)
3. Real subordinate participation, in team configurations, in setting goals.
4. A team approach to reviewing individual and group targets and their achievement.
5. Ongoing individual and team problem-solving discussions with superiors.
6. A continuous helping relationship within teams and in superior-subordinate relationships. (This will not occur quickly; a climate that says "Let's try to help each other succeed" [win-win] needs to emerge.)
7. Attention to personal and career goals in a real effort to make these complementary to organizational goals.

There is some research evidence to support arguments for some of these ingredients. Research at General Electric, for example, found that criticism by the superior tended to produce defensiveness and impaired performance, that goal setting and mutual goal setting between superior and subordinate were associated with improved performance, and that coaching needed to be a day-to-day activity.[19] A follow-up study at General Electric found that appraisals went better in a climate promoting trust, openness, support, and development.[20] Research in a public utility also found the organizational climate dimension of support to be a critical factor in the perceived success of MBO efforts.[21]

Likert and Fisher describe a participative, team approach to MBO in use in a retail division of a consumer products organization and in an automobile plant. They report impressive increases in contribution to corporate profits in the retail sales division and substantially increased productivity and reduced scrap and rejects in the automobile plant. They call the approach Management by Group Objectives (MBGO).[22]

SOCIOTECHNICAL SYSTEMS AND WORK RESTRUCTURING

The term *sociotechnical systems* is largely associated with experiments that have emerged under the auspices of the Tavistock Institute in Britain or have stemmed from the Tavistock approach. These efforts have generally attempted to develop a better "fit" among the technology, the structure, and the social interaction of a particular production unit in a mine, a factory, or an office.

One of the earliest studies was in British coal mining where the consultant-researchers found that by reintroducing a team approach to mining coal, broadening job scope, and providing team pay incentives, a number of benefits accrued, including improved productivity, safety, and morale.[23] An experiment in India in a textile weaving mill also utilized increased job scope and semiautonomous work groups with beneficial consequences.[24] Other experiments and research with semiautonomous work groups have occurred in Norway and Sweden[25] as well as in the United States. Terms like "self-managed groups," "self-managing groups," and "self-regulating groups" are gradually replacing the term "semiautonomous groups."

The more recent heritage of these experiments has been the emergence of *work restructuring* projects such as at the Volvo plants in Sweden, and the General Foods pet food plant at Topeka, Kansas. Common characteristics have been the use of semiautonomous work teams, participative decision making, considerable team autonomy in planning and controlling production and in screening new team members, and pay geared to the number of tasks mastered by each team member.[26] These experiments overlap with programs that have emerged under the rubric of "quality of work life" and have sometimes been given that label.

QUALITY OF WORK LIFE PROJECTS

The term quality of work life (QWL) has been applied to a wide variety of organizational improvement efforts. The common elements seem to be, as Goodman indicates, an "attempt to restructure multiple dimensions of the organization" and to "institute a mechanism which introduces and sustains changes over time."[27] Aspects of the change mechanism are usually an increase in participation by employees in shop floor decisions and an increase in problem-solving between the union and management.

At some General Motors plants, QWL projects have included some of the following features:

Voluntary involvement on the part of employees

Union agreement with the process and participation in it

Assurance of no loss of jobs as a result of the programs

Training of employees in team problem solving

The use of quality circles where employees discuss problems affecting the performance of the plant and the work environment

Work team participation in forecasting, work planning, and team leader and team member selection

Regular plant and team meetings to discuss such matters as quality, safety, customer orders, and schedules

Encouragement of skill development and job rotation within work teams

Skill training

Responsiveness to employee concerns[28]

While the specifics vary from one QWL project to another, both within a given organization and between organizations, several features tend to be common. These features include union involvement; a focus on work teams; problem-solving sessions by work teams in which the agenda may include productivity, quality, and safety problems; autonomy in planning work; the availability of skill training; and increased responsiveness to employees by supervision.

Although many of these QWL projects have had at least modest success, frequently there have been difficulties in sustaining or expanding the process beyond a few years. Some of the reasons, according to Goodman, include changes in union leadership, expectations that were too high, efforts aimed at production and clerical levels with insufficient attention to changes at the managerial and professional levels, and too little attention to long-term financial rewards for the participants.[29] Major resistance from supervisors has frequently occurred when top management has paid insufficient attention to issues of job security and role definition for people at this level.[30]

An example of a QWL project that had some success, yet ran into some of these difficulties, is the experiment at the Rushton Coal Mine in Phillipsburg, Pennsylvania. This experiment, drawing on both Tavistock and American QWL experience, began in 1973 under joint sponsorship by the United Mine Workers and the mine management. The project involved a consulting team headed by Eric Trist who had been involved in the early Tavistock sociotechnical studies and an independent evaluation team headed by Paul Goodman of Carnegie-Mellon University. Basically, the early phases of the experiment, which had safety improvement as the prime objective, and was called a "quality of work program," included the following features:[31]

1. An agreement to the experiment by the president of the company and the president of the United Mine Workers

2. A steering committee comprised of management and local union officers, which met once a week for four months to diagnose the work performance and structure of the mine and to make recommendations

3. Ratification of the emerging plan by the union membership

4. The creation of an experimental section in the mine, involving 27 volunteers constituting a crew of nine for each of three shifts

5. Top pay for all participants, since all would eventually learn all the jobs, including the higher-classified ones

6. Training of all crew members in all jobs of the section, including the jobs of miner operator and helper, roof bolter, shuttle car operator, mechanic, and support person

7. Special training in state and federal mine laws

8. The supervisors to be responsible for safety, on-the-job training, and planning, but not direct supervision of production

9. The crew members to be responsible for the production of coal, and any initial handling of grievances

10. The production to be calculated on a 24-hour basis rather than by shift so as to enhance cooperation between shift crews

11. Training to be provided by the consultants in group problem solving

12. Consultant team assistance to various committees and to supervisors and members of management in meetings to discuss labor-management relations, safety training, the resolution of conflicts, and communications

13. Attendance by the consultant-researchers at union meetings when the project was discussed

14. Preliminary discussions about how any gains would be shared between company and workers

Around the end of the first year of the experiment, reports indicated that:

1. There were fewer violations of the Federal Coal Mine Health and Safety Act in the experimental section in contrast to the other two conventionally operated sections of the mine.

2. Accident and absenteeism rates were lower than those of one conventionally operated section and equal to those of the other section.

3. Crew members perceived themselves as having more job autonomy and perceived supervisors as making fewer decisions about how the work was to be performed.

4. Crew members recognized their interdependence and believed that coworkers had many useful ideas.

5. There was increased job satisfaction and cooperation. One miner, for example, expressed his feelings as follows:

   Suddenly, we felt we mattered to somebody. Somebody trusted us. . . . The funny thing is, in the new system, the crew, we don't really get tired any more. We probably work twice as hard as we did before, but we don't get tired. . . . It's like you feel you're somebody, like you feel you're a professional, like you got a profession you're proud of. . . all 27 guys in all three shifts.[32]

6. The first measurement of results, at the end of about a year, for a one-month period, showed that the experimental section had mined about 25 percent more coal than the poorest section and that its operating costs were 40 percent lower than the poorest section's. The cost of clean coal produced for that month was $1.16 per ton for the experimental section, while the cost was $1.87 for the mine as a whole and $2.74 per ton for the poorest section.[33]

Although the improvement project ran into difficulty when union members voted down a proposal to extend the experiment to the whole mine—the researchers later concluded that, among other mistakes, those workers not directly involved in the first experiment had not been kept adequately informed and that the experiment had not been expanded fast enough.[34] An additional analysis by Goodman suggests that a lack of real consensus on the part of management and union leadership groups as to the desirability of the plan, among other factors, was a serious handicap to the diffusion of the experiment throughout the mine. By 1979, the quality of work program was not functioning at Rushton, although a number of benefits remained, including a more highly trained work force and improved safety practices. Further, a wage incentive plan was under consideration at that time.[35]

In contrast to some job enrichment and MBO efforts that are unilaterally imposed and do not have a work team focus, the Rushton experiment had a fairly high component of collaboration, at least initially between company management and the union, and had a high emphasis on work teams. Of course, the sociotechnical/QWL experiment occurred in the context of a decade of rapidly declining productivity in coal mining and increased concerns about safety in the United States and undoubtedly started with an assumption, based on the Tavistock studies, that job restructuring (i.e., the creation of semiautonomous, interdependent work teams) would be more appropriate than traditional practices involving highly differentiated jobs under the direct guidance of a supervisor. This assumption was, in effect, subscribed to at the outset by the company president and the international union officers. To contrast this to OD, while the OD process does not make the assumption that a given job structure is best, it does make the comparable assumption that a team approach has high merit, particularly under circumstances where interdependency and mutual support are important.[36]

THE COLLATERAL ORGANIZATION: A TASK FORCE WITH A DIFFERENCE

The creation of task forces, a very frequent outgrowth of team-building and intergroup interventions, can be considered structural interventions because these task forces supplement, or are parallel to, the structural subsystem. Task forces temporarily complement the way the organization is structured into units, the organization's regular communications patterns, and its usual planning procedures.

The *collateral organization,* as described by Dale Zand, is essentially a task force but with some differences. The "collateral organization," according to Zand, "is a supplemental organization coexisting with the usual, formal organization." It is created to deal with "ill-structured" (i.e., complex, non-routine, future-oriented) problems that have high priority and that are systemwide, involving more than one unit. In the collateral organization, a deliberate effort is made to develop a set of norms different from those in the formal system. In particular, "careful questioning and analysis of goals, assumptions, methods, alternatives, and criteria for evaluation" are encouraged. Use is made of a change agent, data gathering, data feedback, and process consultation.[37]

In a sense the collateral organization described by Zand is an OD effort in microcosm. A successful effort of this kind would appear to have great promise for providing the interest and skills for a more extensive application of OD technology in the organization.

To an extent, the quality circles discussed earlier create an organizational structure parallel to the existing one. As Lawler and Mohrman point out, "they emphasize different group processes, assign new roles to people, and take people out of their normal day-to-day work activities."[38] However, recommendations are reported back to the existing organization; and the quality circle depends upon the regular organization for its resources.[39]

PHYSICAL SETTINGS AND OD

Some consultants have been active in working with clients and in conceptualizing about how to make physical settings congruent with OD assumptions and the OD process. A notable example of this thrust is Steele's work. To Steele, physical settings are an important part of organization culture that work groups should learn to diagnose and manage, and about which top management needs input in designing plants and buildings.

Steele cites many instances in which physical settings were found to interfere with effective group and organizational functioning. For example,

> A personnel director promoted to senior vice-president, a position inheriting the incredible, mandatory practice of having a secretary share the same office (which was supposed to signal high status), with the resulting lack of privacy and typewriter noise, adversely affecting the executive's ability to hold spontaneous meetings with employees
>
> An executive group wanting to rearrange an office setting to increase interaction and rapport, but locked into status considerations relative to the larger and corner offices
>
> A factory management encouraging group decision making, yet providing no space for more than six people to meet at one time
>
> Classroom and lecture hall arrangement in universities reinforcing a teacher-dominated and low-peer-interaction climate[40]

Many OD consultants have long given considerable attention to the physical arrangements for team-building sessions, and Steele reinforces this approach by urging facilitators to include the dimension of physical arrangements in their "process consultation" interventions.[41] (Steele describes a rating process he uses to examine things such as desks, lights, or machines, patterns of elements such as the arrangement of chairs, and sociological factors such as norms about the use of physical settings.)[42]

While architecture and interior arrangements and design are not OD per se, both the approach used by Steele, which includes a strong emphasis on participative diagnosis, and the outcomes, which tend to meet client needs (e.g., enhancing team efforts when needed and privacy when needed) are highly congruent with OD. Steele's work is a notable example of some of the creative integrations that have occurred between OD and other consultancy modes.

SUMMARY OF DIFFERENCES AND SIMILARITIES BETWEEN
OD AND SELECTED STRUCTURAL INTERVENTIONS

To summarize some of the differences and similarities between OD, job enrichment, quality circles, MBO, sociotechnical approaches, QWL programs, the use of collateral organizations, and a focus on physical settings:

1. *Job enrichment theory* says that many jobs are deficient in one or more characteristics, for example, planning and controlling (Myers) or skill variety, task identity, task significance, autonomy, and feedback from job (Hackman and Oldham). Diverse points of view about implementation exist:
   a. Diagnosis and restructuring of jobs is best done on a top-down, expert basis and that the payoff comes from the motivation that occurs from enhancing the intrinsic aspects of jobs (Herzberg), or
   b. Diagnosis and restructuring of jobs is best done on a highly participative, collaborative basis (Myers). (This approach is congruent with OD.)
   c. Job enrichment can focus on the work of individuals or the work of teams (Hackman and Oldham).

2. *Quality circles,* at least the participative, problem-solving versions, are based on the assumptions that many, if not most, employees are willing to work collaboratively with supervisors in group settings—both natural work teams and cross-functional teams—on problems of product quality and system effectiveness, that they can learn to effectively utilize both technical and process consultants, and that they have considerable insight and capability in doing so, providing they are
   a. Trained in quality-control concepts and the relevant measuring techniques and are
   b. Trained in group dynamics, team leadership, and interpersonal communciations skills.

3. *Traditional MBO theory* assumes there is a need for systematic goal setting linking the goals of superiors to subordinates and that
   a. Objectives or targets should be stated in quantitative terms whenever possible,
   b. Goal setting and appraisal should be a one-on-one dialogue between superior and subordinate. *However,* additional conceptualization and experience indicate that
   c. MBO can vary on an autocratic-participative continuum and that
   d. MBO can feature a participative team approach (French and Hollmann, Likert and Fisher).

4. *Sociotechnical systems/work restructuring theory* says that there should be a good fit between the technological system and the social system and that
   a. The semiautonomous (self-managed) work team is one way to accomplish this,
   b. A union-management committee should agree on the alterations to be made in the structure of work, compensation, staffing, and the like, and
   c. The role of the supervisor should shift to more planning, coordination, and training in contrast to direct supervision.

5. *QWL programs* vary in content but frequently include restructuring of several dimensions of the organization, including
   a. Increased problem solving between management and the union,
   b. Increased participation by employees in work teams in shop floor decisions pertaining to such matters as production flow, quality control, and safety, and
   c. Skill development through technical skill training, job rotation, and training in team problem solving.

6. *The collateral organization* (Zand) is a task force established parallel to the current formal structure and
   a. Is created to deal with complex systemwide problems, and
   b. Uses a facilitator and procedures explicitly congruent with OD approaches.

7. *Physical arrangements or settings* (Steele) can be the focus of interventions that can utilize, and be highly congruent with, OD techniques and assumptions.

8. *OD theory* says that frequently there are aspects to work team, cross-functional team, intergroup and organizational culture that are creating a suboptimization of group and organizational goal attainment and that

   a. Individuals in the context of their natural work teams and in other team configurations usually have the capability to participate in a diagnosis of those cultures and to make action plans to correct deficiencies and to reinforce positive aspects and that this capability can be extensively developed over time,

   b. Skills in interpersonal communications, feedback, group processes, and intergroup processes are important along with technical skills and can be extensively developed, and

   c. The culture of the entire organization, with top-management involvement, can shift in a collaborative, supportive, yet confrontive way toward more effective interpersonal, team, and interteam interaction and more effective organizational coping with the challenges of the external environment.

Although our analysis is brief and perhaps oversimplified, it appears that (1) the collateral organization as described by Zand is an OD effort in microcosm; that (2) some versions of quality circles, team MBO, self-managed work teams, and physical-setting design that feature participative goal setting and problem solving, and that link the efforts of one group to the efforts of other groups, are highly congruent with OD; but that (3) some forms of these improvement strategies are neither OD nor congruent with OD, as we define the process. Through its participant action research and diagnostic features, OD can be an "umbrella" process under which structural interventions can be appropriately and carefully developed. Or, to think of it in another way, OD approaches can provide the common threads that create an internally consistent fabric of a comprehensive organization improvement effort under whatever label, such as "quality of work life," "organizational effectiveness," "employee involvement," "participative management," or "sociotechnical systems."

A critical dimension to which we have alluded only indirectly is the extent of active involvement of the top-management team in processes comparable to those being promulgated for shop floor, office, or supervisory employees. Our hypothesis is that the more top management is involved in and committed to a comparable or complementary process, the more successful the process at lower levels will be. Or, to say it another way, the top-management team will set the stage for how much *real* participation, support, mutual influence, and effective problem solving exists throughout the organization.

SUMMARY

Organization improvement techniques aimed at changes in task, structural, and technological subsystems, which we call "structural interventions," can be supplemental to and congruent with a long-term OD effort. By definition, these techniques are congruent with OD to the extent that the particular strategy includes such features as a collaborative diagnosis of functional and dysfunctional aspects of the client system and joint problem solving and action planning. Some versions of structural interventions, however, appear to be highly incongruent with the OD process, both in the steps leading up to their "installation" and in the leadership styles they reinforce.

In particular, we think it is important for intervention strategies to be examined as to the extent of use of the action research model, the extent to which the strategy is unilateral versus participative, whether the focus of attention is the individual or a group, the consulting mode used, whether of an expert or facilitator variety, the extent to which top management is involved in comparable or complementary processes, and what alterations simultaneously occur in other systems, such as the training and reward systems. (See also Chapter 5, Relevant Systems Concepts, and Chapter 16, System Ramifications and New Demands.) Such an examination should lead to clearer communication about the nature of the OD process and other improvement strategies, less wasted effort, and better research.

NOTES

1. Tichy differentiates between four types of change agents, which he calls "analysis for the top (AFT)," "organization development (OD)," "people change technology (PCT)," and "outside pressure (OP)." Noel M. Tichy, "Agents of Planned Social Change: Congruence of Values, Cognitions and Actions," *Administrative Science Quarterly,* 19 (June 1974), pp. 164–182.

2. Figure 14–2 is adapted from M. Scott Myers, "Every Employee a Manager," *California Management Review,* 10 (Spring 1963), pp. 9–20.

3. See J. Richard Hackman and Greg R. Oldham, *Working Redesign* (Reading, Mass.: Addison-Wesley, 1980).

4. See Harold M. F. Rush, *Behavioral Science Concepts and Management Application* (New York: National Industrial Conference Board Studies in Personnel Policy, No. 216, 1969), pp. 147–148. Although this company had embarked on an extensive Managerial Grid OD program, the job enrichment activities seem to have preceded the more formalized OD effort; nevertheless, both applications at TI appear to be quite congruent (p. 146). For reference to Allan Mogensen's work, see also M. Scott Myers, *Managing with Unions* (Reading, Mass.: Addison-Wesley, 1978), pp. 39–40. Early advocates of work simplification, such as Lillian Gilbreth and Allan Mogensen, wanted to train workers in the techniques rather than to rely solely on engineers, but were largely overruled by the industrial engineers and management hierarchy. See Mitchell Fein, "Motivation for Work," in Robert Dubin, ed., *Handbook of Work, Organization, and Society* (Chicago: Rand McNally College Publishing Company, 1976), p. 481.

5. William Paul, Keith Robertson, and Frederick Herzberg, "Job Enrichment Pays Off," *Harvard Business Review,* 47 (March–April 1969), p. 75.

6. For a more detailed discussion of the advantages and disadvantages of participative versus top-down job enrichment processes, see Hackman and Oldham, *Work Redesign,* pp. 231–235.

7. Peter F. Drucker, "Learning from Foreign Management," *The Wall Street Journal,* June 4, 1980, p. 20.

8. Donald L. Dewar, *Quality Circle Member Manual* (Red Bluff, Calif.: Quality Circle Institute, 1980), p. iii.

9. Robert C. Cole, "Made in Japan—Quality-Control Circles," *Across the Board,* 16 (November 1979), pp. 72–78.

10. Gerald R. Ferris and John A. Wagner III, "Quality Circles in the United States: A Conceptual Reevaluation," *The Journal of Applied Behavioral Science,* 21 (No. 2, 1985), p. 157.

11. Edward E. Lawler III and Susan A. Mohrman, "Quality Circles After the Fad," *Harvard Business Review,* 63 (January–February 1985), pp. 65–71.

12. Based on interviews and observations at Lockheed Shipbuilding; Robert E. Cole and Dennis S. Tachiki, "Forging Institutional Links: Making Quality Circles Work in the U.S." *National Productivity Review,* 3 (Autumn 1984), pp. 417–429; and Mary Zippo, "Productivity and Morale Sagging? Try the Quality Circle Approach," *Personnel,* 57 (May–June 1980), pp. 43–45.

13. Cole, "Made in Japan," p. 76.

14. "Quality Control Circles Pay Off Big," *Industry Week,* October 29, 1979, p. 17.

15. Tom Peters, *Thriving on Chaos* (New York: Alfred A. Knopf, 1988), p. 85.

16. For some of the potential problems with quality circles, see Gregory P. Shea, "Quality Circles: The Danger of Bottled Change," *Sloan Management Review,* 27 (Spring 1986), pp. 33–46; Donald D. White and David A. Bednar, "Locating Problems with Quality Circles," *National Productivity Review,* 4 (Winter 1984–85), pp. 45–52; and Edward E. Lawler III and Susan A. Mohrman, "Quality Circles: After the Honeymoon," *Organizational Dynamics,* 14 (Spring 1987), pp. 42–55.

17. For a description of a federal government MBO program "laid on from the top" and the consequent resistance and token use, see Edward J. Ryan, Jr., "Federal Government MBO: Another Managerial Fad?" *MSU Business Topics,* 24 (Autumn 1976), pp. 35–43. For more on some of the basic faults in many MBO efforts, see Harry Levinson, "Management by Whose Objectives?" *Harvard Business Review,* 48 (July–August 1970), pp. 125–134.

18. See Wendell French and Robert Hollmann, "Management by Objectives: The Team Approach," *California Management Review,* 17 (Spring 1975), pp. 13–22. A workshop participant has suggested we call this "COMBO." See also Wendell L. French and John A. Drexler, Jr., "A Team Approach to MBO," *Leadership & Organization Development Journal,* 5, No. 5 (1984), pp. 22–26.

19. H. H. Meyer, E. Kay, and J. R. P. French, Jr., "Split Roles in Performance Appraisal," *Harvard Business Review,* 43 (January–February 1965), pp. 124–139.

20. Edward E. Lawler III, Alan M. Mohrman, Jr., and Susan M. Resnick, "Performance Appraisal Revisited," *Organizational Dynamics,* 13 (Summer 1984), pp. 20–35.

21. Robert W. Hollmann, "Supportive Organization Climate and Managerial Assessment of MBO Effectiveness," *Academy of Management Journal,* 19 (December 1976), pp. 560–576.

22. Rensis Likert and M. Scott Fisher, "MBGO: Putting Some Team Spirit into MBO," *Personnel,* 54 (January–February 1977), pp. 40–47. Actually, Likert had done some research on such an approach in the mid-1960s but had not called it a form of MBO. See Rensis Likert's discussion of "a group method of sales supervision" in his *The Human Organization: Its Management and Value* (New York: McGraw-Hill, 1967), pp. 55–71.

23. E. L. Trist, G. W. Higgin, H. Murray, and A. B. Pollock, *Organizational Choice* (London: Tavistock, 1965).

24. A. K. Rice, "Productivity and Social Organization in an Indian Weaving Shed: An Examination of Some Aspects of the Socio-Technical System of an Experimental Automatic Loom Shed," *Human Relations,* 6 (1953), pp. 297–329.

25. See, for example, E. Thorsrud, "Socio-Technical Approach to Job Design and Organizational Development," *Management International Review,* 8 (1968), pp. 120–131. See also Calvin Pava, "Designing Managerial and Professional Work for High Performance: A Socio-technical Approach," *National Productivity Review,* 2 (Spring 1983), pp. 126–135; and Calvin Pava, "Redesigning Sociotechnical Systems Design: Concepts and Methods for the 1990s," *The Journal of Applied Behavioral Science,* 22, No. 3 (1986), pp. 201–221.

26. Richard E. Walton, "From Hawthorne to Topeka and Kalmar," in E. L. Cass and Frederick G. Zimmer, eds., *Man and Work in Society* (New York: Van Nostrand Reinhold, 1975), pp. 116–129. See also William A. Pasmore, "Overcoming the Roadblocks in Work-Restructuring Efforts," *Organizational Dynamics,* 10 (Spring 1982), pp. 54–67; and Berth Jonsson and Alden Lake, "Volvo: A Report," *Human Resource Management,* 24 (Winter 1985), pp. 455–465.

27. Paul S. Goodman, "Quality of Work Life Projects in the 1980s," *Labor Law Journal,* 31 (August 1980), p. 487. See also Louis E. Davis, "Guides to the Design and Redesign of Organizations," in Robert Tannenbaum, Newton Margulies, Fred Massarik and Associates, *Human Systems Development* (San Francisco: Jossey-Bass Publishers, 1985), pp. 143–166.

28. Stephen H. Fuller, "How Quality-of-Worklife Projects Work for General Motors," *Monthly Labor Review,* 103 (July 1980), pp. 37–39; Irving Bluestone, "How Quality-of-Worklife Projects Work for the United Auto Workers," *Monthly Labor Review,* 103 (July 1980), pp. 39–41; and Patricia M. Carrigan, "Up From the Ashes," *OD Practitioner,* 18 (March 1986), pp. 1–6. See also Tom Peters, op. cit., pp. 290–291; and Edward M. Glaser and Paul A. Nelson, "A Quality

of Worklife Improvement Effort at Five Mental Health Facilities," *OD Practitioner,* 19 (March 1987), pp. 1–6.

29. Goodman, "Quality of Work Life Projects in the 1980s," pp. 387–494. See also Edward E. Lawler III and Gerald E. Ledford, Jr., "Productivity and the Quality of Work Life," *National Productivity Review,* 1 (Winter 1981–82), pp. 23–36. For further discussion of QWL projects, see Louis E. Davis and Albert B. Cherns, eds., *The Quality of Working Life,* Vol. II (New York: The Free Press, 1975); Richard E. Walton, "Work Innovations at Topeka: After Six Years," *Journal of Applied Behavioral Science,* 13, No. 3 (1977), pp. 422–433; and Richard E. Walton, "Work Innovations in the United States," *Harvard Business Review,* 57 (July–August 1979), pp. 88–98.

30. See Janice A. Klein, "Why Supervisors Resist Employee Involvement," *Harvard Business Review,* 62 (September–October 1984), pp. 87–95.

31. The first part of this discussion is based largely on "Rushton—An Experiment with Miners Regulating Their Own Work Activities," in *Recent Initiatives in Labor-Management Cooperation* (Washington, D.C.: National Center for Productivity and Quality of Working Life, 1976), pp. 51–57; and Ted Mills, "Altering the Social Structure in Coal Mining: A Case Study," *Monthly Labor Review,* 99 (October 1976), pp. 3–10; with some modifications from Paul S. Goodman, *Assessing Organizational Change* (New York: John Wiley, 1979).

32. Mills, "Altering the Social Structure," p. 6.

33. These results are based on ibid., pp. 6–7.

34. Ibid., pp. 7–9.

35. Goodman, *Assessing Organizational Change,* pp. 68, 344–346, 359–376.

36. Other experiments that have involved union-management cooperation include the use of a "relations by objectives" (RBO) technique developed by the Federal Mediation and Conciliation Service, which is aimed at improving relationships between the parties. The RBO technique appears to draw extensively on OD theory and practice, particularly intergroup conflict resolution. See David A. Gray, Anthony V. Sinogropi, and Paula Ann Hughes, "From Conflict to Cooperation: A Joint Union-Management Goal-Setting and Problem-Solving Program," *Proceedings of the Thirty-Fourth Annual Meeting,* Industrial Relations Research Association Series, December 1981, pp. 26–32. For a theoretical discussion of OD as it relates to labor-management relations, see Thomas A. Kochan and Lee Dyer, "A Model of Organizational Change in the Context of Union-Management Relations," *Journal of Applied Behavioral Science,* 12 (January–March 1976), pp. 59–78. For more on the contrasts between QWL and OD, see Neal Q. Herrick, "QWL: An Alternative to Traditional Public-Sector Management Systems," *National Productivity Review,* 3 (Winter 1983–84), pp. 54–67.

37. This discussion is based on Dale Zand, "Collateral Organization: A New Change Strategy," *Journal of Applied Behavioral Science,* 10, No. 1 (1974), pp. 63–89. See also Dale E. Zand, *Information, Organization, and Power* (New York: McGraw-Hill, 1981), Chap. 4; and Barry A. Stein and Rosabeth Moss Kanter, "Building the Parallel Organization: Creating Mechanisms for Permanent Quality of Work Life," *The Journal of Applied Behavioral Science,* 16 (July–September 1980), pp. 371–386. See also Abraham B. Shani and Bruce J. Eberhardt, "Parallel Organization in a Health Care Institution," *Group & Organization Studies,* 12 (June 1987), pp. 147–173.

38. Lawler and Mohrman, op. cit., p. 66. See also S. G. Goldstein, "Organizational Dualism and Quality Circles," *Academy of Management Review,* 10 (July 1985), pp. 504–517.

39. Lawler and Mohrman, op. cit., p. 66.

40. Fred I. Steele, *Physical Settings and Organization Development* (Reading, Mass.: Addison-Wesley, 1973), pp. 101–107.

41. Ibid, p. 131.

42. Ibid., pp. 97–98.

15

CONDITIONS FOR OPTIMAL SUCCESS

A discussion of the conditions contributing to optimal success in the organization development process follows in this chapter. Theory, research, and experience suggest that successful organization development efforts tend to evolve in the ways we will describe, and they have certain distinguishing characteristics. Conversely, unsuccessful efforts tend to feature mistakes or inattention relative to some of these dimensions. Lest the following list of conditions seem overwhelming or discouraging to line managers or consultants assessing the feasibility of an OD effort, we want to emphasize that these are *evolving* conditions for long-term success. One starts where one can, the conditions are never perfect, and there will be mistakes. The more these conditions can be created as the process unfolds, however, the more likely the OD process will be successful and become an integral part of the organizational culture.

The following are the conditions and phases that we see as important to the successful evolution of organization development efforts, which we will elaborate on in this chapter.

1. Perceptions of organizational problems by key people and perceptions of the relevance of the behavioral sciences in solving these problems
2. The introduction into the system of a behavioral scientist-consultant
3. Initial and ongoing top-level involvement and support, and a long-term perspective
4. Participation of intact work teams, with active involvement of the formal leader, and an extension of the process to any parallel structures such as task forces, cross-functional teams, and so forth
5. The operationalizing of the participant action research model

6. Early successes, with expansion of the effort stemming from these successes
7. An open, educational philosophy about the theory and the technology of OD
8. Acknowledgment of the congruency between OD and many previous effective management practices
9. Involvement of personnel and industrial relations/human resources management people and congruency with personnel policy and practice
10. Development of internal OD resources and facilitative skills
11. Effective management of the OD process and stabilization of changes
12. Monitoring the process and the measuring of results

PERCEPTION OF ORGANIZATIONAL PROBLEMS BY KEY PEOPLE

Initially, in successful organization development efforts there is strong pressure for improvement, at least on the top management of an organization or one of its subunits, from both inside and outside the organization. In short, the key people have a real sense of things not going as well as they could. This is one of the distinguishing characteristics of successful change efforts as identified by Greiner in his review of 17 change efforts, of which he labeled 11 ''successful'' and 6 ''less successful.''[1]

> The organization, and especially top management, is under considerable external and internal pressure for improvement long before an explicit organization change is contemplated. Performance and/or morale are low. Top management seems to be groping for a solution to its problems.[2]

We believe, however, that successful OD efforts can emerge in organizations that are in less trouble than that suggested by the quotation from Greiner. From our experience, the important thing is a sense that things could be better. We think that an OD effort can play important ''tune-up'' and ongoing maintenance roles for an organization. In fact, most of the organizations we consult with are basically healthy and successful; they are interested in ''getting better.''

INTRODUCTION OF AN EXTERNAL BEHAVIORAL SCIENTIST-CONSULTANT

A second important condition in the early phases of an organization development effort is that an outside behavioral scientist-consultant is brought in for consultation with a top executive (or the top manager in a subdivision) to diagnose organizational problems. While we do not wish to understate the possibility of an internal person emerging in this role at the beginning, the instances are going to be few when a person with sufficient training, stature, and role congruency can assume a major change-agent role without outside help. The external person is usually freer of the cultural constraints of the organization, is freer of its politics, can take more risks with his or her own career because of not being dependent on one client system for income, and can bring to bear insights from working with numerous systems. We do, however, see a major role for internal consultants as the process unfolds.

INITIAL AND ONGOING TOP-LEVEL SUPPORT
AND INVOLVEMENT, AND A LONG-TERM PERSPECTIVE

The successful OD effort does not necessarily need to start with the chief executive officer, although this is the ideal circumstance. The main thing is that an influential person at the top of some unit recognize the potential applicability of the behavioral sciences to the solutions of problems being faced by that unit and that both support and understanding from this person's superior be forthcoming relative to doing some preliminary exploring and experimenting. As Bennis states it, there needs to be "some kind of 'umbrella' protection from the next highest echelon."[3]

As the OD effort proceeds within a unit, support from additional people outside that unit will become imperative. The surrounding informal social system will tend to become either resistive or supportive; and to accomplish the latter, key people in other units and key people higher in the organization will need to be kept informed of the objectives, activities, and general results of the efforts as they unfold. (This holds true for other improvement strategies as well—the Rushton Mine experiment, cited in the previous chapter, stalled partly because of deficiencies in this area.) Key persons include members of the board of directors, who have a big stake in the success of the organization and who need to interpret the organization to the outside world. Again to quote Bennis, "It can be disastrous if the people most affected by organization development are not involved, informed, or even advised of the program."[4]

Ultimately, there must be top-management support and involvement. As an example, Burke describes how a three-year OD effort in a medical school was aborted when the dean was perceived by the university president as being insubordinate when the dean pressed for more control over his budget. To the dean and medical school faculty, more budget autonomy was logical and necessary to carry out the many changes that were emerging as a result of the OD process.[5]

Obviously, one of the most serious obstacles to the long-range viability of an OD effort is a short-term perspective. As Edward Lawler says, "One of the most common mistakes in change efforts is to expect quick results."[6] Lyman Hamilton, former chief executive of ITT, refers to the distortion that occurs in decision making due to short-term pressures. "Every C.E.O. says he plans for the long term," says Hamilton. "But every C.E.O. lies. He's always temporizing with quarterly earnings."[7] Clearly, there are top executives who have long-term perspectives on the development of their people and their organizations, but, unfortunately, there are many who fit Hamilton's statement.

The awareness of the applicability of behavioral sciences, of course, is a prerequisite for any OD effort. This awareness could occur in one of many ways—for example, through reading, through attendance at a seminar or a workshop, through attendance in a laboratory training session, through discussions with colleagues in a professional association, or through a dialogue with a consultant already doing some work for the organization. This awareness might be at either the cognitive or the experiential level, or both. For example, at the experiential level, a manager might have become aware of the possibility of improved staff meetings through experiencing the way a workshop was handled. More directly, an outside consultant might be brought in to conduct a short workshop or "microlab" to give the client system a brief acquaintanceship with the dynamics of, say, a team-building session. This, of course, presupposes somebody's prior awareness of the potential utility of such prework.

Parenthetically, in OD efforts in public agencies that the mass media tend to watch—such as in a city government—it would seem wise to provide information seminars for members of the media about the nature of the OD process if they are to attend any team-building sessions. News coverage by uninformed reporters and editors can have a seriously adverse impact on an OD effort; unfortunately, the media tend to focus on the problems that are surfaced rather than on positive matters. The effect on participants is predictable: there is an understandable distortion of information about the actual dynamics of the organization. On the other hand, news coverage by well-informed reporters of an ending, summary session in which action plans are reviewed can have a positive impact. Ideally, information seminars for members of the media would have an experiential component so that there would be some appreciation of the process at both the cognitive and the affective levels. Obviously, such seminars would have to be done well. They should probably take place after a solid beginning to the OD effort has occurred, because news stories about a collaborative effort to improve an organization's functioning before collaboration has occurred can create unnecessary internal resistance. Furthermore, reports of successes can assist the OD effort.[8]

ACTIVE INVOLVEMENT OF TEAM LEADERS

We have referred to "intact work teams" several times. It may be obvious at this point, but we want to stress that it is absolutely imperative that the supervisor, leader, or manager of any group participate in any team-building session of that unit. Because of the complex processes involved, sessions without that person can be extremely frustrating, if not downright dysfunctional. We feel so strongly about this that a major condition of our conducting team-building sessions (by whatever name) is the active, continuous presence of the formal leader. One researcher has documented the consequences of the leader's absence and has quoted one subordinate's reaction as follows:

> I'm so frustrated I can't believe it. The material we are exposed to makes so much sense— and I see what the [another, but intact, work team] people are doing in terms of getting their stuff together. But it is impossible for us. What can we do without our boss here? There is no way we can go back and apply these skills. He won't have the slightest idea what we are talking about. We sit down and try to solve our problems, but it is impossible to do it. The boss is too big a part of it all. In a lot of ways this is making things worse instead of better. At least before we came we didn't have as clear an idea of what was available to us. I guess that is what is causing all the frustration—knowing what is available but we can't do anything about it.[9]

It is also imperative that the formal leader make it legitimate for OD activities, in addition to team building, to occur. For example, that person needs to support such activities as process consultation and, eventually, intergroup activities.

OPERATIONALIZING OF THE ACTION RESEARCH MODEL
AND EARLY SUCCESSES

The consultant's initial efforts may be in response to a request for a more traditional intervention, such as an attitude survey or a review of personnel policies and practices. However, the consultant's approach, although the terminology may not be used, quickly begins to take on an action research flavor with the concurrence and involvement of the key client.

Thus, a fifth important characteristic emerges. The action research model of preliminary diagnosis, data gathering, feedback, and action planning is operational, probably through a team-building session or through a survey feedback procedure. These initial interventions are found to be helpful, and additional requests for such assistance emerge laterally or from subordinate units within the organization.

Top management, then, does not commit itself irrevocably to a five or ten year program but, in collaboration with the change agent, makes commitments relative to reasonably sized "chunks" of activities. Successes then lead to additional chunks, and the time perspective grows with the successes.

Herbert Shepard advises that, in the early phases of an OD effort, it is wise to "load experiments for success."[10] In short, it is particularly important for early efforts to be carefully selected and carefully managed in order to maximize the chances of success.

AN OPEN, EDUCATIONAL PHILOSOPHY ABOUT OD

We believe that it is extremely important to the long-range success of an OD effort that the mystery and mythology be minimized and that the technology be understood. This means that a high value must be placed on making the assumptions, theory, and practices underlying the OD effort open and visible. Most people do not wish to be manipulated or have things done to them, particularly in mysterious ways. The external change agent, and ultimately the internal resource people, will continuously need to assume the role of educators who make their knowledge about the OD process and how to go about improving organizations accessible to all. The desired climate is one in which organizational members find that not only have the number of options open to them increased but they are receiving a high return from their own use of behavioral science knowledge. In short, a major emphasis in an OD program must be the opportunity for self-directed personal growth and increased effectiveness of individuals and groups.

ACKNOWLEDGMENT OF THE CONGRUENCY
WITH PREVIOUS GOOD PRACTICE

Another quality of successful OD efforts is an open recognition by internal or external change agents that many OD or behavioral science assertions will be highly congruent with the better managerial practices already in existence in the organization. As a manager once expressed it, "I've been a very successful manager over the years and have worked hard and somewhat successfully to bring about a participative, open climate in my organization. Now people in the personnel department and the OD program are preaching the same stuff to me that I've been practicing for years, and I resent it." He also used the phrase "knights on white horses" with reference to the change agents. A successful OD effort needs such managers as allies and valuable resources, not as people who feel pushed around or unappreciated for their many contributions.

Issues about who is the expert versus who is not, and problems of semantics, tend to diminish as the successful OD effort matures. As the skills learned through various phases of the OD program begin to permeate the organizational culture, and as the action research model becomes internalized, the distinction between the change agents and the nonchange agents, and between what is OD and what is effective management, becomes less and less distinct. It continues to be important, however, that organizational members have a common language and a common understanding relative to the basic underpinnings of OD—for example, action research, emphasis on work team culture, and so forth.

INVOLVEMENT OF PERSONNEL PEOPLE AND CONGRUENCY WITH PERSONNEL POLICY AND PRACTICE

In a company large enough to have a personnel and industrial relations/human resources executive, long-range successful OD activities require that this executive become heavily involved or, at a minimum, highly supportive. This specialist is the one person in the organization whose main function is the design and implementation of human resource systems and to whom such other specialists as the wage and salary administrator, the training director, and the employment manager typically report.

We are obviously talking about a personnel-industrial relations/human resources management role that is much broader than collective bargaining. While OD efforts have considerable promise for shifting union-management relationships toward more of a problem-solving climate, the chief negotiator for the organization may be locked into a "win-lose" stance for a substantial period of time until the entire organizational climate shifts to a different mode. We do know of one labor relations director in a huge multi-national company, however, whose breadth of vision and successful bargaining with the unions resulted in a shift of climate in many of the company divisions toward a more participative and problem-solving leadership style relative to the total work force. On the labor relations side, the basic vehicles for this shift have been new labor contracts that have removed many traditional constraints on job boundaries and that now permit job enrichment activities. Additional features include wage increases tied to productivity and cost savings. On the supervision side in this company, the shift has come, in large part, through a variety of organization development activities, including team building, survey feedback, and management workshops.

Ultimately, it seems to us, it is essential that the entire personnel-industrial relations group, including people in salary administration, be involved in the organization development program. Since internal OD groups have such potential for acting as catalysts in rapid organizational change, the temptation is great, as we will discuss in Chapter 17, for them to see themselves as "good guys" and the other personnel people as "bad guys," or as people carrying out less important assignments. Any conflicts between a separate organization development group and the personnel and industrial relations groups should be faced and resolved. Such tensions can be the undoing of either program. Even in the absence of any serious conflict, the change agents in the organization development program clearly need the support of the other people who are heavily involved in human resources administration, and vice versa.

As we will discuss in more detail in Chapter 16, what is done in the OD program needs to be compatible with what is done in selection, promotion, salary administration, appraisal, and other formalized aspects of the human-social subsystem. For example, substantially improved performance on the part of individuals and groups is not likely to be sustained if financial and promotional rewards are not forthcoming. In short, management needs to have a "systems" point of view and to think through the inter-relationships of the OD effort with the reward and staffing systems and the other aspects of the total human resources subsystem.

This congruency is largely built in at the Space and Defense Sector of TRW. The model there is to make the total personnel and industrial relations group an integral part of the OD program. People in such roles as employment manager and plant personnel director are also change agents. These specialists are supported by line managers who have demonstrated particular skill in consultation and by external OD consultants.

DEVELOPMENT OF INTERNAL RESOURCES AND FACILITATIVE SKILLS

The development of internal resources, as illustrated in the practices at TRW, is an important, if not inherent, feature of successful OD efforts. Continued growth in problem-solving skills, in effectiveness in managing meetings, and so forth is essential in a successful OD effort. In other words, the organization incorporates and builds upon what it learns from the change agent, as suggested earlier in our comments about the open, educational nature of OD.

Ideally, both members of the personnel staff and a few line executives are trained to do some organization development work in conjunction with the external behavioral scientists. In a large organization, in particular, the demands for the help of change agents may soon exceed the immediate supply or may begin to cost substantially more than people employed full time by the organization. In a sense, then, the external change agent tries to reduce the organization's reliance on his or her services by developing internal resources, both because of the growth and development inherent in successful OD and because of the cost or the availability of change-agent skills. We do, however, see an important long-range role for the external consultant, as we will describe later. The training of internal consultants might include group dynamics/T-group training, university courses on OD and related subjects, supervised consultation, and an extensive apprenticeship with an experienced professional.[11]

In addition, the widespread development of facilitative skills by organizational members across specialties and hierarchical lines can be a valuable adjunct to the OD process and to the organization's functioning. The more that organizational members, in general, are helpful to peers, subordinates, and superiors and to customers and suppliers in listening, in examining options, and in running meetings, the more successful both the OD effort and the organization are likely to be. Widespread use of such skills not only will reinforce the OD culture, but it will also enhance the day-to-day functioning of the enterprise, which is, of course, what OD is about. This argues, then, for resources to be invested, not only in training internal OD specialists in the larger organizations, but in widespread training of interested employees at all levels of large or small organizations in facilitative skills. As we suggested in Chapter 2, it is important to think of the *facilitator role* and the *facilitative process* in organizations as well as *facilitator persons.*

EFFECTIVE MANAGEMENT OF THE OD PROCESS
AND STABILIZATION OF CHANGES

A number of aspects relative to the management of the ongoing OD process need careful attention if the program is to meet with continuous success. These dimensions have to do with authenticity, consulting team and client-consultant relationships, coercion versus voluntarism, OD strategy, coordination, and stabilization.

Authenticity, in contrast to gamesmanship, is an extremely important characteristic of successful OD applications. The outside consultant, the internal coordinator, or the key clients need to work together to check periodically on fears, threats, and anxieties centering on the OD effort. Such problems need to be confronted as they emerge, including those stemming from the promises of overzealous advocates.

Not only is the outside change agent needed for his or her skills, but the organization needs that person to act as a ''governor''—to keep the program focused on real problems and to urge authenticity in contrast to gamesmanship. For example, the danger always exists that the organization will begin to punish or reward involvement in group process kinds of activities per se, or reward superficial lip service to OD values, rather than focus on performance. In this sense, the culture of the organization can begin to take on a cultish kind of behavior that may not be in line with meeting its objectives. The consultant can, of course, become part of that problem; in this regard there is simply no substitute for professional competence and self-awareness.

In connection with cultlike behavior, coercion relative to such matters as openness and attendance at T-groups can be highly dysfunctional. While it is difficult to draw a line between persuasion and coercion, OD consultants and top management should be aware of the serious consequences of the latter, particularly when real feelings about it are submerged and a perfunctory acquiescence occurs. What is happening under such conditions, of course, is that the informal system is no longer being managed collaboratively, behavior is not authentic, trust goes down, and communications become guarded. These are consequences diametrically opposed to the objectives of an organization development effort.

The problem of gamesmanship can partially be minimized if the OD consultants constantly work on their own effectiveness in interpersonal relationships and their diagnostic skills so they are not in a position of ''do as I say, but not as I do.'' To elaborate further, from our experience it is imperative that any OD consulting teams, including both internal and external change agents, work intensively at their own team relationships. Lack of attention to their own team relationships and effectiveness will reduce their constructive impact on the broader organization.

Both consultant and client must work together to optimize their knowledge of the organization's evolving culture and to optimize their mutual personal growth. As the consultant needs to be concerned about the personal growth of the key clients, so the clients need to be concerned about the growth of the consultant. For example, this means some investment on the part of the client system to keep the consultant sufficiently tuned in to what is happening in the organization and in providing resources so that consulting teams can pay attention to their own maintenance and development.

Successful OD efforts also require a strategy that can be articulated and made visible. While the overall strategy will evolve, the process can be facilitated by cognitive maps showing where groups have been in their learning experience, where they might go next, and so forth. For example, it can be helpful to realize that follow-up team-building sessions might occur once per year for the purpose of diagnosing and reviewing progress. It can be helpful to realize that, as trust levels go up, it might be productive to focus more intently on conflict reduction and on learning conflict-reducing techniques. Negatively speaking, the constructive gains of the initial OD efforts can be lost if there is no emerging plan relative to what OD means for the long range for both the total organization and its subunits.

Such a long-range strategy is one of the key features of the Grid OD approach as described in Chapter 13. The six phases are deliberately planned to build on each other and to give the effort direction and focus.

The OD strategy as it relates to management development and other programs needs to be planned and articulated. Similarly, there need to be guidelines for subsequent phases or expansion of the OD effort—who has access to the consultants, whether follow-up activities have higher priority than new efforts with new groups, and the like. These are real issues in managing the OD effort and must be faced.

Issues of coordination and control of the OD program also need to be resolved between the key internal OD coordinator, external consultants, and clients. This is particularly relevant to OD activities in large organizations. Lack of coordination can result in incongruous philosophies and practices resulting in dysfunctional tensions between people in different subunits or between OD specialists. For example, high emphasis on T-grouping by consultants in one department or division and a deliberate deemphasis by consultants in another could interject an unnecessary debate into the system which might better have been worked out within the consulting staff. On the other hand, over-control by a central coordinator can choke off useful preliminary and follow-up activities between consultant and client. For example, barriers placed between the client and the consultant can turn an OD effort into a kind of "dog and pony show" in which the consultant displays his or her "tricks" during a team-building session but is prohibited from working with the client group in an ongoing way. In short, we are arguing for a consensual approach to OD strategy, but also for an open, ongoing relationship between consultant and clients in various subunits. Stating the case even more positively, we recommend that the internal OD coordinator encourage a long-range, direct relationship between consultants and key clients in the subunits of the organization.

Further, there needs to be attention to system stabilization as changes occur. It is hoped that people are working smarter and not necessarily harder and that there is more mutual help as an OD effort unfolds. However, there is always the possibility that people and units will take on too many projects or try to move too fast. People can become overloaded, or changes can occur too rapidly for other parts of the system to adjust. People need time to be aware, to discuss, to understand, to look at options, to modify what they are doing, to reflect on where they have been, and to involve others in the examination of the progress made. Thus, effective management of the OD process requires attention to the pace of change and the extent to which changes are being adequately absorbed into the culture of the organization. This is consistent with Lewin's notions about "freezing...on a new level," that is, making the new field of forces relatively stable and secure.[12]

MONITORING THE PROCESS AND MEASURING RESULTS

Finally, successful OD efforts require the application of the action research model to the OD process itself. There needs to be continuous audit of the results, both in terms of checking on the evolution of attitudes about what is going on and in terms of the extent to which problems that were identified at the outset by the key clients are being solved through the process.

The chief executive officer and the "line" executives of the organization will evaluate the success of the OD effort in terms of the extent to which it assists the organization in meeting its human and economic objectives. For example, marked improvements on various indexes from one plant, one division, one department, and so forth will be important indicators of program success. Because of other conditions that will be operating simultaneously, however, the demonstration of cause-and-effect relationships is going to be exceedingly difficult. In fact, both measurement and interpretation are going to be difficult.

Illustration 3 in the first chapter is a case in point. While the OD effort was contributing to a decrease in lost-time injuries and an increase in productivity and quality, the company was losing money because of declining metal prices. A superficial reading of the situation would say that the OD effort was not successful; a deeper analysis indicates that the company might have lost much more money had it not been for the OD effort.

We believe, however, that a substantial contribution has been made by University of Michigan people and others both to the data gathering phase of the OD process and to the measurement of the results of OD efforts. In particular, we would draw attention to questionnaires like Likert's Profile of Organizational Characteristics[13] and to their applicability in measuring changes stemming from an OD program. Likert's Profile, a questionnaire that asks respondents to comment on a variety of organizational dimensions, including leadership, communications, and decision making, essentially taps what Likert calls "causal variables" as well as "intervening variables," e.g. attitudes toward supervision, height of performance goals, and extent of cooperation.[14] This questionnaire, for example, was used at the Weldon Company to measure changes over a two-year period during a major organization development effort. These changes, in turn, were then related to productivity measures and other "end-result" variables.[15]

At a less ambitious level, systematic interviewing or questionnaire polling of participants two or three months after a team-building session could be invaluable for justification of the effort or introducing modifications in the OD program. We think anecdotal evidence, both positive and negative, is also very useful. The informed judgment of participating managers, in particular, is extremely important. For example, we asked a vice president in charge of a large operating divison of a corporation if the team-building sessions and the OD effort in his division had been useful. His response: "You bet. Now we tell it like it is." These kinds of data, supplemented by a more systematic collection of data, including data from subordinates, can be invaluable in diagnosing the utility and the strengths and weaknesses of the OD effort.

SUMMARY

Twelve evolving conditions have been described as important to an optimally successfully OD effort. In addition to skilled interventions per se, these conditions have to do with assessing and managing the context of the OD process. To work well, OD must be conceptualized and managed as a highly participative, evolutionary improvement in the complex fabric of the social system of the organization.

NOTES

1. Larry E. Greiner, "Patterns of Organization Change," *Harvard Business Review,* 45 (May–June 1967), pp. 119–130.

2. Ibid., p. 122.

3. Warren Bennis, *Organization Development: Its Nature, Origins, and Prospects* (Reading, Mass.: Addison-Wesley, 1969), p. 57.

4. Ibid., p. 47.

5. W. Warner Burke, "Systems Theory, Gestalt Therapy, and Organization Development," in T. G. Cummings, ed., *Systems Theory for Organization Development* (New York: John Wiley, 1980), pp. 212–214.

6. Edward E. Lawler III, *High-Involvement Management* (San Francisco: Jossey-Bass Publishers, 1986), p. 233. See also Terrence E. Deal and Allen A. Kennedy, *Corporate Cultures* (Reading, Mass.: Addison-Wesley, 1982), p. 136.

7. *Fortune,* May 31, 1982, p. 111.

8. Whether a team-building session of, say, a city council and the mayor or a state governor and his or her immediate staff must be open to the mass media under any open meeting law needs to be decided state by state. In our opinion, OD sessions involving the examination of such matters as decision-making and communications processes, interpersonal and intergroup relationships, and preliminary discussions of organizational structure should be exempt from these laws. The personal risks to participants in publicly exploring organizational, group, and personal deficiencies will inevitably stifle candidness. At the federal level, the Freedom of Information Act exempts "purely internal management matters," which we interpret as exempting most OD activities. For a further discussion, see Wendell French, Cecil H. Bell, Jr., and Robert A. Zawacki, *Organization Development: Theory, Practice, and Research,* revised ed. (Dallas: Business Publications, 1983). For more on sunshine laws, see Harlan Cleveland, "The Costs and Benefits of Openness," *Academe,* 73 (September–October 1987), pp. 23–28.

9. R. Wayne Boss, "The Effect of Leader Absence on a Confrontation Team Building Design," unpublished manuscript (University of Colorado, 1977). Used with permission.

10. Herbert A. Shepard, "Rules of Thumb for Change Agents," *OD Practitioner,* 17 (December 1985), pp. 1–5. For more discussion on the phenomenon of "success breeding success," see William F. Dowling, "To Move an Organization: The Corning Approach to Organization Development," *Organizational Dynamics,* 3 (Spring 1975), pp. 19, 33.

11. For a discussion of the training of OD practitioners, see Kenneth O. Shepard and Anthony P. Raia, "The OD Training Challenge," *Training and Development Journal,* 35 (April 1981), pp. 90–96. See also "OD Experts Reflect on the Major Skills Needed by OD Consultants," *OD Newsletter* (Academy of Management) (Spring 1979), pp. 1–3; and Fritz Steele, *The Role of the Internal Consultant* (Boston: CBI, 1982).

12. Kurt Lewin, *Field Theory in Social Science* (New York: Harper & Brothers, 1951) pp. 228–229.

13. Rensis Likert, *The Human Organization: Its Management and Value* (New York: McGraw-Hill, 1967), pp. 137, 197–211.

14. Ibid., p. 76.

15. Alfred J. Marrow, David G. Bowers, and Stanley E. Seashore, *Management by Participation* (New York: Harper & Row, 1967). See also William F. Dowling, "System 4 Builds Performance and Profits," *Organizational Dynamics,* (Winter 1975), pp. 23–38; and Edward Lawler III, op cit., pp. 65–81.

16

SYSTEM RAMIFICATIONS AND NEW DEMANDS/ OPPORTUNITIES

In this chapter we will briefly theorize about a few of the more salient ramifications of an organization development effort in terms of new demands that are likely to be made on the system. These demands can be considered opportunities to improve overall organizational effectiveness.

If major organization improvements are to be made and sustained, managerial practices with respect to many subsystems will need to be modified if practices are not already congruent with the OD effort. This is particularly true with respect to the human-social and structural subsystems (see Chapter 5).

Some examples will be provided to show how some managerial practices might be modified to be congruent with the OD process and/or to suggest where innovations might occur. Other examples were given in Chapter 14, Structural Interventions and OD. In that chapter, several examples were given to illustrate what happens if not enough attention is given to the involvement of people in other units, to the interests of middle managers, to top management involvement, and so on.

FEEDBACK

Since more extensive data gathering, including making legitimate the expression of feelings and attitudes, is an integral part of an OD effort, people will have to learn how to give and manage feedback in such a way that it is helpful and not destructive. This means training in giving and receiving feedback, and it means paying attention to the gamut of feedback systems—all the way from interpersonal kinds of exchanges to subunit production or cost data and to the results of organizationwide attitude surveys.

For example, at the interpersonal level, feedback tends to be the most constructive when such conditions as the following are met:

It is solicited.

It is fairly immediate after the event.

It is specific.

It is reported in terms of the impact on the person who is providing the feedback.

It is nonjudgmental in that it does not label the recipient "stupid," "worthless," and the like.

It is given when the basic motive is to improve the relationship (in contrast to a desire to punish, belittle, etc.).

It is given in private or in a supportive group atmosphere.

It is given in the spirit of mutual give-and-take.

It is given in the context of sharing appreciations as well as concerns.

At the level of subunit production or cost data, feedback is most helpful if it is reported

Directly to the manager or team who can take remedial action, in contrast to top management or a staff department

Frequently enough so the manager or team can plan remedial action

Specifically, so that the manager or team can easily identify the problem area (this will usually mean that the using manager or team will need to be involved in designing the reporting system)

In terms of attitude surveys, feedback tends to be the most constructive

When it is sought by the leader and the unit involved

When unit data and aggregate organizational data are reported to the respective manager, but not data specific to other units (direct comparisons with peers tend to be highly threatening at first)

When managers plus their subordinates discuss the dynamics underlying the data with the help of a third party and make action plans

In general, constructive feedback requires intervening at the appropriate depth, as will be discussed further in the next chapter, Issues in Consultant-Client Relationships. In particular, this means that the feedback be *sought* and that it be *provided directly to the person or unit for appropriate action. Constructive feedback also requires that positive data not be withheld.* There is much wisdom in the motto presented in the book *The One Minute Manager:* Help People Reach Their Full Potential—Catch Them Doing Something Right."[1]

STAFFING AND CAREER DEVELOPMENT

Many aspects of the staffing and career development processes, broadly conceived, can be affected by an evolving OD effort, and vice versa. There are implications for selection, orientation and assimilation, transfer and promotion, training and development, and separation.

Selection

In the selection process, for example, there is likely to be an increasing degree of participation by peers in the nomination, evaluation, and selection of candidates. This would be congruent with a broadened level of participation in the organization and with more emphasis on the ability of employees to work interdependently and in team configurations. Training of present employees in effective interviewing of candidates would be important in this evolution. Team member involvement in the selection of both team leaders and new team members is a feature of a number of contemporary work restructuring and QWL projects (see Chapter 14).[2]

Orientation and Assimilation

Substantial attention needs to be paid to the process of introducing new people into the system (sometimes called the "joining up process") if the staffing process is to be congruent with assumptions and values underlying OD efforts. Group methods in orientation and assimilation seem to be particularly useful.[3]

Some experiments with group techniques have been reported. For example, an experiment at Texas Instruments began when a department manager observed that new employees as well as their supervisors experienced high anxiety during the newcomers' first few days on the job and that this anxiety was seriously interfering with communications and training, with one of the consequences being high turnover. An experiment involving both a control group and an experimental group was conducted to test the efficacy of group methods in minimizing some of the anxiety. A control group participated in the usual procedure, which involved a two-hour orientation session with a good deal of information given out; the new employees were then sent to their supervisors for job instructions and from there to their work stations. The experimental group members attended the two-hour orientation seminar but were then sent for the rest of the day to another seminar, which provided information about supervisors and the job environment and presented considerable opportunity for group discussion and questions and answers. The new employees were told what to expect in terms of hazing and rumors from older employees, were given information about the style and practices of their supervisors, and were provided with statistics on their likelihood of success. By the end of four weeks, the experimental group was doing significantly better in job performance and attendance than was the control group.[4]

Group methods would also appear to be useful for groups in preparing for the entry of new members. Such sessions, under the guidance of a facilitator or a supervisor having skills in group processes, can do much to alleviate dysfunctional anxiety on the part of present members and to help them make plans for quickly incorporating the new person into the team. A group session with the new member—for example, involving introductions, descriptions of what each person is currently working on, concerns of the new person—can also be useful.

Career Development and Progression

If a major thrust of the OD process is to shift organization culture toward more honesty, more openness, more mutual support, and improved personal development, the career and growth aspirations of all organization members must be an area of concern. These are matters of considerable interest to employees at all levels and will tend to become more openly talked about. This will probably mean paying more attention to advancement and transfer opportunites and will require more of a commitment of resources to training and management development. There might also be some commitment of resources to "life-planning" or "career-planning" workshops; many organizations have experimented with such learning laboratories. Stranger T-group labs, of course, can be useful in the development of skills that will facilitate OD efforts. Technical courses might not be directly related to the OD process but could be important in a systematic program of career development. These experiences, however, will tend to be more highly specific to individual and system needs than is the usual case; that is, more attention will be given to the diagnosis of training and development needs, with less reliance on "packed" programs.

Another shift will probably occur. The climate could well shift from suppressing dialogue about the merits of leaving the organization toward openly facing the issue of internal versus external career opportunities. A likely outcome, as indicated earlier, will be more effort to increase opportunities for internal mobility. Ideally, new departments, divisions, or subsidiaries could be spawned through paying attention to the entrepreneurial and career aspirations of organizational members. The removal of arbitrary ceilings on responsibility will probably release a good deal of energy for constructive contributions within the system.

To use terminology sometimes found in labor contracts, "job posting" (i.e., notifying present employees of job vacancies) and "bidding" (i.e., permitting people to apply for these vacancies) are possible outcomes of an OD effort. This would be congruent with the open developmental thrust of OD. Another outcome might be more attention to the development of "career ladders," which are diagrams of routes of promotion and transfer within and across various job specialities. These devices are used to advise employees about career opportunities and to assist management in planning the training required for progression from one job to another.[5] As a result of such devices as job posting, bidding and career ladders, more time and effort is likely to be spent in processing internal requests for transfer and promotion and in developing training opportunities. The net effect on employees, however, is likely to be one of higher morale, better placement, better diagnosis of training needs, and improved skills.

The developmental, organic philosophy inherent in the OD process creates a major dilemma relative to the use of psychological tests for selection purposes, especially in the promotion system. On the one hand, some tests, such as intelligence tests, can have sufficient validity in specific circumstances to warrant their use as one additional source of relevant data. On the other hand, tests can leave the candidate feeling subject to mysterious or arbitrary criteria or locked into his or her own personal characteristics which are not subject to modification.

The "assessment center" concept may provide some leads toward solving the testing dilemma. Briefly, companies using assessment centers typically give the candidate, usually a nonsupervisory person interested in promotion, an extensive battery of tests and involve the candidate in an interview and group discussions and other group situations. Trained line managers, who have been observing, then make rankings of the relative performance of the candidates. In general, it has been found that assessment centers increase the proportion of successful to unsuccessful supervisors and higher managers and are useful in identifying management potential among minority and women employees.[6]

The ingredients that can shift the assessment center process from being strictly a matter of selection to one that is developmental are the dialogue that communicates the results to the candidate and the developmental opportunities that are subsequently provided. For example, if the assessment center highlights some deficiencies in group discussion, a center staff member can provide some feedback (ideally, requested by the candidate), and the organization may provide opportunities for developing additional skill. Then, too, the whole process permitting candidates to apply for the assessment center experience and selecting some candidates for promotion tends to create an element of openness and mobility in the system which might not otherwise be there. This is not to say that the use of an assessment center is always constructive. The lack of an effective feedback and discussion process can produce suspicion and hostility. Further, there will be great resentment if the process is perceived as forever cutting someone off from promotional opportunities. Some experimentation has occurred—apparently successful— in dispensing with the selection aspects of assessment centers and focusing solely on using the process as a developmental tool. In this case, no report is given to higher management.[7]

Group input in the selection of formal leaders would also be congruent with the thrust of an OD effort. Although such an approach, like a number of others we have mentioned, can and does occur outside of OD efforts, it would be inconsistent with the OD process not to consider the feelings and perceptions of group members in these important decisions. There may be instances when it would be appropriate to delegate to a group the selection of a new leader. For example, Graphic Controls has used top-management team consensus decision making in the selection of a new president.[8]

Separations, Layoffs, and Other Crises

It follows that exit from the organization is also likely to require more attention. It would be inconsistent to be concerned about job and career needs up to retirement age and to ignore the dynamics of the inevitable formal separation. Resignations and involuntary separations are also occurrences to which an organization moving extensively into an OD effort will want to pay considerable attention, both after the fact and in a preventive way. For example, in a more open, confronting—but supportive—climate, it is likely that inadequate performance would be faced more quickly with the possibility of early correction, in contrast to unspoken resentments building up to a precipitous discharge.

Some organizations, using OD approaches or techniques congruent with the OD process, have reduced the trauma of layoffs stemming from adverse economic conditions. For example, during an aerospace industry downturn, one high-technology firm, having had an OD effort for a number of years, used facilitators and group methods in assisting those being laid off to enable them to overcome their disappointment and anxiety and make plans for a job search. Those being laid off were informed weeks ahead of time, in contrast to the more usual industrial practice of short notice, but overall the performance of those affected did not deteriorate. The company also made great efforts to place these employees with other organizations. (Most laid-off employees subsequently returned when business picked up again.) OD techniques were also used to help groups face up to the realities of the situaiton, to decrease distortions in perception, and to make plans to cope with the cutback.[9] During the OPEC oil embargo, Delta Airlines made extraordinary efforts to retain employees, a posture congruent with the team emphasis of OD. The board chairman, W. Thomas Beebe, told the top-management group: "Now the time has come for the stockholders to pay a little penalty for keeping the team together."[10]

For many years IBM has gone to great lengths to avoid layoffs, using such devices as normal attrition, curtailment of hiring, retraining, transfers, and early retirements to accomplish cost reductions dictated by business conditions.[11] Nucor, Maytag, and Dana Corporation have similar policies.[12] Ideally, the OD process assists top management in examining a wide range of options to follow in a budgetary crisis.

OD interventions can also assist organization members in avoiding a kind of organizational paralysis and the distortions of reality and communications that can occur in other crises as well. The death of a top executive, a serious fire or explosion, or potential plant closures are examples of crisis situations in which OD facilitators can assist in helping people communicate with one another and in making plans.

STARTUP OF NEW UNITS

Team building interventions have been found to be very useful in startup situations all the way from very small units to large, complex plants. For example, Roger Harrison describes a series of team meetings and OD interventions as an integral part of a successful startup of a British chemical plant. In particular, the technique of "role negotiation" was used.[13] Harrison reports some of the benefits:

> They learn one another's "operating characteristics," establish mutual expectations . . . When the startup begins they have . . . built an organization that they are all committed to make work, and they have established and practiced ways of changing it when the need arises.[14]

REWARDS

As in the staffing process, attention must be paid to the allocation of rewards (monetary and nonmonetary) as an OD effort unfolds. We think that any OD effort that improves the performance of organizational members and groups but ignores the total pool of rewards accruing to those members and groups will be self-defeating in the long run. In short, if there is a greatly increased sharing of responsibility and creativity in the attainment of organizational objectives and no proportionate sharing in the rewards, the OD effort will not be sustained.[15] There is no reason to believe that the owners or the top managers of an organization have needs and motives that are drastically different from those of their subordinates and a great deal of reason to believe that they are similar.

The more organic and interdependent the system becomes, the more attention will need to be paid to congruity in the total reward system.

In both profit and nonprofit organizations, this means attention paid to rewards for both individual and team contribution. To place high value on team and interteam cooperation and then allocate rewards solely for individual efforts would clearly be dysfunctional.[16] In a profit-oriented organization, a long-range OD effort might eventually precipitate some form of productivity gain sharing plan or stock ownership plan, or both.

The Scanlon Plan is an example of a plantwide productivty gain sharing plan that can be congruent with an OD effort. Under this plan, when labor costs go down in relationship to productivity, employees share in all or a part of the savings, depending on the particular company. Extensive use is made of committees that meet regularly to consider ways of improving production and to consider employee suggestions. The supervisor of each unit and a representative of the union are members of each committee; recommendations go to a company-wide screening committee consisting of top management and union officials. Ordinarily, all employees are involved.[17]

If an organization moves toward self-managed teams, management and employees will probably also want to move in the direction of "skills-based pay" for team members. Under this concept, such as at TRW, team members are paid in accordance with the number of skills they have mastered.[18] At some of Volvo's plants in Sweden, a bonus scheme is utilized to reward individual skill development as well as the amount of responsibility assumed by teams in such matters as quality control, maintenance, and personnel administration.[19]

At a minimum, it would be important to manage the movement of wage and salary scales consistent with the success of the organization. (The possibility of facing up to temporarily reducing wage and salary levels as one option in a financial crisis would also seem more likely in an organization that has been involved in an OD effort for some time.) Obviously, money is not the only reward accruing from the internal and external environments, and attention would also need to be paid to such matters as recognition and opportunities for meaningful interaction in the broader community.

ORGANIZATIONAL JUSTICE

A shift in team and organizational culture toward more openness and toward more mutual concern should, in large part, facilitate the airing of felt injustices. From our experience, this does occur—and in a more natural and less threatening way. Grievances tend to be raised when they occur and are worked out quickly. (This phenomenon plus others that tend to stem from OD efforts, from our observations, seemingly improves mental health. We see OD as a way of improving mental health in an organization; many of its practices and underlying concepts are congruent with theory and clinical experience in counseling psychology, family therapy, some aspects of psychiatry, and community mental health programs.)

We are not recommending doing away with formalized appeal procedures, however, or what we call *organizational due process.* We have defined the latter as consisting of "established procedures for handling complaints and grievances, protection against punitive action for using such established procedures, and careful, systematic, and thorough review of the substance of complaints and grievance."[20] We believe a formalized appeal system may be needed to protect individuals from gross anomalies in an organization's culture. For example, what if a norm begins to develop that says it is taboo ever to question the usefulness of any part of the OD effort? Or that subordinates should always be "open" no matter what the consequences might be, but that superiors may have hidden agendas? Or that talking about seniority is off limits even though employees feel deeply that length of service is a significant investment to be taken into account in job retention? Such an environment needs a formal appeal system. It is clearly consistent for a system that values openness to retain mechanisms that tend to protect openness.

MONETARY COSTS AND SKILL DEMANDS

The use of external and internal third parties in the role of change agents, and the use of off-site workshops, is obviously going to cost money. If an organization development effort is to be successful, however, there must be a sustained commitment to the notion that the development of human resources is as important as the development of other kinds of resources. Symptomatic of the lack of such a commitment is the assumption that a one-shot team-building exercise will suffice to cure organizational problems. Experience shows that shifting to and maintaining the kind of culture we have been describing must be an ongoing process and that it requires resources.

In addition, the costs in terms of effort and skill demands should not be ignored. In some ways, the environment we have been describing is more difficult and demanding than that found in more traditional organizational cultures. Team members, for example, no longer find it quite so comfortable to let the superior carry the responsibility for decision making or find it convenient to use scapegoats to rationalize why things went wrong. The newer culture is likely to include a commitment to examine all the forces bearing on a problem, including one's own impact.

Thus, while the newer culture may be, and usually is, more exciting and rewarding, it is likely to be more difficult and challenging as well. Implicit demands will be made upon organizational members constantly to improve their skills in managing the human-social subsystem as well as managing the other major subsystems.

SUMMARY

A sustained, successful organization development effort will have extensive ramifications throughout the system. Attention will need to be paid to the design and quality of a wide range of feedback subsystems; to many aspects of the broad staffing and career development processes, including selection, orientation and assimilation, transfers, promotions, and separations; to monetary and nonmonetary rewards; to organizational justice; and to the monetary costs and new demands for upgrading skills. In general, the administration of a wide variety of organizational subsystems—the formal aspects of the human-social subsystem and the communications and feedback components of the structural subsystem, in particular—will have to be congruent with the OD effort if the process of organizational improvement is to be sustained.

NOTES

1. Kenneth Blanchard and Spencer Johnson, *The One Minute Manager* (New York: Berkley Books, 1983), p. 39.

2. Stephen H. Fuller, "How Quality-of-Worklife Projects Work for General Motors," *Monthly Labor Review,* 103 (July 1980), pp. 37–39; and Irving Bluestone, "How Quality of Worklife Projects Work for the United Auto Workers," *Monthly Labor Review,* 103 (July 1980), pp. 39–41.

3. We think that the group methods mentioned in this chapter are likely to be more viable that the selecting, paying, promoting, and firing of groups that Leavitt speculates about in his provocative essay. See Harold J. Leavitt, "Suppose We Took Groups Seriously," in Eugene L. Cass and Frederick G. Zimmer, eds., *Man and Work in Society* (New York: Van Nostrand Reinhold, 1975), pp. 67–77.

4. See Carl A. Gomersall and M. Scott Myers, "Breakthrough in On-the-Job Training," *Harvard Business Review,* 44 (July–August 1966), pp. 62–72.

5. For an illustration, see William P. Fisher and Paul Gaurnier, *Career Ladders in the Food Service Industry* (Chicago: National Restaurant Association, 1971), p. 25; or Wendell French, *The Personnel Management Process,* 6th ed. (Boston: Houghton Mifflin, 1987), p. 302.

6. James R. Huck and Douglas W. Bray, "Management Assessment Center Evaluations and Subsequent Performance of White and Black Females," *Personnel Psycholoyg,* 29 (Spring 1976), p. 13; and Robert B. Finkle, "Managerial Assessment Centers," in Marvin D. Dunnette, ed., *Handbook of Industrial and Organizational Psychology* (Chicago: Rand McNally, 1976), pp. 861–888.

7. See Gary L. Hart and Paul H. Thompson, "Assessment Centers for Selection or Development?" *Organizational Dynamics,* 7 (Spring 1979), pp. 63–77; and Louis Olivas, "Using Assessment Centers for Individual and Organization Development," *Personnel,* 57 (May–June 1980), pp. 63–67.

8. Ernest C. Miller, "Hire in Haste, Repent at Leisure—The Team Selection Process at Graphic Controls," *Organizational Dynamics,* 8 (Spring 1980), pp. 3–26.

9. For a discussion of the use of OD facilitators in layoff situations, see Sheldon Davis and Herbert Shepard, "Organization Develpoment in Good Times and Bad," *Journal of Contemporary Business,* 1 (Summer 1972), pp. 65–73. See also Leonard Greenhalgh, "Maintaining Organizational Effectiveness During Organizational Retrenchment," *Journal of Applied Behavioral Science,* 18, No. 2 (1982), pp. 155–170; and Susan A. Mohrman and Allan M. Mohrman, Jr., "Employee Involvement in Declining Organizations," *Human Resource Management,* 22 (Winter 1983), pp. 445–466.

10. Richard T. Pascale and Anthony G. Athos, *The Art of Japanese Management* (New York: Warner Books, 1981), p. 288.

11. See *Busienss Week,* February 15, 1988, p. 98.

12. Robert H. Waterman, Jr., *The Renewal Factor* (New York: Bantam Books, 1987), p. 229.

13. Roger Harrison, "Startup: The Care and Feeding of Infant Systems," *Organizational Dynamics,* 10 (Summer 1981), pp. 5–29.

14. Ibid., p. 18.

15. Experience at TRW is consistent with this assertion. See Meyer M. Cahn, "Thoughts on Planned Change and Change Diffusion: An Interview with Shel Davis," *Journal of Applied Behavioral Science,* 12 (April–June 1976), p. 235.

16. For example, some of the project teams in one of the Corning Glass Works divisions had becone ineffective and conflict ridden. When a substantial part of the individuals' performance ratings (the mechanism for giving raises and promotions) was based on performance in the project

teams, in contrast to basing ratings solely on performance in the functional areas, effectiveness of the teams was dramatically increased. William F. Dowling, ''The Corning Approach to Organization Development,'' *Organizational Dynamics*, 3 (Spring 1975), pp. 26–27.

17. See Edward E. Lawler III, *High-Involvement Management* (San Francisco: Jossey-Bass Publishers, 1986), pp. 144–169; and James W. Driscol ''Working Creativity with a Union: Lessons from the Scanlon Plan,'' *Organizational Dynamics*, 8 (Summer 1979), pp. 61–80.

18. *Wall Street Journal*, May 22, 1984, p. 1.

19. Berth Jonsson and Alden G. Lank, ''Volvo: A Report on the Workshop on Production Technology and Quality of Work Life,'' *Human Resource Management*, 24 (Winter 1985), pp. 461–463.

20. French, *The Personnel Management Process*, pp. 145–146.

17

ISSUES IN CONSULTANT-CLIENT RELATIONSHIPS

A number of interrelated issues can arise in consultant-client relationships in OD activities, and they need to be managed appropriately if adverse effects are to be avoided. These issues tend to center on the following important areas:

Defining the client system
Trust
The nature of the consultant's expertise
The contract
Diagnosis and appropriate interventions
The depth of interventions
On being absorbed by the culture
The consultant as a model
The consultant team as a microcosm
Action research and the OD process
Client dependency and terminating the relationship
Ethical standards in OD
Implications of OD for the client

There are no simple prescriptions for resolving dilemmas or problems in these aspects of OD, but we do have some notions about managing these areas.

DEFINING THE CLIENT SYSTEM

The question of who the client is quickly becomes an important issue in consultant-client relationships. We think a viable model is one in which, in the initial contact, a single manager is the client, but as trust and confidence develop between the key client and the consultant, both begin to view the manager and his or her subordinate team as the client, and then the manager's total organization as the client. Ideally, this begins to occur in the first interview. Thus the health and vitality of the various organizational subsystems, as well as the effectiveness and growth of all individual members of the client system, clearly become the consultant's concern.

Although this is a controversial point, we find ourselves somewhat dubious about vague notions related to the consultant's representing the total organization when he or she is working with some subdivision of the total. To be effective, the consultant must have a direct relationship with, and be able to influence, the people in the system. The change agent cannot help those with whom he or she does not interact—to attempt to do so would be a projection of one's assumptions about what some vague ''they'' might want. Or, if the consultant is carrying out some secret mandate of higher management, relationships with the more immediate clients are bound to fail. The truth will eventually become apparent, and the consultant will be reduced to impotency. Even if the OD consultant is open about some mandate from the top of the hierarchy, efforts will tend to be minimized simply because an externally directed mission is being attempted. Successful OD efforts involve a process of mutual influence, not an imposed program from any direction.

The total system, however, will not be ignored in an effective consulting relationship with a subdivision. The effective consultant will have some ideas about what courses of action will be helpful and what will be dysfunctional relative to the total system, and will express relevant sentiments—concerns, in particular—to the key client. The key client, moreover, will be the real expert about the broader system, and the key client and the consultant together will be looking for ways to improve the total. The real issue, then, is openness. If the client and the consultant are open with each other, the total system becomes a matter of joint concern.[1]

THE TRUST ISSUE

A good deal of the interaction in early contacts between client and consultant is implicitly related to developing a relationship of mutual trust. For example, the key client may be fearful that things will get out of hand with an outsider intervening in the system— that the organization will be overwhelmed with petty complaints or that people will be encouraged to criticize their superiors. Subordinates may be concerned that they will be manipulated toward their superiors' goals with little attention given to their own. These kinds of concerns mean that the consultant will need to earn trust in these and other areas and that high trust will not be immediate.

Similarly, the consultant's trust of the client may be starting at neutral. The consultant will be trying to understand the client's motives and will want to surface any that are partly hidden. For example, if the client has hopes that a team-building session will punish an inadequately performing subordinate, the consultant and the client will need to reassess the purposes of team building and examine whether that activity is the appropriate context for confronting the matter. On a positive note, the client may see OD as a means of increasing both the client's and the subordinates' effectiveness, plus having hopes that a successful OD effort may bring considerable recognition from superiors. Surfacing such motives and examining their implications for effective behavior will enhance trust between the consultant and the client and will help to assure the eventual success of OD activities.

A related matter is the mystique surrounding organization development and related areas—laboratory training, in particular. In our judgment, the more that assumptions, theory, and technology are shared with the client and the client system, the more that trust develops and the more effective becomes the collaboration.

In this connection a common mistake is for external or internal consultants, in their enthusiasm, to be ''selling'' a kind of utopia instead of concentrating on helping clients with their problems. For example, they may be perceived as selling trust, openness, cooperation, and the like. While we believe that these are good things, they are probably worked on best in the context of helping the client system solve those problems perceived as interfering with organizational effectiveness. In other words, being perceived as helpful enhances trust between client and consultant; conversely, selling philosophy may inhibit trust.

Trust and resistance problems also center on what we call the ''good guy–bad guy syndrome.'' Internal or external OD consultants, through their enthusiasm for an exciting technology, may signal that they perceive themselves as the carriers of the message, that is, that they are ''good guys,'' and implicitly that others are not, or at least are backward. This obviously creates all sorts of trust and resistance problems. People usually want to work collaboratively with others in the pursuit of common ends—but people tend to resist being pushed around, or put down, under whatever banner. No one likes being put in the ''bad guy'' role, and we mistrust and resent those who seem to be doing that to us. This can be a trap not only for the consultant but also for the overly enthusiastic line manager.

Confidentiality must be maintained if trust is to be maintained. Even unintentional errors can be disastrous to the consultant-client relationship. Gavin gives an illustration in which notes made by consultants on the leadership and communication styles of managers were inadvertently duplicated and circulated to participants along with notes on workshop themes and action steps. The consultants had been asked to do the latter; the notes on the managers' styles had been intended to be used by the facilitators in private counseling sessions with individual managers. As Gavin reports it, ''By the time these notes had been circulated, any semblance of trust in the consultants had been destroyed.''[2] We will have more to say about trust later.

THE NATURE OF THE CONSULTANT'S EXPERTISE

Partly because of the unfamiliarity with process consultation and other OD interventions, clients frequently try to put the consultant in the role of the expert on substantive content, such as on personnel policy or organizational structure. *We believe it is possible, and desirable, for the OD consultant to be an expert in the sense of being competent to present a range of options open to the client,* but any extensive reliance on the traditional mode of consulting, that is, giving substantive advice, will tend to negate the OD consultant's effectiveness. The OD consultant needs to resist the temptation of playing the content expert and will need to clarify his or her role with the client when this becomes an issue.

Lapsing into the expert or advocate role on substantive matters frequently stems from an overriding desire to please the client. The consultant wishes to maintain the relationship for a variety of reasons—professional, financial, or ego reasons—and naturally wishes to be perceived as being competent. The consultant therefore gets trapped into preparing reports or giving substantive advice, which if more than minimal, will reduce his or her effectiveness.

There are at least four good reasons why the OD consultant should largely stay out of the expert role. The first is that a major objective of an OD effort is to help the client system to develop its own resources. The expert role creates a kind of dependency that typically does not lead to internal skill development.

The second reason is that the expert role almost inevitably requires the consultant to defend his or her recommendations. With reference to an initial exploratory meeting, Schein mentions the danger of being "seduced into a selling role" and states that under such conditions "we are no longer exploring the problem."[3] In short, finding oneself in the expert role and defending one's advice tends to negate a collaborative, developmental approach to improving organizational processes.

A third reason for largely avoiding the expert role has to do with trust. As shown in Table 17-1, one criterion for resolving whether to provide confidential reports or advice to top management is how such an intervention would affect various client groups in the organization and the consultant's relationship with them. The OD consultant's role is a tenuous one at best. Any impression that the consultant is making recommendations inimical to members of client groups puts the consultant in the role of an adversary. For example, the disclosure that the consultant has made a secret recommendation that the number of divisions and vice presidents be reduced from 16 to 8 is likely to be met with widespread alarm and immediate distrust of the consultant. The question will also immediately arise, What else is the consultant up to that we don't know about? Thus, making recommendations to the top is quite different from confronting the top-management group with the data that three-fourths of the members of the top team believe that the organization has serious problems, partly stemming from too many divisions. In the one instance, the consultant is the expert; in the other instance, the consultant is helping the top team to be more expert in surfacing data and diagnosing the state of the system.

A fourth reason has to do with expectations. The process of soliciting information for use in a confidential report will reinforce expectations that the consultant's role is in the traditional mode of "analysis for the top."[4] Our guess is that OD consultants have enough difficulty getting many clients to move away from this mode without compounding the problem. As organizational members become more sophisticated about different consulting modes or assumptions underlying them, it may be that the OD consultant can increase the frequency with which he or she acts in the expert role.

Table 17–1   Is a Given Intervention Compatible with the OD Facilitator Role?

INTERVENTION	TO OR FOR CEO OR UNIT LEADER	TO OR FOR CLIENT TEAM
Confidential report of advice on qualifications of job incumbents	No	No
Confidential report or advice on structure of organization or unit	No	Usually not; at stake is the trust of the various team members. One question for resolving the issue would be, Who would be hurt?
Technical report or advice in some area of the consultant's expertise, e.g., computer applications or a wage and salary survey	Usually not. One consideration would be, What would this "analysis for the top" mode of consulting do to the client's expectations about my role?	Usually not. One consideration would be, What would this "analysis for the top" mode of consulting do to the client's expectations about my role?
Describing various options open to the client and the implications of those options	Yes and no. Depends on whether the intervention is seen as perspective enlarging or prescriptive for the CEO or other key client, whether the client and consultant are open with others about the request, and whether considerable trust has been earned.	Yes, providing that the intervention is seen as perspective enlarging and not as prescriptive.
Advice on OD strategy	Yes, if it is overall organizational strategy and if shared with top team and more broadly in the organization. Yes, if it is strategy for team, providing that it is shared with team.	Yes, if it is strategy for team. Yes, if it is broad organization strategy providing that advice is shared widely in the organization.
Advice on intervention, e.g., when and how a team-building session should be conducted	Yes, providing that advice is shared with top team.	Yes.
Data feedback from interviews or questionnaires	Yes, if it is data about the leader. Yes, if it is team or organizational data and others have concurred in the strategy of the top person having a preliminary briefing. No, if the understanding was that the data would be fed back to the team first.	Yes, if it is data abut the team. No, if it is data about other teams, unless data have been aggregated to present overall organization averages, ranges, etc., and there has been wide concurrence on the strategy.
Guidance or moderating of a team-building session	Yes, if it is with concurrence of team.	Yes, if it is with concurrence of team.
Process consultation or coaching on individual behavior or style.	Yes, if it is requested.	Yes, if it is requested.

There are exceptions to these reasons, some of which we describe in Table 17–1. For example, it is usually desirable and necessary to give advice on the design of a workshop or the design of a questionnaire. Such advice is usually quite facilitating, providing that the consultant is open to modifications of his or her suggestions by members of the client system. As Schein states it,

> The process consultant should not withhold his expertise on matters of the learning process itself; but he should be very careful not to confuse being an expert on *how to help an organization to learn* with being an expert on the *actual management problems* which the organization is trying to solve.[5]

In other words, the OD consultant should act in the expert role on the *process* used but not on the *task*.

Another exception consists of providing a range of options open to the client. For example, if there are issues about how a unit or organization should be structured in terms of which functions should be grouped together or who should report to whom, it can be helpful for the OD consultant to present some optional forms and to discuss the possible implications of each. However, such an intervention should ordinarily be presented in a team situation so as not to be misinterpreted, must be timely in terms of its relevance and acceptability, and should be essentially perspective-enlarging in contrast to prescriptive. *We believe that the more extensive the OD consultant's knowledge of management and organization, the more effective the OD consultant can be. But there is a difference between being essentially a facilitator-educator and being essentially an advice-giver.* Even the presenting of options can be overdone. If the consultant's ideas become the focal point for prolonged discussion and debate, the consultant has clearly shifted away from the facilitator role. Obviously, this is not an either/or matter; it is a matter of degree and emphasis.

OTHER DIMENSIONS OF THE INITIAL "CONTRACT"

Implicit in our discussion of these issues is the issue of consultant and client formulating the "psychological contract." The resolution of such matters as who the client is, underlying concerns about how the OD effort might evolve, and whether the consultant will make substantive recommendations will have a major impact on subsequent events.

The more formal compensation aspects of the initial contract are also important and need to be confronted for the peace of mind of both client and consultant. We tend to prefer a verbal agreement as to an hourly or a daily fee, with no charge for a brief telephone discussion, and usually no charge for a longer exploration in our offices or over lunch in the key client's office. Thereafter, we like to bill the client organization monthly for any time spent on the organization's behalf, although the approximate time amounts will be based on mutual agreement, with either party free to terminate the relationship should it not be mutually satisfactory. In the case of the internal OD consultant, the amount of time availability will be an important dimension.

Some consultants will charge for the preliminary exploratory discussions. We find this a reasonable practice, since the key client frequently begins to develop new insight into the nature of the problem during the exploratory interviews.[6] Furthermore, in terms of the application of professional knowledge and skill, the initial meeting is as professionally demanding as the interventions that occur later as the OD effort unfolds.

DIAGNOSIS AND APPROPRIATE INTERVENTIONS

Another pitfall for the consultant is the convenience of applying intervention techniques with which the consultant is familiar or particularly likes but which may not square with a current diagnosis of unit problems. Thus the consultant who is an effective T-group trainer may push participants in a team-building session into an intensive interpersonal laboratory session, while the more pressing issues may have to do with goal setting or role expectations. Or a consultant may rely heavily on a few instrumented techniques in his or her ''bag of tricks'' when the need for educational interventions may be minimal and the need for confronting issues directly may be high. In short, as Herb Shepard has said, the consultant should ''start where the system is.''[7]

We think a consultant should do what he or she can do, but the intervention should be appropriate to the diagnosis. The wider the range of interventions open to the consultant, of course, the more the consultant can be free to make a diagnosis unencumbered by anxieties about how to intervene. Inherent in making a perceptive diagnosis is an awareness of the complexity of and the interdependency of the various organizational subsystems.

DEPTH OF INTERVENTION

In addition to the issue of selecting specific interventions from a range of interventions is the question of the depth of intervention. By *depth* we mean the extent to which the change target is the formal system, the informal system, or the self (see Figure 17-1 for a comparision of various group or organizational interventions in terms of depth).[8] In Harrison's terms, this continuum is based upon accessibility and individuality. By *accessibility* Harrison means the degree to which the data are more or less public versus being hidden or private and the ease with which the intervention skills can be learned. By *individuality* is meant the closeness to the person's perceptions of self and the degree to which the effects of an intervention are in the individual in contrast to the organization. We are assuming that the closer one moves on this continuum to the sense of self, the more the inherent processes have to do with emotions, values, and hidden matters and, consequently, the more potent they are to do either good or harm. It requires a careful diagnosis to determine that these interventions are appropriate and relevant. If they are inappropriate, they may be destructive or, at a minimum, unacceptable to the client or the client system.

To minimize these risks, Harrison suggests two criteria for determining the appropriate depth of intervention:

> First to *intervene at a level no deeper than that required to produce enduring solutions to the problems at hand;* and, second, to *intervene at a level no deeper than that at which the energy and resources of the client can be committed to problem solving and to change.*[9]

To Harrison, these criteria require that the consultant proceed no faster or deeper than the legitimation obtained from the client system culture and that he or she stay at the level of consciously felt needs.[10] We think these are sound guidelines.

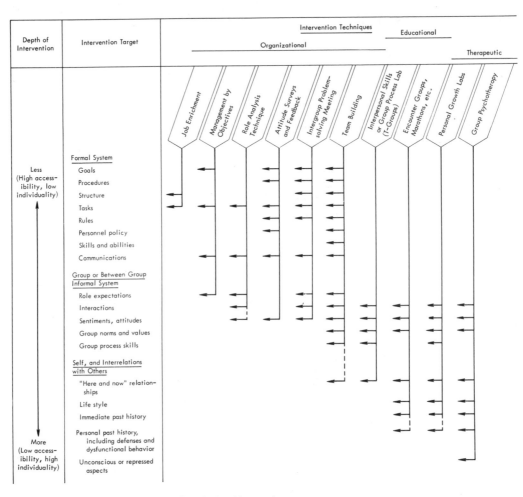

Figure 17-1 Depth of Various Group or Organizational Interventions

Harrison does recognize, however, and we agree, that the change agent is continuously confronted by the dilemma of whether to "lead and push, or to collaborate and follow."[11] Harrison's orientation is to the latter, but we are inclined to be slightly less conservative. We think that, to be effective, the consultant needs occasionally but prudently to take minor risks in the direction of leading and pushing, but these risks should not be quantum jumps. As the consultant develops expertise in diagnosis and in making interventions, the risks that are run are mainly the risks of a rejected suggestion. We do, however, agree with the essence of what Harrison is suggesting and agree with his criteria.

Another way of viewing depth of intervention might be to think about the performance of units by descending order of systems and subsystems. Data about the behavior and performance of the total organization is perhaps the most accessible and the least personal and perhaps creates the least personal anxiety and defensiveness. Performance and behavior data about *me* in an organization are perhaps the least accessible and the most personal. The consultant, then, needs to have the skills to intervene effectively down through these progressively smaller systems—frequently simultaneously—according to whether the issue is

> How well are we performing as a total organization?
> How well are we doing as a large unit?
> How well are we doing as a team?
> How well are you and I working together?
> How well are you doing?
> How well am I doing ?

The concept of depth of intervention, viewed either in this way or in terms of a continuum of the formal system, informal system, and self suggests that the consultant needs an extensive repertoire of conceptual models, intervention techniques, and sensitivities to be able to be helpful at all these levels.

ON BEING ABSORBED BY THE CULTURE

One of the many mistakes one can make in the change-agent role is to let oneself be seduced into joining the culture of the client organization. While one needs to join the culture enough to participate in and enjoy the functional aspects of the prevailing culture—an example would be good-natured bantering when it is clear to everyone that such bantering is in fun and means inclusion and liking—participating in the organization's pathology will neutralize the consultant's effectiveness.

One of us recalls an experience in which the most critical issue to surface in preliminary interviews with members of a professional staff group—we'll call it an engineering organization—was who would be the new manager. The current manager's promotion was to take effect in a few weeks, and he was anxious that the group members provide some input on the selection of his successor as well as that they tidy up a number of unresolved communications and administrative matters. One obvious candidate for the promotion was a senior engineer who was highly respected for his professional competency—clearly an engineer's engineer. However, younger members of the staff privately expressed fears to the consultant that the senior engineer would be too authoritarian if he assumed the manager's role, and they did not want to lose his accessibility as professional mentor. On the other hand they had strong concerns that they would seriously hurt the man's feelings by openly confronting the issue of his style and that he might resign if the matter were confronted. As a result, the consultant team acquiesced in not feeding back to the group the issue most troubling them. In effect, everyone but the senior engineer conspired to protect him, to pretend that he was a strong candidate for promotion, and to postpone the decision. As a result, the group was partly paralyzed for weeks. The immediate effect of the team-building session was one of frustration for all of the participants. In retrospect, the consultant's view is that the client system could probably have worked through the matter and that the senior engineer would have proved to be the strongest and most adaptable there that day, including the consultants.

The dilemma created when a client subgroup describes an issue to the consultant but says, "We won't deal with it and we won't let you surface it in the total group," is a troublesome one. One way out of the dilemma may be to discuss the likely consequences of not dealing with the issue. One consequence may be that the recipient of unclear communication develops a kind of paranoia from the confusing or distorted signals he or she is receiving. Another consequence is that a norm may be implicitly created that says *all* negative interpersonal feedback is off limits, which has the deeper consequence that the entire group is denied data about problem areas that could be constructively worked on. Another consequence might be that the group is denied the capability of sharing much positive feedback for fear that such sharing could spill over into qualifying statements that begin to get into negative areas. Confronting the subgroup with the dilemma and outlining the consequences of inaction, then, may be much more constructive than succumbing to the pressures of the culture:

Reddin provides us with a delightful account of another instance of the consultant's being absorbed by the culture.

> The chairman of a 10,000 employee subsidiary of a British industrial giant invited me to dinner with his board at their country house training centre. It was an epic meal and the vintage port flowed. The conversation was witty and I had to lean on my limited classical education to keep up with the literary allusions. In preparation for an MBO conference I had in fact recently re-read Thucydides' *History of the Peloponnesian War* and this gave me some good lines. My first error was accepting the first invitation and then my next was visiting in similar circumstances yet again. It was a superb, if unconscious, seduction job by the client. My relationship to this client became intellectual witty companion. My attempts to change it were met with incredulity.[12]

Although Reddin did not elaborate, the implication is that once the consultant became the "intellectual witty companion," the chairman resisted any efforts to be guided, along with the board members, toward examining the functional and dysfunctional aspects of the culture of the organization. Perhaps the only course of action open to the consultant, once he realized he had been absorbed by the culture, would have been to express openly his feelings and concerns about the situation to the chairman. Such an intervention might or might not have shifted the relationship more toward an OD consultant–key client mode. This is another illustration in which being absorbed by the culture of the client organization immobilized the change agent.

Internal change agents may be even more susceptible to absorption by the prevailing organizational culture than are external change agents. As long as they work with people and units that have considerable "political distance" from their own unit, their objectivity may not be any more vulnerable than that of a consultant from the outside. On the other hand, if their own unit (whether they are specialists who are part of a personnel or an OD unit or have a home base in some line department) is somehow engaged in maneuvering for resources or power in competition with their client, they may inadvertently be drawn into the politics of the situation. Rather than helping to surface the dynamics of dysfunctional rivalry under appropriate circumstances, the change agents may become part of the problem, thus helping to submerge an issue or contributing to tactics incompatible with the helping role and thereby alienating the client or potential clients.

THE CONSULTANT AS A MODEL

Another important issue is whether change agents are willing and able to practice what they preach. In the area of feelings, for example, the consultant may be advocating a more open system in which feelings are considered legitimate and their expression important to effective problem solving and at the same time suppressing his or her own feelings about what is happening in the client system. In particular, this can be a frequent problem for the less-experienced change agent, and it usually has an impact on this person's feeling of competency: "If only I had said. . . ." The more one learns to be in touch with one's own feelings, the more spontaneous one can be and the greater the options open for interventions. (This is one reason why we recommend extensive T-group experience for OD consultants.) However, the client system is not the appropriate ground for working out any problems the consultant may be currently experiencing. On the other hand, being too aloof emotionally will tend to minimize the possibilities of helping the client.

As another example of modeling behavior, the OD consultant needs to give out clear messages—that is, the consultant's words and apparent feelings needs to be congruent. The consultant also needs to check on meanings, to suggest optional methods of solving problems, to encourage and support, to give feedback in constructive ways and to accept feedback, to help formulate issues, and to provide a spirit of inquiry. We are not suggesting that the OD consultant must be a paragon of virtue; rather, we are suggesting that to maximize one's effectiveness, it is necessary continuously to practice and develop the effective behaviors one wishes to instill in the client system.

THE CONSULTANT TEAM AS A MICROCOSM

The consultant–key client viewed as a team, or consultants working as a team, can profitably be viewed as a microcosm of the organization they are trying to create. In the first place, the consultant team must set an example of an effective unit if the team is to enhance its credibility. Second, change agents need the effectiveness that comes from continuous growth and renewal processes. And third, the quality of the interrelationships within the consulting team carries over directly into the quality of their diagnosis, their workshop or laboratory designs, and their interventions. To be more explicit about the last point, unresolved and growing conflict between two consultants can paralyze a workshop. Or simple lack of attention to team maintenance matters can produce morale problems that reduce spontaneity and creativity in planning sessions or in interacting with the client system.

ACTION RESEARCH AND THE OD PROCESS

A related issue is whether the OD process itself will be subject to the ongoing action research being experienced by the client system. The issue of congruency is, of course, important, but the viability of the OD effort and the effectiveness of the consultants may be at stake. Unless there are feedback loops relative to various interventions and stages in the OD process, the change agents and the organization will not learn how to make the future OD interventions more effective.

Feedback loops do not necessarily have to be complicated. Simple questionnaires or interviews can be very helpful. As an illustration, we recall having lunch with the key people who had been involved in a problem-solving workshop, and upon asking several questions about how things were going "back at the shop," we found that problems had emerged centering on who had been invited to attend the workshop and who had not. This feedback, at a minimum, has caused us to pay even more attention to prework and to helping workshop participants plan how to share effectively what has occurred with those not attending.

THE DEPENDENCY ISSUE AND TERMINATING THE RELATIONSHIP

If the consultant is in the business of enhancing the client system's abilities in problem solving and renewal, then the consultant is in the business of assisting the client to internalize skills and insights rather than to create a prolonged dependency relationship. This tends not to be much of an issue, however, if the consultant and the client work out the expert versus facilitator issue described earlier and if the consultant subscribes to the notion that OD should be a shared technology. The facilitator role, we believe, creates less dependency and more client growth than the traditional consulting modes, and the notion of a shared technology leads to rapid learning on the part of the client.

The latter notion is congruent with Argyris's admonition that if the consultant intervention is to be helpful in an ongoing sense, it is imperative for the client to have "free, informed choice."[13] And to have this free choice, it is necessary for the client to have a cognitive map of the overall process.[14] Thus the consultant will have to be quite open about such matters as the objectives of the various interventions that are made and about the sequence of planned events. The OD consultant should continuously be part educator as he or she intervenes in the system.

An issue of personal importance to the consultant is the dilemma of working to increase the resourcefulness of the client versus wanting to remain involved, to feel needed, and to feel competent. We think there is a satisfactory solution to this dilemma. A good case can be made, we believe, for a gradual reduction in external consultant use as an OD effort reaches maturity. In a large organization, one or more key consultants may be retained in an ongoing relationship, but with less frequent use. If the consultants are constantly developing their skills, they can continue to make innovative contributions. Furthermore, they can serve as a link with outside resources such as universities and research programs, and more important, they can serve to help keep the OD effort at the highest possible professional and ethical level. Their skills and insights should serve as a standard against which to compare the activities of internal change agents. Some of the most innovative and successful OD efforts on the world scene in our judgment, have maintained some planned level of external consultant use.

Another dimension of the issue arises, however, when the consultant senses that his or her assistance is no longer needed or could be greatly reduced. For the client's good, to avoid wasting the consultant's own professional resources, and to be congruent, the consultant should confront the issue.

A particularly troublesome dilemma occurs when the use of the consultant, in the judgment of the consultant, is declining more rapidly than progress on the OD effort seems to warrant. It would be easy to say that here, too, the consultant should raise the matter with the client, and undoubtedly this should occur even if there are risks in appearing self-serving, but we wish more were known about the dynamics of OD efforts' losing their momentum. Such additional knowledge would help consultants and clients to assess more objectively the extent of need for consultant assistance, how to improve the skills of the consultant and the client in managing the OD effort, and how to rejuvenate the OD effort if rejuvenation is warranted.

While much is ''known'' about the conditions that can lead to success or failure, we suspect that some OD efforts languish at the point when the next thrust would be to intensify the development of group and interpersonal skills and to confront those issues at this level that have been avoided. The action research approach can be an efficient way to improve many things in an organization fairly quickly, but some of the more difficult problems can remain submerged unless there is a real commitment to managing the culture in depth.

Tannenbaum believes that many OD programs taper off because there has not been enough attention to helping people and units let go of matters that need to be laid to rest, to die. He believes that in a real sense, facilitators should be able to assist in a mourning process, but to be of help, facilitators must be able to confront their own tendencies to want to hang on and their own vulnerability.

> My hunch is that after we get beyond those attitudes and behaviors most individuals and groups are relatively willing to alter, we then begin challenging the more central fixities that define individuals and organizational units at their cores. Holding on at this level becomes crucial. Yet we keep working on processes that focus on *change,* and do *not* do very much about facilitating mourning and the dying process—helping units let go.[15]

We also suspect that OD efforts frequently flounder because of internal power struggles that have not been sensed early enough by the consultant or understood well enough for anyone to intervene constructively. For example, some relatively powerful person or group may be fearful of losing status or influence and may be mobilizing support for the status quo through such tactics as distorting information or discrediting whoever is seen as the threat. The threat may be the change agent or the OD effort or the threat may be wholly unrelated to the OD process. But if people in the organization get caught up in the political power maneuvering, the OD effort may be immobilized. While not much is known about these occurrences as they relate to OD efforts, it would seem that these situations, if sensed, need to be surfaced and confronted head on. Such shadowy struggles are usually dysfunctional whether or not there is an OD effort under way, and the remedy may need to be a prompt description of reality by the chief executive officer. While a long-term OD effort should replace most such covert maneuvering with an open, working through of issues, these situations can and do occur while an OD effort is under way.

Sometimes the organization may simply be temporarily overloaded by externally imposed crises occupying the attention of key people. Under such conditions, the best strategy may be one of reducing or suspending the more formalized OD interventions and letting people carry on with their enhanced skills and then returning to the more formalized aspects at a later date. If more were known about the dynamics of these and the other circumstances we have described, the resolution of the problem of what to do when the OD effort seems to be running out of steam might take directions other than reducing or terminating the involvement of the change agent.

ETHICAL STANDARDS IN OD

Much of this chapter and, indeed, much of what has preceded in other chapters, can be viewed in terms of ethical issues. Since we have dealt largely with ethics in terms of the dysfuntional consequences or harm that can come from inappropriate interventions, we will not do a separate analysis here. We hope that it has become clear to the reader that the following ethical standards are a minimum for OD practice:

> Interventions must be selected that have a high probability of being helpful in the particular situation.
> The consultant should not use interventions that exceed his or her expertise.
> The client system should be as informed as is practical about the nature of the process.
> The consultant must not be working any personal, hidden agendas that obtrude into high-quality service for the client.
> Commitments to confidentiality must be kept.[16]
> Individuals must not be coerced into divulging information about themselves or others.
> The client must not be promised unrealistic outcomes.[17]

IMPLICATIONS OF OD FOR THE CLIENT

An OD effort has some fundamental implications for the chief executive officer and top managers of an organization, and we believe that these implications need to be shared and understood at the outset. We reach the following conclusions when we ask ourselves, What is top management buying into in participating in and supporting an OD effort?

Basically, *OD interventions* as we have described them, *are a conscious effort on the part of top management*

1. *To enlarge the data base for making management decisions.* In particular, the perceptions, sentiments, and expertise of team members throughout the organization are more extensively considered than heretofore.
2. *To expand the influence processes.* The OD process tends to further a process of mutual influence; managers and subordinates alike tend to be influential in ways they have not experienced previously.
3. *To capitalize on the strengths of the informal system and to make the formal and the informal system more congruent.* A great deal of information that has previously been suppressed within

individuals or within the informal system (e.g., appreciations, frustrations, hurts, opinions about how to do things more effectively, fears) begins to be surfaced and dealt with. Energies spent suppressing matters can now be rechanneled into cooperative effort.

4. *To become more responsive.* Management must now respond to data that have been submerged and must begin to move in the direction of personal, team, and organizational effectiveness suggested by the data.

5. *To legitimatize conflict as an area of collaborative management.* Rather than using win-lose, smoothing, or withdrawal modes of conflict resolution, the mode gradually becomes one of confronting the underlying basis for the conflict and working the problem through to a successful resolution.[18]

6. *To examine its own leadership style and ways of managing.* We do not think an OD effort can be viable long if the top-management team (the CEO plus subordinate team or the top team of an essentially autonomous unit) does not actively participate in the effort. The top team inevitably is a powerful determinant of organizational culture. OD is not a televised game being played for viewing by top management; members of top management are the key players.

7. *To legitimatize and encourage the examination and collaborative management of team, interteam, and organization cultures.* This is what OD is all about.

We think that these items largely describe the underlying implications for top management and that the OD consultant needs to be clear about them from the very beginning and to help the top-management group be clear about them as the process unfolds.[19]

SUMMARY

Numerous issues regarding the client-consultant relationship need to be addressed and managed in a successful OD effort. These issues include establishing the initial psychological contract, clarifying who is the client, clarifying the role of the consultant, identifying the nature of the consultant's expertise, examining the consequences of the consultant's participating in the organization's pathology, viewing the consultant and consulting teams as models, applying action research to OD, and terminating the relationship. These issues have important implications for top management.

NOTES

1. In consulting in the public sector, Golembiewski believes that the OD consultant should work for the "system," not specific individuals or units. See Robert T. Golembiewski, *Humanizing Public Organizations* (Mt. Airy, Md.: Lomond Publications, Inc., 1985), p. 293. W. Warner Burke sees the client as "The relationship and/or interface between individuals and units within and related to the systems." See his "Who Is the Client? A Different Perspective," *OD Practitioner*, 14 (June 1982), pp. 1–6.

2. James F. Gavin, "Survey Feedback: The Feedback of Science and Practice," *Group & Organization Studies*, 9 (March 1984), p. 46. For more on trust, see Dale E. Zand, *Information, Organization, and Power* (New York: McGraw-Hill, 1981), pp. 37–55.

3. Edgar H. Schein, *Process Consultation: Its Role in Organization Development* (Reading, Mass.: Addison-Wesley, 1969), p. 82. See also Edgar H. Schein, *Process Consultation: Its Role in Organization Development*, Vol. I (Reading, Mass.: Addison-Wesley, 1988).

4. Noel M. Tichy, "Agents of Planned Social Change: Congruence of Values, Cognition and Actions," *Administrative Science Quarterly,* 19 (June 1974), pp. 164–182.

5. Schein, *Process Consultation,* 1969, p. 120.

6. Ibid., p. 82.

7. Herbert A. Shepard, "Rules of Thumb for Change Agents," *OD Practitioner,* 17 (December 1985), p. 2. Shepard calls this the "Empathy Rule."

8. This discussion and Figure 17-1 were stimulated by and draw upon Roger Harrison's essay, "Choosing the Depth of Organizational Intervention," *Journal of Applied Behavioral Science,* 6 (April-June 1970), pp. 181–202.

9. Ibid., p. 201. [Harrison's emphasis.]

10. Ibid., pp. 198–199.

11. Ibid., p. 202.

12. W. J. Reddin, "My Errors in OD," paper presented to the Organization Development Division at the Academy of Management 36th Annual Meeting, Kansas City, Missouri, August 13, 1976, p. 3.

13. Chris Argyris, *Intervention Theory and Method* (Reading, Mass.: Addison-Wesley, 1970), p. 17.

14. See Chris Argyris, *Management and Organizational Development: The Path from XA to YB* (New York: McGraw-Hill, 1971), pp. 58, 108, 137, for a discussion of the importance of "maps."

15. Robert Tannenbaum, "Some Matters of Life and Death," *OD Practitioner,* 8 (February 1976), p. 5. See also Robert Tannenbaum and Robert W. Hanna, "Holding On, Letting Go, and Moving On," in Robert Tannenbaum, Newton Margulies, Fred Massarik and Associates, *Human Systems Development* (San Francisco: Jossey-Bass Publishers, 1985), pp. 95–121.

16. Walters looks at confidentiality in the context of the privacy issue in examining ethical issues in OD pertaining to freedom, privacy, and self-esteem. See Gordon A. Walter, "Organization Development and Individual Rights," *The Journal of Applied Behavioral Science,* 20 (Number 4, 1984), pp. 423–439.

17. For more on ethics in OD, see William Gellerman, "Values and Ethical Issues for Human Systems Development Practitioners," in Tannenbaum, Margulies, Massarik and Associates, *Human Systems Development,* op. cit., pp. 393–418; Louis P. White and Kevin C. Wooten, "Ethical Dilemmas in Various Stages of Organizational Development," *Academy of Management Review,* 8 (October 1983), pp. 690–697; Matthew B. Miles, "Ethical Issues in OD Intervention, *OD Practitioner,* 11 (October 1979), pp. 1–10; and American Association for the Advancement of Science, *Annotated Bibliography on Values and Ethics in Organization and Human Systems Development,* 1988.

18. Blake and Mouton refer to "confrontation," "forcing," "smoothing," "compromise," and "withdrawal" as the different modes of conflict resolution. See Robert Blake and Jane Mouton, *The Managerial Grid* (Houston: Gulf, 1964), pp. 30, 67, 93, 94, 122, 123, 163.

19. For more on the implications of OD for behavior changes in the client system, see Jerry I. Porras and Susan J. Hoffer, "Common Behavior Changes in Successful Organization Development Efforts," *The Journal of Applied Behavioral Science,* 22 (Number 4, 1986), pp. 477–494. For more on consultant-client relationships see Diane McKinney Kellogg, "Contrasting Successful and Unsuccessful OD Consultation Relationships," *Group & Organization Studies,* 9 (June 1984), pp. 151–176.

18

MECHANISTIC AND ORGANIC SYSTEMS AND THE CONTINGENCY APPROACH

Two types of organizations, *mechanistic* and *organic,* have been described by Tom Burns and G. M. Stalker; in this chapter we wish to explore the relevance of these concepts to organization development. These terms are used with considerable frequency, and it is important to understand their meanings and the implications of one system versus the other. These terms can be useful shorthand ways of describing the overall "climate" or mode of operating in an organization or its subunits, but, unfortunately, they can also be used as "bad" or "good" connotation. In general, OD activities tend to result in an organization beginning to take on more *organic* characteristics, but some paradoxes and contingencies need examining.

According to Burns and Stalker, these two types of organizations, mechanistic and organic, in their pure form, are seen as located on opposite ends of a continuum and not as a dichotomy.[1] Various organizations will be found at different points between these polarities and indeed may move back and forth along this continuum, depending upon the degree of stability or change being experienced. In addition, an organization may include both types within its subdivisions.

> Both types represent a "rational" form of organization, in that they may both, in our experience, be explicitly and deliberately created and maintained to exploit the human resources of a concern in the most efficient manner feasible in the circumstances of the concern. Not surprisingly, however, each exhibits characteristics which have been hitherto associated with different kinds of interpretation. For it is our contention that empirical findings have usually been classified according to sociological ideology rather than according to the functional specificity of the working organization to its task and the conditions confronting it.[2]

Thus, implicitly, Burns and Stalker do not see the occurrence of one or the other of these two systems as necessarily accidental, but as frequently stemming from the circumstances being faced by the organization. It would also seem to be implicit that the occurrence of one or the other might also stem from an ideological preference—a phenomenon that could represent a trap for overzealous adherents to either type of organization.

MECHANISTIC SYSTEMS

To elaborate on the two types, Burns and Stalker see the *mechanistic* form of organization as particularly appropriate to stable conditions and having the following characteristics:

1. A high degree of task differentiation and specialization, precise delineation of rights and responsibilities and methods to be used, and role incumbents tending to pursue technical improvements in means in contrast to focusing on the overall ends of the organization.
2. A high degree of reliance on each hierarchical level for task coordination, control, and communications. That is, each supervisor is responsible for reconciling the activities below him or her.
3. A tendency for the top of the hierarchy to control incoming and outgoing communications and to be conservative in dispensing information within the system. (Burns and Stalker give an example of a manager who literally controlled *all* correspondence in and out of the firm.)
4. A high degree of emphasis on vertical interactions between superiors and subordinates, with subordinate activities mainly governed by these interactions. (While Burns and Stalker do not say this, clearly there is an informal social system involving lateral peer interactions that stays mainly ''underground'' under these circumstances.)
5. Insistence on loyalty to the organization and to superiors.
6. A higher value placed on internal (local) knowledge, skill, and experience, in contrast to more general (cosmopolitan) knowledge, skill, and experience.[3]

Another characteristic, which is not explicit but is perhaps implied in Burns and Stalker's model and which we believe to be one of the key characteristics of a mechanistic system, is

7. A one-to-one leadership style, that is, with most interactions between superior and subordinate occurring in private discussion and an absence or minimal attention to group processes and the informal system. As seen in this form of organization, the superior-subordinate relationship tends to be a telling-reporting relationship. (See Figure 18–1). To illustrate the existence of such a leadership style, we have had managers tell us that, literally, their superior had never held a meeting involving all his/her immediate subordinates. They also said that most of the one-to-one conversations centered on assignments initiated by the superior, and in his/her office, that is, on his/her ''turf.''

ORGANIC SYSTEMS

In contrast, the *organic* system is seen by Burns and Stalker as appropriate to changing conditions and has the following characteristics.[4]

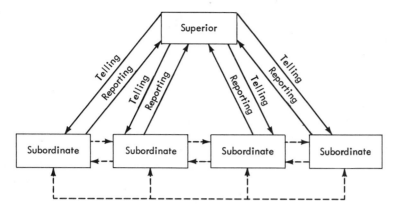

Figure 18-1 Characteristic Pattern of Leadership in a Mechanistic System

1. A continuous reassessment of tasks and assignments through interaction with others and a high value placed on utilizing special knowledge and experience that can contribute to the "real" problems being faced by the organization.

2. A network of authority, control, and communication, stemming more from expertise and commitment to the total task than from the omniscience of the chief executive or the authority of hierarchical roles. Centers of control and communication are frequently *ad hoc,* that is, are located where the knowledge is. Responsibility is viewed as something to be shared rather than narrowly delimited.

Although the organic systems "remain stratified," they tend to be stratified more on the basis of expertise:

> The lead in joint decisions is frequently taken by seniors, but it is an essential presumption of the organic system that the lead, i.e., "authority," is taken by whoever shows himself/herself most informed and capable, i.e., the "best authority." The location of authority is settled by consensus.[5]

3. A tendency for communications to be much more extensive and open in contrast to limited and controlled. (This is more implicit in Burns and Stalker's model than explicit.)

4. The encouragement of a communications pattern and style that is lateral and diagonal as well as vertical and that is more of a consultative, information- and advice-giving nature than of a command or decision-relying nature. By *diagonal* we refer to Burns and Stalker's notion about communications between people of different rank and across functional groups.

5. A greater emphasis on commitment to the organization's tasks, progress, and growth than on obedience or loyalty.

6. High value placed on expertise relevant to the technological and commercial milieu of the organization (cosmopolitan skills). One indicator would be "importance and prestige attach[ed] to affiliations."[6]

And finally, to supplement this model, a characteristic that we believe to be central to a truly organic system:

7. A team leadership style, with an emphasis on consultation and considerable attention to interpersonal and group processes, including methods of decision making and more

frequent decisions by consensus.[7] (See Figure 18–2.) Perhaps symbolically, meetings are frequently held away from the superior's office, with physical facilities designed to further group dialogue. One-to-one interactions occur (perhaps frequently), but there is a strong emphasis on team interactions around matters of mutual concern.

THE CONTINGENCY QUESTION

From our experience, organization development activities tend to shift an organization toward the organic mode as described by the seven characteristics just outlined. The reason, of course, is that there is a deliberate emphasis in an OD program toward collaboratively managed group culture and collaboratively managed organizational culture. Whether we call it collaboration, consultation, or open communications, the theme in OD is effective participation. And that theme pervades most of the characteristics of an organic system.

Paradoxically, however, while the thrust of an organization development effort is toward the organic mode, OD activities sometimes increase the mechanistic quality of some organizational dimensions. For example, consensus might develop in a work team so that it would be functional for duties and responsibilities to be more precisely defined or so that there should be more reliance on the superior for coordination and control in the assignment of routine tasks. At the level of examining its methods, the team has organic characteristics; at the level of routine tasks, the team is deciding to become more mechanistic. As another illustration, an organization development effort might strengthen the organic characteristics of the design and engineering departments of an automobile company, while the assembly-line departments might remain substantially mechanistic in terms of task delineation although becoming more organic in terms of employee involvement in the control function.

Thus it will not suffice to have an ideological adherence to one form of organization over the other. There are unquestionably contingencies that affect the appropriateness

Figure 18–2   Characteristic Patterns of Leadership in an Organic System

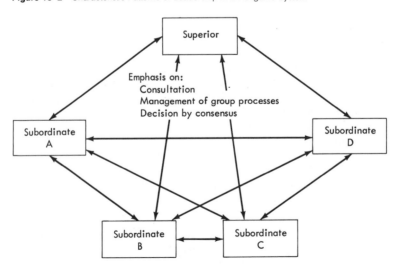

of one system over the other or the appropriateness of a particular mix of characteristics of the two systems.

We have already noted that Burns and Stalker see the mechanistic form of organization as appropriate to "stable conditions" and the organic form to "changing conditions." Joan Woodward in a study in South Essex, England, found that successful manufacturing firms of the "large-batch production" type (assembly-line or large-batch production) tended to be mechanistic, whereas successful firms of the unit and "small-batch" (e.g., prototype production) and "process production" (e.g., continuous flow liquids production) tended to be organic.[8] Another study, by Lawrence and Lorsch, found that production units within six firms had a much more formalized structure than did the research laboratories in the same firms.[9]

Morse and Lorsh, in their important study of less effective and more effective manufacturing plants (two of each), and less effective and more effective research laboratories (three of each), concluded that the more effective units had a better "fit" of characteristics than did the less effective plants. Of particular interest to us, it was found that the more effective manufacturing units, in contrast to the less effective, had a relatively high structure, a directive supervisory style with influence concentrated at the top, and participants who had relatively little "say" in choosing and handling their own work. The more effective research laboratories, in contrast to the less effective, had a relatively low structure, a participative style of supervision with influence widely distributed, and participants who had a relatively high degree of "say" in choosing and handling their own tasks (see Table 18–1).[10]

On the face of it, it would appear that a manufacturing plant, having highly predictable tasks, becomes less effective if it becomes too loosely structured and too participative (i.e., too organic). Conversely, a research laboratory, having highly uncertain tasks, becomes less effective if it becomes too structured and too directive (i.e., too mechanistic). This makes sense to us.

However, this conclusion needs to be qualified relative to at least one important contingency that appeared to be working in the Lorsch and Morse study. It is a contingency not dealt with in Burns and Stalker's model or in the Woodward research. In measuring modes of conflict resolution in the various organizations with Blake and Mouton's "confrontation," "forcing," and "smoothing" categories, Lorsch and Morse found that *organizational members in both the effective plants and the effective laboratories used the "confrontation" mode.* In contrast, the prevailing mode in the less effective plants and laboratories was "forcing."[11] The *confrontation* mode was defined as meaning "that individuals attempt to find the basis for the conflict and ways of resolving underlying issues." The *forcing* mode was defined as when "individuals try to win their own positions at the expense of the other parties to the conflict."[12]

Thus, in the less effective manufacturing plants there was more participation but *less skill* demonstrated in interpersonal, group, and intergroup relationships than in the more effective plants where there was less participation but more skill. Furthermore, Lorsch and Morse cited some data suggesting that in the less effective manufacturing plants where there was the most participation, subordinates felt that they were participating in many matters that could more easily be determined top-side and that too much time was spent in meetings without adequate decisions being made. In the case of the research laboratories, the most effective sites were those that *had higher participation coupled with the*

Table 18–1 Systems Contingencies in Manufacturing Plants and Research Laboratories

TYPE OF ORGANIZATION	TASKS	STRUCTURE	CLIMATE	MODE OF CONFLICT RESOLUTION	ORGANIZATIONAL EFFECTIVENESS
Manufacturing plants	Predictable manufacturing tasks	High formality of structure	Influence concentrated at the top; little "say"; more directive supervisory style	Confrontation	Effective
Manufacturing plants		Low formality of structure	Egalitarian distribution of influence; much "say"; less directive, more participative supervisory style	Forcing	Less effective
Research laboratories	Uncertain research tasks	Low formality of structure	Egalitarian distribution of influence; much "say"; participative style of supervision	Confrontation	Effective
Research laboratories		High formality of structure	Influence tending to concentrate at the top; little "say"; directive style of supervision	Forcing	Less effective

Source: Based on pp. 80–83 and 105–107 from *Organization and Their Members: A Contingency Approach* by Jay W. Lorsch and John J. Morse, Copyright © 1974 by Jay W. Lorsch and John J. Morse. Reprinted by permission of Harper & Row, Publishers, Inc.

most skill.[13] The dimensions of *interpersonal, group,* and *intergroup skills* and *perceived relevance of participation,* then, may be crucial. We conclude, therefore, that there is probably an optimal mix of structure and participation depending upon the technology, that participation must be relevant to the task, and that interpersonal, group, and intergroup skills are critical factors associated with organizational effectiveness generally.

In short, the contingency approach suggests that the question is not "Which is better, an organic system or a mechanistic system?" but that the question needs to be posed in terms of a number of contingencies. For example,

1. What is the most effective mix of organic and mechanistic characteristics for a given organization or unit and its current environment and current technology? or
2. Under what conditions is the organic system superior to the mechanistic, and vice versa? or
3. What is the impact of interpersonal, group, and intergroup skills on the functionality of an organic versus a mechanist system? or
4. Given different technologies, tasks, and human resources, what dimensions do we expect to change with OD-type interventions? or
5. Under what circumstances is an organization development effort particularly relevant and most likely to succeed?

The following are some of the contingencies that we see as the most relevant in answering the second question: Under what conditions is the organic system superior to the mechanistic, and vice versa?

1. *Hierarchical level.* The higher the level, the more extensive the role requirements in terms of planning, coordination, control, and decision making. The higher the level and thus the greater the complexity of these functions, the greater the need for extensive inputs from diverse specialists and for examining many options; thus, the need for acknowledging expertise, for open communications, for clarifying goals, and so forth.

2. *Interdependency.* This relates to the degree to which role performance is directly associated with the discretionary actions of others. (This contingency is related to the preceding one.) The greater the interdependency, the greater the need for open communications, the greater the need for team leadership style, and so forth.

3. *Skills.* This involves the capabilities and talents of the human resources in the system. The greater the cognitive, problem-solving, and interpersonal capabilities of the people in the system, the greater the effectiveness of both systems.

4. *Group process and intergroup skills.* This relates to the degree to which the leader and the subordinates have basic communications, task and maintenance, and intergroup skills. In particular, skills in both processes are a necessary prerequisite to a team leadership style; such skills are also important in the effective functioning of task forces, committees, and so forth. The more participative and loosely structured the system, the greater the need for interpersonal, group, and intergroup skills.

5. *Rapidity of external change.* The more the organization is existing in a rapidly changing environment, the more important the adaptability facilitated by the organic mode. Burns and Stalker see this dimension as particularly important.

6. *Time pressure, danger, or external threat.* For example, although the organic system may be better prepared to cope with future uncertainty, at the time of an unanticipated crisis the organization may need to revert to highly mechanistic characteristics to survive.

7. *Technology.* This involves the degree to which tasks are predetermined by the machinery or methods of a particular industry. For example, the technology of an assembly line serves to preplan tasks and to narrow the interdependency, and so forth.

8. *Attitudes or assumptions about people in organizations.* This involves a "Theory X" versus a "Theory Y" set of assumptions. A Theory X set of assumptions will tend to be incompatible with the culture of an organic system. In contrast, if key executives or subordinates are philosophically committed to a participative or democratic leadership style, such values will tend to be more congruent with the organic style than with the mechanistic.

SUMMARY

Mechanistic and *organic* organizations have been contrasted to provide rubrics for thinking about the outcomes of organization development activities. While, in general, OD strategies tend to increase the organic characteristics of a system, paradoxically they can also lead to an increase in mechanistic attributes along certain dimensions—for example, an increase in task differentiation at lower levels of the organization or more stringent procedures.

Theory and some research suggest that neither the purely organic form nor the purely mechanistic form may be optimal under all circumstances but that there needs to be a good "fit" among technology, tasks, internal and external environments, and skills of the people in the organization. Thus, different organization development interventions may have differing degrees of relevance under different circumstances. And those circumstances may vary by hierarchical levels, interdependency, technical skills and group process skills, time pressure and rapidity of external change, danger of external threat, technology, and values. Interpersonal, group, and intergroup skills appear to be crucial to the success of both organic and mechanistic systems and the *sine qua non* of an effective OD effort.

The genius of OD is that the perceptions, feelings, and cognitive inputs of organizational members are tapped to build an optimal, evolving, organizational design for the unique circumstances faced by the organization and its members. In that sense, OD is a contingency approach. The thrust of OD activities is to be responsive to the data, not to impose an organic system. We see OD as relevant to both organic and mechanistic systems, therefore. Through the OD process, however, some aspects of the organization will inevitably become more organic. Whatever the evolving mix, it is important that changes be accompanied by growing behavioral and conceptual competencies on the part of organizational members.

NOTES

1. Tom Burns and G. M. Stalker, *The Management of Innovation* (London: Tavistock, 1961) pp. 119–125. Rosabeth Kanter uses the terms "segmentalism" and "integrative action" that do not have entirely the same meaning as the concepts from Burns and Stalker but have some

parallels. See Rosabeth Moss Kanter, *The Change Masters* (New York: Simon and Schuster, 1983), pp. 27–36, 396.

2. Burns and Stalker, op. cit., p. 119.

3. Ibid., pp. 119–120. In some respects the mechanistic form of organization is comparable to the "bureaucratic" organization as described by Weber. For example, the features of the bureaucratic form, to Weber, include a "clearly defined hierarchy of offices," emphasis on impersonal rules, and administrators "subject to strict and systematic discipline and control." See Max Weber, *The Theory of Social and Economic Organization* (New York: Oxford University Press, 1957), pp. 333–334.

4. Burns and Stalker, *Management of Innovation,* pp. 119–125. Bennis uses the term *organic-adaptive* in describing a similar type of organization. See Warren Bennis, "Organizations of the Future," *Personnel Administration,* 30 (September–October 1967), pp. 6–19.

5. Burns and Stalker, *Management of Innovation,* p. 122.

6. Ibid., p. 121.

7. Likert contrasts *man-man* and *group* patterns of organization that are comparable to the two types of leadership styles we are contrasting. See Rensis Likert, *New Patterns of Leadership* (New York: McGraw-Hill, 1961), pp. 106–110.

8. Joan Woodward, *Industrial Organization: Theory and Practice* (London: Oxford University Press, 1965), p. 71. A rationale that we see for process organizations to be organic is that the equipment does most of the routine work while employees are largely busy with planning, research, and monitoring functions.

9. Paul R. Lawrence and Jay Lorsch, *Organization and Environment: Managing Differentiation and Integration* (Boston: Graduate School of Business Administration, Harvard University, 1967), p. 32.

10. Jay W. Lorsch and John J. Morse, *Organizations and Their Members: A Contingency Approach* (New York: Harper & Row, 1974), pp. 80–83, 105–107.

11. Ibid., pp. 80, 105.

12. Ibid., p. 79. The reference to these categories, as cited by Lorsch and Morse, is Robert Blake and Jane Mouton, *The Managerial Grid* (Houston: Gulf, 1964), pp. 30, 67, 93–94, 122–123, 162.

13. Lorsch and Morse, *Organizations and Their Members,* pp. 74–76, 99–106. Another dimension, "feelings of competence," also differentiated the more effective organizations from the less effective, Lorsch and Morse discuss the causality aspect; we are including to accept the explanation that the feelings of competence were a result of feedback about effectiveness (pp. 46–48).

19

RESEARCH ON ORGANIZATION DEVELOPMENT

Does OD work? The answer to that crucial question is the topic of this chapter? The answer is, "Yes, OD can have positive effects on individuals, work groups, and organizations in terms of attitude changes, behavior changes, and performance changes." Evaluating organization development programs is a complicated and difficult undertaking, however, as we shall see in this discussion and review of selected research efforts. Teasing out the effects of specific interventions or even a large OD program is an inherently formidable task; field research is prone to confounding from many sources. But evidence that OD is a successful strategy for improving individual and organizational effectiveness is accumulating, and we shall review some of the evidence in this chapter.

An equally important question is, *Why* does OD work? What is it about specific OD interventions that causes positive changes? What are the causal mechanisms occurring in organization development programs that bring about desirable outcomes? The *explanation* of the OD process requires a theory of planned change or a theory of organization development. In addition it requires theory-guided empirical research. Considerably less progress has been made on this front, although some beginnings of theory development are now appearing in the literature.

In this chapter we first explore some of the issues and problems involved in evaluating organization development. Next some positive developments are listed. Finally we present selected examples of research, concentrating on the type of OD program involved, the research design used, and the results observed. The goals of this chapter are twofold: to impart an understanding of the research process as it applies to OD and to recount some actual studies on OD.

ASSESSING THE EFFECTS OF OD: SOME ISSUES AND PROBLEMS

Organization development is a prescription for a process of planned change in organizations that includes concepts, techniques, and interventions. The desired outcomes of organization development are to make the organization and its members and work groups more effective while also making the organization a better place to satisfy human needs. The OD process, then, utilizes various techniques to bring about improvement or change in various target groups—individuals, groups, and the total organization. Viewed from a research perspective, two questions arise: Does OD in fact bring about or cause these desired effects? and If we observe these desired effects in an organization engaged in an OD program, can we attribute the effects to the OD program? Unambiguous answers to these questions can come only from careful, controlled empirical research.

In research terminology the OD program could be called the independent variable (IV), or the treatment, or "cause." It is presumed to cause variation in the dependent variable (DV), or "effect." The independent variable is manipulated (by being either present or absent), and this causes changes on the dependent variable (in this case, increased effectiveness). If we let the independent variable be X and the dependent variable be Y, then the relation between the two is stated as "X leads to Y"; "X is a determining condition of Y"; or "X causes Y." In research on organization development we are interested in determining whether or not OD (X) causes or leads to greater effectiveness of individuals, groups, and organizations (Y). Parenthetically, Pate, Nielsen, and Bacon suggest, and we agree, that it may be incorrect to conceptualize OD or an OD program as an independent variable; rather it is a treatment whereby the independent variable is manipulated.[1]

> Some researchers regarded OD itself to be an independent variable. However, in our view, OD does not generally constitute the independent variable, but is only instrumental in its manipulation. For example, one might expect introduction of participative decision making (OD intervention) to facilitate worker awareness of the rationale for organizational actions (independent variable), which in turn may increase support for and commitment to those actions (dependent variable).[2]

It is not really known in most cases what "causes" the effects of an OD intervention; it is only known that something within the overall activities caused some changes. In the strictest sense, the cause is the independent variable, and since that is usually not identified in OD research, we will loosely refer to the OD intervention or program as a "treatment" that *contains* some independent variables having an impact on dependent variables of interest. Let us look at some problems in conducting research on OD.

Problems with Definitions and Concepts

One of the first problems in research on organization development is that X and Y are not precise terms. There are endless variations of "OD." A program can consist of many activities or only one or two activities, yet it would be referred to as OD. A program can be a one-shot intervention or a multiyear intervention and be called OD. A program can include a particular intervention—say, intergroup team building—or not include it and be called OD. And some programs we would not label OD are called OD. Thus there is no unitary treatment known as OD, and research on OD is therefore not on OD per se but rather on a specific set of treatment activities. In reporting on the research examples later in this chapter, we will specify the treatments involved to know what treatments are causing what outcomes.

Robert Kahn has criticized the field of OD for its lack of precise meaning as follows:

> *Organizational development* is not a concept, at least not in the scientific sense of the word: it is not precisely defined; it is not reducible to specific, uniform, observable behaviors; it does not have a prescribed and verifiable place in a network of logically related concepts, a theory.[3]

We agree with this assessment and believe that lack of precision in definitions has slowed the development of research on the OD process.

Furthermore, the Y, improved effectiveness, is not a precise term. Is it to mean greater efficiency? Greater productivity? Greater profits? More positive attitudes? Is it to mean improvements in individual functioning, group functioning, the functioning of most of the organization, or the funtioning of all of the organization? And how much "better" must the improvement be over the status quo to be called improvement? Answers to these questions are generally not found in the research literature. Thus, improved organizational effectiveness is treated in a variety of ways in research on OD; it is a global term that refers to many different outcomes.

The major means of overcoming the problem of imprecision in definitions is to be more specific in defining X's and Y's. This is done by giving operational definitions to the terms. An *operational definition* is a statement of the specific operations or activities involved in both implementing the treatment and measuring the effects or results.[4] We must also move from describing global treatments and global effects to describing independent and dependent variables—cause-effect linkages.

Problems with Internal Validity

A second problem in research on OD is that of demonstrating that the X of interest, some OD activities, in fact caused the variation in Y and not some other known or unknown X. This is the problem of internal validity. "*Internal validity* is the basic minimum without which any experiment is uninterpretable: Did in fact the experimental treatments make a difference in this specific experimental instance?"[5] This is a problem in all field research and evaluation research: there is simply so much going on in the real-world situation that it is difficult to pinpoint what is causing the changes that occur. The key to overcoming or at least attenuating this problem lies in the research design—the structure of the research effort from start to finish. The research must be so executed that *rival explanations* for the changes in the dependent variables can be systematically discounted. For example, if simultaneously with an OD program everyone in the organization received a substantial salary increase, and if we were measuring the effects of the program on attitudes toward work and the organization, then any positive shift in attitudes could be caused by the OD program, by the salary raise, or by some other unknown factor or factors.

Campbell and Stanley have suggested a number of designs that overcome threats to internal validity.[6] In addition, when conditions do not permit true experimental designs, they suggest ways to build "quasi-experimental" designs that will rule out rival explanations for the changes found. The research designs used in OD are getting better in terms of controlling threats to internal validity: in a review of 37 research studies on OD, Pate, Nielsen, and Bacon found that experimental or quasi-experimental designs were used in 29 of them; in a review of OD research from 1964 to 1974, White and Mitchell found that experimental or quasi-experimental designs were used in only 12 (out of 44) studies.[7] Porras and Berg reviewed 160 organizational change studies conducted between 1959 and mid-1975. Of these, 35 reflected OD interventions that were carefully executed and carefully evaluated. Analysis of the 35 studies showed that 77 percent used quasi-experimental designs and 49 percent used comparison groups.[8]

Several design features enhance internal validity. One of the best methods is to have comparison or control groups that receive no treatment but are measured on the dependent variables. If changes occur in the experimental groups that receive the treatment but no changes occur in the control groups, this is evidence for the treatment's causing the observed effects. It is of course imperative that there be pretreatment and posttreatment measures to register any changes. Posttreatment measures only are of limited value, since one can never know whether the treatment led to the results observed or whether the results would have been there without the treatment. "Time-series" designs offer a compromise between control groups and no control groups. In a time-series design, multiple measures are made on the experimental group over time. If changes in the measures occur after the treatments, this is some support for the hypothesis that the treatment caused the changes.

Norman Berkowitz has discussed the problems inherent in research on OD and has proposed an elaborate time series design.[9] He further suggests that an excessive concern for internal validity in OD research as reflected in trying to use truly experimental designs rather than quasi-experimental designs may be inappropriate at this stage of the research efforts. Finally, random assignment of units (individuals, groups, or organizations) to experimental and control groups is a way of controlling for rival explanations for why the change occurred and controlling for extraneous variables. But random assignment is often difficult to achieve in field research. Organizations involved in OD self-select themselves to engage in such programs and would probably be unwilling to be placed in a "no-treatment" control group for research purposes. Furthermore, an organization hostile to OD is in the "no-treatment" group for very definite reasons. With self-selection it is never possible to know that any changes that occurred were due to the treatment and not to some other unknown factors.

Problems with External Validity

A third problem in research on OD is that of external validity, "*External validity* asks the question of *generalizability:* To what populations, settings, treatment variables, and measurement variables can this effect be generalized?"[10] This question of generalizability to other settings and circumstances is always an important one and will probably become even more important in the near future. Organization development is being applied in an ever-increasing number of settings,[11] and what "works" in one setting may not work in another. For example, organization development techniques are effective in middle-class suburban schools, but are they also effective in ghetto urban schools? Organization development techniques have been shown to increase productivity in private sector business organizations; can they do the same in a federal bureaucracy? It is likely that some techniques or treatments will be found to be situation specific, while others will be more universally applicable.

Problems with Lack of Theory

Another problem is that OD research is not theory-guided research; in fact, there is essentially no comprehensive theory to explain the process of planned change in organizations. Kerlinger defines *theory* as *"a set of interrelated constructs (concepts), definitions, and propositions that present a systematic view of phenomena by specifying relations among variables, with the purpose of explaining and predicting the phenomena."*[12] Without a theory of organization development, the relations among variables and the variables themselves are unknown. Organization development researchers are forced to fall back on a strategy of measuring the effects of global treatments (not independent variables) on a potpourri of dependent variables—things that should *probably* be affected by the intervention.

Theory-guided research is more efficient, more precise, and more definitive. With theory, researchers know what to look for and where to look for it in their research efforts. Research either confirms or does not confirm the theory; if the theory is disconfirmed, it is modified and new avenues for further research are indicated. The first major step in building theory in OD is the identification and specification of the independent and dependent variables that explain the phenomena. Next the relations among these variables are specified with increasing precision. These will be the major chores of OD practitioners, researchers, and theoreticians in the near future.

Significant progress is being made, however, in the development of theory and the identification and specification of relevant independent and dependent variables. Alderfer has coalesced a number of disparate ideas relating to planned organizational change into a coherent theory with research implications;[13] Argyris has proposed a general theory of intervention in human systems based on his experience and research;[14] Blake and Mouton have developed a theory and classification scheme for the consultation process;[15] and Vaill has discussed some of the unique requirements for building a "practice theory"—a theory applicable to applied change problems.[16] Bowers, Franklin, and Pecorella have developed a taxonomy that starts to clarify some of the variables involved in organizational improvement strategies by focusing on both the problems the intervention is designed to rectify and the interventions themselves.[17]

In their review of research on OD, White and Mitchell propose a classification system based on facet theory for independent and dependent variables found in OD interventions.[18] These authors identify three underlying dimensions or facets of OD interventions and the effects of OD interventions: (1) a target or recipient of change, (2) a specific content area of change, and (3) the context or relationships that are supposed to change.

The first facet, *target of change,* consists of three elements—the individual, the subgroup, and the total organization. The *content area of change* facet consists of four elements: conceptual, behavioral, procedural, and structural. The *context of change* facet consists of five elements: intrapersonal, interpersonal, intragroup, intergroup, and organizational.[19] Almost all OD interventions and their desired effects can be specified on these three facets and the twelve elements. For example, a team-building intervention would have as a target the subgroup, the content area of change would be either conceptual or behavioral, and the relationships of change would be either interpersonal or intragroup. With such a classification system in mind, researchers can design their data collection methods better and can start to test for the effects of various interventions on the different facets and elements. This will lead to research based on specified hypothesized relations among variables instead of a "shotgun" approach in which numerous measures are made on variables to "see if anything happened."

Dunn and Swierczek applied a refined content analysis technique (called "retrospective case analysis") to 67 successful and unsuccessful change efforts, many of them case studies, in an attempt to test whether certain hypothesized relations about what causes success would hold up.[20] They examined 11 hypotheses that appear in the literature. These hypotheses consist of such statements as "Change efforts in economic organizations will be more successful than will change efforts in other types of organizations"—not supported by the data—and "Change efforts directed at the total organization will be more successful than will change efforts directed at lower levels"—also not supported by the evidence. Three hypotheses received moderate support as marking successful versus unsuccessful change efforts: first, change efforts in which the mode of intervention is *collaborative* as opposed to other intervention modes tend to be more successful; second, change efforts in which the change agent has a *participative orientation* versus other orientations tend to be more successful; and, third, change efforts employing standardized strategies that involve *high levels of participation* will be more successful than those that involve low levels of participation.[21] This effort toward building a theory of organizational change processes "grounded" or based on empirical research is a laudable one. Benefits derive both from discovering which hypotheses are supported and from discovering which hypotheses are not supported. These hypotheses specify relations among variables that can form the basis for a theory of organization change and development.

PROBLEMS WITH MEASURING ATTITUDE CHANGE

Research on organization development often involves administering preintervention and postintervention attitude questionnaires and observing pre- and postintervention differences on the attitude scores. If responses become more favorable, that is taken as evidence that the intervention helped to produce positive attitude change. If responses stay the same or become less favorable, that is taken as evidence that the intervention had no effect or had a negative effect. In an important article in 1976 Golembiewski, Billingsley, and Yeager suggested that three different kinds of change can occur between the pre- and postmeasures. They labeled these alpha, beta, and gamma change.[22] Alpha change is real or true change; your attitude is more positive or negative after the intervention and the questionnaires accurately reflect that. Beta change is change based on scale recalibration; you view the scale intervals differently after the intervention—for example, a "5" on a 10-point scale of "trust in my group" has taken on a different meaning for you. Gamma change is change based on a reconceptualization or redefinition of the concept being measured; you now view the concept itself in a totally different way.

The problem identified by Golembiewski and his colleagues appears to be valid. What is a researcher to do? Fortunately, researchers such as Armenakis and Zmud,[23] Randolph,[24] and Terborg, Howard, and Maxwell[25] have developed methods to *measure* the three types of change if and when they occur. OD research must be carefully planned to identify these changes, but the methods for doing so are available. Later in this chapter we present a research article by Porras and others on a behavior modeling OD program in plywood mills. The program produced many positive changes. Were they real? Porras and Singh[26] examined the results and found that true (alpha) change occurred as well as some scale recalibration (beta) change; no gamma change was found.

The implications for practitioners and researchers are that additional care and planning must go into research on OD that involves measuring attitude changes.

PROBLEMS WITH "NORMAL SCIENCE"

A controversy is growing within organization development regarding the best way to conduct research on action programs. Specifically, an increasing number of theorists and researchers are rejecting "normal science" with its requirements of replication, control groups, random assignment to treatment conditions, specifying single cause-and-effect linkages, and so forth in favor of less rigorous but richer "action research."

In Chapter 8 we noted Argyris' call for "action science" (a form of action research) as a more effective means for studying complex social change than normal science.[27] Other authors are calling attention to the need for other research methods for OD. Blumberg and Pringle show how the use of control groups in the Rushton Coal Mine experiment distorted the data and even forced the termination of the experiment.[28] Bullock and Svyantek argue the case that it is logically impossible to use random strategies of selection and assignment to study the OD process itself.[29] They say that OD *techniques* can be evaluated using random strategies, but not organization development itself because it is by nature collaborative and diagnosis-based—that is, what one does depends on each specific situation's needs. Bullock and Svyantek state:

> No one has ever suggested that a rigorous OD researcher randomly select organizations from across the country—including, for example, volunteer organizations, work organizations, political organizations, health service organizations—then randomly assign them to OD interventions (the local Boy Scout troop to management by objectives, General Motors to team building, the Ku Klux Klan to T groups, the nursing home to career planning) designed to fundamentally change the organizations as social systems, and with that change to alter the lives and careers of individuals. Yet we continue to evaluate OD research as if such an action were reasonable.[30]

Bullock and Bullock report an experiment involving two kinds of data feedback to an organization, "pure science" and "science-action."[31] Minimal change and usefulness resulted from the pure science feedback approach (giving a one-inch thick book of statistics tables to decision makers); extensive change, problem solving, and energy resulted from the science-action approach in which the scientist acted also as a change agent/ OD facilitator.

Beer and Walton criticize the methods of current OD research on four counts.[32] First, the research attempts to identify causation of a single intervention while overlooking the systemic nature of organizations. Clearly other internal and external forces are operating during OD programs. Second, the research is not sufficiently longitudinal to capture long term change or to identify nonpermanent change. Third, the research is "flat"; it does not describe in enough detail the intervention and the context. And finally, the research does not fit the needs of its users. Beer and Walton conclude: "What we are recommending is a return to the action research traditions of OD with full participation of the client in the research but with much longer time frames and the inclusion of rich descriptions of context and system dynamics.[33] (See also Chapter 21.)

It may be that research on organization development is at a turning point where better methods for understanding the processes of social change will be developed. That would be of great benefit to the field.

CONCLUSION

We have discussed six major problems confronting research on OD: imprecision of definitions and conceptualizations concerning OD research, problems with internal and external validity, the lack of supporting theory to guide research, problems with measuring attitude change, and problems with using normal science methods to study OD programs. These do not appear to be insurmountable problems at this time, although they continue to plague research efforts.

The future of OD research will no doubt see the movement from evaluation and validation studies (the does-it-work-and-can-we-demonstrate-that-it does stage) to a theory-building and hypothesis-testing stage that will signify a more mature level of research. Friedlander and Brown indicate some of the challenges of the future for OD research:

> If the practice and theory of OD is to merge into a broader field of planned change, what role will research play in this transformation? We believe that research will either play a far more crucial role in the advancement of this field, or become an increasingly irrelevant appendage to it. Thus far it has utilized its techniques primarily for evaluation and validation, and its current techniques are well adapted to this. Thus far it has chosen to play a relatively uninvolved and distant role in the change-practice situation. Thus far it has focused on producing data for research needs rather than practice needs. As a result, we have theory from an external research perspective only. We have generally failed to produce a theory of change which emerges from the change process itself. We need a way of enriching our understanding and our action synergistically rather than at one or the other's expense—to become a science in which knowledge-getting and knowledge-giving are an integrated process, and one that is valuable to all parties involved. We believe that a theory of planned change must be a theory of practice, which emerges from practice data and is of the practice situation, not merely about it.[34]

POSITIVE DEVELOPMENTS IN RESEARCH ON OD

Some advances in the area of research on organization development have already been cited, namely, increasing use of experimental and quasi-experimental research designs that really permit us to know what the treatment effects are and increasing attention to the formulation of theory and testable hypotheses. These are recent advances and augur well for the future of OD research.

Another positive feature is the increasing incidence of longitudinal studies on the effects of OD. In the review article by Pate, Nielsen, and Bacon, 18 of the 37 studies examined are longitudinal research efforts.[35] Although these authors end their review with a plea for *more* systematic, longitudinal research, it is a good sign that such studies are becoming more prevalent. Longitudinal research allows both short- and long-term effects of OD interventions to be noted; it permits the use of tighter research designs; and it allows for the differential effects of different interventions to be discovered. Development of theory will go hand in hand with the emergence of more longitudinal research on OD.

Several longitudinal research efforts of a *programmatic nature* are ongoing at the present time. The Institute for Survey Research of the University of Michigan has been engaged for many years in gathering data on a variety of organizations.[36] These data serve as a repository for measuring the effects of a variety of factors impacting on the organizations including planned change programs.[37] Another long-range programmatic research effort directed specifically at measuring the effects of organizational improvement programs is the Quality of Work Life program located at the University of Michigan.[38] This program, under the direction of Professor Edward E. Lawler III, now at the University of Southern California, is monitoring and evaluating a number of quality of work life (QWL) projects initiated in the mid- and late-1970s. Thus far the results look promising: significant gains in productivity and job satisfaction have occurred in several (but by no means all) of the projects.[39]

Advances in measurement techniques and valid measurement instruments have also contributed to better research on OD. Alderfer reviewed the OD research from the 1974–1976 period and noted several advances along these lines:

> there have been significant research developments in OD during the time covered by this review. More rigorous research designs have been employed to evaluate interventions; both positive and negative outcomes have been observed. There is clear evidence that better measuring instruments are being developed, and greater understanding of measurement errors is being obtained.[40]

Research and verified theory can advance only as fast as the measurement capabilities of a scientific field. Therefore, these improvements in measurement techniques are important developments.

In a recent critique of the OD research literature, Nancy Roberts and Jerry Porras find reasons for cautious optimism. They note that substantial progress is being made in four major areas: progress in operationalizing the concept of change, progress in improving measurement processes and also measurement procedures, and progress in developing appropriate statistical and analytical models.[41]

Finally, there is an increased awareness among practitioners and client systems of the value and usefulness of research on OD. In part this may be due to a "coming of age" of OD and research on OD. But credit is probably also due to the numerous excellent reviews and critiques of OD research that have appeared in the professional journals and a number of books. Friedlander and Brown,[42] Alderfer,[43] Faucheux, Amado, and Laurent,[44] and Beer and Walton[45] have written careful comprehensive reviews and critiques of OD research for the 1974, 1977, 1982, and 1987 editions, respectively, of the *Annual Review of Psychology.* Michael Beer[46] and George Strauss[47] have told the broad story of OD in two important handbooks. White and Mitchell,[48] Pate, Nielsen, and Bacon,[49] Porras and Berg,[50] and Golembiewski, Proehl, and Sink[51] have reviewed the research on OD and have offered helpful suggestions for improving it. All these contributions have played a role in emphasizing the need for competent research on OD and have additionally been important in raising the level of sophistication regarding research.

A REVIEW OF SELECTED OD RESEARCH EFFORTS

We will review a number of research reports representing a variety of treatments (interventions) and a variety of research designs. The goal is to explain what was done (the treatment) and what was found (the results) in enough detail to enable the reader to determine the efficacy of various OD interventions. We will briefly describe the organization, the treatment, the research design, and the results.

"Breakthrough in Organization Development," by Robert Blake, Jane Mouton, Louis Barnes, and Larry Greiner[52]

This early, important study of the effects of a comprehensive OD program took place in a plant of about 4,000 employees, including about 800 managerial and professional/ technical personnel. The plant was code named "Sigma" and the parent company was code named "Piedmont" for purposes of disguise. A number of antecedent conditions led to the decision to launch the program: new policies were implemented by the parent company; Piedmont had merged with another company; and in-plant relationships at Sigma were becoming strained, as were relationships between Sigma and headquarters.

The treatment consisted of Grid OD phase 1 and phase 2 activities; in addition, some phase 3 and 4 activities were instituted. (See Chapter 13 for a description of these interventions.) The change program began in November 1962 and was completed in the summer of 1963. This part was done at the direction of Blake and Mouton. All 800 managerial and technical people at Sigma were exposed to a one-week Managerial Grid Seminar (phase 1), and they then applied these Grid principles and concepts in their back-home work teams (phase 2). Some intergroup team-building activities took place (phase 3), and some task forces were established to discover better ways to run the organization (phase 4).

The research design was complicated by the fact that the program was well underway when the decision was made to evaluate the program—not an uncommon event in OD research. The evaluation was performed by Barnes and Greiner and took place between June 1963 and November 1963. Data collection methods included question-naires, interviews, observations, and a combing of company records to separate program effects from nonprogram effects.[53] The researchers looked for changes in three broad areas: productivity and profits, practices and behavior, and perceptions, attitudes, and values. Pretreatment and posttreatment time-series data were available from company records for analyzing effects of the program on productivity and profits. Records permitted some pre-post measures of practices and behavior; and in other cases a posttreatment only measure was used, with people being asked to "think back to what was happening a year ago before the program" and also describe what they were doing today. Posttreatment measures only were available for changes in perceptions, attitudes, and values; again, people were asked to describe "present" and "a year ago" feelings. No control groups were used in the research. All in all, the researchers probably did the best they could in building a "patched-up" design, but it is still a moderately weak design.

The results were positive and impressive, even though we cannot be certain, because of the research design, that they were all caused by the change program. There were significant increases in profits and productivity during 1963, the year the program was in full swing. The authors separated controllable from noncontrollable factors in the profit increase, and they concluded that 44 percent of the profit increase was due to reductions in controllable costs such as wages and maintenence costs—things that the program could be expected to influence. These savings were worth millions of dollars in profit. Of the controllable cost savings, 69 percent came from a work force reduction of 600 people, and 31 percent came from better operating procedures and higher productivity per employee. Higher productivity alone was worth several million dollars in profit. In addition, it was agreed that the *quality* of the work force reduction was enhanced by the OD program—managers felt that better decisions were made as a result of the program; only 84 people were actually laid off; and the reduction took place without hard feelings developing on the part of the union and the community. In sum, productivity and profits increased significantly.

Changes in practices and behavior showed a 31.0 percent increase in formal meetings and a 12.4 percent increase in "team problem-solving meetings" as a result of the program. In addition, there were positive changes in the criteria for promotion, and an increased number of transfers both within the plant and to other parts of the company.

There were also positive changes in perceptions, attitudes, and values. Questionnaire results from 598 respondents showed that 49 percent reported improvement in the way their work groups worked together, and 61 percent reported improvement in the way their work group worked with other groups. These comparisons were between a "year ago" (1962, before the program) and "now" (1963, after the program).

These are impressive results and this study is a good research effort. The results suggest that Grid OD is effective in producing positive changes in individuals and work teams and that these can lead to improved organizational functioning.

Management by Participation, by Alfred Marrow, David Bowers, and Stanley Seashore[54]

This study, probably the best single report of a planned change effort in the literature, is elegant, extensive, and difficult to summarize. The change program was a massive, total organization program; the research project was equally synoptic and complete. We do not claim to do justice to the project in this review.

Harwood Manufacturing Company acquired one of its competitors, the Weldon Company, on January 1, 1962. Both companies manufactured pajamas. Both companies had single plants about 30 years old, and each plant had about 1,000 employees. Harwood was a profitable and healthy organization; Weldon was neither of these. As the new owners and others viewed the two organizations, one striking difference between them became obvious: Harwood's managerial style and concern for the human organization reflected Likert's System 4—participative, democratic, and team oriented; Weldon's managerial style and philosophy reflected Likert's System 1—autocratic, controlling, and authority-obedience oriented.[55] The new owners decided to move the managerial style and philosophy at Weldon to System 4 Management, and they enlisted the aid of researchers at the Institute for Social Research, University of Michigan, to measure the program.

The change treatments started in early 1962 and ended in late 1964. The year 1963 marked the most intensive treatment period. The change program consisted of three overlapping phases: (1) protect the human resources at the Weldon plant, (2) launch an extensive improvement program of an engineering/industrial-engineering nature to improve the plant facilities and work processes, and (3) transform the management system and patterns of interpersonal relations from System 1 to System 4.

Treatments directed toward improving the plant facilities and work flow were extensive. The most basic change was a total reorganization of the work flow throughout the plant—a change from a plantwide mixed-batch production system to a "unit system" of production. In the unit system similar product lines are relegated to departments (units) for easier scheduling and controlling of the work flow. Sales orders and delivery promises were altered to allow for longer job runs and fewer job changes. New record systems were introduced and made available to first-line supervisors. The shipping department was completely changed in terms of work flow, and a different pay system was instituted. The cutting room was modified and work standards were established; incentive pay was initiated in the cutting room. "Nearly every job and person in the plant was affected. All these changes took place over a span of about 12 months."[56]

Treatments directed toward altering the social system were likewise extensive. These treatments were mostly implemented after the engineering changes were well underway. Four major features were involved: extending participative management to all levels of the plant; disrupting the managers' old habits of secrecy, distrust, and noncooperation; initiating problem solving and participation in all work groups of the plant; and pushing responsibility and influence downward throughout the organization. Specific treatments or interventions were as follows: a new personnel department was established; attitude surveys were administered to all employees; incentive pay plans were introduced: sensitivity training sessions were held with all management and supervisory staff; supervisors were instructed in the new management philosophy of System 4; operators and their immediate supervisors held problem-solving meetings to surface complaints and find ways of improving the work process; a vestibule training program was instituted to replace the ineffective old training program; an earnings development program including coaching and counseling substandard operators was initiated; and new policies were initiated in which chronic absentees and employees with substandard performance were terminated. In addition, during the program there was an increase in the federal minimum wage so that everyone got a raise, and the plant became unionized.[57] Thus training and participation activities were going on at all levels of the organization as were various structural and procedural changes.

The research design included both extensive and pre-post measures extending over a long period of time and the use of similar measures on the Harwood plant as a control group. Multiple measures were used, both "hard" data on such objective events as absenteeism, turnover, productivity, and profits and "soft" data on attitudes and perceptions. The data analyses were subtle and extensive as the researchers attempted to tease out the effects of the various treatments.

It is impossible to summarize all the results; we will hit some of the highlights. Most of the comparisons of interest to this discussion are of 1962 (before the program) and 1964 (after the program). Production efficiency improved markedly from the fall of 1962 through 1964, with productivity moving from 85 percent of standard to 115 percent of standard. Operator turnover dropped from a monthly rate of 10 percent to a monthly rate of 4 percent. Absenteeism dropped from 6 percent to 3 percent. In terms of profitability, return on capital invested changed from a -15 percent in 1962 to a $+17$ percent in 1964.

A number of attitudinal changes were measured, centering generally on satisfaction with the company, the work, compensation, and fellow employees, expectations about the future, and the like. In general, attitude changes, where they did occur, were modest though positive. The authors state the situation as follows:

> Rather dramatic changes in policy, in work arrangements, in interpersonal relationships—and in work performance and pay—were in Weldon accompanied by only modest affective and motivational changes....
>
> Such change as did occur was favorable to the firm's program goals. At the end of the change program period there was a more positive view of the company, an awareness of the reduction in disruptive temporary job changes, more satisfaction with the compensation system and with pay, more willingness to plan for continued employment with Weldon. The increase in feelings of having to work hard was accompanied by an increase, not a decrease, in satisfaction and positive attitudes.[58]

These results of a massive change program as measured by a careful, competent research program constitute an important contribution to knowledge in the behavioral sciences. Both the change program and the research program serve as examples to those trying to build a theory of planned change.

But the story is not finished. Seashore and Bowers did a follow-up study of Weldon in 1969, four and one-half years after the termination of the intensive change program.[59] Their purpose was to see if the positive effects of the program would last over time. Questionnaire data from managers, supervisors, and a sample of employees were collected as well as certain company performance information. They found that the positive gains in employee attitudes were maintained and in some cases improved. Managers and supervisors saw the company continuing to move closer to the ideal participative organizational system, System 4. Regarding long-term effects on organizational performance, Seashore and Bowers report,

Briefly, Weldon moved from a position of substantial capital loss in 1962 to substantial return on investment in 1964; this direction of change in profitability has continued through 1968, the last year of record. Employee earnings which rose substantially between 1962 and 1964 have been sustained at a relatively high level. During the period since 1964 there have been substantial gains in efficiency and volume for the factory as a whole. New products and work methods have been introduced.[60]

The Weldon change program thus resulted in many changes, and these changes have been maintained and extended in the years since the program was formally terminated.

"Short- and Long-Range Effects of a Team Development Effort," by Richard Beckhard and Dale G. Lake[61]

This change project took place with 12 managers who were unit and section supervisors in two units of the securities division of a large investment and commercial bank. Nine managers from the Mortgage Production unit and three managers from the Methods unit were selected to become an "experimental team." The managers were a heterogeneous group in that the individuals came from diverse sections and diverse locations. Yet they were all highly interdependently related in terms of getting the work of the Mortgage Production unit done. The Methods people, for example, were charged with helping to improve the work procedures of the Mortgage Production unit and with helping it convert its bookkeeping procedures over to a computerized system. Relationships between the diverse sections of Mortgage Production were generally unsatisfactory, being characterized by distrust, poor communication, and poor coordination. The stated goals of the change project were to improve their operating effectiveness as a problem-solving unit and facilitate the introduction of the computer in the Mortage Production unit.

The treatment was remarkable for two reasons: first, its limited extent and, second, its apparent powerful effects. The first part of the treatment was that all 12 members of the experimental team attend a sensitivity training laboratory; this was "preparation" for the treatment per se. Next the team met for one half-day with the consultant, Richard Beckhard, and discussed the goals of the program, the methods that would be used, and the possible outcomes. During this meeting Beckhard asked each manager to write him an anonymous letter listing the obstacles keeping the group of 12 from functioning as a smooth team. The problems identified in the letters were fed back to the group at the first workshop and were an important part of that conference's agenda. Beckhard suggested that the group have *three team development workshops;* these were weekend conferences and occurred six months apart. These activities constituted the major treatment for this change program. During the three weekend workshops, the group worked at building itself into a more effective team and worked at solving the problems that kept it from effective mission accomplishment.

The change program lasted a little over a year, from late 1963 to the end of 1964. Given the minimal extent of the program, one may wonder why it worked so well. It would appear that in this case the intervention was "right on target" in terms of what the organization needed and that need was better communication, problem solving, and coordination among a group of highly interdependent managers who were not functioning as a team. It also would appear that the intervention served to release a tremendous amount of creative energy that had previously been bottled up by mistrust and suspicion of others. Finally, it appears that what Beckhard created was a kind of "collateral organization" as described by Zand and discussed in Chapter 14. (A *collateral organization* is a special kind of problem-solving task force that cuts across the usual organizational barriers and boundaries.) At the weekend workshops, group members worked on interpersonal problems they had among themselves and also worked on designing action plans to overcome obstacles to task accomplishment. They set up monthly meetings of the group back at the bank (without the consultant), established some task forces to get some long-standing problems solved, asked their boss to set up communication mechanisms with two related departments, and the like. At the workshops they would assess their progress on action steps, establish new priorities for problems, and assign themselves new action steps . At the third workshop they decided that they no longer needed the services of the consultant; they were well on the way to solving their own problems.

The research design was a strong one in several respects. First, the researcher, Matthew Miles of Columbia University, worked completely independently of the consultant, Beckhard. Second, for measuring changes in productivity, turnover and absenteeism, two control groups from other parts of the bank were used. Third, pre-post treatment measures were collected both on the experimental team and on the control groups. Fourth, a variety of measures were used, including hard and soft data. And, finally, a follow-up study was conducted by Lake and Miles three years after the last workshop to determine whether the changes had endured. Data collection methods included pretreatment and posttreatment interviews with the experimental team; similar interviews with the superior of the experimental team members and managers of departments that did business with Mortgage Production; attitude questionnaires given to the clerical subordinates of the experimental team managers and also to two control groups of subordinates; and productivity, turnover, and absenteeism data for Mortgage Production and two control groups.

The results indicated impressive gains in productivity and impressive decreases in turnover and absenteeism data for the experimental unit, Mortgage Production. Productivity moved from about 90 percent of standard in January 1964 to about 120 percent of standard in October 1964. (Yearly productivity did not average 120 percent; this was the highest level, but productivity was consistently above previous levels.) Productivity levels in the two comparison groups did not show similar increases. Follow-up data three years later showed that Mortgage Production was still performing at a high productivity rate and that the two control groups had not increased their productivity. On turnover, Mortgage Production reduced its turnover rate sharply while the two control groups and the bank as a whole increased in turnover rates. Mortgage Production showed a sharp drop in absenteeism while one control group stayed the same and the other control group increased its absenteeism rate. Three years later the turnover rate in Mortgage Production was still well below the total bank rate, and absenteeism, though increasing somewhat, was still low.

Results of the attitude questionnaires given to subordinates of the experimental team and two control groups were not very clear or strong. But subordinates of the experimental managers believed that they had more upward inlfluence, more contact with their managers, and more egalitarian contact with their managers than did subordinates in the control groups. Perceptions of upward influence continued to be found among the experimental team's subordinates three years later.

Finally, organization development activities have spread to the rest of the bank. Numerous team-building efforts are going on. The top 30 officers of the bank had a four-day workshop at which they examined their mode of operation and its impact on the organization. Cross-department task forces have been established to solve intergroup problems.

"Organization Development and Change in Organizational Performance," by John R. Kimberly and Warren R. Nielsen[62]

This is a particularly insightful report of an OD program and its effects in an automotive division of a large multiplant, multidivisional corporation. The organization was an assembly plant employing about 2,600 hourly and 200 salaried employees. The program was primarily directed toward the managerial group of the hourly production employees—supervisors, general supervisors, assistant superintendents, superintendents, and the plant manager. It began in January 1970 and continued through March 1971. The goals of the program were to improve the organizational climate, improve the supervisory behavior of production supervisors, and improve such organizational indexes of performance as productivity, quality of production, and profit.

The treatments consisted of seven different sets of activities, described by the authors as the phases of the OD program. The first phase was an initial diagnosis of the system. The second phase consisted of a series of two-and-one-half-day "team skills training" workshops for supervisors, general supervisors, assistant superintendents, and superintendents designed to increase their effectiveness as supervisors. Phase 3 was a data collection phase in which all supervisors completed two questionnaires, one on organizational climate and one on the supervisory behavior of their immediate supervisors. Phase 4 was termed "data confrontation." In this phase various work groups reviewed the data generated up to this point, identified problem areas and priorities, and developed tentative action plans to correct the problems. Phase 5, "action planning" called for each group to decide on some action plans for change and to assign responsibilities for their accomplishment. Phase 6 consisted of team building in which each natural work team in the system met in a two-day workshop to explore blocks to their effectiveness and ways to improve their functioning. Phase 7 was "intergroup building" consisting of two-day workshops attended by interdependent work groups in the plant. The OD interventions thus focused on the managerial subsystem as the key target group; these managers were given training in supervisory skills, team building, intergroup team building, and problem solving.

The research design was a pretreatment and posttreatment design with no control groups. But an elaborate set of time-series observations on productivity and profits for the plant were obtained. These time-series data on the "hard" variables of organizational performance considerably strengthened the research effort. Selected comparisons with industry-wide data were also made and these gave additional support for the conclusion that the program, not some other factors, caused most of the results found. Finally, the researchers proposed a model of how the change process should work that strengthened confidence in the results. The authors reasoned that since the program was directed toward a specific target group—supervisors—clear-cut changes in the target group could then be expected to impact on other groups, such as the production employees, causing changes in their attitudes and behavior. All these changes should culminate in changes in total organizational performance.

Substantial and positive gains appeared to result from the program. Pretreatment and posttreatment measures of organizational climate showed positive, significant changes on all nine items of the questionnaire. The managerial group perceived positive changes in trust, support, openness of communications, commitment to objectives, and so forth. Pre-post measures were also taken on the supervisory behavior of the supervisor's immediate superiors. All 10 items on this questionnaire showed significant positive gains indicating improvements in such behaviors as listening, relations with others, handling of conflict, and expressing ideas to others. The first part of the model was thus supported: the managerial target group had changed significantly in terms of perceptions of organizational climate and supervisory behavior. Would these changes affect organizational performance?

Data on daily production rates for the 15 months before the program, the 14 months during the program, and the 12 months after the program were collected and analyzed. There were no significant differences found between production levels before and after the program. Production began to decline before the program, continued downward through about half the program, then began to rise substantially, and continued to rise in the period after the program. Curious about this finding, the researchers compared the plant production rates with those for the total industry and found a positive correlation of .90. This suggested that plant production was following the general production level of the industry and thus may not have been under the control of the plant managers but instead may have been determined more by market conditions and other factors. Therefore it may not be reasonable to expect the OD program to affect production rates of a plant in this industry.

The authors had also predicted that, due to the improved communication, planning, and problem-solving skills gained in the OD program, there would be a reduction in the amount of variance in production rates; production rates would be more steady and less sporadic. This prediction was supported: before-after comparisons show significantly less variance in production rates after the program.

Predicted significant gains in product quality were found after the program, as well as predicted significant reductions in quality variance. Quality improvements after the program were substantial.

> The final hypothesis tested focused on the relation between the change program and profit. It was hypothesized that if the OD program led to improved managerial and supervisory skills, these changes would ultimately be reflected in changes in the profit index of the organization.[63]

This hypothesis was supported: the profit index, already in a negative (loss) position, declined before and during the program; about halfway through the program it began to rise and moved to a profit level in the period after the program. But was the significant gain in profits due to the program or due to industrywide factors (as in the case of production rates)? Comparison of plant profits with industrywide profits yielded a positive correlation of .48 suggesting that profits were more under the control of events occurring in the plant. It can be concluded that the program had a significant positive impact on profits for the organization.

To summarize, significant positive changes occurred in organizational climate, supervisory behavior, production variance, quality levels, quality variance, and profits. It is reasonable to attribute these changes to the OD program.

"Participative Decision Making: An Experimental Study in a Hospital," by J. E. Bragg and I. R. Andrews[64]

This change project took place in a hospital laundry containing 32 employees and one supervisor. The formal program lasted 18 months and was still in operation three years later.

The treatment was participative decision making (PDM). *Participative decision making* is an organizational activity in which decision making and problem solving regarding operating practices are done by the people who are most affected by the decisions. Participative decision making usually involves a superior giving over decision making to subordinates about the way they perform their jobs. The authors describe the treatment as follows: "In the present study, decision-making power was transferred from the laundry supervisor to a committee composed of all the laundry employees. Any and all aspects of managing the laundry could be considered by the committee."[65] The program was initiated and explained in a meeting of all employees, the supervisor, and the chief hospital administrator. Thereafter the program consisted of formal and informal meetings of employees and the supervisor to discuss proposals for changes. There were 28 formal meetings during the first 15 months of the program during which 147 specific suggestions were discussed. Most of the suggestions (90) concerned workflow processes and methods; 11 involved working hours and working conditions; 44 involved minor equipment changes; and two involved safety matters. Numerous informal meetings were also held.

The research design and the model for implementing PDM were interrelated. Program implementation followed Lowin's theoretical model for participative decision making; first, the system must be unfrozen; next, participative decision-making activities are implemented; and, finally, the entire program is measured and monitored for its results.[66] The major hurdle for unfreezing the system consisted of convincing the highly effective, authoritarian supervisor to change his leadership style to a participative one. The hospital administrator was able to convince the supervisor, and the program was begun. One factor influencing the supervisor was his satisfaction with the great amount of autonomy *he* was given by the hospital administrator.

Measuring and monitoring the results called for a longitudinal study utilizing pretreatment and posttreatment measurements and several control groups. Use of a longitudinal study (18 months) permitted the short- and long-term effects of the program to be identified and also allowed any results due to Hawthorne effects (the people knowing they were part of an experimental project, novelty, etc.) to be identified and/or dissipated. Attitude questionnaires administered before, during, and after the program allowed measurement of the program's impact on employee attitudes. Two comparison laundries in other hospitals in town were used as control groups for determining the program's impact on productivity. The rest of the hospital nonmedical staff was used as a control group for comparing the effects of the program on absenteeism. This was a good research design for testing the effects of the participative decision-making program.

The results of the program were very favorable. Employee attitudes toward the PDM program, measured every two months, moved from an initial uncertainty about the program (64 percent approval) to a very positive attitude toward it (90 percent approval). Absenteeism in the laundry dropped significantly during the program compared with previous rates; this occurred while absenteeism rates for the rest of the hospital were increasing slightly.

Productivity, always excellent in this laundry, increased significantly during the program. For the year prior to the program, productivity averaged approximately 50 pounds of processed laundry per employee hour. In the first six months of the program, productivity rose gradually to about 61 pounds per employee hour. In the second six months of the program, productivity increased dramatically to 78 pounds per employee hour. In the third six months of the program, productivity dropped back to about 73 pounds per employee hour. It is likely that these significant gains in production can be attributed both to improved workflow procedures stemming from the group's suggestions and to better morale of the group.

This is a good piece of research and an effective, simple intervention. It is clear that a number of factors contributed to the successful outcome. The supervisor's role in implementing the program was crucial. He radically changed his leadership and interaction styles, and it appears from the report that his actions were largely responsible for participative decision making becoming a reality. Another factor was the isolation of the laundry from the rest of the hospital. This allowed them to make some changes in working hours and the like relatively free from outside constraints. Involvement of the total, small group was probably also a factor contributing to success.

The authors describe the impact of this successful experiment in participative decision making on the rest of the hospital:

> The success of PDM in the laundry has encouraged other subsystems in the hospital to follow suit. In a medical records section where there was an adequate unfreezing of the system and strong support (but no involvement) by the chief nonmedical administrator, a serious turnover problem has been eliminated through PDM and a high level of union grievances has been reduced to zero. With the nursing staff, on the other hand, a deficiency of unfreezing activities and substantial resistance by the head nurse caused PDM to flounder badly for the first 6 months. In fact, PDM was a dismal failure until the introduction of a new head nurse with a favorable attitude toward PDM, and until the chief nonmedical administrator found time for some involvement in the program.[67]

"Team Development: Quasi-Experimental Confirmation Among Combat Companies," by Dov Eden[68]

The command teams of seven combat companies in the Israel Defense Forces underwent a three-day team development training session while the command teams of nine similar combat companies did not. All soldiers reporting to the experimental and control group combat companies were asked on preintervention and postintervention surveys to evaluate 13 variables related to managerial practices and organizational climate. The results showed that significant improvements were made in the experimental companies on the dimensions of "teamwork," "conflict handling," and "information about plans." Substantial but nonstatistically significant improvements also occurred in the experimental companies on "personal status" (being treated as a person who can make valuable contributions), "challenge," and "information about performance."

The research design was a quasi-experimental nonequivalent control group design in which the author took care to ensure preintervention similarity between experimental and control groups and to control for other threats to internal validity. In addition, the researcher was not involved in administering the intervention thus negating possible biases. The postintervention measures were collected about three months after the training. Since significant differences were found between experimental and control companies at that time, it may be inferred that the training had induced the command teams (officers and lead noncommissioned officers) to behave differently which in turn led to changes in perceptions on the part of the soldiers.

This is a good, careful piece of research. It suggests that team building/team development activities can change behaviors of leaders which will have a positive impact on subordinates. As Eden observes: "Taken together, these findings constitute prima facie evidence that the [team development] intervention improves teamwork, conflict handling and information flow, and may have other benefits."[69]

"Eclectic Approach to Organizational Development," by Edgar F. Huse and Michael Beer[70]

This article reports on a comprehensive development program in the Medfield plant of the Corning Glass Works Corporation. The plant was relatively new, small (35 hourly employees, 15 technical and clerical people, eight managers and professionals), and nonunion. The program started in 1966, with most of the interventions occurring in 1968 and 1969. The plant manufactures electrical and electronic instruments for medical and laboratory use; most of the jobs are assembly-type jobs. The plant's operations are separated into departments that manufacture different products.

Different treatments were used in the different departments and we shall report the treatments and results for each unit separately. The overall research design was a before-and-after treatment design with observations taken over a long time span. No control groups were used; however, since different treatments were implemented in the different departments, what we have in this report is a series of separate programs, the results of which were carefully documented.

The hotplate department.   In this department the employees assembled hotplates on a standard assembly-line basis. It was decided to introduce a job enrichment program in the department in which each worker would assemble the entire hotplate. Job enrichment efforts attempt to put more challenge into jobs by increasing the amount of planning, doing, and controlling by the individual rather than separating these functions among several people. The results were rapid and dramatic: productivity increased 85 percent, controllable rejects dropped from 23 to 1 percent, absenteeism dropped from 8 to 1 percent, and an inspector position was abolished. The employees, in addition, were very satisfied with the new methods.

The glass shop. In this department glass tubing for electrodes was produced. It was decided to introduce "autonomous or integrated work teams"—cohesive work groups assigned as a group to perform a series of interdependent tasks. It took some time to get the new system running properly, but when it became operational, productivity increased by 20 percent. Involvement and commitment of the employees also increased substantially.

The materials control department. This department was charged with the responsibility for purchasing, inventory control, plant scheduling, and expediting. The department manager implemented a structural change in the way work was done, as follows:

> Rather than have each group specialize in a particular functional area, he decided to organize his department on the basis of product lines. Each group would have total responsibility for a particular product line or department, including all the functions of purchasing, scheduling, inventory control, and expediting.[71]

The results? The employees liked the new system much better, and within three months the parts-shortage lists decreased from 14 IBM pages to one page.

The instrument assembly department. Complex electronic equipment was assembled in this department. The manager decided to institute a "total job concept" program, a program similar to the job enrichment program implemented in the hotplate department. Rather than work on an assembly-line basis, individuals were given the complete assembly of the instruments. Measurements indicated that productivity increased by 17 percent, quality increased by 50 percent, and absenteeism decreased by over 50 percent.

Additional interventions and conclusions. Other interventions in the plant included forming some matrix teams, cross-departmental teams to ensure coordination and better problem solving; monthly meetings of all natural work groups to discuss problems and to share information from superiors to subordinates; a weekly communications meeting of the plant manager with rotating groups of hourly and salaried employees; and intergroup problem-solving meetings.

These results of the OD program at the Medfield plant are impressive. The interventions were designed to complement the individual manager's preferred modes of working and also to take into account the nature of the tasks to be performed.

A considerable amount of OD work has been launched in the rest of the Corning Glass Works Corporation, and it too appears to be quite successful. William Dowling commented on the Corning approach to OD as follows: "Corning's OD effort is perhaps (and, based on personal observation, we should strike out the perhaps) the most complex, in-depth, carefully thought-through, and conscientiously implemented OD program currently in operation."[72]

"Expectation Effects in Organizational Change,"
by Albert S. King.[73]

This research, while not strictly on an OD effort as we define it, is reported here to demonstrate one of the inherent problems in research on organization development, namely, that changes observed as a result of change programs may be due as much to the *expectations* people have about the program's effects as they are due to the *program itself*. The results of the study indicated that when managers were told to expect an increase in productivity due to a "job enrichment program," productivity actually increased, compared with production rates in plants where the managers were told the job enrichment program would improve employee relations but not increase productivity. Two treatments were used in the job enrichment programs: a *job enlargement* program in which three jobs were performed by the same person instead of three persons and a *job rotation* program in which people were allowed to rotate between three separate jobs.

The research was conducted in four different plants owned by the same company. The plants manufactured clothing patterns. In Plant 1 job enlargement was introduced, and the plant manager was told that the program would increase production. In Plant 2 enlargement was also introduced, but the plant manager was told that the program would not increase production although it would improve employee relations. In Plant 3 job rotation was introduced, and the plant manager was told that the program would increase production; in Plant 4 job rotation was introduced, and the plant manager was told that the program would not increase production but would improve employee relations. Thus, job enlargement was introduced in Plants 1 and 2, while job rotation was introduced in Plants 3 and 4. In addition, managerial expectations were manipulated so that the managers of Plants 1 and 3 expected the new programs to lead to higher productivity while the managers of Plants 2 and 4 expected the new programs to lead to improved employee relations but not to increased productivity.

Average daily production rates for the 12 months following the introduction of the new programs showed that production was significantly higher in those plants where the managers were told to expect higher production compared with the plants where the managers were told not to expert higher production. On the other hand, production was not higher for the job enlargement programs compared with the job rotation programs. (It is usually assumed that job enlargement is a more powerful and effective intervention than job rotation.) Expectations about program outcomes had more impact on production than the different programs did.

Were employee relations better in the plants where the managers had been told to expect this outcome of the programs? No, not as indicated by absenteeism, the measure used in this research. (Absenteeism is often considered to be an accurate reflection of employee relations, morale, and job satisfaction.)

Questionnaire data supported the belief that the two experimental conditions differed in their expectations: both managers and hourly employees in Plants 1 and 3 expected their programs to lead to higher productivity compared with managers and hourly employees in Plants 2 and 4. There were no significant differences between members of Plants 1 and 3 and Plants 2 and 4 regarding expectations of improved employee relations due to the programs.

This research demonstrates that expectations can influence both performance and attitudes. And the effects of expectations can be as powerful as or more powerful than the interventions themselves. Since most research on OD interventions does not test for or control for expectation effects, the results of the King experiment raise doubts about the real cause of any positive results that accrue from organization development programs. This is an important, if somewhat disturbing, piece of research for the OD researcher in that it demonstrates that independent variables (causes) other than the ones we think we are dealing with may be operating in organizational change programs.

On the other hand, for the OD *practitioner,* this research has definite positive implications: tell the clients to expect positive gains from the program (any program), and "expectation effects" will help the positive gains to be realized.

"OD Techniques and Their Results in 23 Organizations: The Michigan ICL Study," by David G. Bowers[74]

Pretreatment and posttreatment data from 14,812 people in 23 different organizations in a wide variety of industries were analyzed to determine the relative effects of four different kinds of OD programs: survey feedback, interpersonal process consultation, task process consultation, and laboratory training. Two "control" treatments, data handback and no treatment, were included in the analysis. The measurement tool was the Survey of Organizations Questionnaire, an instrument that measures organizational health and effectiveness as indicated on 16 factors. The questionnaire was developed by Taylor and Bowers.[75] In general, the results showed that survey feedback was the most effective treatment in that it produced positive gains in perceptions of organizational climate and organizational health; interpersonal process consultation was the next most effective treatment; task process consultation produced little or no change; laboratory training and no treatment produced declines in organizational functioning and health. This report analyzed attitude data only, not performance. We will examine this research in some detail.

The data were collected as part of the University of Michigqan Inter-Company Longitudinal Study (ICLS) in which annual, standardized measurements were obtained from a number of companies. Some of these organizations began OD programs during the period and thus the effects of the interventions could be monitored.

The treatments will be described briefly. *Survey feedback* is a data collection and feedback technique in which questionnaire data are fed back to all members of the organization in natural work groups where action plans to correct problems indicated in the data are developed. *Interpersonal process consultation* is an intervention technique in which the consultant teaches the organization members to become more aware of their organizational processes. *Task process consultation* is a consultation mode in which the consultant analyzes and helps the group to analyze its task methods and task objectives. *Laboratory training* is a collection of intervention techniques including sensitivity training, experiential learning exercises, and theory input regarding interpersonal relations. *Data handback* is not a treatment per se. Questionnaire data were given to supervisors of all work groups, but they were not encouraged to do anything with the data (as they would do in survey feedback.) *No treatment* was also not a treatment; data were given to the top executives of the organizations, but nothing was done with the data.

Sixteen factors measuring organization functioning and health were used as the dependent variables. Six factors measure *organizational climate*—human resources primacy, communnication flow, motivational climate, decision-making practices, technological readiness, and lower-level influence. Four factors measure *managerial leadership*—support, interaction facilitation (facilitating ''teamwork''), goal emphasis, and work facilitation. Four factors measure *peer leadership* (these are the same as for managerial leadership)—support, interaction facilitation, goal emphasis, and work facilitation. The last two factors are *group process* (how the group works together) and *satisfaction*. The data analysis examined results both for the total organization and for ''capstone groups''—groups that actually received the various treatments.

The results for survey feedback. Positive and significant changes for capstone groups occurred in every area except managerial leadership. Eleven of the 16 measures were positive and significant at the level of the total organization.

The results for interpersonal process consultation. Positive and significant changes at the level of the total organization were found on seven of the 16 measures, primarily in the managerial and peer leadership areas. Organizational climate, group process, and satisfaction did not change significantly. No firm conclusions could be made on the effects on the capstone groups due to lack of sufficient data.

The results for task process consultation. Two factors, decision-making practices and satisfaction, increased significantly in the positive direction for capstone groups as a result of this treatment. At the level of the total organization, however, five factors changed significantly in the negative direction, and three of the factors were associated with organizational climate.

The results for laboratory training. All six organizational climate factors changed significantly for the total organization—five in the negative direction and one in the positive direction. In addition, managerial support, peer support, and satisfaction decreased significantly for the total organization. The factor *group process* increased significantly for the total organization. Results for capstone groups were similar, but not quite so negative.

The results for data handback. This ''control'' condition showed significant decrease on four factors, and significant gains on five factors, in the analysis of the total organization. For capstone groups, four factors increased significantly while one declined.

The results for no treatment. This ''control'' condition showed significant decreases on 10 factors in the analysis of the total organization. For capstone groups, four factors declined significantly while one increased.

Overall, these results show clear differences in the effects of the different OD interventions. Different organizational variables are impacted by the different programs, and some programs are more impactful than others. In addition, survey feedback and interpersonal process consultation are associated with perceptions of significant positive changes in organizational functioning, whereas laboratory training and task process consultation are associated with negative change or no change.

However, it may be that the treatments are not exactly comparable in that some treatments, laboratory training and task process consultation especially, are not *systemic* in nature. That is, the target is usually a small part of the organization, not the total system. The questionnaire measures systemic problems of a wide range; some treatments are much more narrowly focused.

One further aspect of the research will be mentioned. Perhaps in the organizations where negative or no change occurred as a result of the treatments, the organizational climate was already too negative to allow for gains. Controlling for organizational climate did cause some of the negative effects associated with laboratory training to disappear.

This is an important piece of comparative research in which both absolute and relative effects of different OD interventions were measured. Such longitudinal, comparative research makes a contribution to theory building in OD as well as a contribution to evaluation of OD.

"Modeling-Based Organizational Development: A Longitudinal Assessment," by Jerry I. Porras, Kenneth Hargis, Kerry J. Patterson, David G. Maxfield, Nancy Roberts, and Robert J. Bies[76]

All the first-line supervisors in a plywood mill received training to increase their interpersonal and supervisory skills using behavior modeling. As a result their employees rated them as more effective on key supervisory behaviors, rated the organizational climate as more favorable, increased productivity, and reduced absenteeism and turnover. All changes were significant when compared to two other plywood mills where the supervisors received no training. This research effort is noteworthy for its careful and competent execution; the intervention demonstrates that behavior modeling training is an effective method for promoting organizational improvements.

Let us examine the OD program and the research design. In behavior modeling participants observe a videotaped model solve a problem correctly, examine and discuss the specific behaviors that caused the model to be successful, and then practice the correct behaviors while receiving feedback and reinforcement on their own performance. (See Chapter 12 for a description of this intervention.) Goldstein and Sorcher developed the technique[77] which is based on Social Learning Theory as proposed by Albert Bandura.[78] Behavior modeling is perhaps the single most effective training method for improving interpersonal skills. Latham and Saari used this method with first-line supervisors in a wood products company and produced significant gains in individual performance.[79] Porras and his colleagues extend previous research by showing that behavior modeling can produce total organization change.

All 17 first-line supervisors in a plywood mill with about 700 union employees attended 10 one-half day training sessions based on 10 different problematic situations typically found on the job. Training modules covered such topics as dealing with a worker producing substandard work, dealing with absenteeism, dealing with safety violations, and giving support to a valued employee. The sessions were led by line managers who had received extensive training in how to use behavior modeling. Two other similar plywood mills operated by the company served as control or comparison groups; one mill had eight supervisors and approximately 350 union employees while the other mill had five supervisors and approximately 200 union employees. The mills were not randomly assigned to experimental and control groups, but the nonequivalent control groups design is reasonably strong for making inferences about internal validity.

Five specific supervisory skills were targeted for change in the experimental group as follows:

> Component skills were embedded in a general problem-solving sequence: supervisors learned to describe a problem in a specific and nonjudgmental way (Behavior Description); explain the behavior's impact on organizational performance (Justification); elicit and restate an employee's feeling about a problem (Active Listening); ask the employee for ideas regarding causes and solutions for a problem (Participative Problem Solving); and follow-up on agreed-upon solutions so that reinforcement could be given for improved performance (Follow-up and Reinforcement).[80]

Questionnaires were administered one week before training, one week after training, and six months after training to all the experimental and control supervisors and approximately one-third of the hourly employees selected at random. Measures rated supervisors on the five basic skills and asked for perceptions of overall organizational climate. Company records were examined for changes in produtivity, turnover, absenteeism, and grievances.

The results were favorable, significant, and solid. The experimental supervisors were seen by their employees as improving significantly on all five basic skills compared to the control group supervisors. Moreover, these improvements were found in the six month follow-up questionnaire. Perceptions of organizational climate improved significantly for the experimental group employees compared to the control group employees: this was sustained for six months. The experimental group employees did not feel the increased skill development of their supervisors was "manipulative." Productivity, as measured by Production per Direct Man-Hour, Recovery (lack of waste and spoilage), and Average Daily Production, was significantly higher for the trained supervisors compared to the untrained supervisors. Absenteeism and turnover decreased significantly at the experimental mill compared to the control mills.

This is a competent demonstration of the ability of behavior modeling to improve supervisory behavior which in turn improved employee attitudes and performance. The authors suggest that organization development theorists should consider Social Learning Theory as a valuable resource for understanding planned organizational change.

"Increasing Productivity and Morale in a Municipality: Effects of Organization Development," Christian F. Paul and Albert C. Gross[81]

The 90-person Communications and Electrical Division of the city of San Diego was the target group for this year-long OD project. This group is in charge of the maintenance of street lights, traffic lights, radio and communications equipment, and parking meters. The treatment was thorough and multifaceted, consisting of interviews of all division members, three-day and two-day team-building workshops of all work teams, management skills training, counseling for division managers, and process consulting at various staff meetings. The focus was on identifying and solving the problems that would improve morale and increase effectiveness and efficiency. The program was conducted by the city's internal OD consultants with assistance from an external consultant.

Numerous dependent measures related to productivity and morale were examined in a pre- and postintervention format using both attitude surveys and division records. To improve the interpretability of the results, a variety of comparison groups receiving no treatment were used as quasi-control groups. Some of the comparison groups were from other divisions within the San Diego city government while some were from other governmental jurisdictions engaged in work duties similar to the Communications and Electrical Division. The comparison of results from the treatment group with the comparison groups turned what was an inherently weak research design into a much stronger one. All in all, this appears to have been a competent OD intervention and a careful evaluation of the effects of that intervention.

The results for the experimental group were positive: efficiency as calculated by a number of different measures rose during the intervention year; productivity increased; unit costs decreased; and morale and job satisfaction appeared to increase, although these attitudinal measures were somewhat mixed and weak. Productivity and morale for the comparison groups either remained the same or showed deterioration. The authors concluded that the OD program improved productivity as intended without causing any decrease in job satisfaction.

And, perhaps as important as the actual results, the authors learned that "The present study shows that it is feasible to assess the effects of OD intervention projects that are conducted in municipal government settings."[82] This finding alone made the effort worthwhile.

"Pygmalion at Sea: Improving the Work Effectiveness of Low Performers," by Kent S. Crawford, Edmund D. Thomas, and Jeffrey J. Fink[83]

An interesting and innovative use of organization development techniques is described in this research study conducted with the U.S. Navy. A consultant team in the Navy's OD program received a request from the commanding officer of a combat ship to help him do something about a group of unmotivated, trouble-prone, low performers (LPs). These persons usually cause extensive problems for themselves and their supervisors, get into disciplinary troubles, and often are separated from the Navy with unfavorable discharges. What, if anything, could be done to salvage them? The consultant team developed a theoretical perspective for understanding the problem, developed an intervention plan and implemented it, and evaluated the effects of the intervention plan.

The theory was derived from Albert Bandura's self-efficacy theory[84] that states that efficacy expectations (the belief that one can perform the behavior) and outcome expectations (the belief that desirable outcomes will follow performance of the behavior) play an important role in motivating people to perform. Low performers lack these two sets of expectations; high performers possess them. A further theoretical foundation was

Robert Merton's "Pygmalion effect" or self-fulfilling prophecy, which is defined as "the tendency of people to perform in accordance with what is expected of them as well as their own expectations of success or failure."[85] The LPs had been labeled by themselves and others as "losers." The self-fulfilling prophecy predicts that they would then act out those expectations. The intervention program was designed to substitute positive expectations for negative ones and to put in place an action plan that would allow the positive expectations to lead to positive outcomes for everyone concerned.

The target groups of the intervention were the low performers, all supervisory personnel on the ship, and a subgroup of supervisors who were appointed to act as one-to-one counselors and mentors for the LPs. (Note the systemic nature of the solution: it deals with the larger social system within which the problem sailors operate, not just with the LPs themselves.) The intervention program consisted of three sets of activities described by the authors as follows: "three mutually supportive tracks were used, consisting of: (1) supervisory training; (2) mentor counseling training for selected supervisors; and (3) low-performers' growth workshops."[86]

The supervisory training component was conducted in a one-and-one-half day motivation and training workshop for all supervisors. Ingredients included an examination of the Pygmalion effect, behavior modification techniques designed to reinforce positive behaviors when they occurred, and the general exhortation to replace the negative expectations held for the LPs with positive expectations. The mentor training component was conducted in a one-day workshop for 15 supervisors chosen to serve as role models, mentors, counselors, and "sounding boards" for the LPs. Each mentor would be paired with one low performer. Ingredients of this workshop consisted of training in active listening, counseling skills, and leadership effectiveness.

Twelve LPs attended the low performers' growth workshops, which consisted of two three-day "packages." Ingredients of these workshops were individual planning and goal-setting exercises, examination of self-image and self-expectations, vocational guidance and planning, reading skills, introduction to positive reinforcement techniques, meetings with the mentors, several talks by the CO, and additional exercises linking "how to" do things with positive goal setting.

Three weeks after the intervention program was completed, the ship deployed to the western Pacific for seven months. The OD program was completed; evaluating the effects was next.

The results were positive and measurable. Three treatment group sailors were honorably discharged during the tour at sea and before the evaluation was completed. Interviews indicated that these three had improved in work performance since their training and up to their completion of their enlistments. One person was a clear failure; he was given a disciplinary discharge from the Navy. Eight LPs remained in the Navy during the entire evaluation period, and their work performance after the training was significantly better as compared with two comparison groups. Data collected on these comparison groups substantially strengthened the research effort. The eight experimental sailors showed a decrease in disciplinary actions compared with the comparison groups, although this decrease was not statistically significant. Six of the LPs who were eligible for promotion passed advancement exams and five were scheduled to be promoted. The commanding officer was extremely pleased with the progress made by all eight former low performers. In summary, it appears that 11 out of 12 "problem employees" were turned around and became assets to themselves and the organization. This is an impressive story in applied behavioral science.

OD RESEARCH AND PRACTICE IN PERSPECTIVE

Several excellent recent literature reviews attest to the efficacy of organization development to bring about desired and intended changes. These surveys of OD research and practice cover a broad range of programs conducted over several decades. Such summaries are valuable for providing a perspective of the field. Several conclusions may be drawn from these reports: first, the preponderance of OD programs produce positive results; second, some OD interventions are more effective than others; third, the variables impacted by OD programs are becoming better understood; and, fourth, the actual causal mechanisms of OD programs are not yet well mapped and clarified. Let us examine briefly some of the reviews.

Porras and Berg[87] screened 160 studies and reduced the total to a set of 35 studies exhibiting clear organization development interventions that were evaluated by rigorous research standards. They found that 308 different variables were measured in the 35 studies; these variables were classified into "outcome" variables and "process" variables. Outcome variables are such typical performance measures as profitability, productivity, and turnover, and individual performance measures such as job satisfaction and job understanding. Process variables are such things as goal emphasis, decision making, influence, and human interaction variables such as openness. The typologies are shown in Figures 19–1 and 19–2. Note that the variables relate to different targets of analysis: the individual, the leader, the group, and the organization. These classification models suggest what variables might be amendable to change through OD interventions and offer a roadmap for the practitioner and researcher alike.

In terms of results, Porras and Berg found the following. Outcome variables were measured in 22 studies, and in 51 percent of the cases substantial positive changes occurred. Analyses were made at the level of the individual, leader, group, and organization with changes being found at all levels. Of interest to us is the authors' comment: "At the organizational level, economic performance improved over 50 percent of the times it was measured (in seven of nine projects)."[88]

Regarding process variables, overall 46 percent of the process variables showed positive changes. It was also found that different interventions produced different results: the Managerial Grid had the greatest impact on outcome variables followed by task-oriented laboratory training and survey feedback. The use of multiple intervention approaches was associated with greater positive change. In addition, either relatively short (four to six months) or relatively long (25 or more months) programs seemed to be associated with the greatest amount of change.

This is a most useful survey of the literature. The conceptualization of the change variables is a good addition to the knowledge base of the field. The results suggest that OD works but that there is much we do not know about the causal mechanisms of change.

Margulies, Wright, and Scholl[89] analyzed 30 studies and found positive results in over 70 percent of them. Dunn and Swierczek[90] examined 67 cases and found positive

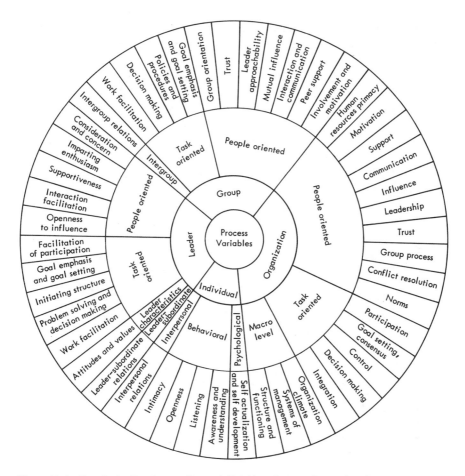

Figure 19–1 Organization Development Research Variables—Process. *Source:* Jerry I.
Porras and P. O. Berg, "The Impact of Organization Development,"
Academy of Management Review, April 1978, p. 252. Used with permission.

gains almost 70 percent of the time. John Nicholas assessed the impact of a variety of
OD interventions on *hard criteria* such as costs, profits, and quantity and quality of
production in 65 studies.[91] Positive outcomes were found in about half of these cases.

Katzell and Guzzo reviewed 207 field experiments using 11 psychological
approaches to improving employee productivity and found gains were reported in
87 percent of the studies. The time frame was from 1971 to 1981 and the interventions
included such activities as sociotechnical systems redesign, goal setting, training and
instruction, appraisal and feedback, and the like.[92] Guzzo, Jette, and Katzell conducted
a meta-analysis on the same set of studies and found that the programs, on average, raised
worker productivity by one-half standard deviation, a substantial gain indeed. These
authors conclude their meta-analysis article as follows:

> *Behavioral science techniques for increasing worker productivity are, on the whole. effective.*
> For industrial and organizational psychologists, that should be great news![93]

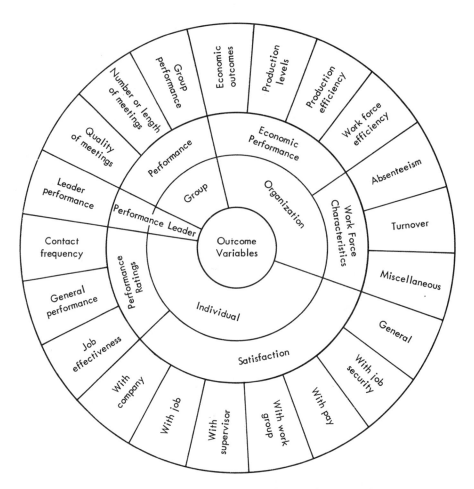

Figure 19–2 Organization Development Research Variables—Outcome. *Source:* Jerry I. Porras and P. O. Berg, "The Impact of Organization Development," *Academy of Management Review*, April 1978, p. 253. Used with permission.

Finally, Golembiewski, Proehl, and Sink report on what is no doubt the most extensive review of the OD literature to date.[94] They found 574 cases of OD applications occurring from 1945 to mid-1980, with 47 percent of these cases being public sector applications and 53 percent being business or private sector programs. A "global estimate of efficacy" was made by examining each case and assigning it to one of four evaluative categories in which the intervention had (1) highly positive and intended effects, (2) definite balance of positive and intended effects, (3) no appreciable effects, and (4) negative effects. The results were favorable: over 80 percent of the cases showed either highly positive or a definite balance of positive outcomes. On the other hand, only 8 percent of the applications showed negative effects. Additional analyses showed that improvements were found at the individual, leader, group, and total organization levels.

We conclude from these surveys that organization development is a viable strategy for organizational improvement. More research is needed—it always is; but the results to date look very favorable.

SUMMARY

In this chapter we have explored the general topic of research on organization development. It can be seen that there are many problems associated with such field research and experimentation, but progress is being made on a number of fronts. Selected research examples and selected literature reviews were examined in some detail to determine what effects, if any, various OD treatments had on individual, work group, and total organization functioning. It appears, from these examples, that there is considerable evidence to suggest that OD works.

NOTES

1. Larry E. Pate, Warren R. Nielsen, and Paula C. Bacon, "Advances in Research on Organization Development: Toward a Beginning," in Robert L. Taylor, Michael J. O'Connell, Robert A. Zawacki, and D. D. Warrick, eds., *Academy of Management Proceedings '76,* Proceedings of the 36th Annual Meeting of the Academy of Management, Kansas City, Missouri, August 11-14, 1976, pp. 389-394.

2. Ibid., pp. 389 and 392.

3. Robert L. Kahn, "Organizational Development: Some Problems and Proposals," *Journal of Applied Behavioral Science,* 10, No. 4 (1974), pp. 485-502. Kahn also criticized the research on OD as being mostly case studies, a condition that was more true then than now.

4. See, for example, Fred N. Kerlinger, *Foundations of Behavioral Research,* 2nd ed. (New York: Holt, Rinehart and Winston, 1973).

5. Donald T. Campbell and Julian C. Stanley, *Experimental and Quasi-Experimental Designs for Research* (Chicago: Rand McNally, 1963), p. 5.

6. Ibid. This little book is generally considered to be one of the best expositions of research designs available.

7. Pate, Nielsen, and Bacon, "Advances in Research on Organization Development"; and Sam E. White and Terence R. Mitchell, "Organization Development: A Review of Research Content and Research Design," *Academy of Management Review,* 1 (April 1976), pp. 57-73.

8. Jerry I. Porras and P. O. Berg, "The Impact of Organization Development," *The Academy of Management Review,* 3, No. 2 (April 1978), pp. 249-266.

9. Norman Berkowitz, "Audiences and Their Implications for Evaluation Research," *Journal of Applied Behavioral Science,* 5, No. 3 (1969), pp. 411-428.

10. Campbell and Stanley, *Experimental and Quasi-Experimental Designs,* p. 5.

11. Clayton P. Alderfer, "Organization Development," in *Annual Review of Psychology,* 28 (1977), pp. 197-223.

12. Kerlinger, *Foundations of Behavioral Research,* p. 9. Italics in the original.

13. Clayton P. Alderfer, "Change Processes in Organizations," in Marvin D. Dunnette, ed., *Handbook of Industrial and Organizational Psychology* (Chicago: Rand McNally, 1976), pp. 1591-1638.

14. Chris Argyris, *Intervention Theory and Method: A Behavioral Science View* (Reading, Mass.: Addison-Wesley, 1970).

15. Robert R. Blake and Jane Srygley Mouton, *Consultation* (Reading, Mass.: Addison-Wesley, 1976).

16. Peter B. Vaill, "Practice Theories in Organization Development," in J. D. Adams, ed., *New Technologies in Organization Development* (La Jolla, Calif.: University Associates, 1974), pp. 71–84.

17. J. G. Bowers, J. L. Franklin, and P. A. Pecorella, "Matching Problems, Precursors, and Interventions in OD: A Systemic Approach," *Journal of Applied Behavioral Science,* 11 (1975), pp. 391–410.

18. White and Mitchell, "Organization Development." For a discussion of facet theory, see L. Guttman, "An Outline of Some New Methodology for Social Research," *Public Opinion Quarterly,* 18 (1955), pp. 395–404.

19. See White and Mitchell, "Organization Development," pp. 59–66, for this discussion.

20. William N. Dunn and Frederic W. Swierczek, "Planned Organizational Change: Toward Grounded Theory," *Journal of Applied Behavioral Science,* 13, No. 2 (1977), pp. 135–157.

21. Ibid., p. 149.

22. R. J. Golembiewski, K. Billingsley, and S. Yeager, "Measuring Change and Persistence in Human Affairs: Types of Change Generated by OD Designs," *The Journal of Applied Behavioral Science,* Vol. 12 (1976), pp. 133–157.

23. A. A. Armenakis and R. W. Zmud, "Interpreting the Measurement of Change in Organizational Research," *Personnel Psychology,* Vol. 32 (1979), pp. 709–723.

24. A. Randolph, "Planned Organizational Change and Its Measurement," *Personnel Psychology,* Vol. 35 (1982), pp. 117–139.

25. J. A. Terborg, G. S. Howard, and S. E. Maxwell, "Evaluating Planning Organizational Change: A Method for Assessing Alpha, Beta, and Gamma Change," *Academy of Management Review,* Vol. 5 (1980), pp. 109–121.

26. J. I. Porras and J. V. Singh, "Alpha, Beta, and Gamma Change in Modeling-Based Organization Development," *Journal of Occupational Behavior,* Vol. 7 (1986), pp. 9–24.

27. C. Argyris, R. Putnam, and D. M. Smith, *Action Science,* (San Francisco: Jossey-Bass, 1985).

28. M. Blumberg and C. D. Pringle, "How Control Groups Can Cause Loss of Control in Action Research: The Case of Rushton Coal Mine," *The Journal of Applied Behavioral Science,* Vol. 19 (1983), pp. 409–425.

29. R. J. Bullock and D. J. Svyantek, "The Impossibility of Using Random Strategies to Study the Organization Development Process," *The Journal of Applied Behavioral Science,* Vol. 23 (1987), pp. 255–262.

30. Ibid., p. 260.

31. R. J. Bullock and Patti F. Bullock, "Pure Science Versus Science-Action Models of Data Feedback: A Field Experiment," *Group and Organization Studies,* Vol. 9 (March 1984), pp. 7–27.

32. Michael Beer and Anna Elise Walton, "Organization Change and Development," *Annual Review of Psychology,* 38 (1987), pp. 339–367.

33. Ibid., p. 344.

34. Frank Friedlander and L. Dave Brown, "Organization Development," in *Annual Review of Psychology,* 25 (1974), p. 336.

35. Pate, Nielsen, and Bacon, "Advances in Research in Organization Development," pp. 390–391.

36. J. Taylor and D. G. Bowers, *The Survey of Organizations: A Machine-Scored Standardized Questionnaire Instrument* (Ann Arbor, Mich.: Institute for Social Research, 1972).

37. See, for example, David G. Bowers, "OD Techniques and Their Results in 23 Organizations: The Michigan ICL Study," *Journal of Applied Behavioral Science,* 9, No. 1 (1973), pp. 21–43.

38. See, for example, the *Michigan Organizational Assessment Package Program Report II* (Ann Arbor, Mich.: Survey Research Center, August 1975). This program is partially sponsored by the National Center for Productivity and the Quality of Working Life, an independent agency of the federal government.

39. Edward E. Lawler III and Gerald E. Ledford, Jr., "Productivity and the Quality of Work Life," *National Productivity Review,* 1, No. 1 (Winter 1981–1982), pp. 23–36; and G. E.

Ledford, Jr. and E. E. Lawler III, "Quality of Work Life Programs, Coordination, and Productivity," *Journal of Contemporary Business,* 1982, 11, No. 2, pp. 93–106. This issue of the *Journal of Contemporary Business* is devoted to addressing behavioral science strategies for organizational improvement and is worthwhile reading.

40. Alderfer, "Organization Development," p. 219.

41. Nancy C. Roberts and Jerry I. Porras, "Progress in Organization Development Research,"*Group and Organization Studies, 7,* No. 1 (March 1982), pp. 91–116.

42. Friedlander and Brown, "Organization Development."

43. Alderfer, "Organization Development."

44. Claude Faucheux, Gilles Amado, and Andre Laurent, "Organizational Development and Change," *Annual Review of Psychology,* Vol. 33 (1982), pp. 343–370.

45. Beer and Walton, "Organization Change and Development."

46. Michael Beer, "The Technology of Organization Development," Dunnette, ed., *Handbook of Industrial and Organizational Psychology,* pp. 937–993.

47. George Strauss, "Organization Development," in Robert Dublin, ed., *Handbook of Work, Organization, and Society* (Chicago: Rand McNally, 1976), pp. 617–685.

48. White and Mitchell, "Organization Development."

49. Pate, Nielsen, and Bacon, "Advances in Research on Organization Development." In addition, a model for evaluation of OD programs has been proposed by John M. Nicholas, "A Systems Analysis Approach for Planning Evaluations of OD Interventions," in Robert L. Taylor, Michael J. O'Connell, Robert A. Zawacki, and D. D. Warrick, eds., *Academy of Mangement Proceedings '77,* Proceedings of the 37th annual meeting of the Academy of Management at Orlando, Florida, August 14–17, 1977, pp. 358–362.

50. Porras and Berg, "The Impact of Organization Development," pp. 249–266.

51. Robert T. Golembiewski, Carl W. Proehl, Jr., and David Sink, "Estimating the Success of OD Applications," *Training and Development Journal,* 36, No. 4 (April 1982), pp. 86–95.

52. From *Harvard Business Review, 42* (November–December 1964), pp. 133–155.

53. Ibid., p. 135.

54. This book is published by Harper & Row (New York, 1967).

55. See Chapter 13 for a description of Likert's System 4 Management and references to Likert's work.

56. Marrow, Bowers, and Seashore, *Management by Participation,* Harper & Row, 1967, p. 69. This discussion is taken from pp. 68–69.

57. Ibid., pp. 69–74.

58. Ibid., p. 200.

59. Stanley E. Seashore and David G. Bowers, "Durability of Organizational Change," *American Psychologist,* 25, No. 3 (March 1970), pp. 227–233.

60. Ibid., p. 232.

61. This article is in Harvey Hornstein, Barbara Benedict Bunker, W. Warner Burke, Marion Gindes, and Roy J. Lewicki, eds., *Social Intervention: A Behavioral Science Approach* (New York: The Free Presss, 1971), pp. 421–439.

62. From the *Administrative Science Quarterly, 20* (June 1975), pp. 191–206.

63. Ibid., p. 201.

64. From the *Journal of Applied Behavioral Science, 9,* No. 6 (1973), pp. 727–735.

65. Ibid., p. 730.

66. A. Lowin, "Participative Decision Making: A Model, Literature Critique, and Prescriptions for Research," *Organizational Behavior and Human Performance, 3* (1968), pp. 68–106.

67. Ibid., p. 734.

68. Dov Eden, "Team Development: Quasi-Experimental Confirmation Among Combat Companies," *Group and Organization Studies,* Vol. 11 (September 1986), pp. 133–146.

69. Ibid., p. 142.

70. From the *Harvard Business Review, 49* (September–October 1971), pp. 103–112.

71. The *Harvard Business Review,* p. 108.

72. William F. Dowling, "The Corning Approach to Organization Development," *Organizational Dynamics, 3,* No. 4 (Spring 1975), pp. 16–34. This quotation is from page 17.

73. From *Administrative Science Quarterly,* 19 (1974), pp. 221–230.

74. From the *Journal of Applied Behavioral Science,* 9, No. 1 (1973), pp. 21–43.

75. Taylor and Bowers, *The Survey of Organizations: A Machine-Scored Standardized Questionnaire Instrument.*

76. From *Journal of Applied Behavioral Science,* Vol. 18 (1982), pp. 433–446.

77. A. Goldstein and M. Sorcher, *Changing Supervisory Behavior,* (New York: Pergamon, 1974).

78. A. Bandura, *Social Learning Theory,* (Englewood Cliffs, N.J.: Prentice-Hall, 1977).

79. G. P. Latham and L. M. Saari, ''Application of Social-Learning Theory to Training Supervisors Through Behavioral Modeling,'' *Journal of Applied Psychology,* Vol. 64 (1979), pp. 239–246.

80. Porras et. al., ibid., p. 438.

81. From *Journal of Applied Behavioral Science,* 17, No. 1 (1981), pp. 59–78.

82. Ibid., p. 77.

83. From *Journal of Applied Behavioral Science,* 16, No. 4 (1980), pp. 482–505.

84. Albert Bandura, ''Self-efficacy: Toward a Unifying Theory of Behavioral Change,'' *Psychological Review,* 84, No. 2 (1977), pp. 191–215.

85. This quotation is from Crawford, Thomas, and Fink, *The Journal of Applied Behavioral Science,* 16, No. 4 (1980), p. 486. The self-fulfilling prophecy concept was first proposed by Robert K. Merton, *Social Theory and Social Structure,* rev. ed. (New York: The Free Press, 1957).

86. Ibid., p. 488.

87. Porras and Berg, ''The Impact of Organization Development.''

88. Ibid., p. 256.

89. Newton Margulies, Penny L. Wright, and Richard W. Scholl, ''Organization Development Techniques: Their Impact on Change,'' *Group and Organization Studies,* 2, No. 4 (December 1977), p. 449.

90. Dunn and Swierczek, ''Planned Organizational Change.''

91. John M. Nicholas, ''The Comparative Impact of Organization Development Interventions on Hard Criteria Measures,'' *Academy of Mangement Review,* 7, No. 4 (October 1982), pp. 531–541.

92. R. A. Katzell and R. A. Guzzo, ''Psychological Approaches to Productivity Improvement,'' *American Psychologist,* (April 1983), pp. 468–472.

93. R. A. Guzzo, R. D. Jette, and R. A. Katzell, ''The Effects of Psychologically Based Intervention Programs on Worker Productivity: A Meta-Analysis,'' *Personnel Psychology,* Vol. 38 (1985), pp. 275–291.

94. Golembiewski, Proehl, and Sink, ''Estimating the Success of OD Applications.''

20

POWER, POLITICS, AND ORGANIZATION DEVELOPMENT

Power and politics are indisputable facts of social and organizational life that must be understood if one wishes to be effective in organizations. In this chapter the concepts of power and politics are examined in relation to organization development. The OD practitioner needs both awareness (knowledge) and behavioral competence (skill) in the arenas of organizational power and politics. As Warner Burke observes: ''Organization development signifies change, and *for change to occur in an organization, power must be exercised.*''[1]

Organization development has been criticized in the past for not taking account of power in organizations.[2] That criticism was essentially correct for many years although it is less valid today. Recent years have seen a sizable outpouring of theory and research on power and politics,[3] and OD practitioners have attempted to derive implications and applications for the field of OD.[4] But we are still in the early stages of knowing how power and organization development should be related. One goal of this chapter is to advance our understanding of the role of power in OD and the role of OD in a power setting.[5]

POWER DEFINED AND EXPLORED

Let us examine several representative definitions of power.

> ''Power is the intentional influence over the beliefs, emotions, and behaviors of people. Potential power is the capacity to do so, but kinetic power is the act of doing so. . . . One person exerts power over another to the degree that he is able to exact compliance as desired.''[6]

"A has power over B to the extent that he can get B to do something that B would otherwise not do."[7]

Power is "the ability of those who possess power to bring about the outcomes they desire."[8]

"*Power is defined in this book simply as the capacity to effect (or affect) organizational outcomes.* The French work 'pouvoir' stands for both the noun 'power' and the verb 'to be able.' To have power is to be able to get desired things done, to effect outcomes—actions and the decisions that precede them."[9]

Analysis of these definitions shows some common elements: effectance—getting one's way; the necessity of social interaction between two or more parties; the act or ability of influencing others; and outcomes favoring one party over the other. We therefore define interpersonal power as *the ability to get one's way in a social situation.*

The phenomenon of power is ubiquitous. Without influence (power) there would be no cooperation and no society. Without leadership (power) in medical, political, technological, financial, spiritual, and organizational activities, humankind would not have the standard of living it does today. Without leadership (power) directed toward warfare, confiscation, and repression, humankind would not have much of the misery it does today. Power-in-action may take many forms, both positive and negative. Leading, influencing, selling, persuading—these are examples of positive uses of power. Crushing, forcing, hurting, coercing—these are examples of negative uses of power. Power per se is probably neither good nor bad although Lord Acton observed that "power tends to corrupt; absolute power corrupts absolutely." A moment's reflection, however, suggests that many problems with power stem from some of the goals of persons with power and some of the means they use, not the possession of power as such.

Two Faces of Power

This discussion is based on the important distinction articulated by David McClelland who identified "two faces of power"—positive and negative.[10] McClelland observed that while power has a negative connotation for most people, it is through the use of power that things get done in the world. According to him, the negative face of power is characterized by a primitive, unsocialized need to have dominance over submissive others. The positive face of power is characterized by a socialized need to initiate, influence, and lead. This positive face of power is intended to enable others to reach their goals *as well as* let the person exercising power reach his or her goals. The negative face of power seeks domination and control of others; the positive face of power seeks to empower self and others. It seems to us that this is a good insight into the concept of power.

In most organizations the positive face of power is much more prevalent than the negative face of power. Patchen found in organizational decision making that coercive tactics were "noticeable chiefly by their absence" and problem solving and consensus seeking were much more prevalent.[11] The positive and negative faces of power appear to be what Roberts calls "collective power" and "competitive power" respectively. Her research in four organizations showed both kinds of power being exercised, with collective power being the predominant mode.[12]

THEORIES ABOUT THE SOURCES OF SOCIAL POWER

Power exists in virtually all social situations. It is especially salient in coordinated activities such as those found in organizations. In fact, for organizations to function, the authority or power dimension must be clarified and agreed upon in a more or less formal way.

How do some people come to possess power? How is power generated, bestowed, or acquired? In this section we will examine four differnt views about who gets power and how: Emerson's "power-dependence theory," French and Raven's "bases of social power," a "strategic-contingency model of power" by Salancik and Pfeffer, and Mintzberg's observations concerning the genesis of power in organizations.

Power-dependence theory states that power is inherent in any social relationship in which one person is dependent upon another. The sociologist Richard Emerson states that "the dependence of Actor A upon Actor B is (1) directly proportional to A's motivational investment in the goals mediated by B, and (2) inversely proportional to the availability of those goals to A outside of the A-B relation."[13] In other words, if a person has something we want badly and we cannot get it any place else, that person has power over us. The components of this theory are *a social relation* between two parties, *resources* (commodities, goals, rewards), *that are controlled* by one party, *and desired* by the other party.

Power-dependence theory is related to a broader framework of social interaction called *social exchange theory* which posits that what goes on between persons in interaction is an exchange of social commodities: love, hate, respect, power, influence, information, praise, blame, attraction, rejection, and so forth. We enter into and continue in exchange relationships when what we receive from others is equivalent to or in excess of what we must give to others. When the net balance for us is positive, we will continue the exchange relationship; when the net balance for us is negative, we will terminate or alter the relationship. Social interaction represents an exchange of social goods and services. Viewed in this light, giving someone power over us is the commodity we exchange when we are dependent on that particular person for something we want.

Closely related to these ideas is the classic statement by John R. P. French and Bertram Raven on "the bases of social power."[14] These authors suggested five sources, or bases, of social power as follows:

1. *Reward power*—power based on the ability of the powerholder to reward another, that is, to give something valued by the other.
2. *Coercive power*—power based on the ability of the powerholder to punish another, that is, to give something negatively valued by the other.
3. *Legitimate power*—power based on the fact that everyone believes that the powerholder has a legitimate right to exert influence and that the power-receiver has a legitimate obligation to accept the influence.
4. *Referent power*—power based on the power-receiver having an identification with (attraction to, or feeling of oneness with) the powerholder.
5. *Expert power*—power based on the powerholder possessing expert knowledge or expertise that is needed by the other. *Informational power* is a form of expert power where the powerholder possesses important facts or information needed by the other.

It can be seen that power belongs to the person who has control over or mediates desired commodities. Exchange theory and power-dependent theory are quite compatible with the bases of social power proposed by French and Raven.

The strategic-contingency model of power asserts that power in organizations accrues to organizational subunits (individuals, units, or departments) that are most important for coping with and solving the most critical problems of the organization.[15] These critical problems are generally "uncertainties" posed by the environment. This theory, like the ones discussed previously, supports the notion that those who have something highly valued by others—in this case, the special expertise most needed for the organization's survival—have power.

Once power is gained, Salancik and Pfeffer suggest how it is then used: "Power is used by subunits, indeed, used by all who have it, to enhance their own survival through control of scarce critical resources, through the placement of allies in key positions, and through the definition of organizational problems and policies."[16] These authors view organizational power as a good thing, for power in the hands of the critical problem solvers helps the organization cope with the various realities it faces.

Henry Mintzberg has developed a theory of organizational power drawn from the organization theory literature and his own creative synthesis abilities.[17] This theory, "is built on the premise that organizational behavior is a power game in which various players, called *influencers,* seek to control the organization's decisions and actions."[18] The three basic conditions for the exercise of power are (1) some source or basis of power, coupled with (2) the expenditure of energy in a (3) politically skillful way when necessary. There are five possible bases of power according to Mintzberg: first, control of a resource; second, control of a technical skill; and, third, control of a body of knowledge. All of these must be critical to the organization. The fourth basis of power is legal prerogatives—being given exclusive rights or privileges to impose choices. And a fifth basis of power is access to those who have power based on the first four bases.[19] In addition to a base of power the influencer must have the "will" to use it and the "skill" to use it.

There are many potential influencers in and around an organization such as the board of directors, the managers, the top executives, the employees, the unions, suppliers, customers, regulators, and so forth. The important aspects of the theory for our purposes here are that the sources of power derive from possession of a commodity valued and desired by others, that power-in-action requires will and skill, and that the organization is the setting or context for the exercise of power.

In summary, these four views of the sources of power are remarkably similar—power stems from possession of or mediation of desired resources. The resources may vary from ability to reward and punish, being in control of critical skills, knowledge, or information, being able to solve critical problems or exigencies, or anything that creates dependence of one actor or set of actors on another.

ORGANIZATIONAL POLITICS DEFINED AND EXPLORED

Let us now examine the concept of politics in organizations. Several representative definitions of politics are the following:

Harold Lasswell defined politics simply as: the study of who gets what, when, and how.[20]

Organizational politics inovlve those activities taken within organizations to acquire, develop and use power and other resources to obtain one's preferred outcomes in a situation in which there is uncertainty or dissensus about choices.[21]

Organizational politics involve intentional acts of influence to enhance or protect the self-interest of individuals or groups.[22]

Organizational politics is the management of influence to obtain ends not sanctioned by the organization or to obtain ends through non-sanctioned influence means.[23]

We view *politics* as a subset of power, treating it . . . as *informal power,* illegitimate in nature. Likewise we also treat authority as a subset of power, but in this sense, *formal* power, the power vested in office, the capacity to get things done by virtue of the position held.[24]

Analysis of these definitions suggests that the concepts of power and politics are very similar. Both relate to getting one's way—effectance. Both relate to pursuit of self-interest and overcoming the resistance of others. For our purposes, organizational politics is power-in-action in organizations; it is engaging in activities to get one's way in an organizational setting.

One important feature in these definitions should be examined further. The first three definitions treat politics as a neutral set of activities: the last two definitions view politics as illegitimate or unsanctioned activities. We are inclined to consider politics as neither good nor bad per se and believe that *politics, like power, has two faces.*

Organizational politics can have a positive and a negative face. The negative face is characterized by *extreme* pursuit of self-interest; unsocialized needs to dominate others; a tendency to view most situations in win-lose terms—what I win, you must lose— rather than win-win terms; and predominant use of the tactics of fighting such as secrecy, surprise, holding hidden agendas, withholding information, deceiving. The positive face of politics is characterized by a *balanced* pursuit of self-interest and interest in the welfare of others; viewing situations in win-win terms as much as possible; engaging in open problem solving and then moving to action and influencing; a relative absence of the tactics of fighting; and a socialized need to lead, initiate, and influence others.

Pursuit of unsanctioned organizational goals or the use of unsanctioned organizational means might be examples of the negative face of politics. Illegitimate uses of authority, information, or resources might also be examples of the negative face of politics. But a positive face of politics is shown whenever ''hard decisions'' must be made, are made, and most organizational members feel good about what was decided and how it was decided. In this regard, Jeffrey Pfeffer argues that politics are *necessary* if organizations are to function effectively and efficiently. This concept of the two faces of politics handles the two sides of the phenomenon that we all see in our common experience. Some organizations reflect a mostly positive face of politics and other organizations reflect a mostly negative face of politics.

Organizational politics tend to be associated with the decision making, resource allocation, and conflict resolution processes in organizations. These are the key decision points; these are the areas where actors win and lose; these are where the ''goods'' are distributed and the goals are decided. In fact, one gains a quick understanding of the overall ''political climate'' of an organization by studying its methods of resource allocation, conflict resolution, and choosing among alternative means and goals.

Organizations often display modal patterns in the way their decision-making, resource-allocation, and conflict-resolution processes operate. Patterns identified in the organization theory literature include the bureaucratic, rational, and political models.[25] In a bureaucratic mode, decisions are made on the basis of rules, procedures, traditions, and historical precedents. In a rational mode, decisions are made on the basis of rational problem solving: goals are identified and agreed upon; situations are analyzed objectively in relation to goals; alternative action plans are generated and evaluated; and certain alternatives are chosen and implemented. In a political mode decisions are made on the basis of perceived self-interest by coalitions jockeying for dominance, influence, or resource control. Most organizations exhibit all these modes in the conduct of their business. Some organizations exhibit one predominant mode. It is important to realize that a predominantly political orientation is only one of several possibilities.

FRAMEWORKS FOR ANALYZING POWER AND POLITICS

Two conceptual models will provide a picture of the component parts of situations involving organizational power and politics. The first is taken from Pfeffer's book, *Power in Organizations*. The second is derived from the literature on game theory. A useful model of the antecedents and conditions for power is shown in Figure 20–1.

In this diagram, political activities are seen to be the outcome of a number of conditions. When these conditions exit, power and politics result. According to Pfeffer, the environment of the organization imposes demands and constraints that will be accommodated to in the form of "means" and "ends"—that is, what the organization does and how the organization gets its job done. Ends are the goals pursued by the organization. Often heterogeneous or incompatible goals are sought by different members

Figure 20–1 A Model of the Conditions Producing the Use of Power and Politics in Organizational Decision Making. *Source:* Jeffrey Pfeffer, *Power in Organizations.* Marshfield, Mass.: Pitman Publishing, Inc., 1981, p. 69. Used by permission.

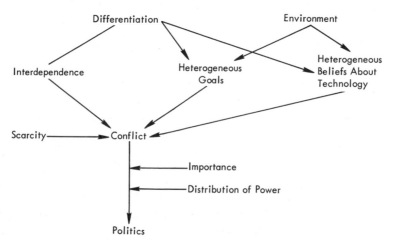

of the organization. Likewise, different or incompatible ways to accomplish the goals may be sought by different members of the organization. Preferences for different means to the goals is what is meant by the term ''heterogeneous beliefs about technology.'' Differentiation refers to the fact that division of labor in organizations causes the creation of many subgroups, which in turn produces different world views, different subgroup goals, and ''tunnel vision'' of subgroup members.

The three primary conditions giving rise to conflict are scarcity (there are not enough desired resources to allow all parties to have all they want), interdependence (the parties are related to each other in such a way that the distribution of resources affects everyone in some way), and incompatible goals and/or means to goals. When these conditions exist, conflict is a probable result. And when conflict exists, power and political behavior are a likely result if two additional features are present. As Pfeffer states:

> Together the conditions of scarcity, interdependence, and heterogeneous goals and beliefs about technology produce conflict. Whether that conflict eventuates in politics, the use of power in organizational settings depends upon two other conditions. The first condition is the importance of the decision issue or the resource. In the case of our example, the resource was very important—necessary for survival. In situations in which the decision may be perceived as less critical, power and politics may not be employed to resolve the decision because the issue is too trivial to merit the investment of political resources and effort. The second condition is the distribution of power. Political activity, bargaining, and coalition formation occur primarily when power is dispersed. When power is highly centralized, the centralized authority makes decisions using its own rules and values. The political contests that sometimes occur in organizations take place only because there is some dispersion of power and authority in the social system.[26]

It is possible to increase or decrease the amount of political activity in organizations by manipulating the conditions of power shown in the model. For example, if resource scarcity were replaced by resource abundance, conflict would be reduced and politics would be reduced. If organizational actors were made less interdependent (for instance, through the use of profit centers and other structural arrangements), conflict and power would be reduced. Likewise, increased consensus about goals and means and more centralized power would reduce conflict and, hence, reduce political activity. The model suggests the factors that can be changed if less political activity is desired.

A second model is taken from the game theory literature. The conditions giving rise to cooperation and competition and to the use of power have been studied extensively by economists and behavioral scientists in an attempt to understand wars, strikes, and arguments as well as collective cooperation and altruism.[27] Several concepts have been identified that provide a framework for understanding power and politics. Some of these concepts are conflict, the payoff matrix, the nature of interdependent relationships, and integrative and distributive bargaining.

In game theory, conflict is viewed as a critical condition leading to power and political behavior. There can be *conflict of interest* in which different parties prefer different goals. There can be *conflict or competition for scarce resources* where different parties want the same resources but both parties cannot possess them.

Thus conflict arises because of the real or perceived nature of the *payoff matrix,* the way in which the goods and services sought by two or more parties are to be distributed.

Some payoff matrices promote cooperation and minimal power use; other payoff matrices promote competition, conflict, and maximal power use. Understanding the nature of the payoff matrix is the key to understanding conflict, which in turn is the key to understanding most political behavior. An outside observer who wants to analyze a particular situation for its potential for organizational power and politics thus would want to know answers to the following questions:

> What is the commodity or issue that is under decision?
> How important is the commodity or issue?
> What are the possible payoffs that are available?
> What are the likely payoffs?
> Can all parties get their desires, or must one party win and one party lose?

These questions lead to another concept involved in power and politics—the nature of the relationship between the parties. Two parties in interdependent interaction can have one of three possible relationships based on the nature of the payoff matrix: *purely competitive* (a win-lose or zero-sum situation in which what one party wins the other party loses and the total payoffs always sum to zero), *purely cooperative* (a situation in which both parties have completely compatible interests but must engage in communication or coordination in order to receive their payoffs), and *mixed or mixed motive* (a situation in which both a push to compete and a push to cooperate are inherent in the payoffs).[28] Power and politics will predominate in the purely competitive, win-lose situation. Power should be absent from the purely cooperative, win-win situation; here the appropriate behaviors are communication, coordination, and cooperation. Power may or may not prevail in the mixed-motive situation; here each party needs the other to transact an exchange, yet each party is seeking to maximize its own gains. In the mixed-motive situation too much competition may cause both parties to lose; yet "too little" competition by one party may allow the other to gain a significant advantage.

Mixed-motive relationships are prominent in many social and organizational settings. In fact, many everyday situations are mixed-motive in nature. Examples are found in labor-management relations, the relations between two peers both of whom are working for a promotion that only one can obtain, and relations among members of a sports team all of whom want the team to win but each of whom wants to be the "star." Mixed-motive situations thus contain a push and a potential for both cooperation and competition, and which of these occurs depends on the behaviors of the two parties. But the important thing to realize is that to cooperate effectively and to compete effectively require quite different kinds of behaviors. Cooperation usually requires problem solving; competition usually requires power-orineted action.

This brings us to the concepts of integrative and distributive bargaining proposed by Walton and McKersie.[29] They studied labor-management bargaining situations and concluded that for best results for both parties the bargaining process should be conceptualized as a two-phase process: (1) a problem-solving, collaborative phase in which the total joint payoffs are maximized, and (2) a bargaining phase in which the payoffs are divided between the parties. In the first phase, called integrative bargaining, the parties try to identify the areas of mutual concern, search for alternative courses of action, and identify the largest joint sum of values possible. This is a cooperative, problem-solving phase. In the second phase, called distributive bargaining, the parties are in a conflict situation. Here each party tries to establish norms and procedures that will help to maximize its gains while trying to keep the gains of the other party to a minimum. Integrative bargaining calls for problem solving, honesty, open communication, and mutual exploration of all ideas. Distributive bargaining calls for secrecy, suspicion, deception, and not accepting the ideas of the other party. By separating bargaining into these two phases, better solutions can be achieved for both parties involved in the bargaining.

These concepts from game theory are applicable to understanding political processes in organizations. The sources of conflict are competition for scarce resources and conflict over incompatible goals and means to goals. A key factor is the nature of the payoffs to all parties—what they stand to win or lose. Positive outcomes for both parties can often be enhanced through a two-phase bargaining process in which integrative bargaining precedes distributive bargaining.

THE ROLE OF POWER AND POLITICS IN THE PRACTICE OF OD

A number of ideas concerning power and politics have been discussed. In this section we shall attempt to integrate those concepts with organization development and offer advice to the OD practitioner for dealing with the political realities found in organizations.

The Nature of Organization Development in Relation to Power and Politics

Organization development was founded on the belief that using behavioral science methods to increase collaborative problem solving would increase both organizational effectiveness and individual well-being. This belief gave rise to the field and is the guiding premise behind its technology. To increase collaborative problem solving is to increase the positive face of power and decrease the negative face of power. Thus from its inception OD addressed issues of power and politics in that it proposed that collaboration, cooperation, and joint problem solving are better ways to get things done in organizations than relying solely on bargaining and politics. The nature of OD in relation to power and politics can be inferred from several sources—its strategy of change, its interventions, its values, and the role of the OD practitioner.

Organization development is a particular approach that rests heavily on behavioral science interventions, systematic joint problem solving, and collaborative management of the organization's culture and processes. As such, OD programs implement normative-reeducative and empirical-rational strategies of change, not a power-coercive strategy, to use the framework of Robert Chin and Kenneth Benne.[30] The normative-reeducative strategy of change focuses on norms, culture, processes, and prevailing attitudes and belief systems. Change occurs by changing the matrix of norms and beliefs, usually through education and reeducation. The empirical-rational strategy of change seeks out facts and information in an attempt to find ''better'' ways to do things. Change using this strategy occurs by discovering these better ways and then adopting them. The power-coercive strategy of change focuses on gaining and using power and on developing enforcement methods. Change occurs when people with more power force their preferences on people with less power and exact compliance. OD practitioners advocate normative-reeducative and empirical-rational strategies of change and OD interventions are designed to implement these strategies. In addition, OD values legitimate these two strategies. Organization development thus has a distinct bias toward a normative-reeducative strategy of change and against a power strategy.

Examining OD interventions demonstrates that problem solving and collaboration are emphasized while power and politics are deemphasized. Virtually all OD interventions promote problem solving, not politics, as a preferred way to get things accomplished. OD interventions are designed to increase problem solving, collaboration, cooperation, fact-finding, and effective pursuit of goals while decreasing reliance on the negative faces of power and politics. We know of no OD interventions designed to increase coercion or unilateral power. For example, OD interventions typically generate valid, public data about the organization's culture, processes, strengths, and weaknesses. Valid, public data are indispensable for problem solving but anathema for organizational politics. OD interventions do not deny or attempt to abolish the reality of power in organizations, rather, they enhance the positive face of power thereby making the negative face of power less prevalent and/or necessary. Given the nature of OD interventions, it can be seen that not only is organization development not a power/political intervention strategy, it is instead a rational problem solving approach that is incompatible with extreme power-oriented situations.

OD values are consistent with the positive face of power but not with the negative face of power. Values such as trust, openness, collaboration, individual dignity, and promoting individual and organizational competence are part of the foundation of organization development. These values are congruent with rational problem solving and incongruent with extremely political modes of operating. "Power equalization" has long been described as one of the values of organization development, and that is correct. But emphasis on power equalization stems from two beliefs: first, problem solving is usually superior to power coercion as a way to find solutions to problematic situations; second, power equalization, being one aspect of the positive face of power, *increases* the amount of power available to organization members, and by so doing adds power to the organization.

The role of the OD practitioner is that of a facilitator, catalyst, problem solver, and educator. The practitioner is not a political activist or power broker. According to Chris Argyris, the "interventionist" has three primary tasks: (1) to generate valid useful information, (2) to promote free, informed choice, and (3) to help promote the client's internal commitment to the choices made.[31] The practitioner works to strengthen skills and knowledge in the organization. But organization members are free to accept or reject the practitioner, his or her program, and his or her values, methods, and expertise. The OD consultant, like all consultants, is providing a service that the organization is free to "buy" or "not buy." The facilitator or educator role is incompatible with a political activist role because cooperation requires one set of behaviors and competition requires a different set of behaviors, as was seen earlier in this chapter. Cobb and Margulies caution that OD practitioners can get into trouble if they move from a facilitator role to a political role.[32] We believe that is true.

In summary, organization development represents an approach and method to enable organization members to *go beyond* the negative face of power and politics. This is a major strength of OD, and it is derived from the strategy of change employed, the technology of OD, and the values and roles of OD practitioners.

Operating in a Political Environment

General observations will be presented followed by some rules of thumb for the OD practitioner.

First, organization development practitioners operate from a potentially strong power base that may be used to advantage. Using the framework of French and Raven, the OD consultant possesses power from the following bases: legitimate power (the OD program and consultant are authorized by the organization's decision makers); expert power (the consultant possesses expert knowledge); informational power (the consultant has a wealth of information about the strengths and weaknesses of the organization); and possibly referent power (others may identify with and be attracted to the consultant). These sources of influence produce a substantial power base that will enhance the likelihood of success. Michael Beer has identified additional means by which an OD group can gain and wield power in organizations:[33]

1. *Competence.* Demonstrated competence is the most important source of power, acceptability, and ability to gain organizational support.
2. *Political access and sensitivity.* Cultivate and nurture multiple relationships with key power figures in the organization. This will ensure timely information and multiple sources of support.
3. *Sponsorship.* "Organization development groups will gain power to the extent that they have sponsorship, preferably multiple sponsorship, in powerful places."[34] This maxim has been recognized for years under the heading of "get top-level support for the program."
4. *Stature and credibility.* This item is related to point 1. Beer notes that power accrues to those who have been successful and effective. Successful efforts lead to credibility and stature. Early successes in the OD program help promote this reputation. Usefulness to key managers of the organization helps promote this reputation.
5. *Resource management.* Power accrues to those who control resources—in this case, the resources of OD expertise and ability to help organizational subunits solve their pressing problems.
6. *Group support.* If the OD group is strong internally, it will be strong externally. If the OD group is cohesive and free of internal dissention, it will gain more power.

Paying attention to these sources of power will enhance the likelihood of success of OD programs.

Second, the models presented in this discussion suggest ways the OD practitioner can help organization members reduce the negative face of power. Creation of slack resources, replacing tight coupling of interdependent relationships with more loose coupling, gaining agreement on goals and means for goal accomplishment, centralizing some decision making, and addressing mixed-motive situations in two phases as indicated by integrative and distributive bargaining—all these processes have been demonstrated to reduce the negative consequences of intense power and politics. The OD practitioner can help implement these conditions in the organization thereby modifying the political climate.

Third, the concept of the positive and negative faces of power and politics suggests where the practitioner is likely to be more effective and less effective. We believe that OD programs are likely to be unsuccessful in organizations with high negative faces of politics and power: the OD program will likely be used as a pawn in the power struggles of the organization, and the OD practitioner can become a logical scapegoat when conditions require a ''sacrifice.'' On the other hand, OD programs are likely to be highly effective in organizations with positive faces of power and politics: the practitioner helps organization members to build multiple power bases in the organization (more power to everyone); he or she promotes collaborative problem solving, which leads to better decisions being made; and the practitioner teaches organization members how to manage mixed-motive situations to ensure the best outcomes.

Fourth, the OD practitioner is encouraged to learn as much as possible about bargaining, negotiations, the nature of power and politics, the strategy and tactics of influence, and the characteristics and behaviors of powerholders. This knowledge is not for the purpose of becoming a political activist but rather to understand better those organizational dynamics where power is an important factor. This knowledge will make the OD practitioner a more competent actor in the organization and a more effective consultant in helping organization members solve their problems and take advantage of opportunities.

Fifth, the OD practitioner realizes that power stems from possessing a commodity valued by others. If the OD program indeed improves individual and organizational functioning; if the OD practitioner has indeed learned his or her craft well, then a valuable commodity has been produced that will be welcomed by the organization powerholders.

What advice is available for OD practitioners who want to operate more effectively in a political environment? Several rules of thumb are implied by the fact that power accrues to persons who control valued resources or commodities.

Rule One.   Become a desired commodity, both as a person and as a professional. Becoming a desired commodity as a person means being interpersonally competent and trustworthy. OD practitioners are likely to have high interpersonal competence by virtue of their training, experience, and expertise. Skills such as listening, communicating, problem solving, coaching, counseling, and showing appreciation for the strengths of others are components of interpersonal competence. Good OD practitioners will have learned and practiced these skills. Being trustworthy means being reliable, dependable, and honest in dealing with others. These skills and traits are highly valued in social exchanges; persons who possess them become desired commodities and accrue power.

Making oneself a desired commodity as a professional is related to the issues of competence, stature, and credibility mentioned above by Beer. Good OD consultants are experts on people, organizations, and change. Such expertise is a rare and valuable commodity. Becoming an expert on people, organizations, and change requires hard work, learning the craft of organization development, continuously learning from experience, gaining exposure to a wide variety of problematic situations, and lots of practice. OD practitioners who get results, help solve long-standing problems, help create successes for organization members, and give credit for success to others become desired commodities and gain power. Such expertise is especially valued in today's rapidly changing world because it is critical for organizational survival.

Rule Two.   Make the OD program itself a desired commodity. OD programs become desired commodities when they are instruments that allow individuals and organizations to reach their goals. OD programs should be results-oriented and goal-oriented. Another way the OD program becomes a desired commodity is by focusing on important issues, those issues vital to the organization's success. In this regard, Greiner and Schein challenge OD practitioners to become more involved in the strategic management process.[35] They state:

> We argue that a "new OD" must emerge to help the power structure change not only itself but the strategic alignment of the firm with its environment. OD can, if properly devised, provide a more effective process than political bargaining for assisting the dominant coalition to address pressing strategic issues. In essence, OD must enter the arena that has long been sacred ground to the power elite—the strategy of the company, its structure for delivering on it, the positions that key leaders will hold in the structure, and the manner in which they will lead.[36]

We agree with Greiner and Schein on the need for OD practitioners to extend their activities to include strategic management issues and senior executives. We also agree that OD methods are superior to political bargaining. However, we do not agree that a "new OD" is needed since many OD practitioners are already assisting top management on strategy planning and implementation, and since OD interventions have already been developed to deal with strategic management issues. If the OD program itself is to become a desired commodity, though, it must be instrumental in addressing and resolving crucial issues.

Rule Three.   Make the OD program a valued commodity for multiple powerful people in the organization. When the OD program serves the needs of top executives it gains an aura of respect and protection that sets it above most political entanglements. Although the program should be of value to persons at all levels of the organizational hierarchy, paying special attention to the needs of top executives is a useful rule of thumb. Again the issue is goal achievement—helping people realize their important goals. The powerholders can be expected to reciprocate with endorsement, support, and protection of the OD program. Being of value to multiple powerholders rather than a single one both increases support and protection and reduces the likelihood that the program will become the target of poilitical activities.

Rule Four.   Create win-win solutions. The nature of organizations and the nature of organization development suggest this rule. Organizations are social systems in which members have both a history and a future of interacting together. Effective conflict management techniques are required in organizations to enhance stable, constructive social relationships. Many OD interventions are specifically designed to promote win-win solutions in confilct situations. OD professionals who are skilled in conflict management techniques and OD programs that encompass conflict resolution activities become valued commodities.

The above rules of thumb describe ways to increase or solidify one's power base. The following rules describe ways to avoid becoming involved in one's own or in others' political struggles. Each is derived from the general principle: Mind your own business.

Rule Five. Mind your own business which is to help someone else solve his or her major problems. Sometimes OD practitioners overlook the fact that they are hired by others, usually managers, to help them achieve *their* goals and solve *their* problems. The OD consultant is successful to the extent that the manager is successful; the OD consultant is competent to the extent that the manager's goals are met through collaboration between consultant and key client. OD consultants are not hired to instill OD values in an organization, or to cause the widespread use of participative management, or to "do good and expunge evil" (as defined by the consultant). Instead, OD consultants have a formal or informal contractual agreement with managers to help them do what they are trying to do—better. The role of the OD consultant is to help others upon request. Beer and Walton argue that field or organization development should move from being practitioner-centered to being manager-centered.[37] That is sound advice. *The OD program belongs to the manager, not the OD consultant.* A valuable byproduct of this fact is that if the program runs into political turbulence, the manager will defend it, probably vigorously.

Rule Six. Mind your own business which is to be an expert on process, not content. Organizational politics revolve around decisions: Should we seek Goal A or Goal B? Should we use Means X or Means Y? Should we promote Mary or John? The proper role of OD consultants is to help decision makers by providing them with good decision-making *processes,* not by getting involved in the answers. The processes used are the business of the OD consultant, the answers chosen are not. Abiding by this rule keeps the consultant from becoming entangled in politics, while at the same time increases his or her usefulness to the organization's powerholders. The principle is simple but powerful: know your legitimate business and stick to it.

Rule Seven. Mind your own business because to do otherwise is to invite political trouble. A subtle phenomenon is involved here: when people engage in illegitimate behavior, such behavior is often interpreted as politically motivated thereby thrusting the actors into political battles. Illegitimate behavior encroaches on others' legitimate "turf," which arouses defensive and protective actions. Illegitimate behavior reduces predictability, causing others to try to exert greater control over the situation. We believe the legitimate role of the OD practitioner is that of facilitator, catalyst, problem solver, and educator, not poweractivist or powerbroker.[38]

More rules of thumb could be articulated, but these give the flavor of the issues that must be considered when operating in a political environment. Attention to these rules can save OD practitioners time and energy that can be more profitably invested in the OD program.

SUMMARY

In this chapter we have examined the concepts of organizational power and politics with the goals of understanding the phenomena and deriving implications for the OD practitioner. Power and politics were seen to be similar in nature, to stem from known conditions and to be amenable to positive control. The well-trained practitioner is a facilitator, catalyst, and educator who understands power and can perform effectively in that arena.

fNOTES

1. W. Warner Burke, *Organization Development: Principles and Practices.* (Boston: Little, Brown and Co., 1982), p. 127.

2. See George Strauss, "Organization Development," in Robert Dubin, ed., *Handbook of Work, Organization, and Society* (Chicago: Rand McNally, 1976), pp. 617–685; Robert L. Kahn, "Organizational Development: Some Problems and Proposals," *Journal of Applied Behavioral Science,* 10, No. 4 (1974), pp. 485–502; Warren G. Bennis, *Organization Development: Its Nature, Origins, and Prospects* (Reading, Mass.: Addison-Wesley, 1969), pp. 78–79; and Wendell L. French and Cecil H. Bell, Jr., *Organization Development,* 2nd ed. (Englewood Cliffs, N.J.: Prentice-Hall, 1978), Chap. 20.

3. Important contributions to management and organization thought are Jeffrey Pfeffer, *Power in Organizations* (Marshfield, Mass.: Pitman, 1981); Henry Mintzberg, *Power In and Around Organizations* (Englewood Cliffs, N.J.: Prentice-Hall, 1983); Kenneth Thomas, "Conflict and Conflict Management," in Marvin D. Dunnette, ed., *Handbook of Industrial and Organizational Psychology* (Chicago: Rand McNally, 1976), pp. 889–935; and John P. Kotter, "Power, Success, and Organizational Effectiveness," *Organizational Dynamics,* March–April 1976, pp. 27–40.

4. Important contributions to the OD literature are Anthony T. Cobb and Newton Margulies, "Organization Development: A Political Perspective," *Academy of Management Review* (January 1981), pp. 49–59; Virginia E. Schein, "Political Strategies for Implementing Organizational Change," *Group and Organization Studies,* 2 (1977), pp. 42–48; Andrew Pettigrew, "Towards a Political Theory of Organizational Intervention," *Human Relations,* Vol. 28, No. 3 (1979), pp. 191–208; and Burke, *Organization Development,* Chapter 7.

5. This chapter draws on material from our book of readings in OD, W. L. French, C. H. Bell, Jr., and R. A. Zawacki (eds.), *Organization Development: Theory, Practice, Research* (Plano, Tex.: Business Publications Inc., 1983), Part 6.

6. R. G. H. Siu, *The Craft of Power* (New York: John Wiley, 1979), p. 31.

7. R. A. Dahl, "The Concept of Power," *Behavioral Science,* 1957, pp. 202–203.

8. Gerald Salancik and Jeffrey Pfeffer, "Who Gets Power—And How They Hold On To It: A Strategic-Contingency Model of Power," *Organizational Dynamics,* 5 (1977), p. 3.

9. Mintzberg, *Power In and Around Organizations,* p. 4. [Mintzberg's emphasis.]

10. David C. McClelland, "The Two Faces of Power," *Journal of International Affairs,* 24, No. 1 (1970), pp. 29–47.

11. M. Patchen, "The Locus and Bases of Influence in Organization Decisions," *Organization Behavior and Human Performance,* Vol. 11 (1974), pp. 195–221. This quotation is from p. 216.

12. Nancy C. Roberts, "Organizational Power Styles: Collective and Competitive Power Under Varying Organizational Conditions," *Journal of Applied Behavioral Science,* Vol. 22, No. 4 (1986), pp. 443–458. Roberts has developed a Power Styles Inventory that measures five different influence styles: directive, impression management, transactional, consensual, and charismatic. See N. C. Roberts, *Organizational Power Styles: Their Determinants and Consequences,* unpublished doctoral dissertation, Stanford University, 1983.

13. Richard M. Emerson, "Power-Dependence Relations," *American Sociological Review,* 27 (1962), pp. 31–40. This quotation is from page 32.

14. John R. P. French, Jr. and Bertram Raven, "The Bases of Social Power," in Dorwin Cartwright, ed., *Studies in Social Power* (Ann Arbor: Institute for Social Research of the University of Michigan, 1959), pp. 150–167.

15. This discussion is taken from Salancik and Pfeffer, "Who Gets Power—And How They Hold On To It." An earlier treatment of this view is "A Strategic Contingencies Theory of Intraorganizational Power," by D. J. Hickson, C. R. Hinings, C. A. Lee, R. E. Schneck, and J. M. Pennings, in *Administrative Science Quarterly,* 16, No. 2 (June 1971), pp. 216–229.

16. Salancik and Pfeffer, "Who Gets Power," p. 3.

17. Mintzberg, *Power In and Around Organizations.* This book is an important contribution to the concept of power in general and organizational power in particular.

18. Ibid., p. 22.

19. This discussion is taken from ibid., Chap. 3, especially pages 24–26.

20. Harold Lasswell, *Politics: Who Gets What, When, How* (New York: McGraw-Hill, 1936).

21. Pfeffer, *Power in Organizations,* p. 7.

22. Robert W. Allen, Dan L. Madison, Lyman W. Porter, Patricia A. Renwick, and Bronston T. Mayes, "Organizational Politics: Tactics and Characteristics of Its Actors," *California Management Review,* 22 (1979), p. 77.

23. Bronston T. Mayes and Robert W. Allen, "Toward a Definition of Organizational Politics," *The Academy of Management Review,* 2, No. 4 (October 1977), p. 676.

24. Mintzberg, *Power In and Around Organizations,* p. 5.

25. Pfeffer, *Power in Organizations,* Chapter 1. See also Jay M. Shafritz and J. Steven Ott, eds., *Classics of Organization Theory,* 2nd ed. (Chicago, Ill.: The Dorsey Press, 1987).

26. Pfeffer, *Power in Organizations,* pp. 69–70.

27. See, for example, J. Von Neumann and O. Morgenstern, *Theory of Games and Economic Behavior* (Princeton: N.J.: Princeton University Press, 1947); R. D. Luce and H. Raiffa, *Games and Decisions: Introduction and Critical Survey* (New York: John Wiley, 1957); T. C. Schelling, *The Strategy of Conflict* (Cambridge, Mass.: Harvard University Press, 1960); and J. W. Thibaut and H. H. Kelley, *The Social Psychology of Groups* (New York: John Wiley, 1959).

28. Schelling, *The Strategy of Conflict.*

29. R. E. Walton and R. B. McKersie, *A Behavioral Theory of Labor Negotiations* (New York: McGraw-Hill, 1965).

30. Robert Chin and Kenneth D. Benne, "General Strategies for Effecting Change in Human Systems," in Warren G. Bennis, Kenneth D. Benne, Robert Chin, and Kenneth E. Corey, eds., *The Planning of Change,* 3rd ed. (New York: Holt, Rinehart and Winston, 1976).

31. Chris Argyris, *Intervention Theory and Method: A Behavioral Science View* (Reading, Mass.: Addison-Wesley, 1970), pp. 17–20.

32. Cobb and Margulies, "Organization Development: A Political Perspective," *Academy of Management Review,* 6, January 1981, pp. 50–59.

33. Michael Beer, *Organization Change and Development: A Systems View* (Santa Monica, Calif.: Goodyear, 1980), pp. 258–261.

34. Ibid., p. 259.

35. Larry E. Greiner and Virginia E. Schein, "A Revisionist Look at Power and OD," *The Industrial-Organizational Psychologist,* Vol. 25, No.2 (1988), pp. 59–61.

36. Ibid., p. 60.

37. Michael Beer and Anna E. Walton, "Organization Change and Development," *Annual Review of Psychology,* 38 (1987), pp. 339–67.

38. A growing number of authors assert that OD practitioners should be political activists and/or powerbrokers. We disagree. For this other point of view, see: R. G. Harrison and D. C. Pitt, "Organizational Development: A Missing Political Dimension?" (pp. 65–85), and P. Reason, "Is Organization Development Possible in Power Cultures?" (pp. 185–202), both from the book *Power, Politics, and Organizations* edited by A. Kakabadse and C. Parker (Chichester: John Wiley

and Sons, Ltd., 1984). See also W. R. Nord, "The Failure of Current Applied Behavioral Science—A Marxian Perspective," *Journal of Applied Behavioral Science,* 10 (1974), pp. 557–578; Andrew Pettigrew, "Toward a Political Theory of Organizational Intervention"; Virginia Schein, "Political Strategies for Implementing Organizational Change"; and N. Margulies and A. P. Raia, "The Politics of Organization Development," *Training and Development Journal,* 38 (1984), pp. 20–23.

21

THE FUTURE OF OD

Organization development represents one of today's leading edges of applied behavioral science as organization theorists and practitioners endeavor to find ways to improve organizational effectiveness and achieve organizational excellence. Organization development appears to be coopting a sizable portion of the behavioral science and practitioner talent; it seems to be absorbing increasing amounts of internal resources of organizational time and personnel; there continues to be growth in the number of practitioners and concomitant professional groups; in sum, it appears as though OD is well established as an organization improvement strategy in the United States and abroad. A panel of leading professionals in the OD field predicts that the number of full-time and part-time practitioners will double by the year 2000.[1]

In this chapter we look at organization development—a social invention and a change technique—from the point of view of its permanence as a form of applied behavioral science. We believe that some of the foundations of OD and some of its practices augur well for its continued value and validity in improving organizations. However, there are some problems and challenges.

There is the possibility, of course, that OD is a fad. *Fad* is defined as "a practice or interest followed for a time with exaggerated zeal."[2] Clearly OD is being embraced enthusiastically by many applied behavioral scientists, organization theorists, and organizations. The critical issues, then, have to do with whether it will last on the social science practice scene and also whether it has substance and a fundamental quality. Let us examine some of the strengths and the weaknesses of organization development. Following that we will express our opinion in answering the question, "Is OD a passing fad?"

SOME OF THE STRENGTHS OF OD

Organization development draws upon a large number of models, theories, and practices; it borrows freely from the proven procedures for improving the functioning of individuals, groups, and organizations. Organization development is an amalgam, a culmination from diverse sources, and as such represents the resultant of some of the best thinking from the behavioral sciences. The foundations and characteristics of OD discussed in Chapter 7 suggest to us that OD is solidly grounded in practice, theory, and research. The action research model, a systems approach to understanding organizational dynamics, and a change strategy that focuses on the culture of work teams and the organization—all these features of organization development serve to make it more powerful and relevant than change strategies of the past. In addition, a systematic, planned approach utilizing an overall improvement strategy assures that the desirable features of OD are capitalized upon.

The action research model, for example, is a model for *tracking*—for staying on target, for discarding alternatives that do not meet the test of efficacy in the real world. Not only is it a good model for improvement of an organization (with its emphasis on goal setting, data collecting, and action planning by the organization members themselves), it is also a good model for keeping the practice of OD flexible, responsive to changing demands, and open to new ideas and practices. In effect, we are suggesting that application of the action research paradigm to the practice of OD will keep it from becoming irrelevant to the needs of individuals and organizations.

The focus on organization culture is another strong feature of OD that portends future success. Individual beliefs, values, attitudes, and behaviors are so overwhelmingly determined by, and are part of, organization culture that change efforts directed toward other facets of the individual, such as personality and physical environment, will probably have only minimal impact, while change efforts directed toward culture will have significant impact. But OD as a process does not just recognize the importance of culture—it also suggests ways of analyzing culture and changing culture. These are the real steps of progress. Mastery over one's culture rather than subjugation to it is a profound concept. Organization development represents definite steps in this direction and thus distinguishes itself from many other change efforts.

There seems to be historical evidence that permanent change in individuals and groups is facilitated by working with the intact group rather than with isolated individuals. This finding is no doubt related to the importance of culture in determining behaviors. For example, in part, the laboratory training movement attempted to improve organizational functioning by having key individuals attend sensitivity training labs. This practice had only limited payoff in terms of organizational change. On the other hand, working with real, intact work groups, including cross-functional groups, has been found to have tremendous potency for increasing effectiveness of individuals and groups.

This notion seems to have extensive support. Evidence of widespread and increasing emphasis on building and maintaining effective teams can be seen in a multitude of sources. For example, in his conclusion to an exhaustive study, Robert Guest states:

> From hundreds of studies and commentaries the evidence is conclusive that American management is (1) designing organizations and work processes to make more effective use of teams in accomplishing the goals of the organization, and (2) using techniques drawn from the behavioral sciences to improve the orientation and training of people at work to help them function as effective team members.[3]

Rosabeth Moss Kanter, in her study of high-innovation companies, finds extensive use of both functional and cross-functional teams and points to their energizing qualities when used properly:

> So "American-style" participation does not and should not mean the domination of committees over individuals, the submergence of the individual in the group, or the swallowing of the person by the team, but rather *the mechanism for giving more people at more levels a piece of the entrepreneurial action.*[4]

The airlines provide another example. United Air Lines, for instance, is focusing on the quality of the teamwork of flight-deck crews as a major factor in air safety. This is in contrast to the traditional chain-of-command mentality that has been pervasive in the operation of both military and civilian aircraft. [Incidentally, the United Air Lines program is called Cockpit Resource Management (CRM) and was developed using Blake and Mouton's Managerial Grid concepts.][5] Thus, since there is widespread interest in the creation and maintenance of effective teams and since theory and research point to the importance of group behavior on individual and organizational improvement, and since a central tenet of OD is that of working with teams, OD is on solid ground.

While organization development facilitates changes in individuals, teams, and organizations, there is a genuine sense in which OD also brings continuity and stability. Organization development represents an application of the scientific method of problem solving to human, social, and organizational problems. There is great solidity and stability in having such a model to base solutions upon. Change occurs, of course, when people move from a traditional, or haphazard, problem-solving modality to that of the scientific method. But stability occurs when individuals, groups, and organizations learn to apply this method to all sorts of events in the organization. Change occurs when the win-lose, boundary-defending, competitive relations between groups are altered by organization development efforts aimed at improving intergroup relations and intergroup effectiveness. But stability occurs when the awareness of interdependence of goals and efforts and the benefits of cooperation lead to reward for the groups.

James O'Toole refers to the importance of continuity and stability in organizational change efforts, and uses the strategies of successful presidential candidates to illustrate the point: "Every one of these agents of change has known that success depends on the active support of the people, and for the people to become involved in change they must see some familiar elements of continuity."[6] We believe that the OD process provides strong aspects of continuity and stability as well as managed changes. If this is so, OD has a much stronger chance of survival.

SOME PROBLEMS AND CONTINGENCIES

Diffusion of Technique

We see a number of problems and contingencies that can affect the future viability of OD. One phenomenon is both a tribute to the basic soundness of OD and a challenge to its survival, at least in recognizable form. Many, many practitioners—training specialists, industrial engineers, quality control specialists, management consultants, labor relations specialists, human resources/personnel directors, attitude survey people, teachers, clinical psychologists, psychiatrists working with organizations, and more— have learned OD techniques and are successfully adapting them to their practices. This has resulted in, for example, quality circle programs that include group dynamics training and the use of facilitators, and that are labeled QC and not OD. As another example, some QWL efforts have a strong OD component, but the OD label is not used.

Similarly, some programs labeled Organizational Effectiveness (OE) or Organizational Improvement (OI) or Employee Involvement (EI) have strong OD components. Further, it seems to us that articles in popular business publications that deal with participative approaches to organization improvement rarely make mention of the OD roots or processes that underly many such programs.

There is nothing wrong with these developments; this widespread diffusion of OD approaches is undoubtedly helping to create more effective and more humane organizations. The potential problem lies in the possibility that people may lose sight of the basic ingredients that give OD its vitality and enables the core technology of OD to be so useful to so many occupations. We see this as a healthy challenge to the field: How do theorists, researchers, and practitioners continue to focus on, study, and improve on the use of such matters as the action research model, group and intergroup dynamics, the facilitator role, and change processes? The danger, although perhaps not great, is that the attention and emphasis will shift to programs and away from understanding the dynamics of developmental kinds of change processes.

Semantics and Definitions

The problems associated with diffusion are partly related to semantics and definitions. We have already mentioned the absence of the OD label in many improvement programs that have an OD foundation. The opposite also occurs: some change programs are labeled OD when they have few or none of the features of OD, at least as we describe the process. If all sorts of techniques get slotted under the rubric "OD" without much thought to any criteria for using that label, it will be very difficult to ascertain the boundaries of the field, let alone being able to develop a coherent theoretical framework for it. As Miles has perhaps overstated it, "OD by attempting to become everything has become nothing—at least nothing which we can clearly get our minds around, nothing which gives us a distinct identity, nothing which provides clear goals for future development or criteria by which to measure reasoned growth."[7] While we hope we have lent some clarity to defining the field, the semantics and definitional problems require continuous attention by practitioners and theorists as the field evolves.

One term that has been used with increasing frequency in recent years is Organizational Transformation (OT). In our view, OT is largely synonymous with OD. However, the OT concept is frequently used to describe change efforts that have a strong future orientation and/or where there is a massive attempt at changing the culture and direction of an organization using participative, OD-like approaches. We believe that OD approaches can be used across a broad spectrum of change efforts—all the way from helping organizations fine-tune and maintain generally successful practices to helping organizations make major shifts in culture or mission. The terms OD and OT, then, are not mutually exclusive, in our opinion.[8] Again, it is not the terminology that is so important—it is identifying and understanding the underlying processes involved that is important.

Organization of Tomorrow: Genuinely Participative or Autocratic?

The future viability of OD will undoubtedly be a function of prevailing management philosophy about how people in organizations should be treated and managed. There are probably at least four interrelated aspects to the creation of management philosophy: (1) what management practices are suggested by experience and research to be the most effective, (2) expectations and influences among members of the work force, (3) values that top managers hold about how people should be managed, and (4) stimuli imposed by the external environment.

As to (1), we believe there is a great deal of evidence and experience that suggests that participatory, organic-type approaches to managing organizations have wide applicability. Regarding (2), there appear to be widely held expectations among members of the work force across occupations and across hierarchical levels that reinforce the applicability of such forms of organization. We refer to expectations that people have about increased participation, job autonomy, and the meaningfulness of work, in particular.

These expectations become translated into expected leader behaviors. Toffler's, Naisbitt and Aburdene's, and Peters' views of the future suggest the general type of leadership that will be required. Toffler:

> The requisite qualities of Third Wave leaders are not yet entirely clear. We may find that strength lies not in a leader's assertiveness but precisely in his or her ability to listen to others; not in bulldozer force but in imagination; not in megalomania but in a recognition of the limited nature of leadership in the new world.
>
> The leaders of tomorrow may well have to deal with a far more decentralized and participatory society—one even more diverse than today's. They can never again be all things to all people. Indeed, it is unlikely that one human being will ever embody all the traits required. Leadership may well prove to be more temporary, collegial, and consensual.[9]

Naisbitt:

> The guiding principle of this participatory democracy is that people must be a part of the process of arriving at decisions that affect their lives. Whether or not we agree with the notion or abide by it, participatory democracy has seeped into the core of our value system. Its greatest impact will be in government and corporations.[10]

Naisbitt and Aburdene:

> . . . The best people want ownership—psychic and literal—in a company: the best com-
> panies are providing it . . .
> . . . Authoritarian management is yielding to a networking, people style of
> management . . . [11]

Peters, in examining the choices faced by American industries, concludes that to remain
competitive over the long term and to "maintain and improve America's standard of
living over time," organizations must follow a path in which

> . . . all those associated with the firm become partners in its future. . . . Each member of
> the enterprise participates in its evolution. All have a commitment to the firm's continued
> success . . . [12]

Such values and expectations are powerful factors in the shaping of managerial
values and philosophy. In the last analysis, the way in which top managers and boards
believe people *should* be treated will have a powerful influence on the culture of the
organization, what management techniques are used, and whether OD approaches will
be rejected or welcomed.

Pascale and Athos provide us with interesting contrasts in management philosophy among Konosuke Matsushita, head of Japan's Matsushita Electric Company,
Edward Carlson, formerly CEO of United Airlines, and Harold Geneen, formerly CEO
of International Telephone & Telegraph (ITT).[13] Matsushita's and Carlson's emphases
on the development of people and on participation and teamwork are placed in vivid
contrast to Geneen's use of fear of humiliation and the use of checks and balances to
make sure he got what he called "unshakeable facts."[14] We would speculate that an
OD effort might have an excellent chance of flourishing under an executive with the
philosophy of a Matsushita or a Carlson, but would be an anathema to an executive with
Geneen's philosophy.

How executives respond to stimuli and crises imposed by the external environment may reinforce OD efforts or may negate or cancel any OD process underway. In
an era of intense international competition, unpredictable energy shortages, and fluc-
tuating stability in the international monetary scene, it is possible that management
philosophy in some organizations may swing widely as budgetary crises arise, particularly
if philosophies are only partly developed or have incompatible aspects. An example of
stability under crisis was Delta Airlines' policy to make extraordinary efforts to retain
employees during the oil embargo. This policy stemmed from a well-articulated philosophy
that stressed teamwork and the development of people.

On the other hand, we have seen organizations abandon reasonably humane
personnel policies in periods of budgetary crises and treat employees as though they were
so many unneeded machines when other options would have worked just as well from
a fiscal point of view. O'Toole describes how the managements of Arco, Levi Strauss,
and Control Data abandoned high principles when confronted with crises and the resulting
long-term, serious consequences, and contrasts their actions with those of the executives
at Motorola under similar circumstances. With reference to Motorola,

> Motorola plans ahead and is often—but not always—able to use reduced workweeks in lieu of morale-destroying layoffs...When recessions hit Motorola, the company...does nothing fundamentally different. Of course, the company makes appropriate strategic, tactical, and product changes; but the fundamental principles—including employee participation in decision-making, sharing of productivity gains, "open and complete argument on controversial issues," honesty, integrity, and the goal of "zero product defects"— are never compromised.[15]

Abandonment of such principles, which O'Toole calls the "high road," would bode ill for the beginnings of any OD effort or portend the abandonment of one if already underway. On the positive side, as discussed in Chapter 16, if values congruent with OD are sustained, an OD effort can assist in planning a much wider range of options to choose from in times of crisis, and can assist in the management of crises whey they occur. As Beckhard says, "The best interventions from a values point of view are those that help clients prepare for their place in the future, whether it's creation, adaption, or reorientation."[16] Assisting top managers, governing boards, and organizational members in preparing for uncertainties of the future, then, is a major contribution that OD practitioners and approaches can make.

Underattention to Task, Technology, and Structure

Probably the most serious handicap of OD as it has emerged historically has been its overpreoccupation with the human and social dynamics of organizations to the detriment of attending to such matters as the task, technological, financial, and structural aspects and their interdependencies. This statement reflects an imbalance of effort and perhaps a lack of skills on the part of the practitioners, not a total disregard to these other areas. Bennis addressed this point some years back in an editorial in the *Journal of Applied Behavioral Sciences* as follows:

> I have yet to see an organization development program that uses an interventional strategy other than an interpersonal one, and this is serious when one considers that the most pivotal strategies of change in our society are political, legal and technological. We call ourselves "change agents," but the real changes in our society have been wrought by the pill, the bomb, the automobile, industrialization, communication media, and other forces of modernization.[17]

This statement is substantially less true today than when Bennis made it; we see many OD efforts that have paid a great deal of attention to such matters as intergroup dynamics, role clarification, goal setting, strategic planning, and the modification of structure. Some have paid substantial attention to pay systems as the OD process unfolded.[18] But Bennis' point is still worth examining.

In the future, organization development specialists must know much more about such matters as goal setting, strategic planning, and structural changes and must establish linkages with practitioners in such fields as corporate planning, human resources management, labor relations, compensation, clinical psychology, management information systems, and industrial engineering to provide a broader range of options for organizational intervention. Much of this is already happening. Such broader knowledge, when integrated with OD techniques, will be particularly relevant in the second or subsequent phases of OD efforts, that is, probably after the first cycle of diagnosis, data feedback, problem discussion, and action planning. For example, the job description exercise in Illustration 6 of Chapter 1 is a marriage of OD and personnel management techniques and was used in the second phase of an OD effort.

Limited Models

Another significant contingency to the viability of OD lies in the conceptual foundation underlying OD strategies. OD is limited to the model of planned change that it utilizes. OD represents the state of the art, but the current state is that we have a rather limited number of models for effecting permanent change. For example, OD seems restricted in its model regarding effective use of power in organizations. Stemming from the laboratory training method background, models of change underlying OD interventions typically involve love-trust, collaborative models rather than those involving power, coercion, or competition.[19] We have no quarrel with the collaborative model but rather are appealing for the development of additional, perhaps contingency, models.

It seems to us that contributions such as Walton's in the area of third-party peace-making[20] increase the range of models available for more effective management of power issues in OD efforts, and Ouichi's[21] and Pascale and Athos's contrasting and comparing firms having certain constellations of characteristics, both Japanese and American,[22] provide us with useful typologies or patterns to help us to be aware of a wider range of variables and their interrelationships. Peters' and Waterman's *In Search of Excellence,*[23] Waterman's *The Renewal Factor,*[24] Peters' *Thriving on Chaos,*[25] Kanter's *The Change Masters,*[26] and O'Toole's *Vanguard Management*[27] distill systems of attributes these researchers see as characteristic of innovative, constantly improving organizations. (OD approaches can assist organizations in developing these attributes, by the way. A number of companies identified as best run by these authors have made extensive application of OD techniques and values.) Goodman's longitudinal depth analysis of the complexities of a QWL project[28] is another example of research and conceptualization that has promise for adding to the repertoire of models available for OD practice and theory.

Quality and Extent of Research

Implicit in the preceding is that more and better research on OD will obviously also be a major aspect of the future viability of OD. There are many hopeful signs in this regard, as suggested by Chapter 19. It seems to us that what Alderfer said several years ago is increasingly true: "The overall quality of research on OD is showing increasing signs of both rigor and vigor as more careful studies of OD processes and outcomes are being conducted and reported."[29]

However, Beer and Walton suggest an emphasis that is needed in OD research. Fundamental to this research is the development of "a theory of organizational adaptation that incorporates *all* types of interventions."[30] They then go on to describe the research methodology appropriate to this orientation:

The primary research methodology . . . would not be that of normal science, which attempts to answer little questions precisely. Instead, we should be more concerned with broader longitudinal designs, creating knowledge that could be used. We suggest a return to the action research traditions of the field but with a longer time frame and a more thorough investigation of the context in which episodes occur. OD need not become lax in its search for knowledge, but we must recognize that our sphere of inquiry is fundamentally different from that of normal science. We cannot borrow the tools and techniques of another paradigm; we must develop our own.[31]

Case studies of both success experiences and failures in OD can also be immensely useful. Although failures tend to go unreported, the book by Mirvis and Berg about failures in OD is a very healthy development.[32]

Cross-Cultural Assumptions

Cultural assumptions underlying OD need to be examined vis-à-vis the unique cultures of different localities around the world. It may be that some of the assumptions underlying OD may not hold for some societies. To illustrate, the Chinese on Taiwan have a long tradition of deference to authority, and criticism of the practices of superiors in that setting may need to be much more oblique at the outset of an OD effort. On the other hand, some cultures may have characteristics that are uniquely supportive of OD efforts. Japan, for example, has a long tradition of group discussion and decision by consensus. These cultural aspects may make OD approaches readily adaptable to Japanese organizations.

A number of cultural dimensions may be critical. What does a given societal culture say about openness? About the expression of feelings? About participation? About authority? About hard work? What does the culture say about examining the culture? What differences exist in these dimensions between organizations within a given country? (Between-organization differences may be greater than differences across national boundaries in many instances.) We think these are important questions that need to be researched. The answers may facilitate OD efforts and/or help create realistic expectations about OD approaches in different cultures. Some helpful research is beginning to emerge.[33]

Quality and Extent of Laboratory Training

The number of managers who participate in laboratory training experiences—T-groups in particular—and the quality of these experiences, we believe, will have a major impact on the future viability of OD. Organization development that pays no attention to feelings, no attention to interpersonal and group dynamics, and no attention to personal and group development is not OD at all, at least as we define it. It is some form of sterile, mechanistic exercise in super-rationality.

As Freidlander says, OD is an interplay of the values of rationalism, pragmatism, and existentialism[34] (we would add idealism).[35] A suppression of OD's existential aspects of experiencing, subjective perception, and the confrontation of one's existence would kill OD, we believe. Although we do not see T-grouping as central to OD, we do see the T-group as one of the most effective training vehicles for developing some of the insights and skills upon which effective OD must be based. Thus the long-range viability of the OD field partially rests on the availability and quality of laboratory training, T-groups in particular, in the United States and abroad.

Impact on Both Managers and Subordinates

The impact that potential and actual OD experiences have on executives and supervisors is also an area that needs to be examined. It may be that OD never emerges in some organizations because of the fear and anxiety aroused in managers by the real or imagined things that might happen in an OD effort. As Miller says,

> Open-endedness is often found frightening by managers (and also by some OD consultants) who therefore often seem to impose limits on the development of participative processes: thus far and no further. Part of managers' fear, I think, is that their competence will come under close scrutiny; part, too, is that if the managerial role and authority are called into question, this poses a threat to all the trappings of "management"—the assumption of power, status, privileges, the sense of self-importance, and so on. Such fears are not without foundation. Unbridled participation certainly does invite scrutiny of the ways in which roles are performed. But what tends to get forgotten is that appraisal of superiors by subordinates does not originate with participation. Judgments are constantly being made; and corresponding patterns of behavior are developed as a means of exploiting weaknesses or expressing contempt. Sometimes these take the form of adjustments to the work-role itself; sometimes the union role is used as the vehicle.[36]

Therefore, we need to know more about such matters as: How much anxiety is there? What kind of feelings do managers have as they approach and participate in a team-building exercise? What can consultants do to be more helpful to the key client? After all, as Beer and Walton say, "The general manager is the central character in the drama of organization development."[37]

Of course, the fears and anxieties of the subordinates are also important and need to be examined. But we are emphasizing the impact on managers because we suspect this is a more potent dimension than is usually assumed. While we agree with Friedlander and Brown that "OD as a field runs the risk of encouraging and implementing subtle but persuasive forms of exploitation" (of subordinates)[38] OD can also be viewed as a vehicle for "clobbering" the boss. The behavior of the manager of any group is obviously an important feature of team dynamics, and positive and dysfunctional behaviors are frequently examined in OD efforts. While team members are ordinarily prepared to work constructively together to solve problems, and competent practitioners will always assess team readiness to do so, the possibility exists that there can be some behind-the-scenes collusion to unload negative feelings on the superior. Fear of criticism in a group setting is very understandable, whether or not escalation in the informal system is involved. (This is one illustration of why facilitators exercise a certain amount of control in the use of various OD interventions, as discussed in a number of places in this book.) More knowledge about and sensitivity to the impact of prospective and actual OD interventions on the formal leader as well as group members will assist facilitators in being more helpful to client groups, and it should enhance the future viability of the field.

Rediscovering the Past

Another factor that will affect the future viability of OD is the extent to which practitioners and theorists rediscover effective past practice and theory. For example, one of the skills brought to the OD field in its early days was the design and management of large conferences. These can be very productive in change efforts involving large departments, total management groups, or associations having delegates from a number of organizations. Very little about running large conferences appears in current literature; an exception is Marvin Weisbord's description of "the future search conference" in his book *Productive Workplaces*. [39] Some of the earlier literature includes a book edited by Burke and Beckhard entitled *Conference Planning*. [40]

Another example of an early component of OD that might profitably be rediscovered is the area of insights from family therapy. As the reader will recall from the chapter on the history of OD, insights from the practice of family therapy influenced both the laboratory training stem of OD and Tavistock sociotechnical and socioclinical approaches.

Time and Cost

Another possible handicap to the viability of OD is that it represents a long-term and expensive investment on the part of client organizations. OD technology has developed to the state that client systems and consultants working together can in fact bring about organization improvement when there is enough time—when there is a long-range change project. While OD techniques can help groups address crises and short-range issues, OD does not have many quick remedies. OD does not offer shortcuts to total organization improvement. Significant organization improvement requires that there be a stabilization of the complicated fabric of organization culture at successively more effective levels—this takes time and much effort on the part of organizational members.

OD and the External Environment

Another major issue affecting the future viability of OD is the degree of congruence between the emerging internal organizational culture resulting from OD efforts and the cultures of the organization's various external interfaces. Our hypothesis is as follows: the higher the congruence, the greater the potential viability of the OD effort. As an illustration, if the internal culture of a manufacturing company professes honesty, but if that part of the interface between company and consumer under the control of the company has elements of deception, the internal environment will ultimately take on some of the same quality. If a company cheats its customers, it's going to be difficult for Division A within that company not to believe it is being cheated by Division B. As another example, if "quality of work life" is the internal slogan but resource exploitation is the external practice, a spreading internal cynicism among organizational members can be predicted. One can, however, also be optimistic about such incongruities. A long-range OD effort is likely to result in people confronting such issues and greatly improving the quality of the external interfaces.

To elaborate on the relationship between OD and the external environment, there are a number of likely occurrences that we believe will have an impact on the interest shown in OD. The rapid awakening to the grave dangers of environmental pollution and exploitation is likely to provide—and probably already has—impetus to an examination of the quality of life in organizations. We believe that people are increasingly concerned with the quality of organizational life, particularly in those organizations where people earn their livelihood. For example, more and more managers and professionals are realizing the important linkages between mental health on the one hand and leadership style and group processes on the other and the similar linkages between physical health, motivation, and the meaning of one's work. People are increasingly going to be intolerant of organizational cultures that treat human resources as relatively passive entities mainly to be selected, directed and evaluated. People want much more control over their destinies than that, and their impatience with such cultures will become more and more evident. Such concerns for the quality of life in both the physical and the organizational environment will provide, we believe, an acceleration of interest in organization development.

Reciprocally, it should be recognized that internal OD activities will have important effects in the community. For example, the marketing executive who has developed skill in group methods is likely to become influential in such matters as meeting improvement, problem diagnosis, and climate setting when on a church board or on the executive committee of a civic organization. The director of nursing who has had a long-range collaborative involvement in a hospital OD effort is likely to be an extraordinarily effective participant in professional associations or clubs. The machinist who is familiar with attitude surveys and problem-solving meetings may become a catalyst around whom union meetings become more participative, more problem solving oriented.

WILL OD BE A PASSING FAD?

We have three points to make relative to whether or not OD will be a passing fad. First, we are convinced that OD will be around and will survive for many years to come; second, current OD technology will undoubtedly be superseded by additional or modified practices as the years unfold; and, third, there will always be a need for something like OD. Organization development is partially a response to the needs of both individuals and organizations for improvement strategies that will bring individual aspirations and organizational objectives together. There will always be that need.

We do not believe that OD is a passing fad. Organization development (perhaps under a new name or names) will evolve new forms, new technologies, new concepts, and new models in the future as it changes and grows with new inputs from practitioners and clients in many different situations. It will continue to reflect the state of the art even as that art changes. We believe that OD will be on the increase through the 1990s; it will become more widely used by different kinds of organizations. Long-term relationships may permit and encourage more evaluation research on OD; in addition, the causal dynamics of interventions may increasingly come under scrutiny.

SUMMARY

Historically, organization development has largely emerged from three interrelated origins: (1) innovations stemming from attempts to utilize laboratory training in the solution of work team and larger system problems; (2) innovations centering on the effective feedback of attitude survey data; and (3) the emergence of action research techniques and approaches. Paralleling these developments was the emergence of sociotechnical and socioclinical approaches to improving organizations.

Organization development is based on a set of assumptions and values about people and groups in organizations, about the nature of total systems, and about the nature of the client-consultant relationship, and it has a substantial base in behavioral science research and theory. Intervention strategies of the behavioral scientist-change agent tend to be based on an action research model and tend to be focused more on helping the people in an organization learn to solve problems rather than on prescribing how things should be done differently.

Successful organization development efforts require skillful interventions, a systems view, top-management support and involvement, an open and shared technology, a value system, and a long-range perspective. In addition, to be sustained, changes stemming from organization development must be linked to changes in such organization subsystems as the appraisal, reward, staffing, bargaining, and leadership subsystems.

The future viability of organization development efforts has many dimensions, including the degree to which the OD efforts accurately reflect the perceptions, concerns, and aspirations of the participating members. Other dimensions include the degree to which OD practitioners are innovative and successful in helping bring about congruence with other programs aimed at organization improvement, such as job redesign, management by objectives, self-managed groups, quality circles, and QWL; the degree to which theorists and practitioners develop additional conceptual models; the degree to which conceptualizers add clarity and focus to the field of OD; the quality and extent of research on the effectiveness of various intervention strategies; and the extent to which theorists and practitioners retain and build on the insights of the past.

Successful organization development is a total system effort, a process of planned improvement—not a program with a temporary quality; it is aimed at developing the organization's internal resources for effective change in the future. Its real thrusts are for organizational members to draw out and help develop the resources of each other and to increase the range of behavioral options open to individuals and teams. Furthermore, it is a collaborative process of managing the culture of the organization—not something that is done *to* somebody, but a transactional process of people working together to improve their mutual effectiveness in attaining their mutual objectives.

NOTES

1. Anthony P. Raia and Kenneth O. Shepard, ''The Future of OD Study: Summary of Findings for the Panel,'' mimeographed, Graduate School of Management, UCLA, July 1981, p. 1.

2. *Webster's New Collegiate Dictionary* (Springfield, Mass.: Merriam, 1976), p. 410.

3. Robert H. Guest, *Work Team and Team Building Highlights of the Literature* (New York: Pergamon Press, 1986), Work in America Institute Studies in Productivity No. 44, p. 10.

4. Rosabeth Moss Kanter, *The Change Masters: Innovation for Productivity in the American Corporation* (New York: Simon and Schuster, 1983), p. 364.

5. Kenneth F. Englade, "Better Managers in the Friendly Skies," *Across the Board,* 25 (1988), pp. 36–45.

6. James O'Toole, *Vanguard Management: Redesigning the Corporate Future* (Garden City, N.Y.: Doubleday & Company, 1985), p. 277.

7. Raymond E. Miles, "OD: Can It Survive?—And Should It?" *OD Practitioner,* 9 (January 1977), p. 5.

8. For more on Organizational Transformation see Linda S. Ackerman, "Development, Transition or Transformation: The Question of Change in Organizations," *OD Practitioner,* 18 (December 1986), pp. 1–8; John D. Adams, editor, *Transforming Work: A Collection of Organizational Transformation Readings* (Alexandria, Va.: Miles River Press, 1984); and William G. Dyer and W. Gibb Dyer, Jr., "Organization Development: System Change or Culture Change?" *Personnel,* 63 (February 1986), pp. 14–22.

9. Alvin Toffler, *The Third Wave* (New York: Bantam Books, 1980), p. 404.

10. John Naisbitt, *Megatrends* (New York: Warner Books, 1982), p. 159.

11. John Naisbitt and Patricia Aburdene, *Re-inventing the Corporation* (New York: Warner Books, Inc., 1985), p. 53.

12. Tom Peters, *Thriving on Chaos: Handbook for a Management Revolution* (New York: Alfred A. Knopf, 1988), p. 22.

13. Richard T. Pascale and Anthony G. Athos, *The Art of Japanese Management* (New York: Warner Books, 1981).

14. Ibid., p. 288.

15. James O'Toole, "Sic Transit Excellence," *Across the Board,* 23 (October 1986), p. 6.

16. Richard Beckhard, "Who Needs Us? Some Hard Thoughts About a Moving Target—The Future," *OD Practitioner,* 13 (December 1981), p. 5.

17. Cited in W. G. Bennis, *Organization Development: Its Nature, Origins, and Prospects* (Reading, Mass.: Addison-Wesley, 1969), pp. 78–79.

18. See the preface to Edward E. Lawler, III, *Pay and Organization Development* (Reading, Mass.: Addison-Wesley, 1981).

19. For an elaboration of this point, see Bennis, *Organization Development,* pp. 77–79.

20. Richard E. Walton, *Managing Conflict: Interpersonal Dialogue and Third-Party Roles,* 2nd ed. (Reading, Mass.: Addison-Wesley, 1987).

21. William Ouichi, *Theory Z: How American Business Can Meet the Japanese Challenge* (Reading, Mass.: Addison-Wesley, 1981).

22. Pascale and Athos, *The Art of Japanese Management.*

23. Thomas J. Peters and Robert H. Waterman, Jr., *In Search of Excellence: Lessons from America's Best-Run Companies* (New York: Harper & Row, 1982).

24. Robert H. Waterman, Jr., *The Renewal Factor* (New York: Bantam Books, 1987).

25. Peters, *Thriving on Chaos.*

26. Kanter, *The Change Masters.*

27. O'Toole, *Vanguard Management.*

28. Paul S. Goodman, *Assessing Organizational Change* (New York: John Wiley, 1979).

29. Clayton P. Alderfer, "Organization Development," *Annual Review of Psychology,* 28 (1977), p. 197.

30. Michael Beer and Anna Elise Walton, "Organization Change and Development," *Annual Review of Psychology,* 38 (1987), p. 362.

31. Ibid.

32. Phillip H. Mirvis and David N. Berg, eds. *Failures in Organization Development and Change* (New York: John Wiley, 1977).

33. See for example, L. David Brown, "Global Development and the Potentials of Organization Development," *OD Practitioner,* 20 (June 1988), pp. 1–5; Alfred M. Jaeger, "Organization Development and National Culture: Where's the Fit?" *Academy of Management Review,* 11

(January 1986), pp. 178–190; Carl Rogers and Ruth Sanford, "Reflections on Our South African Experience," *Organization Development Journal,* 4 (Winter 1986), pp. 8–10; A. Desreumaux, "OD Practices in France: Part Two," *Leadership & Organization Development Journal,* 7 (Number 1 1986), pp. 10–14; Kenneth L. Murrell and E. H. Valsan, "A Team-building Workshop as an OD Intervention in Egypt," *Leadership & Organization Development Journal,* 6 (Number 2 1985), pp. 11–16; and Risto Tainio and Timo Santalainen, "Some Evidence for the Cultural Relativity of Organizational Development Programs," *Journal of Applied Behavioral Science,* 20 (Number 2 1984), pp. 93–111.

34. Frank Friedlander, "OD Reaches Adolescence: An Exploration of its Underlying Values," *Journal of Applied Behavioral Science,* 12 (January–March, 1976), pp. 7–12.

35. Wendell French, "Extending Directions and Family for OD," *Journal of Applied Behavioral Science,* 12 (January–March 1976), pp. 51–58.

36. Eric J. Miller, "Organizational Development and Industrial Democracy: A Current Case-Study," in Cary L. Cooper, ed., *Organizational Development in the UK and USA: A Joint Evaluation* (New York: Petrocelli, 1977), p. 59.

37. Beer and Walton, "Organization Change and Development," p. 362.

38. Frank Friedlander and L. Dave Brown, "Organization Development," *Annual Review of Psychology,* 25 (1974), p. 335.

39. Marvin R. Weisbord, *Productive Workplaces: Organizing and Managing for Dignity, Meaning, and Community* (San Francisco: Jossey-Bass Publishers, 1987), pp. 281–295.

40. W. Warner Burke and Richard Beckhard, *Conference Planning,* 2nd ed. (San Diego: University Associates, 1970).

INDEX